Record Book
for
Oregon's Big Game Animals

First Edition

Oregon Big Game, Inc.
Irrigon, Oregon

Dedicated to
and
in Memory of Brian Byrd

For more information concerning entries and submitting photographs or stories, contact:

Record Book for Oregon
P.O. Box 759
Irrigon, Oregon 97844
(541) 922-2959

Book Production & Project Management: ETP Harrison
Printing: Paramount Graphics
Binding: Lincoln and Allen Bindery

Oregon Big Game, Inc.
Record Book for Oregon's Big Game Animals
P.O. Box 759
Irrigon, Oregon 97844
(541) 922-2959

First Edition

Printed in Oregon

ISBN: 0-9656283-0-2 Collector's Edition ISBN: 0-9656283-1-0

Contents

Color Photographs

Artist Profiles

Tales of the Hunt

Oregon's Big Game Records

In Memory of Fred Bean

Fred Bean, 1910–1996

I had the fortunate opportunity a few years ago to meet Fred Bean. I first heard of Fred through his cousin Wayne Berry in John Day. Wayne said, "If you're interested in some big blacktails and you're ever down in Central Point, go by and talk to him." When I did go, I was absolutely astounded with the incredible number of trophy blacktail deer Fred and his son, Riley Bean, had accumulated over their years of hunting. I instantly knew Fred was a very special man, a man who had devoted his entire life to hunting, a man similar to the men we have grown to love and cherish from our childhood.

Fred Bean was born on July 15, 1910, in Gold Hill, Oregon. His father was Purl Riley Bean, the now-famous hunter who killed the legendary giant California grizzly bear "Reel-Foot." Purl taught his son the ways of the land from a very early age. Fred spent most of his early years growing up in a cabin on Sucker Creek in the Grayback Mountain area of southwestern Oregon. Hunting was a matter of survival, a necessity, for food was hard to come by. To teach Fred to become a good hunter, each time he went hunting Purl gave him only three .22 shells. Ammunition was scarce back then. If he returned

with game he was given more shells. It was on one of these occasions, when he was nine years old, that Fred killed his first deer. Fred became an experienced hunter at a very young age and an excellent marksman. As Fred would say, "Hell, that's all we've ever done, hunt and shoot." Even with the vast amount of hunting and shooting experience passed down from his father and a growing passion for the pursuit of game, little did he know he was destined to become a legend in his own right.

Like many other people in his time, hunting was his line of work. He ran hound dogs, chased bears, cougars, bobcats and raccoons, and ran trap-lines in the pursuit of fur. But Fred's greatest passion in life was hunting big blacktail deer.

Fred did have one other passion and that was mining. He worked in mines in several western states and it was on one of these excursions that he told me the following story. "I was working in Arizona near an Indian reservation and stopped in a store where the conversation concerned all the wild burros in that area. One man jumped up and said, "Something's got to be done about all these damn burros. They've taken over this country." Fred replied, "The burros are about the only thing the natives have to eat." The man got real mad and said, "Well they don't belong here—they're foreigners!" Fred stood up and pointed toward the man and sternly said, "Mister, let me tell you something! So are you and I!"

After telling me the story Fred said, "So-what-the-hell, some of them guys get as smart as hell." He had a very deep respect and appreciation for the native American Indians. He had grown up in an area where he had had the opportunity to know many Indians and learned the ways of their culture. He said, "The Indians are good people. They told me a lot of things, and you could learn a lot if you would just listen! God-damn-well-right they did!"

At one time Fred had planned to live with some Indians high up in the Siskiyous because a man had falsely accused him of stealing from a neighbor. He put together a pack and was planning a thirty-day walk through the mountains because of the shame he had brought to his family. Then his father Purl, without Fred knowing, confronted the accuser, telling him to do what was right or face the consequences. The man then admitted Fred had been falsely accused and apologized for the distress he had caused. When Fred told me the story, I could clearly see that Fred was disappointed that he had not left to join the Indians. He said, "What an adventure that would have been!"

Fred Bean was a man of character. He was raised when a handshake meant more than any written contract and he always stood by his word.

Fred told me, "You know, you see a lot of things happen in a lifetime, and a lot of things just happened a certain way."

"I was eating lunch one day by a log deck. We were working up around Anderson Peak and a big four-point buck came running down the road. He turned and ran right up on the log deck. A log rolled and he broke his neck, just like that! You see, he had lived in that area all his life and I guess was disoriented because of the logging."

"You know, another time we were hunting, me and my brother, up in that same area and we jumped a big buck up across the canyon. We had both shot at it, so we decided we'd better go over and take a look. You know, we never hit that buck, except for just clipping some hairs from off his tail, but the damn thing had jumped off the other side and hung his horn right in the fork of a laurel tree. And there he hung, must have been close to ten feet off the ground."

"But I'm going to tell you one of the damnedest things I think I've ever seen. I was walking down the street in Redding, California. You know where that is, don't you? I looked over and there, sitting on the front porch of a store, was this Indian woman in a rocking chair. Now I'm going tell you, she had hair—her braids were as big around as a man's fist and her hair was so long that it came right down her back and onto the floor, clean out to where her feet were. I just stopped and stared as she just kept rocking. Finally I walked up to this woman and said, 'Ma'am could I just touch your hair,' and she said yes, so I did! Now I've seen lots of things but this was something else!"

Fred worked hard as a logcutter for fifty-five years and being out in the woods was his way of life. As his true passion was hunting big blacktail deer, he always kept his eyes open for big buck sign and kept his ears open for talk of a big buck.

In 1953 he was told by several people about a big buck west of Eagle Point, so he decided that he'd better go take a look. This was the first and only year that Fred hunted with a bolt action .30-06 Springfield. Being left-handed, he had always hunted with a lever action. From 1922 until 1953 he hunted with a .30-40 Krag Model 95 Winchester and he had killed many deer with that gun, but a guy had talked him out of it in a trade. Fred was hunting with his son and life-long hunting partner, Riley, named after Fred's father, Purl Riley Bean. They started in an area where the buck had been spotted, and it wasn't long before they were onto his tracks. Fred decided to take the tracks, with Riley moving along above him. The wind from the night before had blown leaves and moss from the trees, so they were taking it real slow when Fred decided to sit down and think out the situation. He was eating a sandwich when he caught movement out of the corner of his eye. There was the buck, not more than ten feet away, lying down, and chewing on a piece of moss nearly two feet long. Just as Fred laid eyes on the buck, the buck turned and looked at him. Then all hell broke loose. Fred's gun was coming up as the buck was bounding away, but he was not used to this gun and he couldn't find the safety. After looking down to release the safety, he looked back up as the buck began to disappear out of sight and he fired instinctively from the hip. Riley, having witnessed the shot, stated, "We always knew when Dad's gun went off, a buck died, but this was something else."

Fred let out a loud war whoop that could be heard for miles because he knew he had killed an exceptional deer. "Old Moss Mouth" won the big buck contest that year, weighing 203 lbs. He was later measured at 173 1/8 B.C.; but an error in the measurement had been made, and he now officially measures 169 5/8 B.C., the fourth largest blacktail taken in Oregon. With the $100 first-place prize Fred bought the gun he would hunt with from then on, a .348 Winchester Model 71. The .30-06 was given to Riley, and that very next year he won the big buck contest with another exceptional buck.

Riley told me, "I'm the luckiest man alive to have a father like Fred. He truly had an undying passion to hunt blacktails. We hunted every season just about the entire season. We had two real good areas to hunt—we cut horse trails into the Grayback country and also the Anderson Peak country. Both areas we knew like the back of our hand, and Dad had a very unique way of locating big bucks. He could sit down, study an area, and tell you exactly where the bucks would be. He would look for something different in the lay of the land, whether it was a big tree or a rock that stood out from the rest of the surroundings. Dad was adamant that the big bucks picked out and used landmarks so as to know where they were. Dad was perhaps one of the finest shots there ever was. If a buck gave him one split second to get his gun up, he was dead."

I asked Fred how deer reacted to the different weather conditions and this is what he told me. "When it's hot and dry, you want to hunt the dense brush. If it's rainy, hunt the big timber, way back in the cover. If it's windy, look for open areas in the timber, and if it's snowing, well, look for tracks."

"When we hunted, one of us would find a vantage point, while the other one would work the brush. You would have to make two or three passes through the same area to jump them up—you have to literally step on them. On several hunts we could see a buck out in front of the other hunter and would be talking back and forth, telling him just exactly where the buck was lying and the buck would just lie there."

I asked Fred his opinion on the future of big blacktail bucks, and he made me promise him to tell it like he did.

"There will always be a few big bucks around, but nothing like it was back then. There were times in the better areas that we would see fifty to sixty bucks, not in a season but in a day. As soon as they started those damn does seasons, the deer numbers went down. Anyone's a fool to think of killing a doe. Where the hell do they think the bucks come from! With all the roads they got nowadays and with houses being built all over the country, no it probably won't ever be like it used to be. Hell, we rode horses for miles back into that country. Now it just makes me sick. Right where our old hunting cabin was is a God-damn clearcut, with roads going every which a way! Now I'm going to tell you something. When we hunted, we never killed any little bucks. We passed them up. Just as soon as you kill a little buck, you give it all away because somewhere close is a bigger buck. Now that's the way you got to think or you might as well sit at home. No sir!! I wouldn't let anyone shoot a little buck and I'm for damned sure against shooting any does. Now, I talked to them fellows who make all those decisions until I was blue in the face, and you know what, they're just like that guy I told you the story about down in Arizona, with the burros. Hell, they haven't been around long enough to evaluate the situation. They went off, got themselves educated, and came back thinking they're as smart as hell. You know what I mean? It's pure hogwash. I didn't go down there talking through my hat. I've been in this country all my life and I've seen a lot of things.

"What most people don't realize is them old does never become nonproductive. They're the ones that teach the young how to survive, not only their fawns but the fawns they had two or three years ago. You see, deer are a lot more complex than cattle. They are a lot more like coyotes or wolves. They will continue to live in the same area for a long time; hell, they know one another throughout their entire lives. The older deer teach the younger deer how to migrate, when to migrate and where to migrate. Sure, some of it is instinct but most of it is learned. Now, over in eastern Oregon there used to be big migrations of mule deer. For miles the deer travel; these migration routes were established long before we ever came here, and they were taught these routes by the old barren does, you know, the ones they call nonproductive. Well, a lot of those migrations don't even exist now. Well, I wonder why!

"The blacktail migrate too, from all along the Cascades and down out of the Siskiyous and now you have people telling you true blacktails are only from west of I-5. The blacktail range is from right up around the crest to the Cascades to the coast. Because of the feed, blacktail from the Cascades and the Siskiyous are larger than the deer from the coast, but there are true blacktail."

Fred and Riley Bean have taken thirty-one blacktail that qualify for the *Record Book for Oregon's Big Game Animals,* and twelve bucks that qualify for Boone and Crockett, including three bucks in the high 160s. Fred's 203 1/8 B.C. nontypical blacktail from the 1930s taken up in the Grayback country ranks number one in Oregon for Columbian blacktail. (Boone and Crockett currently doesn't recognize non-typical blacktail deer.) They also have several other non-typicals that rank high in the record book. Fred also killed a forked-horn buck that measures 125 0/8 B.C.

Fred and Riley Bean are undoubtedly two of the greatest deer hunters to have lived. The passion, desire and effort they have put forth reflect the characters of these truly extraordinary hunters. I, for one, will always remember and cherish every moment of time I spent listening to their stories. Fred Bean was truly a man of great character, a very warm and compassionate man and a very knowledgeable man.

One of the last stories Fred Bean told me was about how the elderly Indians would go out and set up a wigwam, taking along with them some food and firewood; when they ran out, they died. He said, "Now I want to tell you, what the hell's the matter with that?"

May he always be remembered, like his father, as "The Legendary Hunter of the Siskiyous." Fred, you will be missed dearly.

Fred passed away in February of 1996.

David M. Morris

Foreword

This is the first edition of the *Record Book for Oregon's Big Game Animals.* Future editions of this book will be printed every four years. In association with this book an annual publication titled *Oregon's Big Game Yearly* will be printed every fall. This magazine will feature the photographs and stories from the entries recorded from July 1st through June 30th of each calendar year.

The entries recorded in this edition were submitted either by the hunters who harvested these animals or by the present owners. Exhaustive efforts were made to reach the people who have entries in other record books; however, we cannot list animals recorded in other books unless that information is submitted to us.

This book also features photographs taken during the early 1900s through the 1960s. These historical hunting photographs exhibit Oregon's deep hunting heritage.

There are three separate categories established for the different methods used to harvest big game animals. They are: Rifle (which includes hand guns), Archery and Black Powder. There is a separate category for recording shed antlers. In each of these categories there are separate listings for each of the big game species. This book features categories currently not listed in most other record books, including Columbian whitetail deer, California bighorn sheep, Cascade Roosevelt elk, Cascade blacktail deer, Pacific Northwest blacktail deer and nontypical blacktail deer.

In the first edition, the minimum score requirements in the Rifle categories were based upon either eighty or ninety percent of the current Boone and Crockett minimum standards. In the Archery and the Black Powder categories, the minimum score requirements were the same as those used in Pope and Young and the Long Hunters Society record books. After further evaluation and input, the minimum score requirements for the second edition have been revised. All entries received from July 1,1996, through June 30, 2000, will be accepted under the revised minimum scores.

The *Record Book for Oregon* will hold an annual awards ceremony to recognize exceptional animals for each of the big game species. It will also be enacting the Big Game Hunter Award Program, developed to recognize hunters who have successfully taken outstanding animals. The information and requirements for this program are clarified further in this book.

It is our goal to establish and maintain a complete and accurate record book for the recognition of Oregon's big game animals and the hunters who pursue them. It is our hope that this book will increase awareness among the various sporting organizations, so that we become a common voice, dedicated to the preservation and enjoyment of hunting for present and future Oregonians.

Measurements may be different for some entries than those that appear in *Records of North American Big Game* (Boone and Crockett) or *Bowhunting Records of North America* (Pope and Young).

The Records Committee, consisting of Measuring Coordinator Rusty Lindberg and two committee members, will evaluate any discrepancies in measuring and will have final approval of all entries.

The *Record Book for Oregon's Big Game Animals* discourages entrants from having their entries measured by more than one scorer, thus eliminating the practice of "shopping around" for a higher measurement. However a request can be made to the Records Committee concerning a discrepancy in the measurement or validity of an entry.

Entries ranked in the top ten must also meet the qualifications for Boone and Crockett or Pope and Young; however, they do not have to be entered in or accepted by either organization. An asterisk will be used to identify these entries and they will not be ranked accordingly.

Acknowledgments

I would like to express my appreciation to the people who have submitted entries to this book. Without your faith, patience and understanding, this book would not be possible. My thanks also to the official measurers, photographers, artists, contributing authors and the advisory committee for their contributions to this book. A tremendous amount of time and effort has been devoted by many to assure its success.

I would like to thank Eldon "Buck" Buckner for the experience and knowledge he provided in forming the structure of this book; Roger Selner of Trophy Show Productions for his encouragement, dedication and time taken to assure the success of this project; and Greg Smith of Northwest Trails Outdoor Shows for providing exposure and support of the record book.

I would especially like to thank each of the following people for their outstanding contributions and for devoting a great deal of their time in helping create this book:

Charles "Rusty" Lindberg for his invaluable expertise as measuring coordinator, instructing the measuring clinics, and for his insight in establishing this book; Stan Neitling and Jerry Egbert for their knowledge and assistance with the measuring clinics and scoring entries; Chuck and Toni Lynde, Vic Masson, Stanley Miles, Eugene Smith, Charles Sarrett and the other scorers for their assistance in measuring entries; Vic Coggins, District Game Biologist for the Oregon Department of Fish and Wildlife, who has been an essential member of the advisory committee, providing valuable insight in developing, structuring and promoting this project; Paula Jessel, who designed and developed a computer program with the essential components for our record keeping and who also helped design the Oregon score sheet and spent many hours entering data and processing information; Oregon artist Tom Schillinger, selected by the record book for his extraordinary talents as an artist, who worked countless hours painting the first six of a set of Oregon state records, "Taft" and "Tarzan" at Wallowa Lake, and who drew the divider page illustrations and graphics for the new Oregon score sheets (other examples of Tom's work can be seen throughout the book).

A very special thanks goes to Todd and Suz Hueckman, Greg and Lisa Robirts, Rusty Lindberg, Doug and Shannon Weaver, Larry and Robin Griffin, Joe and Paula Jessel, Ben and Mary Cook, Huston and Norma Hansen, Tom and Melanie Schillinger, Jeff Gritz, Josh Zabransky, Lee Rhoden and Gordon Childers, first and foremost for their friendship, and also for their support and encouragement and the tremendous amount of time and effort that they have devoted.

Above all, I would like express my deepest appreciation to my family for their confidence and support, especially to my son Holt for his sacrifice of personal time.

David M. Morris, Director
Record Book for Oregon

Advisory Committee Members

Vic Coggins—Oregon Department of Fish and Wildlife
Enterprise, Oregon

Chuck Lynde—Oregon Bow Hunters/Pope and Young Measurer
Clackamas, Oregon

Dave Doran—Oregon Hunters Association/ODFW/Pope and Young
Bend, Oregon

Eldon Deardorff—Oregon Guides and Packers
Richland, Oregon

Rusty Lindberg—Boone and Crockett Measuring Coordinator
St. Helens, Oregon

Stan Neitling—Boone and Crockett Measurer
Lake Oswego, Oregon

David M. Morris—Director/Oregon Measurer
Irrigon, Oregon

Introduction

The *Record Book for Oregon's Big Game Animals* was established to record and increase the recognition of Oregon's big game animals, to recognize those hunters who take such animals legally under fair chase conditions and to enhance the awareness of Oregon's rich hunting heritage. It is our hope that this book will promote more selective, ethical hunting by sportsmen as they enjoy this traditional sport.

This record book is directed by David M. Morris and is advised by a seven-member committee, appointed to serve by their various hunting organizations in Oregon. The format for this book has been a correlation of ideas gathered from this committee and from hunters throughout Oregon.

History

The idea for this book began in December of 1993. Several other states had successfully established record books. After reviewing these books, a meeting was scheduled with Boone and Crockett Measurer Eldon "Buck" Buckner, who served as chairman and measuring coordinator of the Arizona Wildlife Trophies. The information and experience provided by Buck was instrumental in the conception of the *Record Book for Oregon*. In February of 1994, authorization for the use of the Boone and Crockett measuring system was granted by Jack Reneau, director of the Boone and Crockett Big Game Records.

The following organizations were contacted with a request to appoint a member to serve on an advisory committee for the record book: the Oregon Department of Fish and Wildlife, the Oregon Hunters Association, the Oregon Bow Hunters, the Oregon Guides and Packers Association, the Boone and Crockett Club and the Pope and Young Club. Once this committee was in place, the rules and requirements, minimum scores and categories for the *Record Book for Oregon* were established. Official Measurers from Boone and Crockett and from Pope and Young were notified of the opening of the *Record Book for Oregon's Big Game Animals*. In my conversation with several measurers, a concern was raised that the number of entries needing to be measured could be overburdening to them. Other states facing the same dilemma have certified state measurers, instructing them in measuring clinics using Certified Instructors who are either Boone and Crockett or Pope and Young Official Measurers.

Rusty Lindberg, who serves as the measuring coordinator, Dr. Stan Neitling and Jerry Egbert instructed measuring clinics for Oregon, certifying fifty-nine Oregon Measurers. Geographically dispersed throughout the state and selected for their qualifications, they will be available to measure entries for the *Record Book for Oregon*.

Minimum Score Requirements

July 1, 1996–July 1, 2000

Species	Rifle	Archery	Black Powder	Shed Antler
Rocky Mountain Elk (Typical)	310	260	255	135
Rocky Mountain Elk (Non-typical)	335	300	265	150
Roosevelt Elk (Typical)	260	225	225	100
Roosevelt Elk (Non-typical)	285	250	250	110
Cascade Roosevelt Elk (Typical)	260	225	225	100
Cascade Roosevelt Elk (Non-typical)	285	250	250	110
Mule Deer (Typical)	170	145	146	70
Mule Deer (Non-typical)	200	160	175	85
Columbian Blacktail Deer (Typical)	125	90	95	50
Columbian Blacktail Deer (Non-typical)	150	110	115	60
Cascade Blacktail Deer (Typical)	125	90	95	50
Cascade Blacktail Deer (Non-typical)	150	110	115	60
Northwest Blacktail Deer (Typical)	110	90	90	50
Northwest Blacktail Deer (Non-typical)	135	110	110	60
Whitetail Deer (Typical)	130	125	125	60
Whitetail Deer (Non-typical)	160	140	160	70
Pronghorn (Antelope)	76	64	63	
Rocky Mountain Bighorn Sheep	165	140	136	
California Bighorn Sheep	155	150	140	
Black Bear	18 8/16	18	18	
Cougar (Mountain Lion)	14	13 8/16	13	
Columbian Whitetail Deer (Typical & Non-typical)	We are accepting all entries for this species.			
Rocky Mountain Goat	Twenty Rocky Mountain Goats were taken during 1965–68.			

Rules and Requirements for the
Record Book for Oregon

1. All entries must have been taken in the state of Oregon.
2. All entries must have been taken legally as prescribed by the Oregon Department of Fish and Wildlife and in accordance with the fair chase rules as defined by the Boone and Crockett Club.
3. All entries must be measured by an official Boone and Crockett or Pope and Young measurer, or a measurer certified by the *Record Book for Oregon*.
4. All entries must have a sixty-day air-drying period.
5. All entries are subject to final approval by the *Record Book for Oregon* Committee.
6. Each entry must be submitted with a $15.00 recording fee.

Official Measurers for Oregon

David Powell
810 SW 7th
Pendleton, OR 97801
(541) 276-2859

Sam L. Wilkins, Jr.
2218 E. 14th
The Dalles, OR 97058
(541) 298-7900

Jerry Donovan
2750 6th St.
Columbia City, OR 97018
(503) 397-6737

Danny Benson
750 South 8th
Lakeview, OR 97630
(541) 947-5107

Todd Hueckman
P.O. Box 362
Hines, OR 97738
(541) 573-5934

Diana Shields
3412 NE 169th
Vancouver, WA 98682
(360) 254-4709

Bob Staples
P.O. Box 1665
La Grande, OR 97850
(541) 963-9348

Mark Penninger
2104 Leo Ln.
La Grande, OR 97850
(541) 963-4238

Eugene Erwin
2435 Century Loop
La Grande, OR 97850
(541) 962-0592

Leonard Erickson
20th St.
La Grande, OR 97850
(541) 963-9014

Steve Hawkins
266 Norman Ave.
Coos Bay, OR 97420
(541) 888-2524

Rich Lebsock
3208 SW Isaac
Pendleton, OR 97801
(541) 276-2399

Randy Higley
35230 SE Divers Rd.
Estacada, OR 97023
(503) 630-5098

Larry Wolfgram
4850 Appaloosa Ln.
Pendleton, OR 97801
(541) 276-6829

Ken Moore
Hcr 56 Box 720
John Day, OR 97845
(541) 932-4475

Ron Russell
P.O. Box 743
Coquille, OR 97423
(541) 396-2029

David M. Morris
P.O. Box 759
Irrigon, OR 97844
(541) 922-2959

Lloyd Christenson
422 SW 18th
Pendleton, OR 97801
(541) 276-3196

Delbert Moulton
2307 Main
Baker City, OR 97814
(541) 523-5934

Scott Ritner
P.O. Box 604
John Day, OR 97845
(541) 820-3511

Walt Gentis
P.O. Box 243
John Day, OR 97845
(541) 575-0593

Jim Cadwell
107 20th St.
La Grande, OR 97850
(541) 437-1718

Gary L. Broadhead
1227 N.W. Galveston
Bend, OR 97701
(541) 382-8396

Ken Lebsock
3715 SW Marshall
Pendleton, OR 97801
(541) 276-0013

Rick Kelly
29835 S. Molalla
Molalla, OR 97038
(503) 829-3867

Lee J. Dohaniuk
P.O. Box 1130
Cannon Beach, OR 97110
(503) 738-3689

Gordon Childers
322 SE Jackson
Redmond, OR 97756
(541) 548-8929

Mark Johnston
P.O. Box 1113
Bandon, OR 97411
(541) 347-3155

Rodney Wilson
150 Rattlesnake Rd.
Glendale, OR 97442
(541) 832-2653

Dan Smith
Rt. 5 Box 882
Astoria, OR 97103
(503) 325-6044

Robby Porter
P.O. Box 132
Haines, OR 97833
(541) 856-3654

James Ward
57923 Foothills Rd.
La Grande, OR 97850
(541) 963-6977

Russ Powell
551 W. Bryan
Union, OR 97883
(541) 562-6287

Jerry Grover
2995 Hughes Ln.
Baker City, OR 97814
(541) 523-4743

Brent Beagley
19115 Bedford
Oregon City, OR 97045
(503) 655-2694

Larry Powell
P.O. Box 751
Prineville, OR 97754
(541) 447-1112

Shirley Andrews
28297 Ridge Way Road
Sweethome, OR 97386
(541) 367-4892

Randy Curtis
Rt. 2 Box 2146
Hermiston, OR 97838
(541) 567-4232

Larry Griffin
12688 SE 162nd Ave.
Clackamas, OR 97015
(503) 658-7112

Huston Hanson
P.O. Box 895
Hood River, OR 97031
(541) 352-6215

Brian Samuel
812 Corey Dr.
Phoenix, OR 97535
(541) 512-9436

Chuck Link
64443 Lostine River Rd.
Lostine, OR 97857
(541) 569-2484

Nathan Hull
415 David Eceles Rd.
Baker City, OR 97814
(541)-523-3308

Bill Spears
2403 Birch St.
La Grande, OR 97850
(541) 963-3147

David Carroll
1207 N Avenue
La Grande, OR 97850
(541) 963-5898

Dale Dotson
85711 Grote Lane
Joseph, OR 97846
(541) 432-0104

Armone Foulon
7220 Hwy. 234
Central Point, OR 97502
(541) 826-8308

R.J. Simington
3025 Debbie Dr.
Klamath Falls, OR 97601
(541) 882-1314

Official Measurers for Oregon (continued)

Eddie Heid
P.O. Box 44
Jamieson, OR 97909
(541) 473-3345

Terry W. Smith
P.O. Box 323
Siletz, OR 97380
(541) 444-2311

Dennis King
5300 Hwy. 238
P.O. Box 567
Jacksonville, OR 97530
(541) 899-7330

John Milleson
4908 Pioneer Rd.
Ontario, OR 97914
(541) 262- 3232

Tom Schillinger
P. O. Box 332
Hines, OR 97738
(541) 573-6398

Gary Nyden
92871 Kinser Lane
Cheshire, OR 97419
(541) 729-4868

Jerry Pressley
P.O. Box 1508
Yreka, CA 96097
(916) 842- 4556

Mike Parks
155 S. Gordon Way
Grants Pass, OR 97527
(541) 955-8400

Paul H. Larsen
P.O. Box 1113
Tenino, WA 98589
(360) 264-5264

Parry Hurliman
21100 Wilson River Hwy.
Tillamook, OR 97141
(503) 842-5190

Doug Weaver
467 Trails End Rd.
Eagle Point, OR 97524
(541) 830-0654

Oregon's Official Boone and Crockett Measurers

J.D. Gore
445 South 46th
Springfield, OR 97478
(541) 746-8045

Elvin Hawkins
4950 Crater Lake Ave.
Medford, OR 97504
(541) 776-7605

Rusty Lindberg
58724 Timber Crest Ln.
St. Helens, OR 97015
(503) 397-4608

John E. Stone
190 Crowfoot Rd.
Lebanon, OR 97355
(541) 259-2697

W.V. Masson
Box 128
Hines, OR 97738
(541) 573-2785

Stan Neitling
14143 Taylors Crest Ln.
Lake Oswego, OR
(503) 635-1120

Eldon "Buck" Buckner
Hunt Mt. Rt. 2 Box 128
Baker City, OR 97814
(541) 523-6109

Curt Harrison
P.O. Box 367
Fossil, OR 97830
(541) 763-2127

Larry Griffin
12688 SE 162nd
Clackamas, OR 97015
(503) 658-7112

Jerry Egbert
3412 NE 169th Ave.
Vancouver, WA 98682
(360) 254-4709

Oregon's Official Pope and Young Measurers

Ben R. Cook
2125 S.E. 139th
Portland, OR 97233
(503) 255-7689

Larry D. Jones
4015 Main St., Suite A
Springfield, OR 97478
(541) 741-0263

Stephen Herrara
702 West Central
Sutherlin, OR 97479
(541) 459-9577

Stanley Miles
1425 NW 13th
Corvallis, OR 97330
(503) 753-8945

Eugene Smith
P.O. Box 17
Joseph, OR 97846
(541) 432-7015

Dave Doran
60562 East Lake Dr.
Bend, OR 97702
W (541)-388-8400
H (541)-388-6363

Donald Ranjus
30485 Transformer Rd.
Malin, OR 97632
(541) 723-4371

Chuck Lynde
P.O. Box 84100
Vancouver, WA 89684-0100
(503) 632-3022

Charles Sarrett
509 Benton Court
La Grande, OR 97850
(541) 963-6685

Gary Madison
101761 Hill St.
Prineville, OR 97754
(541) 447-5930

Annual Awards Ceremony

The purpose of this program is to recognize Oregon's outstanding big game animals. A secondary purpose is to recognize the hunters who have taken such animals. The award ceremony will be held annually in conjunction with the Oregon Association of Taxidermists Wildlife Show and Art Competition.

Each animal must have been harvested legally according to the Oregon Department of Fish and Wildlife and in the state of Oregon.

There are two types of award programs established as of July 1996. The first type of award will be given annually in recognition of Oregon's exceptional big game animals. The qualifying scores are listed below. One award in this category will be given to recognize each outstanding animal that qualifies by meeting or exceeding the required score for their species. Another award will be given to recognize the largest animal taken in each calendar year for each big game category.

Species	Minimum Score for the Award Program	Minimum Score for the Record Book for Oregon
Rocky Mountain Elk (Typical)	335	310
Rocky Mountain Elk (Non-typical)	350	325
Roosevelt Elk	275	260
Mule Deer (Typical)	175	170
Mule Deer (Non-typical)	215	200
Blacktail Deer (Typical)	130	120
Blacktail Deer (Non-typical)	155	150
Whitetail Deer (Typical)	150	130
Whitetail Deer (Non-typical)	170	160
Pronghorn	78	76
Rocky Mountain Bighorn Sheep	170	165
California Bighorn Sheep	165	155
Black Bear	19	18 8/16
Cougar	14 8/16	14

The second type of award is the Accomplished Hunter Award. This award will be given to hunters who have taken qualifying animals in three different programs:

Oregon's Big Eight, Nine, Ten and Eleven. This award is in recognition of those hunters who have taken animals from the following categories and meet each requirement:

Rocky Mountain Elk: Must be a bull elk other than a spike.

Roosevelt Elk: Must be a bull elk other than a spike.

Mule Deer: Must have five points to each side, counting the eye guard.

Whitetail Deer: Must have four points to each side, counting the eye guard.

Blacktail Deer: Must have four points to each side, counting the eye guard.

Pronghorn: Must have horn length exceeding thirteen inches.

Bighorn Sheep: Must be a legal ram of either species (California or Rocky Mountain).

Black Bear: Must be an adult bear.

Cougar: Must be an adult.

Turkey: Must be an adult male.

Mountain Goat: Must be a legal adult.

Ultimate Hunter Award. The Ultimate Hunter Award will be given to hunters who qualify for one of the Accomplished Hunter Awards, with five of their animals meeting the minimum score requirements, for either Archery, Black Powder or Rifle categories in the *Record Book for Oregon.*

Trophy Hunter Award. This award will be given to hunters who have qualified for one of the Accomplished Hunter Awards, with each animal meeting the minimum score requirements, for either Archery, Black Powder or Rifle categories in the *Record Book for Oregon.*

Dedication

For each of us, there are very special people who have influenced our lives; through their efforts and devotions they have enhanced our understanding of life. With some we have lived our entire lives, with others we may have met only once, but in each, we can recall the influence they made in our lives. Some were our fathers and mothers, uncles and aunts or cousins; others were our grandparents, friends or neighbors. All of these people were cut from the same mold yet each were their own individual selves. These were people of character, people of honor, people we looked up to. These were tough, hard-working people, yet they all possessed a certain warmth and understanding. They were raised in and lived through an era when times were hard; most of them worked from daylight to dark to provide for their families. Whether they were loggers or ranchers, farmers or worked in other professions, their hearts were never far away from the outdoors.

They somehow always found the time to do what they loved the most, to take us out to experience life and to show us the adventures they had found in nature. They were there when we shot our first buck; they baited the hook when we caught our first fish. They smiled when we returned with a handful of wild flowers or a shed deer antler. They showed us where to pick huckleberries and raspberries or taught us which mushrooms were edible, and watched our faces pucker as we tasted chokecherries or elderberries for the first time. They broke the trail through the deep winter snow to cut a Christmas tree, pointing out the rabbit tracks along the way. They taught us how to hunt, to shoot, to swim, to fish, to build a fire and to survive. We have in our possession the antlers of their game, the guns they hunted with, the knives they carried, the watches they wore and the many lasting memories we hold dear to our hearts. The relationships that have been built while sharing this passion withstand the test of time.

We've listened to the sounds of elk bugling in the fall and the call of the sandhill cranes and Canadian geese as they flew south for the winter. Together we have seen the magnificence in the mountains, the valleys, the desert and the rivers. We have seen spectacular colors, the reds, purples, pinks, oranges and yellows at sunrise and sunset. Together we have endured the rains of spring, the heat of summer, the chill of fall and the bitter cold and snow of winter.

We have sat around camp fires for hours and hours, spellbound, listening to their stories. They told us stories about Indians, bears, cougars, a big buck or big bull and our families' struggle to inhabit this land. When I hear the sound of a lonesome coyote cut through the still night air, I often wonder what it must have been like to have lived back then.

These people have instilled in us the same passion that they possessed. They have helped in the building of our characters, through their direction we have been forged. In our character they have built a spirit, created honor, compassion, warmth and understanding. Our lives mirror a reflection of their spirit, their fortitude, their determination and their strength, and through our adventures they will live forever because they live within us.

We will forever cherish the time we have spent together, reminiscing in the stories they have told and treasuring the invaluable lessons they have taught us. We would like to express our deepest appreciation to all of those who took their time and exposed us to the many wonderful adventures in the outdoors.

As outdoorsmen, we have an ethical responsibility to our environment, to nature and to the game we pursue. I feel it is also our duty as sportsmen to take the time to continue to expose our youth to the adventures in nature, as did those before us.

The Last California Grizzly in Oregon

by David M. Morris

Fred Bean's father was Purl Riley Bean. Purl Bean was a legend in his own right: On April 10, 1890, not yet seventeen years old, while hunting with Billy Wright, Purl killed a notorious California Grizzly Bear, named "Reel-Foot." This tremendous brown bear weighed over two thousand pounds. He stood twelve feet tall, measured twenty-two inches from the tip of his nose to the top of his head, and fourteen inches between his ears. This was not your average grizzly, he was a giant among bears.

Reel-Foot waged a one-bear war for over forty years with the ranchers of northern California and southern Oregon. He ranged over an extremely large area: north almost to Roseburg, west to the Pacific, east to Klamath Lake, and south almost to Redding, California. His favorite haunt was the Pilot Rock area near the California-Oregon border. He traveled the wagon trails and roads almost exclusively at night. He had learned how to open gates and negotiate fences, breaking into well-built corrals to carry off a calf if he was hungry. This bear showed no fear of anything or anybody. As a matter of fact, they took nearly a quart of lead out of his body when they skinned him. He killed hundreds of sheep simply for the sport; he had acquired a lust for killing, leaving their carcasses fully intact.

On one occasion in 1882, witnessed by a sheep herder named J. D. Williams from a secure vantage point in a tree, Reel-Foot stealthily approached some cattle in a pasture, led by a large bull. He suddenly made a charge for a calf standing by its mother's side. Reaching the speed of a good saddle horse, he snatched the calf. Naturally, the mother tried to defend her calf, but with one swift blow from his paw, she was dispatched. Then the bull charged the grizzly and so enraged was he at this interloper that the bear was knocked into the brush. Undaunted, Reel-Foot charged the bull again and again, at last seizing the bull by the nose and, with a powerful twist, broke his neck. Triumphant, the bear inspected his kill, then ambled over to a nearby spring for a drink and a leisurely swim. He then returned to eat his dinner and finally shuffled off into the brush. The terrified sheep herder remained in the tree until nightfall. (How was he to know that Reel-Foot never returned to the scene of a kill?)

Experience through the years had taught Reel-Foot that there was danger in returning to a kill. Gifted with enormous strength, wonderful agility and almost human instinct, he reigned supreme among the wildlife of the Siskiyous. He had eluded all attempts to capture him, until one day he killed a two-year-old heifer belonging to Bruce Grieves, near Hornbrook. Grieves had set a trap near the kill and what a trap it was: about four feet long and weighing forty-two pounds. Reel-Foot was passing down a trail that had a large clump of brush on either side of it. Passing through the center, he stepped into the trap and was caught. He ran with the trap, which was fastened to a drag (a black oak about eight inches in diameter and ten to twelve feet long). Once the drag became lodged between two trees, the trap came tight. Fighting desperately to free himself, he twisted and pulled with all his might, finally freeing himself by severing part of his foot and three of his toes. His deformed stump of a foot was to forever give away his presence and earned him the name of Reel-Foot. (He was also called "Slewfoot" or "Clubfoot.")

His rage against man would never subside. He never forgot his pain and was never caught in a trap again. He didn't stay away from traps, he would simply rob them; as the years went by, innumerable traps were set to no avail.

When traps failed, an attempt was made to kill the old grizzly with a set gun. His tracks were found on a dim trail that led through tall firs and underbrush, and an old trapper decided to outwit the bear this time. Choosing a point where the trail passed between two trees, he placed a loaded gun pointing across the trail, attached a strong string to the trigger, then placed a tempting morsel of meat as bait at the other end of the string. Smugly, he took his position in a nearby tree, where he would spend the night waiting for the bear.

Along about daylight he was rewarded with the sight of Reel-Foot's massive form moving in the shadows toward the bait. The bear scented the tempting bait and was instantly suspicious. He stopped, reared up and sniffed the air. His keen nostrils caught the scent of the human and his cunning came into play. Cautiously, he moved toward the bait. As he approached the nearest tree, he reached around the tree with his paw, clutched the bait and dragged it toward him. At that precise moment the trigger fell. There was a loud report and the rifle's slugs were buried into the tree trunk. With a mighty roar, old Reel-Foot rushed off and the amazed hunter was left behind, shaking his head disbelievingly.

Rewards offered by cattlemen and sheepmen for his destruction grew with the years, but for four decades he continued on a rampage of depredation of their stock. Countless stories were told of his cunning and stealth. Reel-Foot was credited with killing over five thousand head of livestock, and on many encounters he had been shot at and hit, but because of his tremendous size, bullet holes were just superficial wounds.

As the legend of Reel-Foot grew, so did the reward money. On Soda Mountain a reward tree had been posted for $2750.00 and the fascination with this bear by Billy Wright and Purl Bean began.

Billy Wright was born in 1849 and crossed the plains in a covered wagon. He settled in Siskiyou County on Camp Creek in 1879, where he raised cattle. Purl Bean was born in 1873 and was a neighbor of Billy Wright's. He had yet to turn seventeen but even at this young age was an experienced hunter and a very fine shot.

On several occasions, hunting parties were formed to rid this region of the notorious bear. They had assembled some of the finest hounds in the county to begin the task of hunting down Reel-Foot. For several months they had searched for signs of the bear. On more than one occasion they had found his tracks, only to be eluded by the cagey old veteran. Billy and Purl were members of the party that had started on his tracks near Pilot Rock. Having only his clubfoot track to guide them, he led them across the upper Rogue River Valley through what is known as Dead Indian country, then along the shores of Lake of the Woods. After continuing the hunt to the shores of Crater Lake, they finally gave up. What they didn't know was that Reel-Foot was now following them. That night, while they camped, he killed a young steer near their camp in what seemed an act of utter contempt. This wasn't discovered until the next day, long after he had vanished again.

One day Reel-Foot came across two Klamath Indians drying salmon along the banks of the Klamath River. That day he had a craving for dried fish—approaching from upriver he could smell delicious odors from quite some distance. As he ambled closer his presence was detected by one of the Indians, who fired upon him. This only enraged the bear: he charged as the second Indian fired, the bullet lodging in his cheek. As the Indians tried to escape, he quickly attacked, killing both with swift blows from his powerful arms and sharp claws. They were discovered shortly following the attack; it appeared he had savagely taken out his frustrations for man on these unsuspecting victims.

On another occasion, Billy Wright and Purl Bean were hunting cougar when they came across Reel-Foot's tracks. They were on the Smith River, in Preston Peak country, and they had followed his tracks for several days. This bear would simply wear hound dogs out: once the dogs caught up with the bear they would tire from fighting, as the bear wouldn't or couldn't climb a tree. With Billy and Purl too far behind the chase to be of any assistance to the dogs, it became a routine to follow Reel-Foot day after day, only to have each day end like the last, with no sighting of the bear. It was during one of these hunts that they finally lay eyes on Reel-Foot. After four or five days of following the dogs, they made camp. Exhausted and soaking wet, they crawled into bed. During that rainy night they awoke to the sound of their dogs barking savagely, and then all hell broke loose as Reel-Foot came crashing into camp, slashing at everything and anything, reminding them of who he was and what his intentions were.

Billy or Purl didn't see Reel-Foot again until sometime later. One day, while looking for stock high in the Siskiyous, they located his tracks somewhere around Bald Mountain. Billy and Purl followed the bear deep into the snow. The bear would plow through the snow up to his throat, and the men, on snowshoes, had a definite advantage. They were closing the distance between them and the bear when they spotted Reel-Foot. Their dogs had him cornered up against the face of a rock bluff. Eight shots were fired into the hulk of the bear as he fled the scene, but the hunters were too far out of range. Fate prevailed again, as their snowshoes began to fall apart and the chase had to be abandoned.

Bears are usually in poor condition following a long winter. The *Yreka Journal* reported a quote from Billy Wright about Reel-Foot:

> He was in good flesh and as strong as a grizzly can get or he would never have escaped. The reason for his good condition was found in the discovery that his headquarters were in the midst of the carcasses of some forty horses that had been caught in the deep snow and had perished during the winter.

A short fourteen days later, in the same *Yreka Journal*, dated April 16th, 1890, was printed the following:

> Billy Wright and a boy named Bean killed the celebrated grizzly "Clubfoot" one day last week, about seven miles from here. Wright and Bean found his tracks at 9 a.m. and followed it until noon when they located him in a thicket of scrub oak near Deihl Springs. Rocks were rolled down the hill and the bear came out. Both fired at the same time and the great grizzly fell, but

immediately got up again and started for the boys.

There have been several different versions of the story about the day Reel-Foot died. The following one was told to me by Fred Bean.

Billy Wright and Purl Bean had tracked the bear from the morning until sometime in the early afternoon, when the dogs had caught the bear heading up a steep hill. As they approached, the bear saw them and instantly charged downhill toward them. Billy was shooting a .52-56 Spencer rim fire, and Purl was shooting a .44-40 model 73 Winchester, with Purl's gun having superior fire power. Billy had already told Purl, "If the bear charges, hold your ground and fire every round into his head or chest." Purl was steady as he fired his gun as fast as he could, working the action with lightning speed. They had both anticipated and envisioned this scene over and over, around the many campfires they shared while in pursuit of this bear. He continued to fire as the enormous grizzly quickly closed the ground between them. He could hear Billy coaching him on every shot. Finally, the giant bear went down, only fifteen feet from where they stood. After some forty years, the reign of one of the greatest creatures on this planet was over. One of the last California grizzly bears, the rogue bear of the Siskiyous, the legendary Reel-Foot, was dead.

All eleven rounds from Purl's model 73 had hit the bear. Upon skinning the bear they recovered nearly a quart jar of bullets that had been shot into him, including those shot by the unfortunate Indians on the Klamath River.

There was great excitement and interest when the old monarch was finally killed. So much so that the bear was mounted life-size. His teeth were worn off to not more than one-half inch in length, but what he lacked in teeth he made up in size: close to two thousand pounds, he stood twelve feet tall. His head measured twenty-two inches from nose to base and fourteen inches between his ears. Several of his claws exceeded six inches in length; there were only two claws left on one foot from the time he was trapped. The bear went on the road with Billy and Purl, advertised as the "World's largest grizzly bear," and drew outstanding crowds wherever they appeared.

In 1893, he was exhibited in Chicago at the Columbian Exposition. Some say that he was then purchased by the Native Sons of the Golden West, to be displayed in the lobby of their headquarters in San Francisco, and that he was destroyed in the San Francisco earthquake and fire in 1906. Rumors say that he was seen after the earthquake as late as 1914, in Jordan's Museum of Anatomy in San Francisco. Some say he was exhibited by a doctor across Europe, who made a great deal of money displaying him. Whatever became of Reel-Foot is uncertain. What is certain is that his legend will live on forever as the giant, silver-tipped grizzly of the Siskiyous.

Southern Oregon blacktail hunting. Photographs courtesy of Fred and Riley Bean

Left: the Bean hunting party

Left: They called this buck the Banana Buck for the shape of his drop tines.

Riley Bean, Jackson County

Klamath Falls, Oregon, Klamath County, 1930s, Riley Bean

Riley and Fred Bean

Fred Bean and his Model 71 .348 Winchester

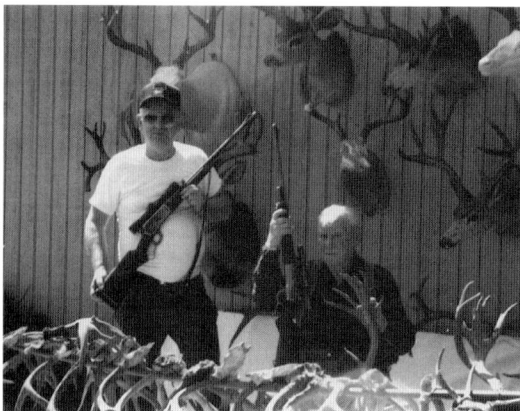

Fred and Riley Bean: father and son

These two pages: Fred and Riley Bean Collection:
Photographs courtesy of Fred and Riley Bean.

Fred Bean, 169 5/8 B.C., Jackson County 1953

Fred with his 168 6/8 B.C., Jackson County

Fred and Riley Bean, thirty-one record blacktail

This page: William Sherman Phillips Ranch, Izee, Oregon, 1930s. Photographs courtesy of Rick Page

Historical Photographs Taken from early 1900s–1960s

Columbus Phillips, 1930s. Photograph courtesy of Rick Page

Alan McFetridge on horseback with a large bull elk. Taken in the Chesnimnus Unit on the first elk hunt in 1933, Alan was hired by these men (unknown) to pack the elk out whole to Kirkland Springs, where they were camped. With his mules, two fir poles, a wool sack, rope and determination, they succeeded. Photograph courtesy of Alan Birkmaier.

Edward Emerson,
Grant County, 1940s,
Howard Emerson

Sharon Polley,
157 7/8 Columbian whitetail,
Douglas County, 1960s

Bill, John and Bill Gardner, Jr.,
Vinegar Mountain, Grant County, 1940s.
Photograph courtesy of Tony Gardner

Julia Balance and Kate Flynn
with a black bear

Fred Reed, 167 7/8 B.C.,
Gilliam County, 1953

Fred Reed, 165 0/8 B.C. 3pt., Gilliam County, 1950

Andrew Radinovich, Grant County, 1959, Seneca, Oregon

Buck Matson,
242 5/8 B.C.,
Deschutes County, 1960,
Tim Rozewski

17

Vern, Lamon and Chris. Photograph courtesy of Vernon Case.

Marvin Burnette, 1952

Irene Burnette, 1950

Buster Burnette's bull elk, 1938

Ben Burnette, 1953

Marvin, Fred, Vivian and Buster Burnette, 1947

Buster and Irene Burnette Ranch, Ritter, Oregon.
Photographs courtesy of Irene Burnette.

Jimmy Winslow and Buster Burnette

Oregon State Record, Hugh Evans, 418 0/8 B.C.,
Crook County, 1942, Joe Jessel

Oregon Game Officer, 1964,
with Ray Gage's 376 4/8 B.C. bull,
Mitchell, Oregon, 1957, Bill Powell

Wayne Simmons, 172 4/8 B.C.,
Fox Valley, Grant County, 1958

Wesley Townsend, 357 0/8 B.C.,
Upper Grande Ronde River, 1935, DeMoss

Arbogast's deer hunting, 1915, Evert, Elmer and Ernie

Mrs. French 1939, Drake Park, Bend, Deschutes County, Oregon

Elk Hunting in the 1930s near Pilot Rock, Umatilla County, Oregon, Paul Ellis

Harley Hill, 1930s, Milton-Freewater, Oregon, Umatilla County, Bob Mawhin

Taft

One of the Original Bull Elk Imported from Wyoming and a Victim of Mistaken Identity

by David M. Morris

On March 3, 1912, in Jackson Hole, Wyoming, twenty-three elk were loaded onto sleds for the ninety-mile trip over the Tetons to Anthony, Idaho. A heavy snowstorm was encountered on the pass and for four days men and teams did little except buck through big snow drifts. The caravan of sleds pulled into Anthony on March 8. Here the elk were unloaded into the stockyard, where the fifteen strongest animals were selected for the first introduction of elk to Oregon.

The idea of moving the animals from Jackson Hole to the Wallowas had originated in the Biological Survey of the Department of Agriculture in Washington, D.C., and the mind of William L. Finley, Oregon's first State Game Warden. After a meeting in Joseph with W.E. Leffel, game warden for Wallowa County, and Mr. Finley they met with the game commission in Portland and were allotted thirty head of elk for the Wallowa country. The elk were to be shipped in two shipments of fifteen elk, the first one in 1912 and the second in 1913. The native elk in the state at this time had become almost extinct. It was estimated that there were only a half dozen elk left in Wallowa County. Early settlers throughout Oregon had hunted elk as a primary source of meat, and the elk harvest during the

Taken from a Postcard at Wallowa Lake

early days was unregulated. "Market hunting" and encroachment on elk range had already resulted in reports of elk scarcity by the late 1880s. At the turn of the century, elk populations were reduced to a few small herds along the coast, in the Cascades and in northeast Oregon.

Almost too late, the Oregon legislature started providing some protection for elk by passing a law making it illegal to sell meat from wild animals in 1899 and then by making it illegal to hunt elk at all from 1909 to 1932. With the once plentiful elk nearing the point of annihilation, conservation efforts turned to the reintroduction of elk into Oregon.

The winter of 1911–1912 was very severe and the elk in Jackson Hole were starving. The Biological Survey came out with the statement that any state or any sportsmen's association could procure elk for the purpose of restocking. With strong support from the people of Wallowa County, the Oregon Game Commission, the Elk's Lodges in the state and the Biological Survey, the first reintroduction was under way. The total cost of the reintroduction was estimated at $1100.00. The amount collected for the purpose of bringing the elk to Oregon, according to a report from William Finley, was $532.25 (the people of Wallowa County raised $300.00 and the Elk's Lodges of Oregon donated $232.25) with the remainder being jointly financed by the Oregon Game Commission and the U.S. Biological Survey.

The reintroduction site was selected by the Oregon Game Commission. This was a 2560-acre enclosure built in 1907 by the United States Bureau of Forestry, known as Billy Meadows. This enclosure had previously been used for grazing studies conducted by the U.S. Bureau of Forestry. In the fall of 1911, this pasture had been turned over to the Oregon State Game Commission to be used as a refuge for the elk. The caretaker J. Ross Leslie had prepared the way for the elk by building corrals, a feedlot and a cabin at Billy Meadows.

The elk were captured at Jackson Hole, Wyoming, where a large number of elk wintered every year. The bulls were lassoed and thrown and their antlers were cut off so they could be hauled in crates. In the first shipment were seven cows, six calves and two mature bulls, the larger nicknamed "Roosevelt" and the other nicknamed "Taft," appropriately named after presidents Theodore Roosevelt and William Howard Taft.

William L. Finley personally accompanied the elk from Anthony, Idaho, by train to Joseph, Oregon, and then continued on horseback to Billy Meadows, forty-six miles north of Joseph. Fortunately W.L. Finley documented the entire trip by photographing the event from the beginning in Anthony, Idaho, to the release site at Billy Meadows.

Once the train arrived in La Grande, the interest became intense. Half the town turned out at every station. Photographs taken by Finley at the rail stations in Imbler, Elgin, Wallowa, Lostine and Enterprise show large crowds gathering to view the crates containing the elk. Arriving

in Joseph on the evening of March 14, the elk were allowed to rest for a while, and were fed and watered, while crates were built on wagon beds.

On the morning of March 16, the wagons were loaded and the trip to Billy Meadows was begun. Several Joseph area men furnished the wagons and drove the teams. Among the men on the trip were W. E. Leffel, William L. Finley, Dan Warnock, George Saladay, Andy Heaverne, John Blevans, Frank Marr, Harry Gibson, Ed Rodgers, F.I. Vergere, George Emmons, Carl Rapp, James H. Fisk and Deputy Wardens Tom Craig and Ed Averill. Eight wagons were used to transport the elk from Joseph: five wagons containing three elk in each, two wagons loaded with hay and a cook wagon loaded with provisions for the men. In all there were twenty-one men, nineteen teams and two saddle horses (ridden by Finley and Leffel).

Saturday morning March 16, 1912, the caravan departed for Billy Meadows. Then the real difficulties began. Weather conditions were very much against them.

We had expected plenty of snow so the elk could be hauled in sleds, but all the snow had melted in the valley. We could not let the elk stay in Joseph until the roads opened in the spring, so it was necessary to get them to permanent pasture as soon as possible.

From the first day out we encountered snow. We found the roads heavy and almost impassable in places. In two days of hard traveling we did not make over twenty-five miles. We had to double up [the teams,] eight horses to a wagon in some places, and in others all hands had to help [a wagon] out of a hole or prevent a wagon from tipping over.

At the end of three days we were still some twelve to fifteen miles to go further in wagons. Finally we reached the deeper and more stable snow. A number of rough sleds or go-devils, as they were called, were constructed to use for the remaining part of the journey. It was impossible to take

the elk out of the crates so as to change them from wagon to sled. We pulled in under a big pine and with block and tackle hooked to a big limb . . . hoisted the crates and lowered them down on the sleds.

The pasture was reached on March 19. The elk were released into the corral and fed hay. The new arrivals had completed the long journey to their new home in the Chesnimnus District of the Wallowa Forest. The trip had begun March 3 and ended March 19 and encompassed ninety miles by sled over the Tetons to Anthony, Idaho; by train from Anthony, Idaho to Joseph, Oregon; and forty-six miles by wagon and sled to Billy Meadows.

Excerpts from the *Enterprise Record Chieftain*, May 16, 1912. Headline: "Elk Turned Out In Big Pasture."

The elk taken to the Billy Meadows pasture in the Chesnimnus range have been turned out into the big grazing ground. When first taken there, they were confined within the corral because it was so early in the season that the grazing was not good and, also, the fences needed rebuilding. Two additional wires have been placed around the whole pasture, making the fence seven wires high.

The period of falling trees has passed so that this fence should be in no danger of being broken down. Hence the game has been given their liberty.

The original herd of fifteen has now dwindled to twelve. Two of the cows died shortly after arrival and now the big bull "Roosevelt" has died. The three were injured while being shipped from Wyoming.

When the big bull Roosevelt first showed signs of distress it was thought it was suffering from the effects of cutting off his horns. But an examination after death showed three ribs broken. This was done, it is believed, during the clashes with a

rival bull which has been nicknamed "Taft." Attendants had thought Roosevelt had the best of these tussles, as he seemed more aggressive than Taft.

However, one calf was also born, the first of many descendants in Oregon of the original transplant. A year later another shipment of fifteen elk arrived in Wallowa County to join the first herd, "attracting much attention but not as much as the band did last year."

The elk from Billy Meadows were eventually transferred to other areas in Oregon, with the first retransplant occurring in 1917, when fifteen elk were shipped to Crater Lake National Park. A band of elk was placed at Wallowa Lake in 1918 where they became a very popular tourist attraction. In 1922, ten years after they arrived, the elk were turned out of the Billy Meadows pasture and winter feeding ceased.

Excerpts from the *Enterprise Record Chief-tain*, February 1, 1923. Headline: "Off To The Pasture To Kill Bill Taft."

The executioners have started in search of their victim. Charlie Ryason, Art Lyman, George Rodgers (Deputy Game Warden) and P.C. Bond left last Monday for Billy Meadows pasture with the purpose of killing Bill Taft, the large bull elk. The State Game Commission ordered that he be killed as he is old and troublesome.

Bill Taft is old and could not live more than a year at best. With age he has become vicious and has frequently attacked visitors at the pasture.

Excerpts from the *Enterprise Record Chieftain*, February 8, 1923.

Roaming in the forests and thickets of the big country north of the upper Chesnimnus, Bill Taft, the old bull elk, is still lord of his herd. The sentence of death, passed by the State Game Commission, was not executed last week. In fact the old elk has not been notified of the decree. The hunting party, organized as if for African game trails, reached the cabin in Billy Meadows pasture last Wednesday. In the expedition were the official marksman, official taxidermists, gun bearers, porters, beaters of the bush, cooks, interpreters, guards and guides.

As the cabin was in good repair they entered and fortified themselves for the night and, after throwing out guards, they slept soundly. In the morning they sent the beaters of the bush to scare out the big game. The gun bearers, marksmen and scientists followed on snowshoes.

Here and there elk tracks were observed

and excitement ran high. All day spoor was followed, but the party returned at night to the security of the cabin without having seen an elk. The operation was repeated the next day with no better results.

On the third day the hunt was abandoned and the venturesome party thought it time to turn back to civilization. The trip was made in sleds both ways. It is rumored that some of the Joseph Creek hunters will be drafted for the task next time.

Excerpts from the *Enterprise Record Chieftain*, February 15, 1923.

As the hunters failed to find and kill Bill Taft, the big bull elk on the Chesnimnus, the State Game Department and forest officials have decided that he is not dangerous or vicious, but that the bull elk at the head of the lake is the vicious and dangerous animal.

Old Bill Taft has been the victim of mistaken identity. But the bull at the lake is a very, very dangerous animal.

He is said to have pursued several men

who barely escaped with their lives, by climbing trees."

Excerpts from the *Enterprise Record Chieftain*, September 25, 1930.

Game Warden George Rodgers received word yesterday morning by telephone from the head of the lake that a dead elk lay near the dock. He immediately went to

1927   *1930*   *1925*

the lake and near the dock found a dead bull elk and around him the ground was plowed up and blood and hair was scattered around indicating that two bull elk had staged a terrific battle for supremacy.

The dead elk had both eyes gored out and was slit from throat to tail. Mr. Rodgers sent the head and horns to the State Game Commission for mounting, and went to the lake to seek out Taft and ascertain how badly he was hurt.

Excerpt from the *Joseph Herald*, September 25, 1930. Headline: "Bill Taft Executed, Disposition Cause."

Old Bill Taft, lord of the twenty-odd elk at the head of Wallowa Lake, is dead. He came ignominiously to his end yesterday afternoon from a slug of lead from the rifle in the hands of Ben Sutton after his execution has been ordered by Deputy Game Warden George Rodgers.

It was not a very honorable death for such an old aristocrat as Old Bill, but the handwriting had been on the wall for several years. Old Bill's disposition had been getting increasingly vicious, and last night when he gored to death another rival to his honors as head of the band, Mr. Rodgers made up his mind and passed the death sentence. The elk he killed is said to have been a larger and more magnificent specimen than Old Bill himself, but unluckily perished when he caught his horns in some brush and was unable to extricate them. Old Bill's disposition had been causing considerable trouble the last few months. He treed several tourists during the summer and in the last few days has caused several residents at the lake to run for cover. Mr. Rodgers decided it was best to do away with him now before he caused someone serious injury. Several men with rifles went out to hunt him and Mr. Sutton found him first, it is understood.

The head of the elk which Old Bill killed was sent to Portland to be mounted yesterday afternoon, while only the hide of Old Bill will be saved.

Excerpt from the *Enterprise Record Chieftain*, October 2, 1930.

In their fight for leadership of the band of elk at the head of the lake last week, the two big bulls, named Bill Taft and Tarzan, were not on equal terms. Mr. Rodgers received the following letter Sunday from Art M. Fish, Chief Law Enforcement Officer of the Oregon Game Commission at Portland: "In skinning the elk head sent to the office to be mounted by a taxidermist, it was discovered that Tarzan had been shot full in the face with a charge of beebe shot evidently fired from a shotgun. Several of the shot took effect in his eyes, which no doubt caused his blindness. We are just wondering if it is not likely and altogether probable that Big Bill sensed Tarzan's helplessness and therefore the

attack. Had Tarzan not been in the helpless condition, the final outcome of the battle that ensued might have been different."

Tarzan, 364 6/8 B.C.

Having assumed someone had researched the story of Taft the bull elk shipped from Wyoming in 1912, I was quite shocked by these articles found by Elaine Dickenson of the Wallowa County *Chieftain*. Keying on the excerpts highlighted in these articles it has been determined that the elk in the La Grande Elk's Lodge is not Taft, the original bull transplanted in Billy Meadows. The visitors to Wallowa Lake have been looking at a very large bull elk, one they presumed to be Taft, thus starting the rumor that Taft once had lived at the lake.

Photographs taken of the original Taft, found in the Oregon Historical Society in Portland, re-

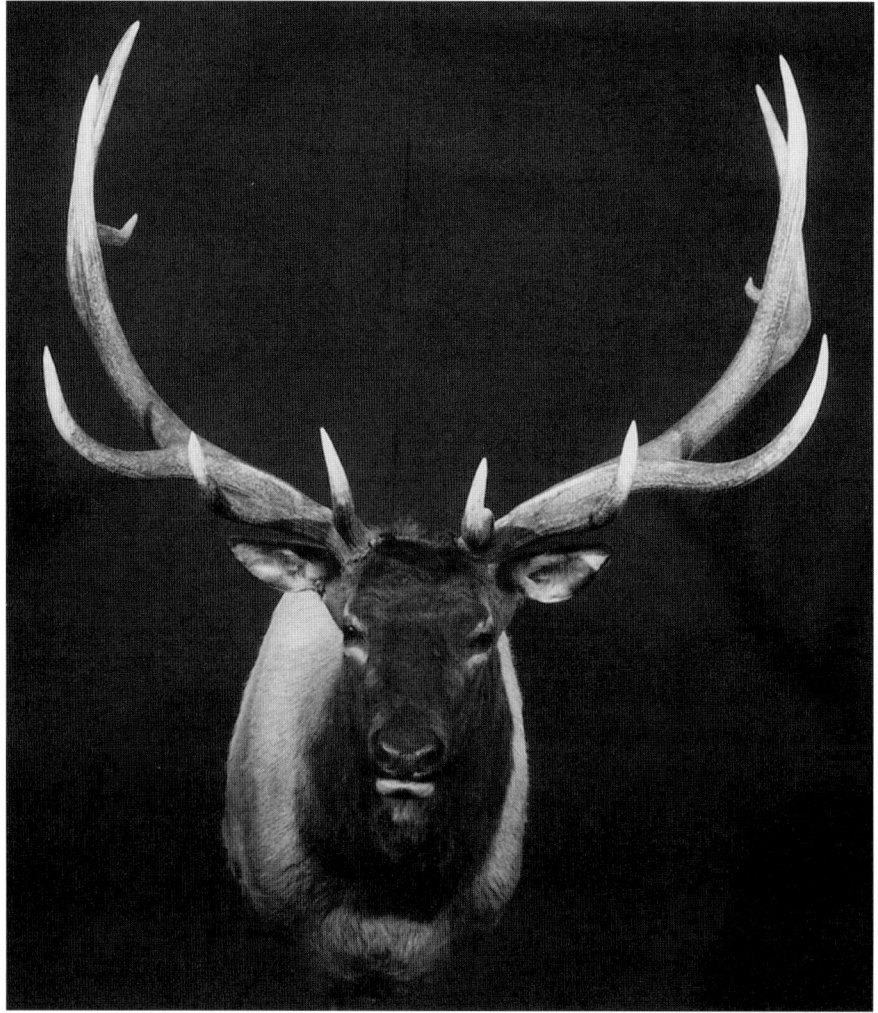

Tarzan

veal that the conformation of his antlers does not resemble that of the bull at the lake.

The *Chieftain* article dated February 1, 1923, stated: "Bill Taft is old and could not have lived more than a year at best." The article written February 15, 1923, stated Old Bill Taft had been a victim of mistaken identity. He is not the mean and vicious bull; the mean and vicious bull is the one at the head of the lake. This indicates there were two bulls being called "Taft."

This also explains why, in the *Chieftain* article dated February 1, 1923, Deputy Warden George Rodgers, having received many reports of a mean and vicious bull called "Taft," went to Billy Meadows and not to the head of the lake. With the death sentence passed to kill "Taft," George Rodgers knew Bill Taft was still up at Chesnimnus and that was why the hunting party was taken to Billy Meadows.

The antlers from the bull at the lake that now grace the walls in the La Grande Elk's Lodge Local #433 were recently measured by the Record Book for Oregon and Boone and Crockett Official Measurers at 411 0/8 B.C. Tarzan was measured at 364 6/8 B.C., certifying him as the state record non-typical American Elk. Further research into the battle that took place on September 23, 1930, indicates that perhaps the elk named Taft did not kill Tarzan, but that Tarzan killed Taft.

In the *Joseph Herald* article dated September 25, 1930, George Rodgers is quoted as saying, "The bull he killed [the elk lying dead near the dock] is said to have been a more magnificent specimen than Old Bill himself," and that the head of the elk Old Bill killed will be sent to Portland to be mounted, but only the hide of Old Bill would be saved. In looking at the two elk, Taft and Tarzan, the more magnificent of the two specimen is Taft, measuring 411 0/8 B.C., not Tarzan, measuring 364 6/8 B.C. It is altogether likely that the mean and vicious bull was also the one shot full in the face with a blast from a shotgun and blinded. Tarzan, being the younger bull and sensing his rival's helplessness, would have killed the bull mistakenly named "Taft."

A photograph was taken of the bull lying dead by the docks and if it is located, it will write the final chapter about the bulls at the head of Wallowa Lake. The final fitting touches to the story of the bulls at the lake will be painted by Oregon artist Tom Schillinger, commissioned by the *Record Book For Oregon*. The setting will be Wallowa Lake September 23, 1930; the subjects will be the two bull elk in Tom's challenge series, "Taft" and "Tarzan."

Compiled by David M. Morris: *Record Book for Oregon's Big Game Animals.* Organizations providing the reference and source material used to compile this story:

Wallowa County Chieftain
Wallowa County Museum
Oregon Historical Society
The La Grande Elk's Lodge #433
The Elk of North America
Oregon Department Of Fish and Wildlife

A Ram Called "Spot"

by Vic Coggins

The story of this legendary ram started on November 19, 1971, when five Rocky Mountain bighorn rams and fifteen ewes from Jasper National Park, Alberta, were released in the Lostine River Canyon at the base of the Wallowa Mountains. The site selected was a 1966 burn in the Silver Creek drainage with open south-facing steep grass-covered slopes. This habitat was very similar to the Jasper Park area where the sheep had been captured. The animals wintered above the release site and the following spring moved south along the Hurricane Divide for the summer. The migratory behavior of wintering at lower elevations in the Lostine drainage (now the Lostine Wildlife Area, owned by the Oregon Department of Fish and Wildlife) and summering in the high elevation alpine basins of the Wallowas was thus established. This migratory tradition allowed the bighorns to be on excellent forage through most of the year and the source stock had the genetics to produce large sheep.

On May 26, 1972, I located the first bighorn lamb of three that survived that first year. One of these lambs was "Spot" and he was probably born in the white cliffs aborve Dry Hollow on the Lostine Range, where I first saw them.

The Lostine herd prospered and their numbers increased to the point that we started a trapping and transplanting program in 1977 and limited ram hunting in 1978. At this time it was obvious we had some very good rams coming on and several potentially great rams. The first hunting seasons were highly successful, with most of the rams utilizing the high alpine basins along the Hurricane Divide. Spot survived these first hunts by luck, since the majority of the rams were generally in a bachelor herd of fifteen to twenty animals. After those first years, the rams became harder to find and wcrc in smallcr groups, with some moving across Hurricane Creek to the Hurwal Divide out of the hunt area. The hunt boundary was later changed to include the Hurwal Divide.

The day Spot was named, Jim Warrenner and I were conducting a sheep and goat survey in the Hurricane Creek drainage and had climbed to Pipit basin on the west side of Sacajawea. My records say the date was July 11, 1981, and that there were ten rams in the basin above timberline. I was able to approach within twenty yards of them to take some pictures and read eartag numbers on two of the animals. The special ram was in the group. He had the largest horns and they were over full curl with broomed horntips coming up well above the bridge of his nose. The ram, now nine years old, also had a white spot (giving him his name) about one inch in diameter in the center of his throat and, of course, no scars on his face.

We were into an annual trapping and transplanting program on the Lostine Range during the winter and were baiting the sheep to the trap site. Many of the sheep became very tame, including some of the large rams, so we were able to keep track of Spot and another large ram named "Flare," for his long horns that flared out at the tips. Spot and Flare survived all the hunting seasons from 1978–86, with fifty-six tagholders hunting rams in the Wallowas during that time. Also 152 bighorns were trapped and transplanted off the Lostine range, although some returned home from distant ranges as far as sixty air miles away and we didn't move any mature rams. A plot to poach Spot was uncovered and fortunately Oregon State Police officers, ODFW personnel and volunteers prevented that from happening. Many wildlife photographers spent countless days on the Lostine winter range photographing the sheep and especially the large rams. They were very protective of the sheep, but most of them were especially attached to Spot, who by this time was also known as "Scarface" (because the bridge of his nose and his right eye were badly scarred from fights).

The last time I saw Spot alive was on April 9, 1985. I was walking a deer survey route on the

Spot and Flare lived in the same area of the Wallowa Mountains, though they were seldom seen together. This picture of the two, taken by Galen Clark, is considered by many to be a record photograph—the largest two rams ever photographed in the same frame. Photograph courtesy of Galen Clark. This and other photographs available for sale by contacting: Galen Clark, Elgin, Oregon 541-437-6591

ridge east of the Lostine River to Wade Point and ten of the largest rams had moved down to feed on the new green grass. I spent some time close to the sheep, photographing them. Spot was now nearly thirteen years old and nearly blind in his right eye, but what a magnificent bighorn! Spot now seldom came to the sheep trap for feed and salt in the winter but spent most of his time in the Silver Creek drainage with a few other old rams.

In November 1986, disaster struck the Lostine herd and all but thirty-four of an estimated 120 sheep died from a bacterial pneumonia outbreak. All the rams over four years of age died from the disease. I spent much of the winter of 1986–87 capturing and treating sick bighorns and, of course, hoping the special one had sur-

vived. We located a number of dead bighorns that winter, but Spot wasn't among them.

In October 1986 we received a report of a large dead ram in Ice Lake but were not able to find it. There had also been some calls regarding a large ram found dead but the callers would not give their names. A later investigation revealed a Washington College student had taken the head and kept it through the winter until OSP and U.S. Fish and Wildlife Service officers "encouraged" him to return the head. Spot had been found! Elvin Hawkins and I scored him in April 1987 at 202 7/8 points—larger than the former U.S. record ram scoring 200 points taken in the Wind River Range of Wyoming in 1883. Unfortunately Spot was not officially scored at that time

Spot and Flare lived in the
Wallowa Mountains
from the early 1970s
until the fall of 1986.
Spot was 14 1/2 years old,
measuring 202 7/8 B.C.
Flare was 12 1/2 years old;
he was never found.
Photographs taken in the
summer of 1986.
Spot died that October.

Photographs courtesy of Jerry
Partin.

by Boone and Crockett judges. He was on display in a number of locations prior to being officially scored in 1989 at 197 7/8 points.

The Lostine herd recovered slowly, with almost no lamb survival for two years after the die-off. Lamb survival returned to normal in 1990 and the herd is presently estimated at about eighty animals. The rams are coming back as well, but need some years to grow to pre-die-off-sized rams. The genetics and forage conditions are still available to produce great rams. Hopefully, in future years "Spot"- and "Flare"-sized rams will again roam the Wallowas.

Flare, considered to have had 50" horns with a tip-to-tip spread of 30"

Oregon State Record
Martin Pernoll, 21 10/16 B.C., Lake County, 1967

Brian Day, 21 2/16 P.Y., Jackson County, 1989

Mark Moncrief, 20 14/16 P.Y., Wallowa County, 1985

Dan Stanfield, 19 12/16 B.C.,
Jackson County, 1994

Black Bear

Brian Day, 18 9/16 P.Y.,
Jackson County, 1993

Oregon State Record
Mark Moncrief, 15 14/16 B.C.,
Wallowa County, 1994

Cougar

Dan Leizure,
15 10/16 B.C.,
Umatilla County, 1993

Joe West,
15 8/16 B.C.,
Grant County, 1992

Ron L. Lay, 15 10/16 B.C., Union County, 1966

Cougar

Thomas Campbell, 14 5/16 B.C.,
Union County, 1984

Wallowa County

Brian Day, 14 6/16 P.Y., Josephine County, 1990

Laimon Osis, 42 4/8 B.C., Wallowa County, 1965

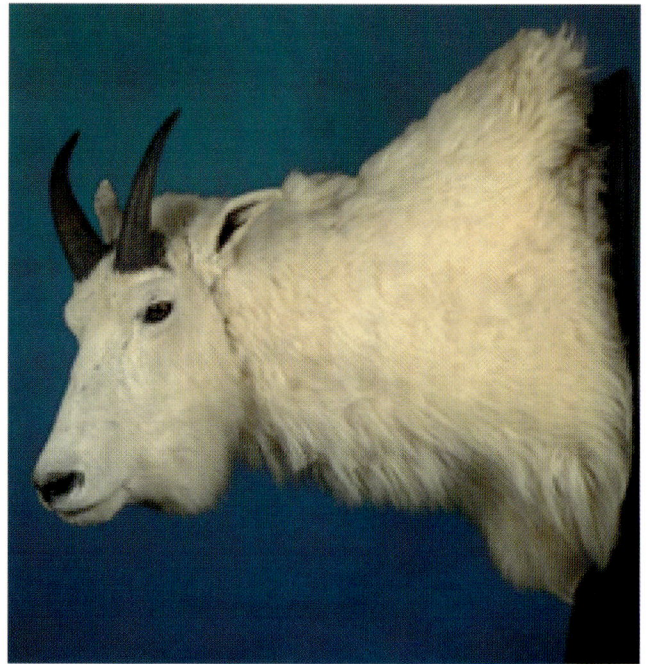

Oregon State Record, Dr. John Waterman, Wallowa County, 1968

Mountain Goat

Hurwal Divide, courtesy of Laimon Osis

Virgil Thornton, 39 4/8 B.C.,
Wallowa County, 1967

Gary Martin, Wallowa County

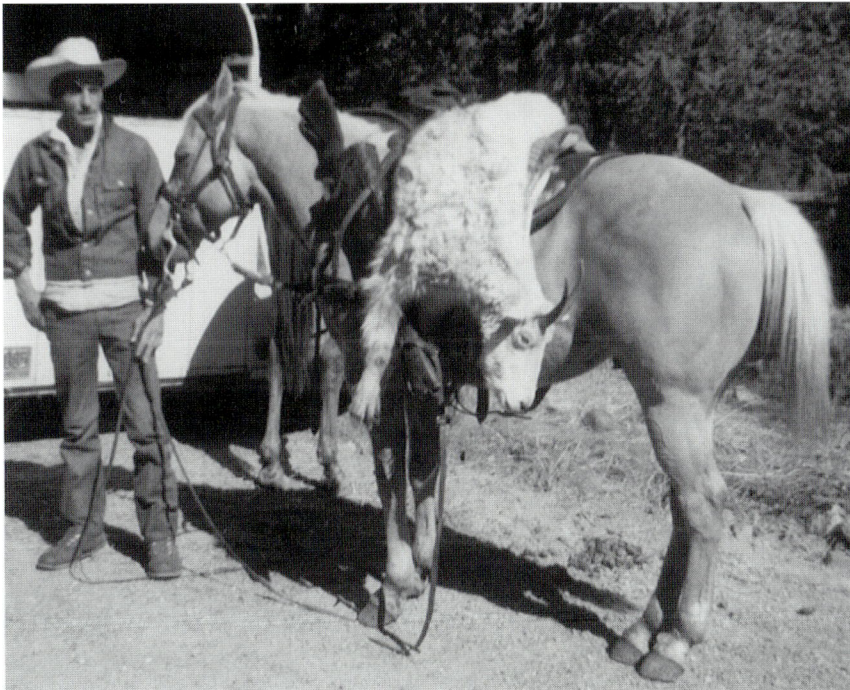

Virgil Thornton, 39 4/8 B.C., Wallowa County, 1967

Carl Hunter, 39 6/8 B.C.,
Wallowa County, 1968

California Bighorn
Sheep

Oregon State Record
Red Iler, 176 0/8 B.C., Malheur County, 1991

Red Iler, Upper Owyhee

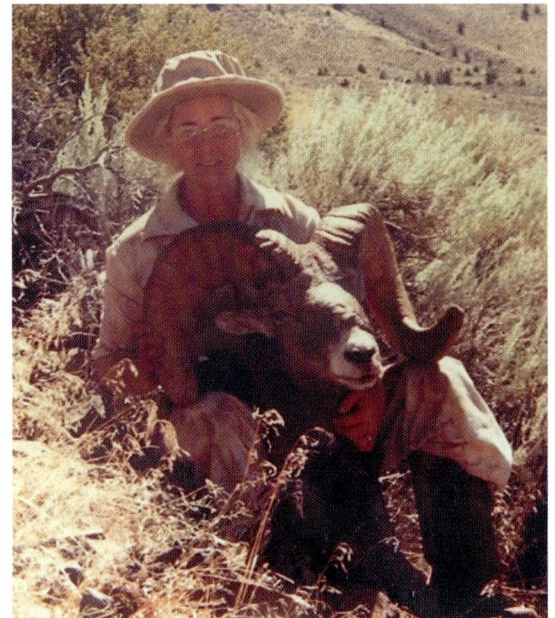

Sherrain Glenn, 173 0/8 B.C., Lake County, 1984

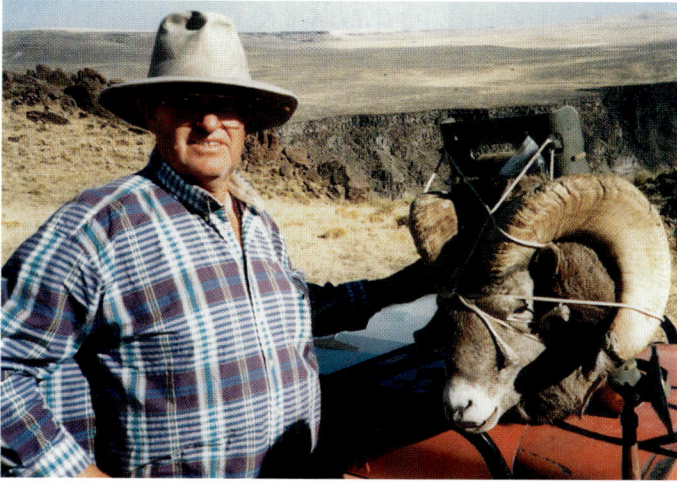

Jerry Gardner, 167 4/8 B.C., Malheur County, 1994

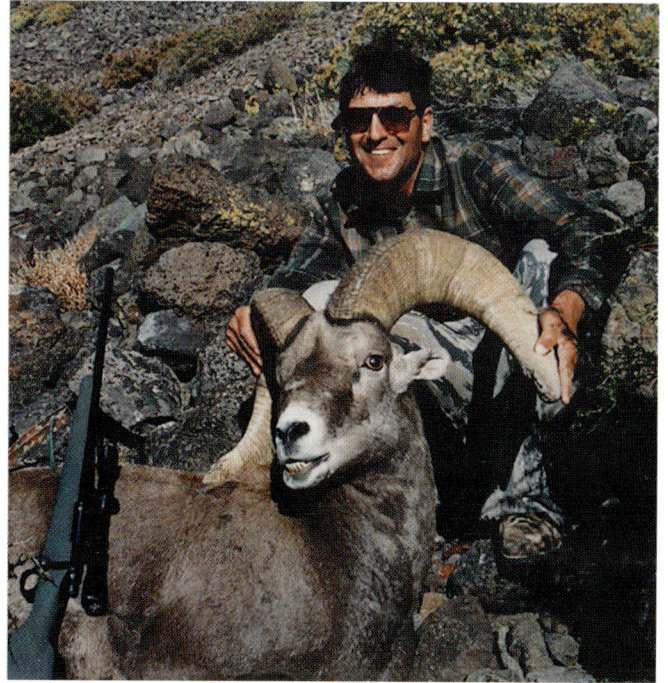

Robert Klink, 168 2/8 B.C., Lake County, 1994

Doug Vandehey, 167 7/8 B.C., Malheur County, 1987

Robert Arnott, 163 7/8 P.Y., Lake County, 1992

Peter Bollinger, 200 6/8 B.C., Wallowa County, 1989

Todd Jaksick, 198 0/8 B.C., Wallowa County, 1988

Jim Tonkin, 192 0/8 B.C., Wallowa County, 1991

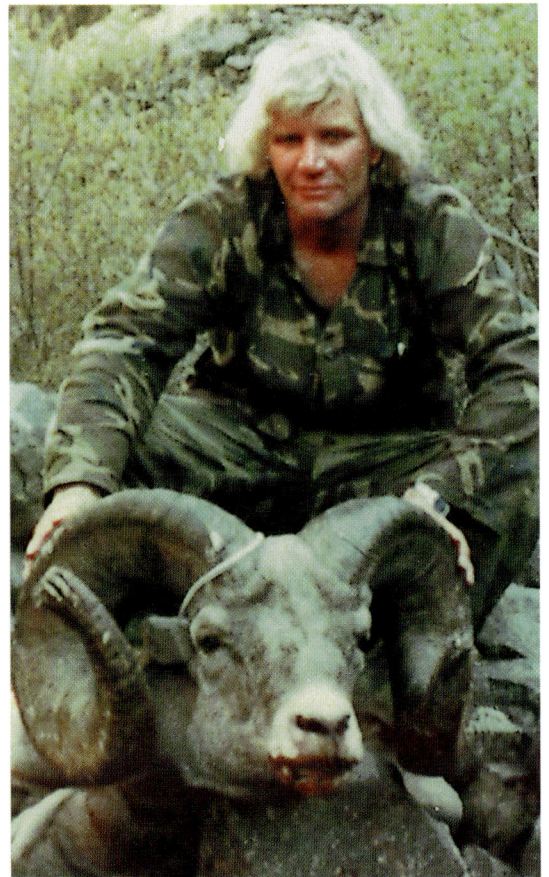

Sam Jaksick, 191 4/8 B.C.,
Wallowa County, 1987

Rocky Mountain
Bighorn Sheep

Ken Kirsch, 183 1/8 B.C., Wallowa County, 1994

Tom Croswell, 183 6/8 B.C.,
Wallowa County, 1992

Mike Taylor, 181 3/8 B.C., Wallowa County, 1987

Jerry Donovan, 169 6/8 B.C., Wallowa County, 1994

3/4 curl ram?

Hermaphroditic Bighorn

On August 24, 1995, Tim Hueckman was hunting bighorn sheep in the Upper Owyhee unit. Having spotted two rams in Antelope Creek, a tributary of the Owyhee River, he shot a three-quarter curl ram, measuring 145 1/8 green and officially 144 6/8 B.C. Upon further analysis, when they began to field dress the animal, they realized there were no male genitalia—it had the external sexual components of a ewe. According to the Oregon Department of Fish and Wildlife, this is extremely rare. Upon further investigation, through other state game offices and the Foundation for North American Wild Sheep, no evidence of another case of this kind has been found. Call it a ram-ewe or ewe-ram, this animal, having features of both male and female, predominantly male but with genitalia of a female, may be one of a kind.

Tim Hueckman, 144 6/8 B.C.,
Malheur County

See anything missing?

Roger Clarno, 90 0/8 P.Y., Lake County, 1994

Pronghorn

Douglas Modey, 84 2/8, Harney County, 1990

Charles Waite, 82 4/8 B.C., Lake County, 1969

JoAnn Hathaway, 87 0/8 B.C., Lake County, 1976

George Terril, 81 2/8 B.C.,
Crook County, 1994

47

Pronghorn

Sam Wilkins Jr., 86 4/8 B.C., Harney County

Brian Day, 80 6/8 P.Y., Lake County, 1994

Jim Baley, 80 2/8 B.P., Klamath County, 1995

Sharon Ganos, 85 2/8 B.C., Harney County, 1992

Jake Baley and Jesse Hickey
with Jim Baley's black powder antelope

Randy Allen, 172 3/8 (T) 188 3/8 (NT),
Jackson County, 1995

David Baird, 166 2/8, Jackson County, 1991

Blacktail
(Archery)

Charles Endicott, 137 7/8 P.Y., Linn County, 1995

Loren McLaughlin, 130 7/8 P.Y., Marion County, 1993

Brian Day, 103 0/8 P.Y., Josephine County, 1994

49

Mike Schaffeld, Dr. Bill Monson, 192 1/8 B.C. (typical); 224 3/8 B.C. (non-typical), Malheur County, 1995

Mule Deer (Rifle) typical

Wade Evans, 180 7/8 B.C., Grant County, 1995

Mike Schaffeld and hunting partner, Malheur County, 1995

Ed Pugh, 177 2/8 B.C., Jefferson County, 1995

Kimberly Wirth (seven and a half months pregnant), Grant County, 1991

Glenn Dobson Jr., 192 2/8, Harney County, 1994

Malcolm Cameron, 191 5/8 B.C., Grant County, 1975

Mule Deer (Rifle) typical

Ron Robinson Jr., 190 3/8 B.C., Deschutes County, 1995

Tony Cop, 184 2/8 B.C., Grant County, 1986

Jerry Donovan, 167 0/8,
Harney County, 1995

Ed and J.J. Pugh, Jefferson County, 1995

Nancy Yancy's son, 190 4/8 B.C., Union County, 1995

Bob McClean, 183 6/8 B.C. 3 pt., Umatilla County, 1995

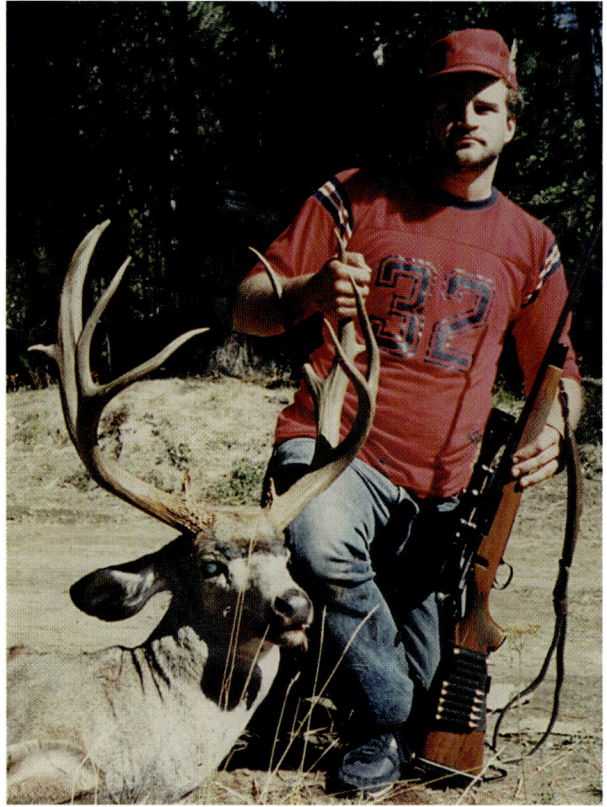

Leslie Brady, 186 2/8 B.C., Grant County, 1992

Mule Deer (Rifle) typical

Jeff Riley, 168 0/8 B.C. 3 pt., Harney County, 1995

Mule Deer
(Rifle)
non-typical

Bradley Barclay, 297 1/8 B.C., Malheur County, 1971

Ken Pruitt, 283 B.C., Harney County, 1964

55

Lige Davis, 268 5/8 B.C., Grant County, 1941

Right: Tim Rozewski with his grandfather Buck Matson's 242 5/8 B.C., Deschutes County, 1960

Stoney Geinger, 250 6/8 B.C., Grant County, 1993

Logan Girrard, 236 6/8 B.C., Union County, 1995

Glen E. Park, 262 0/8 B.C., Grant County, 1962

Mule Deer
(Rifle)
non-typical

Tony Gardner, 200 4/8 B.C,
Grant County, 1991

Charles Kies, 240 2/8 B.C., Crook County, 1995

Oregon State Record (typical)
Hop Jackson, 195 7/8 B.C., Crook County, 1990

Oregon State Record (non-typical)
Brad Smith, 252 0/8 P.Y., 1992

Mule Deer
(Archery)

Jon Silver, 236 7/8 P.Y., Union County, 1995

Glen Shelly,
213 4/8 P.Y.,
Harney County, 1994

Patrick Wheeler, 163 2/8 P.Y., Harney County, 1994

Bob Reed, 177 1/8 P.Y., Harney County, 1991

Oregon State Record (typical), Doug White, 203 0/8 B.P., Harney County, 1994

Oregon State Record (non-typical) Delwyn Hendrickson, 194 4/8 B.P., Malheur County, 1995

Mule Deer (Black Powder)

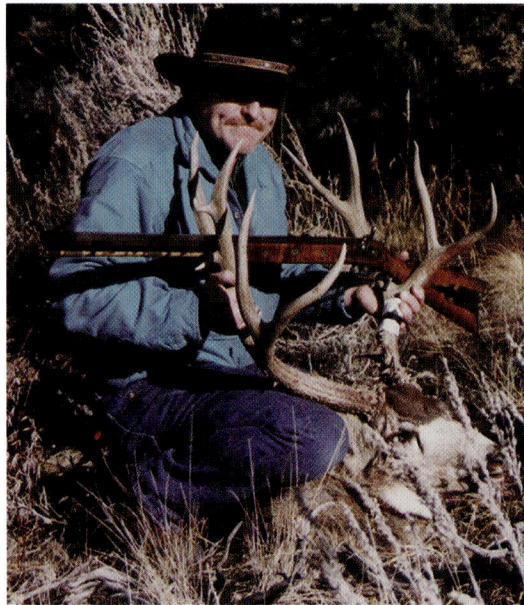

Left: Mike DeWitt, 188 4/8 B.P., Harney County, 1995

Larry Powell, Doug White, Bruce Hawkin, Dave Noble, Harney County, 1994

Larry Richards, 157 4/8 B.P., Malheur County, 1995

Whitetail

Oregon State Record—Black Powder
Jim Hambleton, 165 5/8 B.P., Wallowa County, 1992

Jeffrey A. Koorenny,
163 1/8 B.C.,
Umatilla County, 1987

Dick Kyriss, 170 0/8 B.C., Wallowa County, 1994

Gary Bertleson, 166 4/8 B.C., Umatilla County, 1983

Whitetail

Larry Bennett, 163 6/8 B.C., Union County, 1994

Danny Evans, 143 2/8 B.P., Umatilla County, 1995

Oregon State Record
Robert Sharp, 384 3/8 B.C., Clatsop County, 1949

Rusty Lindberg with Fred Williamson's bull, 378 5/8 B.C.,
Clatsop County, 1947

Roosevelt Elk

Floyd Lindberg, 366 5/8 B.C.,
Columbia County, 1966

John McIllhenny, Gary Larson, Allan Johnson, John May,
338 4/8 B.C., Clackamas County, 1993

World Record—Archery
Dale Baumgartner, 367 3/8 P.Y., Tillamook County, 1985

John Beavers, 294 1/8 B.C., Clatsop County, 1976

Left: Ernest Thomas, 336 4/8 B.C.,
Douglas County, 1969

Roosevelt Elk

Ron Stone

World Record Roosevelt Elk Antlers

by Roger Selner

When Harold and Belva Burroughs from Molalla, Oregon, came to the International Sportsmen Exhibition show in Portland, Belva told me they had a set of sheds that were as big as anything in our World Record Elk display. Several weeks later, I measured the sheds at the Northwest Trails show in Pendleton, confirming they were indeed the greatest set of Roosevelt elk antlers ever recorded. Fred King, who is an official measurer for Boone and Crockett and the Shed Record book, and I panel-measured the sheds as the new World Record Roosevelt.

In the current record book, the world record scores 388 B.C., with the number two antlers scoring 384 B.C. When the Burroughs' sheds were mounted, we used a thirty-nine-inch inside spread whereas forty-inch spreads are quite common in Roosevelt elk. The sheds scored a whopping 431 0/8 B.C., forty-three inches larger than the world record. It is hard to believe this animal lived a good share of its life just thirty miles away from three million people.

The largest set of sheds from this bull was found in the spring of 1990 by Harold and his son-in-law, Sam Aho. Due to the fact there was some thirty feet of barbed wire wrapped around the antlers, it made finding the pair quite easy!

The bull was well-known in the area, with other neighbors finding the earlier sheds as well as photographing and filming the great bull. The sheds from 1986 scored 384 7/8 B.C. while the 1988 set scored 378 3/8 B.C. The bull has been seen for some eight years wintering in the area, with the last sighting occurring in the spring of 1994. We are guessing that his age is between thirteen and fifteen years old.

(Notes: Roger, who is a Boone and Crockett scorer and owner of Trophy Show Productions, travels throughout the United States with The Eastmans' Journal World Record Elk Tour. *The Burroughs' great trophy was one of those featured in the 1996 Tour.)*

Reprinted from *The Eastmans' Journal*, Vol. 8, Iss. 32 (November/December) 1995.

1986   1988   1990
World Record Roosevelt Shed Antlers

Oregon State Record Rocky Mountain elk
Hugh Evans, 418 0/8 B.C., Crook County, 1942

Wayne Marks, 392 1/8 B.C. (non-typical), Wallowa County, 1947

Rocky Mountain Elk (Rifle)

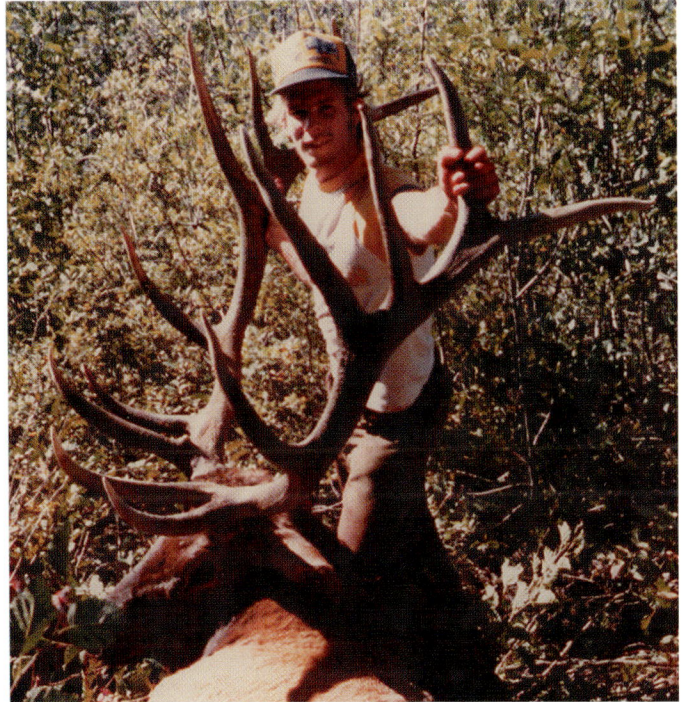

Bill Tensen, 390 2/8 B.C., Hood River County, 1980

Del Howard, 372 0/8 B.C., Grant County, 1981

Bob Abbott, 372 7/8 B.C., Grant County, 1989

Pete Hettinga, 362 2/8 B.C., Grant County, 1981

Rocky Mountain Elk
(Rifle)

Hettinga hunting party with Pete's 362 bull

W.W. York, 324 1/8 B.C., Wallowa County, 1993

Roy Hempel, 349 3/8 B.C., Grant County, 1975

Greg Willmore,
368 5/8 P.Y.,
Grant County, 1988

Rocky Mountain Elk (Archery)

Robert Reed,
332 0/8 P.Y.,
Grant County, 1992

Pat Wheeler,
304 0/8 P.Y.,
Harney County, 1993

Introduction to the Artists

Wildlife artist Tom Schillinger, from Hines, Oregon, was commissioned by the *Record Book for Oregon's Big Game Animals* to paint each of the Oregon state record animals. The first six, featuring Rocky Mountain bighorns "Spot" and "Flare," Rocky Mountain elk, "Taft," Hugh Evans's 418 0/8 bull, Robert Sharp's 384 0/8 Roosevelt elk and Fred Bean's blacktail deer, have been completed and are available through the *Record Book for Oregon*. He was also selected to paint two of Oregon's most renowned bull elk, Taft and "Tarzan"; set at Wallowa Lake on September 23, 1930, the ensuing battle between these two bulls ended in death on that fateful day in September. Tom is destined to be recognized as one of the nation's finest wildlife artists; he paints with a photographic style that lends a convincing realism to each painting.

Wildlife sculptor Dale Dotson, from Joseph, Oregon, was selected by the *Record Book for Oregon* to sculpt pieces featuring several Oregon state record animals. Dale's first series featured four African pieces: a bongo, sable, kudo and Cape buffalo. Dale was selected for the distinctive realism by which he gives life to each of his subjects.

The first of the Oregon series, "Taft," is named for the state record, non-typical Rocky Mountain elk. This truly magnificent bull measured 411 0/8 B.C. Taft's extraordinary conformation has been recreated by Dale on a one-quarter life-size scale. Taft's colorful history combined with Dale's exquisite artistry makes for a terrific combination. Fifty limited edition "Taft" pieces and Dale's African pieces are available through the *Record Book for Oregon*.

Renowned sculptor and taxidermist Rip Caswell, from Troutdale, Oregon, has been selected by and will be featured in the *Record Book for Oregon*. Rip will be sculpting many of Oregon's big game animals as full-size pieces, adding to this extremely talented artist's diverse collection of bronzes. The Mule Deer Foundation selected Rip Caswell as Artist of the Year and has commissioned him to produce another piece for their fund raisers.

Rip Caswell and Dale Dotson offer two different and distinctive styles in their work as bronze sculptors; their work along with Tom Schillinger's will be displayed in the Tour of Oregon's Big Game Animals and are available through the *Record Book for Oregon*.

Wildlife Artist
Thomas W. Schillinger

The great outdoors, wildlife and sports have played a big role in the life of artist Tom Schillinger. He was born and raised in remote southeastern Oregon, in the small town of Hines.

Tom enjoys the outdoors, from hiking, camping, hunting and fishing, to photography and pursuing subjects for his art. Studying Art and Fish and Wildlife Management at the University of Wyoming, Tom transferred to Oregon State University in 1976 and added photography and journalism to his studies. He also played varsity football and track while attending college, where he was probably better known for his athletic pursuits than for his art.

Graduating in 1980 with a B.S. degree in Art, Tom returned to OSU and received his teaching certificate in 1982. Tom taught high school art and yearbook courses for three years at Grant Union High in John Day, Oregon, where he was also head coach for both football and track.

Opening a gallery in Burns with his mom in 1984, he quit teaching in 1986 to pursue his career in art and participated in various shows throughout the Northwest (the CM Russell Art Show and Auction in Great Falls, Montana and the Rocky Mountain Elk Foundation Annual Banquet, to name a few).

This past year Tom became involved in the

Record Book for Oregon with David Morris, and is currently working on art for the book and tour.

Tom still maintains a studio at his home in Hines:

Saddle Butte Studio
350 N. Roanoke
P.O. Box 332
Hines, OR 97738
(541) 573-6398

He also has his art on display at the Wayside Deli in Burns, Oregon and various other businesses.

"Spot"

"Flare"

Oregon State Record Rocky Mountain elk (non-typical)—411 0/8 B.C., "Taft" 1930

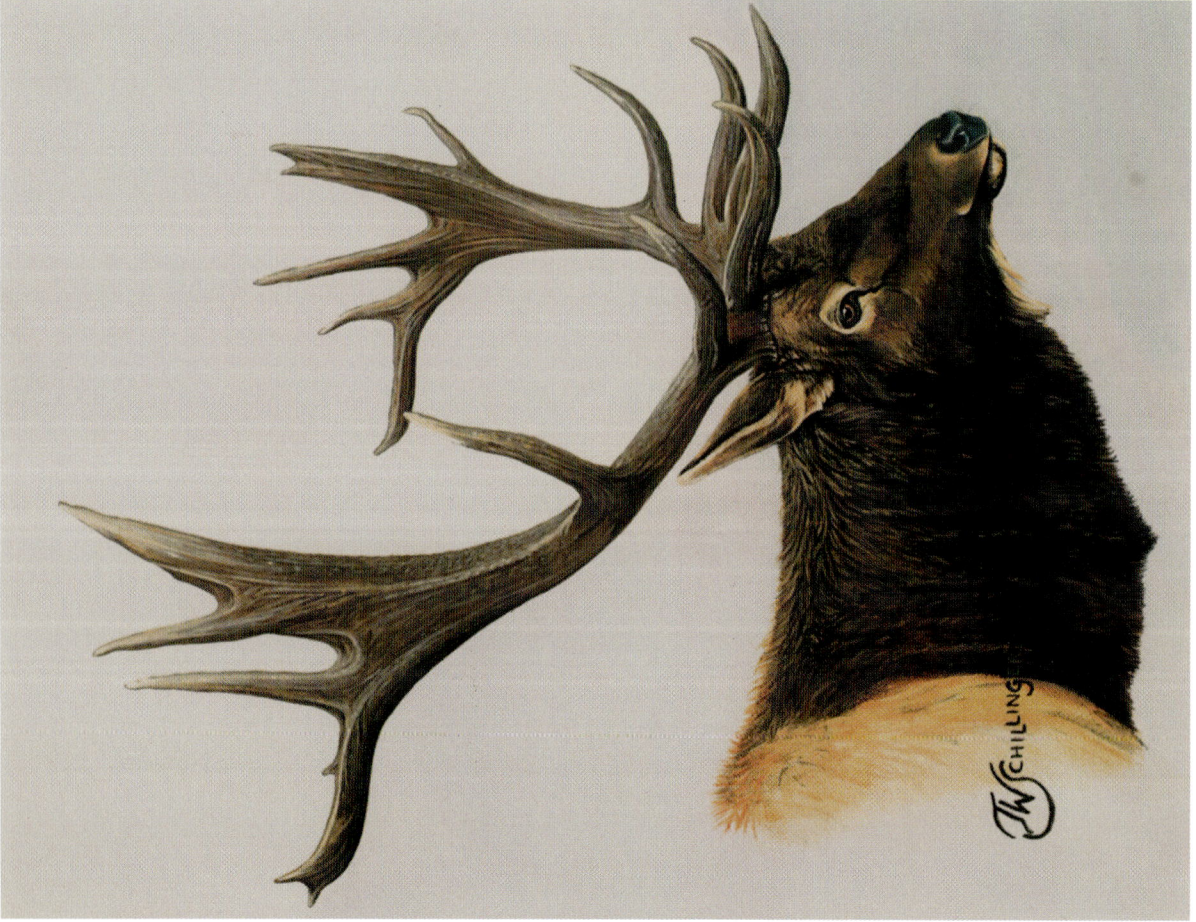

Oregon State Record Roosevelt elk—384 3/8 B.C., Robert Sharp, 1949

"Taft and Tarzan at Wallowa Lake"

Blacktail Deer—169 5/8 B.C., Fred Bean, 1953

Oregon State Record Rocky Mountain elk (typical)—418 0/8 B.C., Hugh Evans, 1942

Above: "The Bighorn Challenge"
Below: "The Pronghorn Challenger"

Above: "The Challenger"
Below: "The Challenging Mulie"

Above: "Winter Mulie"
Below: "Two Old Snags"

"Top Cat"

"Cougar"

"Pined Cougar"

"Evil Eyes"

"Little Wolf"

"Grizzly"

"Wapiti"

"Two Old-Timers"

"Buffalo Hunt"

"The Watering Hole"

"Steens Mountain Pronghorn"

"Last Call"

"The Prince of the Prairie"

81

RIP CASWELL

1996 MULE DEER FOUNDATION SCULPTOR OF THE YEAR

Troutdale, Oregon—The son of a professional guide and outfitter, Rip Caswell moved to the Northwest when he was just six years old. Everything about art attracted the young boy. When his family lived in northeastern Washington for a time, he sculpted animals from the water-based clay of the shores of the Pend Oreille River.

Rip's father saw his son's talent and encouraged the boy to study taxidermy. For several summers Rip understudied with the well-known taxidermist, Bill Lancaster of Beaver Creek, Oregon. In 1985, Lancaster offered Rip a full-time job and the two teamed up to become lead contenders in Northwest taxidermy. In 1988, their entries swept the Northwest Regional Taxidermy competition by winning all bird and mammal categories. The competition had ninety-six entries and the Lancaster/Caswell team took every award at the event. Caswell repeated this effort on his own in 1989, again winning every award.

In 1990, Caswell made a decision to compete at the national level, planning eight months in advance what he would need to do in order to stand a chance of winning. He chose to combine contemporary sculpture and traditional taxidermy. Those concepts were applied to his work on a green-winged teal that sat on a feather-shaped rock of green jade soapstone that Caswell carved. The piece took six months to complete and was revolutionary enough in its approach that Caswell had no idea how it would be received. In the end, the eight judges couldn't decide which of Caswell's pieces should receive Best of Show. The green-winged teal won and almost everyone in the taxidermy field concurs that today taxidermy should emphasize presentation as well as technical accuracy. Caswell's inclusion of presentation has perhaps helped taxidermy in its battle for acceptance as fine art.

Inspired by the prestigious win at Nationals, Caswell's friends suggested that he cast images in bronze. The decision to move into sculpture had merit and resulted in the opening of the Caswell Gallery in December, 1992. Adjacent to a foundry, American Art Casting, Caswell is able to nurture his pieces through the casting process. Rip Caswell has completed an amazing forty-four pieces in four years. He also completed a double–life-size portrait of a Grand Ronde ancestor for that tribe in 1995. His life-size mule deer is part of the permanent collection at the High Desert Museum in Bend, Oregon.

"Noble Presence"
(Miniature)
3.5" x 5" x 5"

"Noble Presence"
(Life-size)
23" x 58" x 50"

"RMEF Bust"
12" x 12" x 18"

"Bighorn Sheep Bust"
14.5" x 14" x 17.5"

"First Retrieve"
3.5" x 5" x 6"

"Wolf Bust"
12" x 12" x 18"

RIP CASWELL

Award-winning sculptor and National Taxidermy Champion, Rip Caswell is popular with corporate and private collectors world wide. He has created more than 50 bronze sculptures of various subjects in both realistic and contemporary styles.

After years of in-depth artistic study and research, Caswell opened his gallery adjacent to a foundry where he is able to oversee his work from start to finish.

Caswell Gallery & Studio
201 W. Columbia River Hwy., Troutdale, OR 97060 (503) 492-2473

Artist—Dale Dotson

Dale Dotson was born in Clarkston, Washington. He grew up in northeastern Oregon, graduating from Joseph High School in 1970 and from Oregon State University in 1974 with a degree in Wildlife Science.

Sketching wildlife was always one of Dale's most enjoyed hobbies. His formal training included mixed-media art classes at Joseph High as well as various drawing classes taken as electives at Oregon State. After graduation, Dale returned to Wallowa County and began working as a timber faller. This gave him ample opportunity to study his subjects on a daily basis. In 1980, he began doing taxidermy on a part-time basis; he credits this with helping him to develop his knowledge of the muscle and bone structures essential to creating life-like wildlife sculptures. Dale's first bronze was cast in 1992.

While his first love is North American big game, his current interest is in African wildlife. He recently spent three weeks in Zimbabwe sketching and photographing the wildlife there. Nothing can replace studying the subject in its natural environment when it comes to doing artwork in any medium.

Dale still resides in Joseph with his wife and two children. Joseph is fast becoming a focal point for sculptors and art buyers alike: With its two foundries, and a third in nearby Enterprise, local artists can keep close tabs on work in progress. The quality of workmanship exhibited by these foundries is nationally recognized and can be appreciated by anyone viewing the finished products.

"Taft," the first in a series depicting a selection of Oregon's record heads, was commissioned by David Morris for the *Record Book for Oregon's Big Game Animals.*

Front and side views of Dale Dotson's "Taft"

"Greater Kudu"
25" × 16" × 8"
Edition of 35

"Bongo"
17 1/2" × 12" × 10"
Edition of 35

Here are a few more examples of bronzes by
Dale Dotson. His work can be seen in the
Bronze Coast Gallery, Joseph, OR;
Whitt/Kraus Galleries, San Diego, CA;
Planet Bronze Art Gallery, Bozeman, MT.

"Defiance" (sable antelope)
19" × 17 1/2" × 8 1/2"
Edition of 35

"Beauty and the Beast"
16" × 16" × 9"
Edition of 20

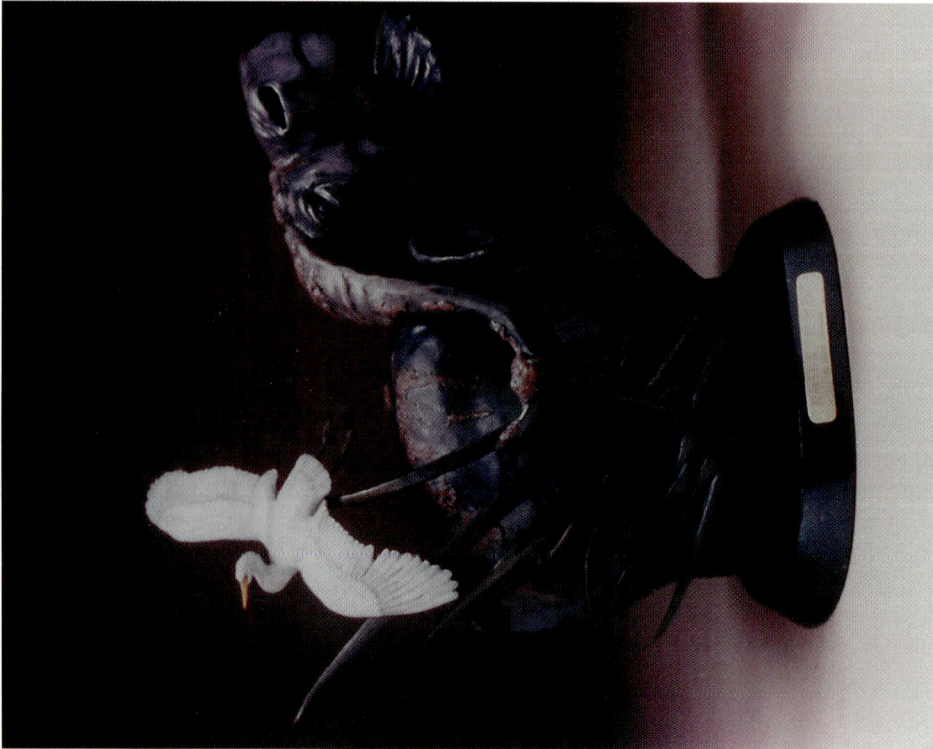

Otto Lawson

Born in northern California on April 14, 1965, Otto Lawson spent most of his childhood near Eureka, California, with the redwoods and the Pacific Ocean providing him an endless source of inspiration. Otto's passion for wildlife and painting was evident early in life, and by age sixteen he was producing saleable artwork. In 1988, he moved to Eugene, Oregon, where he currently resides.

Otto's first important mentor was a high school biology/art teacher, Jim Welsh. Mr. Welsh has been invaluable to his learning.

Gallery International, Portland, Oregon; Stevenson's Gallery, Corvallis, Oregon; Criterion Gallery (formerly Soaring Wings), Eugene, Oregon; and Humboldt's Finest, Eureka, California exhibit Otto's artwork and his work will be featured in the *1997 Oregon Wildlife Calendar*. In addition to completing commissions for many private collectors throughout the United States, Otto has donated artwork to help the efforts of the Sequoia Zoological Society, Eureka, California; the Willamette Wildlife Rescue and Rehabilitation Center and the Cascade Raptor Center in Eugene, Oregon.

Otto has the privilege of working privately with artist Jim Daly at his studio. Mr. Daly is someone Otto admires and looks to for guidance in his art.

In May, 1993, Otto attended a John Seery-Lester workshop in Denali, Alaska. Instructors included John Seery-Lester, Alan Hunt and Ray "Paco" Young. In May 1996 he attended a Pro Arte Workshop with instructors Terry Isaac, Jessica Zemsky and Jack Hines in Big Timber, Montana.

"In each painting, I try to understand how each subject thinks and feels to bring out the personality that makes each an individual and unique within itself. The combination of that and genuine depiction of its habitat is essential to achieve a veritable piece of artwork."

Above: "Campground Companion"
Left: "Silent Watch"
Below: "Spring Light"

Above left: "Quiet Morning"
Above right: "Rosebud"
Left: "Morning Passage"
Below: "Silent Pause"

Otto Lawson Studio
3003 West 11th Avenue #224
Eugene, OR 97402
Phone (541) 689-6107
Fax (541) 345-0877

To Hunt

by David M. Morris

I could feel the autumn chill through the school bus window as we headed down the gravel road toward school. The colors of fall were everywhere: yellow, in the aspen and cottonwood; red, in the willow and snow brush; all shades of blue and gray in the cool autumn skies; with green grasses still remaining along the winding riverbanks. I was swallowed up in yet another morning of my childhood, wishing I was experiencing life two hundred years ago instead of traveling to school. Trapped inside of civilization, I had only to close my eyes and I was there.

Shoshone hunters were now within sight of the village overlooking the upper John Day River. They were returning from a successful elk hunt, with antlers draped across their horses. The village was full of excitement because here in the heart of the Oregon country the game was plentiful. Lush green valleys held large numbers of elk, deer and bighorn sheep were plentiful up in the mountains and the rivers were full of spawning steelhead and salmon. From here to the Rockies this was paradise, the place to be, so that was why I was here, planning my daily routine of hunting, trapping and fishing. I was either Indian or mountain man, or I could have been half of each, but regardless of that I was alive, I was alive and living the good life. The good life was living like an Indian, and there wasn't any other life for me to live. What more could you ask for? It was plain and simple—this was it.

Then all of a sudden there he was, the buck of my dreams, standing amongst all those does right in the middle of Bud Walton's wheat field. I was wishing that all of the hunters I had told to follow the school bus were behind us now, maybe then they would have believed me. I was wishing that I was old enough to hunt deer, but I had to wait three more years until I was twelve. That's what I remember, waiting for the deer hunters to show up just after we were told to go back to school, how exciting each year became, talking to the same nice old men who showed up, hoping they remembered to bring us some candy or peanuts, and never being disappointed. Let's see, there was Paul and Pearl Blackwell from Willamina, Jerry Cook from Portland and Eldon Walker from Eugene. I sat quietly listening to them tell how my dad or grandfather had made a real nice shot on that buck or this buck. Secretly I wished somehow I could be involved, and then one day it happened. Pearl Blackwell had stayed down in camp that day because his knees hurt him pretty bad. I had gotten up early in the morning to see what was going on, and to my surprise, Pearl was out in his camper. I asked him if he wanted to go hunting and he said sure, so away we went. It probably took us a total of five minutes before I spotted the first buck, a nice forked horn just under Shivers Rim. The buck was two or three hundred yards off, so we decided to get closer. Once we were closer, we were looking

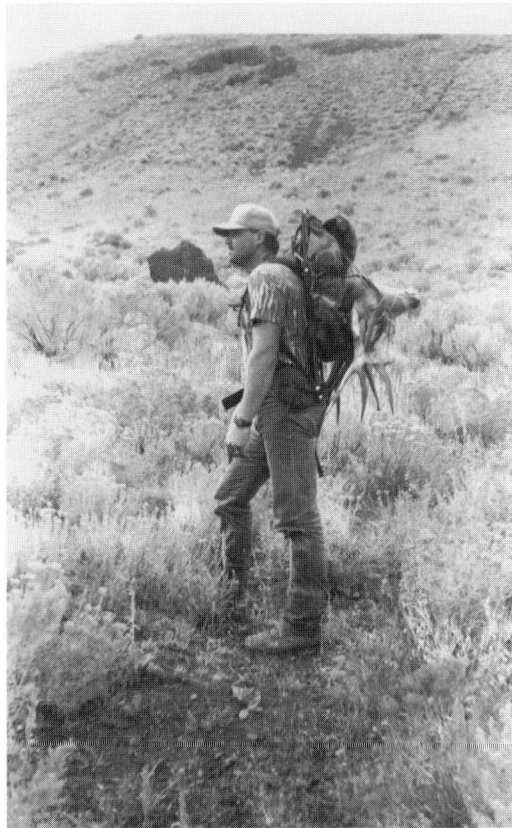

right into the morning sun. Pearl had shot at least two shots when I heard him say, "I can't see him very good, do you think you could hit him?" Well, of course I said yes. Pearl placed the .30-.40 Craig into my eager young hands. I leaned back against the juniper tree and jerked the trigger. To my surprise the buck never moved, so I reluctantly loaded another shell into the chamber and prepared to have my shoulder torn off again. Remembering how pleasant it was to shoot that old Marlin .22, I held the gun up toward the buck, and with Pearl shading the barrel with his hat, I jerked the trigger again. To my surprise, the deer finally decided to run. I had hit the buck on the second shot and later Pearl finished him off. From that moment on, Pearl and I shared a very special relationship with one another. Perhaps because one of us had become too old to hunt and the other was yet too young to hunt. Whatever it was I experienced, it was something that stirred in my blood forever.

Was it the act of killing that put me on an emotional high? What is it in hunting that we find so exciting? Why is it that for many of us hunting has become a way of life? Why is hunting so highly addictive? I'm sure we have all asked ourselves similar questions.

Hunting is an emotional cleansing. It is an adventure in nature, whether it be hunting big game animals, upland birds, fishing, trapping or looking for shed antlers. Hunting is an experience between man and an inner stirring that calls to us, telling us to go out in nature and experience what it has to offer.

There is nothing like looking down into a river canyon dusted with pure white snow and listening to the sound of the dogs as their excitement runs high, nearing the end of the chase. Taking the time to reach out to touch a giant pine tree or old-growth fir, looking up to admire its size: it's old enough to remember the first hunters upon this land. Spending countless hours behind the spotting scope, hoping to get a glimpse of a big mule deer buck as he leaves the golden aspens high in the Oregon desert, the smell of the sage after a refreshing rain. Looking

down you notice something black, it's an arrowhead chipped out of obsidian by another hunter of the great basin. Watching your dog first scent the bird, then express his excitement with his tail as he works and works, finally flushing a brilliantly colored pheasant, you can feel the cold morning air numb your fingers as you raise your gun toward the bird. The exhilaration as you set your hook into a pesky smallmouth bass; the singing of your line as a bright steelhead makes another run; the excitement of your children's faces as they hook into yet another fish. Or the sting of the cold wind as it blows across your face, as the first glimpse of the morning's sun peaks over the distant horizon and you await its warming rays. Hunting elk high in the mountains, the fall has burst into many colors: yellows, reds, greens; and the sky is full of blues and grays. Pausing to take in the many smells of the forest, the pine, the fir, and then you can catch a whiff of elk and your hunt begins. Many thoughts race through your mind, the experience you have gained from all your past hunts, the mistakes you have made but won't make again. Checking the wind, you have formulated a plan, your strategy has been carefully laid out. Success is only moments away because you have already felt the stirring spirit within you, the spirit that moves your primeval instincts that thrive when you hunt. Suddenly a Steller's jay sounds off his warning, joined by a pine squirrel with his scolding chatter that startles you back to reality. Using your senses, your ears listening to the sounds, your nose smelling the many different scents, your eyes seeing yet another magnificent panorama constantly changing as the day passes on. Secretly hoping that somehow your adventure won't end, but always knowing that you must return to civilization, only to dream of what the next adventure may bring. One day to recall the memories from the hunts you have experienced in the past.

No, hunting isn't just about killing, it's about living, feeling alive. Many of my most memorable hunts have ended without even firing a shot. Personally, I hunt to harvest only a mature animal; hunting simply to kill doesn't even enter my mind. A great deal of satisfaction can be felt after you have matched your wits with a big, old, wise mule deer buck and outsmarted him, but ultimately it comes down to whether you choose to shoot or not. There is always a sense of sadness that accompanies the act of killing. I believe each of us has the right to choose to hunt and also has an ethical responsibility to the game we love to hunt: to honor the animals we pursue with the highest level of respect and admiration.

My thoughts drift back to that first buck. Little did I know it would be Pearl's last one. Finally, after almost thirty years of hunting, I realized what had stirred me so: it was that big smile across Pearl's face, to see his excitement, watching this old man enjoy his right to hunt and for me to share this moment in life with him.

My Oregon Super Slam

by Duane Bernard

As a boy in Columbia County, Oregon, I was like many others yearning to kill my first deer. It would be a buck of course. Any buck would do and there were lots of blacktails near my rural home. My mother managed to scrape together enough money to buy me, her eldest child, a hunting license and tag when I was eleven years old. I hunted near home by myself but to no avail. The next year was a repeat performance.

When I was thirteen, a neighbor family asked me if I'd like to join them on a deer hunt in the then famous Tillamook Burn for the opening weekend of the season. I was elated, but still failed to connect with a buck.

By the time I was fourteen, I had just about reconciled myself to the fact that I'd probably never be a deer hunter. Then one Saturday morning in October 1952, after I'd ridden my horse several miles from home, I tied him up and hunted for about an hour. In that hour my luck changed. I spotted a nice big buck across the big canyon I was walking in. Nobody had ever told me that my old Winchester Mod. #94 in 30-30 caliber wasn't a long-range, flat-shooting, deer-killing marvel. I was so far away from that buck that he never bolted at the first few shots; in fact he probably didn't realize I was in the same canyon as he was. Finally, after several more shots, he bolted straight down the canyon toward the large stream at the bottom. When I finally got across the canyon and up the other side to the spot where he'd been, I found no blood, no hair and no sign of a hit. But I followed his twenty-foot leaps to the bottom of the canyon and into the thick brush covered with logging debris where I lost the track. Talk about discouraging! I looked upstream and I looked downstream. Then I went to my horse and rode home, down and discouraged.

On the way, I stopped in at a neighbor's and told him about my bum luck. Unknown to me, he went hunting in that same area the next morning and, probably due to his thirty-plus years of experience, was able to find my 4×4 blacktail dead on the opposite side of the creek from where I'd been looking. The meat wasn't good, but the horns sure were. When he called that night and said he'd found them, I was elated but at the same time very disappointed in myself for not being able to locate my buck. Consequently I told him to keep the horns and they hung on his porch for many years before I finally took them home.

Since then I've gone on to hunt blacktails in most of the western Oregon hunting units and so far I have one B&C buck and three SCI bucks out of the many I've killed.

When you could legally hunt deer any place in the state, I'd usually chase the blacktails for a couple of weeks and then go to the John Day area for some mule deer hunting. I've never taken a real big Oregon mule deer, but I did get a nice 4×4 with forked eye guards in 1969. Of all the mulies I've taken there, he is my best, taken in a snow storm at close range on a very memorable trip.

My Roosevelt elk hunts have taken place mostly in Columbia and Clatsop counties. I've taken numerous spikes and rag horns in the 1960s, 70s, and 80s and a nice 4×4 in 1991 (the most recent bull). Dale Trautman of Philomath and I killed our bulls together that year, with my son-in-law Bill Harrel helping out.

Bear hunting has never been a real big thing for me. I've only taken two Oregon black bears. One of those was an "incidental" kill in Hells Canyon and the other was in a bear trap.

In 1978, Dale Trautman and I applied for an antelope tag for the first time (Beulah unit). With tag in pocket, I located a nice buck about 7 a.m. that same day. The buck was killed as he lay in his bed and as my son Dave, who was celebrating his birthday that day, watched from about a mile away. I've never applied in Oregon again.

Nearly all of my elk hunting in Oregon has been for the Roosevelt elk, making only a couple of trips to eastern Oregon to hunt Rocky Mountain elk. However, October 1987 found me hunting elk in the Sumpter unit with friends, Tim Combs and Dan Baugher. We killed our three bulls in two days, with me taking the smallest, a two-point.

I had been applying for one of Oregon's sheep tags for years and repeatedly told my sheep-hunting friend, Elvin Hawkins, that if I ever drew a tag, he and I were going hunting. This was in the years before he started guiding for sheep. I finally drew a Hart Mountain tag in 1988 and on September 27th in the company of Elvin, my son Dave and son-in-law Jim Usherm, I shot the fifty-first ram that I'd seen on that trip. This ram scored 160 3/8 the next day by Elvin and the rangers.

It was, in fact, on that trip that I first shared my desire to bag each of Oregon's nine legal big game animals. Both Elvin and I knew many, if not most, of the successful Oregon sheep hunters and we were quite sure none of them had taken all eight other animals. Some very discrete detective work on our part in the next few months seemed to confirm this. My desire to be the first to do so increased while I made plans to harvest cougar and whitetail in Oregon.

In 1989, I applied for and got a permit to hunt whitetails in northeast Oregon with a muzzle loader. I hunted hard but never saw a buck. Prior to the next season I phoned my friend, Galen Clark, in Elgin to get some tips on hunting whitetail there. He invited me over for the 1990 season and said we'd hunt together. Maybe I still had a chance at what I was now calling "The Oregon Super Slam." That fall, near Elgin with Galen's assistance, I took a very nice 5×6 whitetail buck with a muzzle loader.

Ah-hah! Eight down and one to go. I had already drawn a cougar tag for the Sled Springs unit for 1990. Mike Rahn of Enterprise had recommended Mike Shirley of Joseph because of his pack of good cougar hounds. I got a motel room in Joseph, called Mike and we started scouting. When the season opened on December 3rd, we were out hunting way before daylight, with my 4×4 Dodge and Mike's hounds. It was fresh tracking in two inches of new snow, and after a fairly long race I took the large male with one shot from my .50 caliber muzzle loader through his heart.

This fulfilled my goal of getting the Oregon Super Slam and to the best of my knowledge, it is the first one ever!

Exceptional Cougar

by Ron L. Lay

Ron Lay owned and ran hound dogs from the time he was nine years old until the age of fifty five. As a boy, he hunted bobcats for a $5.00 bounty and worked his entire life as a cattle rancher in the Med-

ical Springs area. Ron's son, Joe, also killed an extremely large cat in 1981, measuring 15 4/16 B.C.

I cut a large cougar track near Catherine Creek State Park and decided to turn my dogs on it. The cat crossed the creek and headed up over the ridge. The snow was thigh deep, making the going very difficult. For me, cougar hunting was

trying to stay up with the dogs and seeing if I could last. Eventually, the cat headed back across Catherine Creek, where my five dogs had him treed. I had a .22 pistol, so I shot the cat in the head. He jumped out of the tree, with the dogs trailing close behind, and they treed him again a short distance away. As I approached the cougar, he jumped right for me. I fired a second shot, the cat jumped and the dogs tore into him. It was quite a fight, and the cougar seriously injured one dog. I stuck the barrel of the revolver down next to his head and began firing shots into him. He got hold of my boot and bit in as he died. I shot him a total of twelve times, and the dogs had torn holes in him big enough to stick your fingers into. I packed the injured dog out to the road and a passerby helped me pack out the cougar. I weighed him on a certified scale: he weighed one hundred eighty-four pounds and measured 8′11″ from the tip of his nose to the tip of his tail. The lion's skull measured 15 10/16 B.C., the state record for a cougar and ranked number nine in the world, winning the first place award at the Boone and Crockett Competition in Pittsburgh, Pennsylvania. Over the many years of hunting with dogs I've treed around forty-eight cougars, but this Tom was very exceptional, holding the state record for thirty years.
(Final score: 15 10/16 B.C.)

First Antelope

by Sharon Ganos

My enjoyment of hunting began because of the patience of my father when I was the age of five. As his little "tag along," he offered me the wonder of the outdoors and inspired my ambition to become a confident and accomplished sportswoman. Scoring 85 2/8, I dedicate to my father the entry of this pronghorn into the *1992–1994 Boone and Crockett Club Records of the North American Big Game Book.*

On August 25, 1992, my sister, her husband and I drove from Joseph, Oregon to the hunting unit of East Beatys Butte, located in Oregon's southern high desert. As we arrived that evening at the location where we planned to establish base camp, our enthusiasm for the hunt was tempered by the distant glow of a raging prairie fire. With a watchful eye on the blazing grasslands we cautiously established an encampment, leaving ourselves an avenue for escape. The coolness of the night's air calmed the flames and, with an irrigated field in its path, the fire eventually ran out of life. At daybreak we were greeted with a surprisingly clear sky.

By 6:00 a.m., we were hunting the northern section of the Catlow Valley. Luck was with us and we began spotting animals right away, although at considerable distances. After observing over a dozen animals, a pair of antelope came into view that appeared distinctly darker than the others. Through my scope I discerned both

to be bucks, either of which would qualify as a respectable trophy. Just as I began to focus on the lead buck, they quickened their pace, heading toward a knoll behind which they would soon disappear. I had only a split-second to decide. The report from my 300 Savage broke the silence and sent the front pronghorn spilling forward. Quickly he regained his feet, wheeled immediately to the right, continued for twenty yards and fell. At 7:30 a.m., we approached my first antelope, stepping off two hundred and sixty-five yards.

He was an older buck with thick horn tips, which twisted slightly to a height of seventeen inches. A third horn almost an inch in length emerged from the middle of his forehead, a remnant from a few million years ago when antelope displayed a second full set of horns for defense.

My feelings at that moment were complex: part elation, part sadness and grateful reflection for such moments during the past forty years. (Final score: 85 2/8 B.C.)

Blind Luck Antelope

by Brian Day

My antelope hunting started in 1992. I got a Juniper unit tag, and from the statistics I saw and the people I talked to, this was going to be easy. Boy, was I wrong. I never felt so feeble and intimidated with a bow. I like to feel in control

when I shoot, but every time I turned an arrow loose, the antelope would jump the string.

I probably shot at and missed the biggest buck the most. I was lying on a bald flat like a decoy. This buck came right up to within twenty yards and looked at me, but I couldn't shoot lying down, so I sat up, drew and almost shot my kneecap off with the lower limb. This exceptionally dumb critter let me shoot four more arrows at him, all at less than forty yards, but every time I shot, he'd jump. I had already missed three other antelope from this same position, so I had to start whistling at him so he would leave and let me gather up my arrows.

The next morning he came back and let me miss him twice more. All this had me believing that you had to be a poor shot to get an antelope. That way, maybe he would run into an arrow when he jumped. Well, all of this kind of took the enthusiasm out of antelope hunting, but I applied for and got a Hart Mountain tag for 1994. It was almost the end of the season and I

still hadn't gone antelope hunting, so one day I finished work at 4:30 in Gold Beach and drove home to Eagle Point. I was so tired that I knew if I went to sleep I wouldn't get to Hart Mountain until the next night, so I unloaded my tools, threw in my camping gear and took off. I got there after daylight. I drove around a little to look the area over and found a nice saddle in which to build a blind. I dug a small hole, stacked a bunch of sagebrush around it, put some camo netting on for a roof to keep the sun out of my eyes and settled down for a nap. About two hours later I had to wake up and stand up to fill my specimen bottle. I looked over my shoulder and there was a nice buck watching me. I sat right back down and watched him. After about thirty minutes, curiosity finally got the best of him and he came over and looked in my blind. Then he walked around to the other side and let me shoot him. All of a sudden, antelope hunting was more fun again. Final score was 80 6/8. I guess I wouldn't mind applying for another tag.
(Final score: 80 6/8 P.Y.)

Rocky Mountain Bighorn (#5 in Oregon)

by Sam Jaksick

In September of 1987, I hunted Bighorn in the Joseph Creek area of northeastern Oregon. Two companions and I walked into the area from a county road approximately four miles to the east. From a previous scouting trip, we knew the general area we wanted to hunt, an area very close to the Oregon/Washington state line.

Upon arriving at the area, we located a large ram that we estimated would score in excess of one hundred and ninety Boone and Crockett points. This ram was just entering a cave to escape from the extreme heat of that September day. There was no easy way to approach the ram without spooking it, due to the fact that three other smaller rams lay just outside the cave. There were two possibilities: (1) to wait out the ram in hope he would leave the cave later that day, or (2) take a shot in excess of three hundred yards from across a main canyon approximately one-half mile away. I decided to try the latter. I had the wind in my favor and was able to stay in the shadows of a rim rock to get in the position to take the shot. Once I arrived at a predetermined spot, I took the rifle off safety, held my breath and squeezed the trigger. I immediately heard the sound that every hunter hopes to hear: the thud of the bullet as it finds its mark. The sheep was down. As I approached, there was no doubt that the ram met my expectations.
(Final score: 191 4/8 B.C.)

Rocky Mountain Bighorn (#3 in Oregon)

by Todd Jaksick

In June of 1988, I was lucky enough to acquire a permit that allowed me to hunt in Oregon throughout the month of September. On the opening weekend I was unable to locate any sheep due to smoke created by a local fire. The next weekend my father, Sam, a friend, Rob Bichols, and I flew back to Oregon, hoping to have better success.

The morning after our arrival, the three of us started glassing in hopes of finding a record-book ram. Throughout the morning we saw a few small rams, but none of them satisfied what I was looking for. Later on that morning, my father finally spotted five rams in a small basin in the Joseph Creek area. We felt that one ram, in particular, could exceed one hundred and ninety-five Boone and Crockett points.

After carefully planning a stalk, my father remained at the glassing point where he could continue to observe the sheep. Rob and I dropped into the canyon and after about three hours we had positioned ourselves two hundred yards from the sheep. Although we could not see

the sheep, my father signaled that the sheep had not moved. One hour later, when the sheep got up to feed, I watched as each sheep crossed through my scope. When the largest ram of the five began to cross my path, I was ready to shoot, but my hands were shaking and my heart was beating so quickly that I had to stop and take a deep breath before I could shoot. As I squeezed the trigger, the sound of my heart beating was louder than the gunshot itself. I hit the ram with the first shot! A wave of excitement ran through me, and I then realized that although I had hit the ram, it did not go down. The ram continued slowly down the hill and I positioned my gun once more on the ram to finish it off. Pulling the trigger again, I saw the ram fall to the ground. After taking a rough score of the ram, I knew I had shot one of the largest bighorn rams ever taken.

(Final score: 198 0/8 B.C.)

My Ram and I

by Sherrain Glenn

I shot him at about 8 a.m. Unbelievable shot, across a canyon . . . just zipped his belly and broke his left leg (his insides fell out). My rifle is a 6 mm and shoots very straight. I had my crosshairs aimed at the top of his back: that's where Jack said to put them, since the rams were across the canyon; six rams grazing across the hillside. My sights never left this one. I knew he was a legal ram—heavy, full curl, gray in color across the face and not much daylight between his horns. Jack was tossing rocks up in the air and said "Let me know when you're going to shoot!" I decided I wasn't going to tell him. Time stood still . . . the shot echoed across the canyon, my ram bucked, ran up the hill and around a ledge. Another ram ran down and came right up in front of me. Jack was yelling for me to shoot! I told him I had already shot another one. He had not seen it, as he was not looking when I shot. Jack crossed the canyon in, I believe, two steps. I just sat down and thought: well . . . now the chase . . . another canyon . . . what the heck? He yelled at me to get over there *right now.* Those were strong words so I crossed the canyon. It was so steep you would slide down for every step you took to go sideways, and I had to climb back up the other side! To this day, I believe I have from this hunt a permanent spot in my back from the bolt of my rifle. After reaching the other side, Jack came around the ledge, and said, smiling, "Get over here." My ram was lying down, licking his belly. He jumped up on a ledge, out of sight, with his guts and leg hanging. We had to go around and down the ledge, and there my ram stood up. Jack said to shoot him, and I did, just as he jumped off the ledge at ME. I missed. Ram, rifle and I slid down the shale (note the photo).

My hunt was over . . . and the work began as we packed out. We got to headquarters about 6 p.m. to have the ram scored. September 9 was the next to the last day of my hunt. I had hunted for three hard days, across the top of Warner peak from the bottom up, Poker Jim ridge by way of the whole ridge, and the front Hart.

Hunting the California bighorn sheep was truly a once-in-a-lifetime experience. To my mentor, my husband and guide: Jack, thank you! (Final score: 173 0/8 B.C.)

The Hunt I Will Never Forget

by Robert Staples

There he is! Yes, a nice 28- or 30-inch, 4×4 buck. He keeps getting closer, and I get ready for a close shot. There, ten yards away, is an old monarch. I'm ready to pull my bow back . . . but I left my bow back at my house!

This was just a scouting trip to check out a couple of big bucks my friend had told me about. I continued to scout this area and saw two very large bucks in velvet. Oh, how huge they looked in velvet!

Finally, I got my chance to hunt these ol' bucks. I got off from work late, so I rushed home to grab my bow and meet my friend, who also wanted to go along.

When we got to the hunting spot we had about one and a half hours of daylight left. My friend went one way and I another. After about fifteen minutes, I got to where I had seen that wide buck while scouting earlier. I stopped and started to look around and I heard this crackling sound. I thought it was my friend. Well, it wasn't; it was a nice little 2×3 buck. He was too close for me to pass up a shot, but I could only see his head and his neck: not my kind of shot. I went ahead and pulled back my bow and hoped he would take just one more step, then I'd shoot him. Well, he didn't, he just kept looking to his right. At this time I heard a rustling sound where this buck was looking, and out stepped a heavy, symmetrical 4×4 buck. I held my sights right on his chest and let him keep walking toward me. Finally, at twenty-five yards, he saw me as something out of the ordinary and stopped.

I was ready for that moment! My Wasp CCL-tipped Beman carbon arrow flew true to aim, hitting him in the center of his chest and breaking his neck. Down he went to stay. I was excited but I didn't approach him yet. I first went to find my friend and tell him about the buck. We waited for about half an hour and then went to check him out. Wow, a dream come true! Now the hard work begins . . .
(Final score: 178 3/8 P.Y.)

Enormous Buck

by Bob Vinson

It was getting toward the latter part of the general rifle season in October of 1981—only a couple of days left—when I thought about going out for an afternoon hunt. My son was in high school at the time and would be getting home early enough to go along with me. It was a clear, hot, sunny day as we were heading out to a favorite hunting spot that I'd been hunting for the last twenty years.

We were heading west out of Klamath Falls on Highway 66 when we decided to turn off onto the Ward Ranch Road and into the Fox Lake Reservoir area; it was about ten miles from the highway into an old burn that has been successful for me in years past. As we approached the east end of the old burn—about three miles across from the west end, which I've always liked to hunt—my son asked if he could put down the tailgate of the Chevy Blazer and ride there, knowing we would have to go slowly along the old rough road that cut through the middle of the burn. The manzanita brush was about four or five feet high, and the trees that Weyerhauser had planted several years earlier were probably eight to ten feet tall, with areas that were impassible even on foot.

When we got toward the west end there was an old road that went a couple hundred yards and came to a dead end. My thought was to park there and walk over to the edge of a small ravine and sit on a stand until dusk.

Just as I pulled up and shut off the motor, I glanced over and saw an enormous buck jump up out of its bed and just stand there, frozen. My son jumped off the tailgate, grabbing his gun, and took a quick shot at him from about sixty yards

away. When he fired, the deer dropped out of sight and I yelled out, "Good shot, you got him." I then jumped out of the rig and we started over toward him. I got about halfway there when he jumped back up and took off running. Of course, I didn't have my gun with me and my son couldn't get off another shot because the brush was too thick.

My son took off after the deer while I ran back to the vehicle and grabbed my gun out and took off in another direction, hoping to cut him off. I headed over toward the ravine, thinking he may go down through the middle of it. When I got to where I could see well, no sign of any deer. I stood there for a few moments and then heard some thrashing behind me: Here he was, coming toward me full speed. I was standing in the trail that he was traveling on, so I threw the gun up, put the cross hairs right on his head and pulled the trigger to hear a "click," as I had forgotten to put a shell in the chamber. About that time he saw me and whirled away, jumping over the high manzanita thickets. On the last bounce he made before going completely out of sight, I put the sights on the back of his head and fired, and I could see him go down. When my son heard me shoot he came running over to see what I had shot at. There lay one of the biggest blacktail bucks I've ever seen. When we checked out the animal, we saw that I had put a bullet behind his ear that had come out through the eye on the same side. If it had been about an eighth of an inch to one side, he still would have been running. We also noticed a small piece of horn that had been shot off, and that's where my son had hit the deer earlier, knocking him out momentarily.

I shot the deer with a 270 Remington 700 at approximately seventy-five yards.
(Final score: 172 3/8 B.C.)

The Monster Buck

by David Baird

Like great yellow ghosts, the elk drifted through the young pines into the open, old-growth timber. The old cow in the lead had her nose into the wind, leading the others up the mountain slope. Was there a bull with them? I quietly nocked an arrow without alerting the elk. I was beginning to worry that they would see me, simply because I was looking at them with such intensity. The lead cow was fifty yards in front of me and nervously looking everywhere as she moved deeper into the open timber. Would I take a cow, or wait in hopes of taking a bull?

Horns, there they were! The last one, hanging back from the others, was a bull. I could just make out the brow tines through the branches as it stepped out of the young pines into the open. My G—, it's a BUCK.

It was August 1991, and it was hot! I was hunting out of my brother-in-law's camp in the upper elevations of the Rogue River Valley, in Jackson County, Oregon. Dan Reed was more like a brother than a brother-in-law. Whenever I showed up at his hunting or fishing camps, I was always welcomed with a hot meal and a dry place to sleep. Dan and his son, Kevin, age 14, were hunting with Tim Cluster and his two sons, Caleb, age 11, and Theron, age 12.

Late August to early September is the Roosevelt elk/Columbian blacktail deer archery season. Western Oregon deer, a separate species from the mule deer, are classified as Columbian blacktail deer. They are generally smaller in size than mule deer. The coastal and inland habitat these deer thrive on produces some fantastic-sized antlers. This season I had archery tags for both Roosevelt elk and blacktail deer.

We had hunted hard for three very hot, dry days. On the evening of the third day, dark ominous thunderheads began building up against the coastal mountain range to the west. As darkness came so did the much-prayed-for rain; all night it pounded on the roof of the tent. It was the last thing I heard as I drifted off into dreams of bulls and bucks.

Coffee never tastes so good and air never smells so clean as it does in the predawn mountain air after that first autumn rain. What a great place to live! At least I thought so until Dan outlined the day's hunt. They had not located the herd yet. With the rain washing out old tracks, today's first rule of business was to find fresh tracks, and the herd. The morning hunt was going to be a hard one: miles of uphill climbs and rough terrain.

At noon I dragged myself back into camp. I was exhausted, and I had not seen an elk or a deer. I had not prepared for rain, and my clothes and shoes were soaked. The heat from the wood stove in the cook tent was as good as any Jacuzzi. Heat soaked into my tired body and steam drifted lazily off my clothes as they dried.

A cup of hot coffee, lunch and a nap sounded good, but the others were back. Dan had spotted a record-class, non-typical blacktail buck and Tim had found the elk. The elk were feeding toward the same general area as the buck. It was time to hunt and put all those hours of practice at the archery range to use,

Dan and Kevin went low, where timbered ridges broke off into pine thickets and small open meadows. I took the middle, where second-growth pines opened into old-growth forest. This was the prime feeding location, below the area where the buck was spotted and ahead of where the elk were seen feeding. Tim, taking the high ground, would hunt where the steep slopes were constantly shaded by the old-growth canopy. The wind was drifting into my face and the rain sneaked down the middle of my back as we took on our assigned tasks.

About three miles into the hunt all thought of sleep was gone from my mind. The cool damp air was invigorating and the quietness of the forest floor led to thoughts of great bulls and monster bucks. This is it, this is when it's supposed to happen, at least it always does in my dreams: the ideal weather, a great location and deer and elk in the vicinity. Then there they were, like great yellow ghosts drifting through the trees.

I had thoughts of shooting a cow and not waiting to see if a bull was with the herd. I had only a couple more days left before I had to be back at work. The elk were crossing about forty yards ahead of me in the open timber. Dropping down on one knee behind a huge old pine tree, I watched as nine or ten elk cows moved out to feed for the evening. Then I saw the horns.

The last animal in line was farther away and more concealed by the trees than the cows, which is typical of bulls. The cows passed beyond my view as the bull stepped out forty yards away. Except it wasn't a bull following the cows, it was a blacktail buck with a rack of incredible horns.

The buck stopped and put his head down to eat. Unable to shoot from the kneeling position, I eased slowly up. Behind the tree, I pulled my bow to full draw and leaned out to the right. The buck still had its head down as I anchored my hand up against my jaw and looked through the peep sight. Wait! I can't see through the peep sight; what's going on? I held at full draw and moved the string away from my face until I could see the peep. It had water in it that was blocking the hole. I couldn't hold full draw any more and wasn't going to take a guessed-at shot. I leaned back behind the tree as I glanced at the buck. He was looking directly at me. Darn!

I quietly let the bow off full draw, hoping the arrow wouldn't bounce off the rest. I raised the string and blew through the peep sight to clear it of water. The sound of my blowing resounded like a fog horn in the quiet of the forest. Praying the buck was still there and not wanting to lean out and look without being ready, I pulled the bow to full draw. I anchored it against my face and checked the peep.

Raising the bow to approximately where I judged the buck to have been last, I leaned out from behind the big pine. My G—, he's coming at me! The buck had obviously seen me and evidently heard me blow through the peep. What he thought I was, I'll never know. But he had turned and begun walking right up to me. Instead of a forty-yard shot, I now had a fifteen- to twenty-foot shot.

We obviously saw each other simultaneously. Fortunately, I was at full draw and anchored to shoot before I leaned out. As I released the arrow, the buck swung his head to the right and jumped. Everything happened so fast I lost sight of the arrow. The buck gave no evidence of being hit. And then he was gone.

I scrambled around the tree and saw the buck disappearing up the mountain. Quickly I went to check for evidence of a hit. Blood in his tracks or on the arrow; whatever indication of a hit I could find. The tracks were evident in the soft damp pine needles where he had jumped. Just beyond, buried a quarter of the way into the

ground, was my arrow and it was red, with blood, from end to end. I had hit him, but where and how bad?

Time to slow down, and review where I was, what time it was and what was happening. It was 6:00 p.m. and I was two miles up the side of a mountain I had never hunted before. I was at least three miles from camp and two miles from the closest road. Dan had given me an exact compass bearing to take when it was time to end the hunt. "Be headed out by 6:30," he had said, "it'll be black by 7:30." Ever the prepared one, he insisted that I have a compass, a flashlight and flagging tape before I left.

I figured on waiting half an hour before going after the buck, but that would be too late to track it. Better to track it now. Maybe it was hit hard and would go down soon. The running tracks were easy to follow on the wet ground. Almost immediately there was a blood trail, bright red and foamy, and almost as fast the rain turned from a light sprinkle to a heavy shower. The tracks and the blood were being obliterated by the rain. As fast and as hard as I could, I followed the tracks straight up the side of the mountain.

Suddenly it was getting hard to see the tracks and I realized it was getting dark. I checked my watch and it was 7:00, past time for heading to the road. Taking a compass bearing, I hung flagging ribbon at the last blood sign and began heading out. I hung flagging ribbon every fifty yards, so I could get back to this spot in the morning and continue the track. The rain I had been so glad about was now destroying the evidence I needed to locate the biggest buck I had ever seen.

I made it to the road just as it was too dark to see and walked the two miles back to camp in the dark. Never had a walk been so lonely and so long. My dream of a monster buck had just been realized and was slipping away just as fast.

At camp the fire burned brightly and felt good, but it couldn't warm the cold inside that I felt. I knew the tracks and the blood trail were gone. The rain had lasted for two hours before it quit. Only Tim's boys were at the fire. Dan, Kevin and Tim were still out. As the minutes passed away, so did my dream of killing a monster buck. He was gone, and I knew it.

When the others walked into camp

together, I was glad for their safety and sorry that they had seen nothing. Then I told them of the buck. Dan and Tim looked at each other and never said a word. They began to gather lanterns and rain gear, and got the boys dressed and outfitted to be out all night if necessary. These two had hunted together so long that words were not necessary. They thought and acted alike, each knowing what the other would do in any given situation. Within minutes we were all equipped with day packs, meat packing frames, foul-weather gear, lights and food. Half an hour later we found my flagging ribbon on the road and headed in. It was now 9:30 p.m.

Finding flagging tape at fifty yards in fairly open timber in daylight is one thing, but at fifty yards away on a dark overcast moonless night is something else. The red ribbon I had used did not show up in the dark. You had to be right on top of it before you could see it. Although I had followed a compass bearing out, it wasn't a straight line. I had followed the least obstructed path in the growing darkness and drifted left and right. Finding my ribboned path was going to be harder than tracking the buck.

We discovered that a lantern passing behind a length of ribbon made a reflection like a red brake light coming on. We adopted this technique. One of us would stay at the last ribbon and the others would work away from it in increasingly large half circles, until the next ribbon showd in the light.

Feeling somewhat guilty about everyone being out on my account, I suggested that we could do this more easily in the daylight, but they never hesitated. If you have an injured animal, you stay with it until you know it's down or that it's going to make it. You make exceptions for personal safety and when common sense tells you to. This, however, was not one of those times. It just happened to be dark. Dan's big concern was that a black bear sow and her cub had been seen earlier in the week on the mountain. If the bear caught scent of the blood trail before we found the buck, there wouldn't be much left.

At 11:30 p.m., we finally found the last ribbon. With the aid of the bright propaned lanterns we could see that the rain had washed away all blood signs. Knowing the color of the blood and the foam that I had seen, Dan and Tim both agreed that the buck had been hit hard, probably low in the lungs near the heart, and wouldn't go very far.

Knowing that these blacktail bucks typically make a hook to the right just before they lie down from a fatal arrow wound set the stage for what was to happen next. Dan stayed on the tracks with Tim's two boys. Tim, Kevin and I each took a propane lantern and began circling out to the right in hopes of finding the buck. We kept our bearings from Dan's propane lantern as he kept on slowly working out the faint tracks.

At 1:00 in the morning, all traces of the buck were gone and my hopes with them. Everyone agreed to give it another half hour and then head out. We would pick up again in the morning and hope the bears, coyotes, etc. didn't find the buck first. And suddenly, there it was, lying dead right in front of me, not twenty yards from where I had given up and headed out. It had gone uphill, turned to the right and then headed downhill. Had I waited awhile the first time out before turning back, he would have walked right into me.

The yelling and hollering from that mountain side on that dark quiet night still rings in my head. Thank you, Lord, for good friends, a good hunt and the monster buck of my dreams.

The buck was unofficially scored at 172 6/8 the following year. Its first official scoring was at the 1995 Pope and Young conference in Travis City, Michigan. It scored 160 7/8 and was ranked number one for the two-year scoring period, and officially ranked as the number-four all-time record. In 1996, the buck was displayed at the Safari Club convention and scored for their records at 172 2/8. It was ranked as the number-one Columbian blacktail in the world. (Final score: 166 2/8 P.Y.)

Buck

by Kevin Robins

I bagged this buck at the end of the second week of the season. I was driving down a forest service road when I saw him cross the road about one hundred and fifty yards in front of me. I immediately pulled over and parked. I guessed that he might be moving in my direction. There was a fifty-foot-high hillside parallel to the road. I worked my way up and over the hill and down into some timber. I had waited about ten minutes when he suddenly appeared to my left. He was about seventy-five yards away and working his way toward me. When he was about forty yards away, standing broadside, I released my arrow, hitting him low in the shoulder. He jumped in the air and took off, running up and over the hill. I waited thirty minutes and then started tracking him. I found him just over the hill, dead. My arrow had hit him through the heart and he had run about sixty-five yards.

This was my first time hunting with a bow and I really enjoyed it. I just hope I can top this buck with a bigger one in the future. (Final score: 176 4/8)

Christmas Tree Buck

by Dwight A. Homested

My friend Jim and I decided to leave work a little early on that dreary November day so we could get some hunting in before sundown. There were only a couple of days of deer season left and we wanted to get as much hunting in as we could before our tags ran out. We decided to go to Rock Creek outside of Sheridan. I had hunted the area a few times prior to this. The last time I went up there I had only seen a few does and a herd of elk. With elk season just around the corner, we figured we could scope out the area for future reference.

We stepped out of the truck into the light rain and grabbed our rifles. The fog began to settle among the surrounding oak trees. We were hunting in a Chrismas tree field that was surrounded by tall oaks and a variety of other trees and underbrush. My partner started off into the three- to four-foot Christmas trees, and I decided to walk the fence row that outlined the field. After a while we noticed a lot of elk sign ahead of us. Then, about one hundred yards ahead of us, a four-point bull elk walked into the Christmas trees from behind a tall oak. It just stood there. We must have watched it for about ten to fifteen minutes before we decided to move on. We still had quite a way to go before it got dark, and the fog was getting thicker.

We had gone about twenty yards past the bull elk when I noticed something ahead of me. About eighty yards up the hill I could make out a pretty nice rack in the Christmas trees. I took a look through my binoculars. The rack was too dark and too big to be a buck, or so I thought. About the same time that I was taking a look, my partner shot.

"That rack looks too big for a buck!" I yelled over to Jim.

"No, it's a buck. I'm right in the same line of trees he is!" he yelled in response.

The animal just stood there, unaware of where we were. My partner's scope was shooting about a foot too high and he had missed. I had a good shoulder shot and didn't hesitate. The buck dropped where it stood.

Hunting Is Hard Work

by Leah Robertson, age 14

We had been hunting hard all week and Daddy promised we could go for a short hunt this morning. We walked out of camp and twenty minutes later we spotted a deer across the canyon. I didn't know if it had antlers or not, but Daddy yelled "Shoot it!" so I did. Everyone at camp was excited. I was just happy to get it over with so I could sleep in.
(Final score: 197 7/8 B.C.)

Deer Diary

by Mike DeWitt

Day 1, (Sat.) 11/25/95
Walking southwest from the gravel pit for three-quarters of a mile, I didn't see any deer until 9:45 a.m. Then I sat down to watch a medium-size 3×4 chase a doe in heat. It started to rain about 10:30. I was on my way to get a better look, but wild horses got in my way. Then I saw him! He was chasing a doe up the hill to the west and was about twenty-five yards away. It was raining harder, so I returned to the pickup, and arrived there at 12:00. From there, I drove north on the pavement and took a road I had seen during my earlier scouting. I spotted some deer under a ridge and could see there were two bucks and one doe through my binoculars. Using the spotting scope from the window was difficult, due to the rain. At around 1:30, I could see there was a small forked horn and a medium-size 4×4, maybe 24″ to 25″ wide, but not very heavy-horned. As I watched, they moved back and forth from one draw to another for almost an hour, then they lay down. It was 3:30 by this time and raining very hard, so I decided to come back in the morning to try to get a better look.

Day 2, (Sun.) 11/26/95
I went to the same place as last night. The deer were in the second draw, but there were more of them. I could not see any horns in the bunch. The rain had stopped and the wind was out of the northeast and cold, so I headed toward the deer on foot. Getting above and behind them was fairly easy, with junipers and the rolling hills giving me cover. I was hoping they were in the same spot and as I crept over the ledge, five does stood up and ran toward the pickup. They were closer to me than I had expected, but, such was my luck, no bucks were with them. I returned to my pickup as the wind was blowing colder and coming more from the west. The sky was overcast. I decided to do some road scouting, as I did not see any more deer in the area. It was about 10:30 when I got to the pavement and headed down along the refuge, stopping several times to use the spotting scope. Down the road a ways, I unloaded "Big Bear," the four-wheeler, and went up the steep hill toward where I had seen the 3×4 on opening morning. After reaching the top, all

I saw was another hunter in his pickup and the wild horses, so I went back to the pickup for lunch. By 4:00 p.m. I had spotted several small bucks and does, along with one pretty good-looking bigger buck. He was about three-quarters of a mile into the refuge and didn't seem to be coming out. I could not get a good look at him, since it was raining again. I could tell he was bigger than the one I had seen last night, but how much bigger, I couldn't tell. For the next couple of hours, I drove on a gravel road, stopping several times to spot. It was around 4:00 when I got back to where the bigger buck had been earlier. He was farther off than before and it was getting dark, so back to camp I went. No deer liver for supper; just scallops I had brought from home.

Day 3, (Mon.) 11/27/95
Monday was another overcast day—no rain or snow, but the wind was colder and still blowing out of the northwest. Closer to camp this time, I decided to unload the "Big Bear" out of the pickup to do some rough road scouting. My fingers were very cold, even with good Gortex mittens on. I saw lots of country, and checked a few waterholes for deer traffic, finding them to be only lightly frozen over. By 10:00 a.m. I had not seen any fresh sign, let alone any deer. I parked the four-wheeler and walked out east on a high ridge that gave me a good vantage point for scouting the basin and draw of juniper and sagebrush below. At around 10:30, I spotted a group of thirteen does with a very small three-point, 18″ to 20″ and very spindly. The deer were feeding up the hill to the road I had come in on. I decided that trying to plan a vantage point was better than a stalk, as they were moving at a pretty good pace. Positioning myself about thirty yards off the road behind a rock fence proved to be an advantage. Cocking the gun and peering over the fence with my naked eyes, I could see the deer were headed my way. The buck changed places two, three or maybe four times in the lineup, as they moved single-file, closer and closer. The first doe went through the gate on the road, then another, then another three or four, and then the

buck. Finally, all fourteen deer stood on the road. The buck was at a good side-angle shot on my side of the fence, only twenty-five yards away. Watching those twenty-eight eyeballs for thirty seconds seemed more like thirty minutes. Knowing this was only my third day, I decided not to shoot. The deer either winded me, or I twitched. At any rate, they just moved off the road and uphill. It was 12:30 when I loaded "Big Bear" and headed up the pavement to spot where I had seen the 4×4 on Saturday afternoon. No luck.

At around 2:00 p.m., I set up the spotting scope. After glassing a little while, I decided to go for a walk to check out the country above. By 4:00, I did not see any fresh sign and it was starting to rain lightly. In the pickup again, I headed back to camp. Along the way I saw a few bucks in the refuge, but they made up their minds to stay inside the fence.

That evening the wind was from the west, and it was snowing like hell. I called home and my wife told me not to come home until Saturday. My son Bradley was sick and had stayed home from school. Back at camp, I told Josh I was going to leave the immediate area and head farther north to check out another area. He agreed this was a good idea, as a lot of hunters were pressuring the deer along the pavement.

Day 4, (Tue.) 11/28/95
I left camp at 5:30 a.m. to get a good start on the distance I had to travel. Along the way, I saw five really big does off the pavement, when it was just breaking daylight at about 6:30. Turning west on a gravel road, I traveled about ten miles and came upon posted private ground on one side and a lot of cows. The private side looked promising for hunting, but with maps and good judgment I could not find a way past the private land to where I could scout, so I turned around and went back. Heading south, then turning west, the road I came upon was really muddy and rutted from previous rains. At around 10:30, I saw a pickup coming toward me. I stopped it to be courteous. Two guys were coyote hunting and told me they had seen a pretty good buck over 50″ behind the

private land that I had just left. Following their directions was not easy, due to the fact they had a small Nissan pickup that was not as heavy as mine. After backing up, turning around and almost getting stuck in four-wheel drive, I found what looked like the location where they had seen the buck. By that time it was raining lightly and the wind was blowing hard out of the west. From the rig I spotted three does lying under a ridge among the rocks and sagebrush. They were about six hundred yards off the road and I could see no vantage point to get close to them. Hoping the big buck was with them, I headed into town for a few supplies and fuel. The trip to town and back to camp gave me time to plan my hunt for early morning. The coyote hunters had told me an easier way to get past the private ground so my route would be about half the distance off the pavement as before.

Day 5, (Wed.) 11/29/95
It rained and blew hard all night long. I awoke several times and thought to myself that it was going to be a really hard day for hunting. Leaving camp at 5:00 a.m. with my hunt planned, I was hoping to find the buck I was looking for. I was not even discouraged when I spilled my coffee on the seat on the journey. By daybreak, at 6:30, it had stopped raining, and I had just spotted six does with a small buck, and also what looked to be a 30″×20″ heavy-horned buck.

They were close to the spot where I had seen the three does the night before. They were about seven hundred yards away and were feeding uphill to the west. The wind was slight, from the north, so I headed out on foot to try to get above them for a shot. They might have seen me park the pickup due to open range between us, but they didn't seem worried. Losing sight of the eight deer and heading uphill, I saw two does running fast to the north, but no buck. After getting above the eight and arriving at the spot where I had thought they would come out, I saw nothing. The wind had picked up out of the north and was getting colder. I sat down and rested, spotting for less than five minutes. Then, I saw two, three, six or seven deer walking. They came from the top of the ridge and headed for the rolling hills of grass that seemed to go for five or six miles. Counting again, I registered six does and two bucks. They headed for the open grass and I followed, maybe four hundred yards behind. After one swale, they went halfway up the rise, turned as if to look at me or just behind me, and then they all lay down. I was in a really bad spot, two hundred yards away and nothing but scattered two-inch-high dead grass between us. The does were pretty alert and watchful, but the bucks, especially the larger one, were ready to rest. The smaller buck was a 2×3, maybe 16″ to 18″ and light-horned.

By now it was 9:00 a.m., and I had watched the bigger buck for thirty minutes and could tell he was a keeper. He was not what I was really wanting, but I would take him if conditions were right. He looked to be 30″×20″ and real heavy-horned, with four points on both sides with deep tines, except for the left rear. He rested for over an hour with his head turning side to side. His horns really looked wide compared to his body and judging from how tall the grass was. The does often got up and lay back down. By 10:30, there was no rain but it was overcast, and the wind from the west was blowing directly in my face. By 10:45, I decided to get a better vantage point, crawled backward about one hundred yards, and then got up and walked toward a draw on my left. The four-point was sleeping. Three does were up and looking my way, still about two hundred yards away. With no chance for a shot, I lay down behind a rock. After using the binoculars for the next hour or so, I made my mind up. I wanted to get my hands on those horns. At 11:45, they all got up and headed over a grassy knob, out of sight. Picking up my backpack, I headed around a rocky knoll to try and cross their path. At 12:05, creeping on my belly over the knoll, I saw five does scattered in the dry grass less than fifty yards below me. The 4×4 was less than forty yards away, walking away from me. His horns really looked huge this time. The buck walked toward the five does and lay down behind them. Then and there I capped and cocked my .50 caliber gun. I didn't see the other doe or buck at all, but maybe they had seen or winded me, and that's what made the big buck and five does suddenly take off. No matter what the cause, I had to shoot now. He was angling away broadside and running fast when my 370-grain maxiball hit him. I heard the ball hit, and then I re-loaded with my speed loaders. After watching him go across the draw and fall down over one hundred yards away, I kept walking toward him. There were two does waiting just above him, and he stood up to look at me. As I fired a second time, he moved up the hill and out of sight. Cresting the grassy knoll, I saw nothing but two-foot-high grass for three or four miles. Knowing he was hit pretty good, I turned back downhill. After going only a couple hundred yards, I saw him lying down again. He was bleeding badly from the left rear and he stood up again to head for his two does. Downhill at over eighty yards, I could not hit my mark. As he stumbled away, I headed after him with ninety grains of 2F and another maxiball stuffed away. I lost sight of him again; then I lost the blood trail. The does were headed uphill, but he had been going down. After traveling for about half a mile through sagebrush, rocks and grass, I went to the pickup and headed in the direction I had last seen the buck. I spotted a coyote on the uphill side. Knowing the deer was hurt pretty bad and bleeding, I got out and walked in the direction of the coyote. Then I saw another one, and then there were three coyotes uphill. Figuring the coyotes were on the blood trail, I turned and looked back downhill toward the water. At about four hundred yards with the binoculars, I spotted the deer lying next to the water. With the coyotes uphill and the water below me, I sat down to spot the area and collect myself. It was 4:00 p.m., and almost dusk. Then downhill, around eight hundred yards away, I saw the buck lying on the water's edge. I headed downwind from him and then turned straight for him in the wide open. At one hundred yards I could tell he was done for. At fifty yards, I made a finishing shot, seeing his body was in poor shape.

His ears were only 19″ wide and that was what had made me think he was 30″ wide. I didn't know all the time I was stalking and chasing him that he had two cheaters on the right and one on the left. The deer was not in very good shape and he weighed a little over one hundred and fifty pounds. I pulled him up and lifted him up on the back of the 4×4, and tied him down for the trip back to the pickup to dress him out. The terrain was rough and slippery, even for the four-wheeler, and it was raining and dark. I guess I didn't see that the ropes had loosened, but I sure knew it when the deer fell off on the right side and I ran over it with a tire. Okay—one more time. I loaded him up and this time I tied him a

lot better. It was dark, but I had only about a quarter mile to go. I used the pickup lights to gut him, making sure I kept the liver and heart. I was glad I had stayed with him. He is the biggest buck I've taken with a muzzle loader. He was 27″×24″, close to the estimated 50″ T-square that the coyote hunters had judged him to be. (Final score: 188 4/8 B.C.)

September Buck

by Jon Silver

My name is Jon Silver. I am a bow hunter and this is the story of the big buck I shot on September 12, 1995.

My father and I had decided to go for an evening hunt. So far I had not seen anything worth shooting, so Dad said he knew where I might find a buck. We loaded up and headed out.

We drove for about an hour. As we got closer to the area, I decided to ride in the back of the pickup, so that in case we saw something, I could get out quicker. We drove maybe another mile. Then we saw two deer up the road, one doe and one that looked like a nice buck. They became nervous and ran into a patch of timber on top of the ridge we were driving on. Dad decided to drive on past them and let me out, in hopes I could get back on them. As we drove up to where they had been, another buck sprang out of the brush and followed the previous two.

Dad drove past where they had run into the trees and continued up the road about one hundred yards. I jumped out of the pickup and headed into the wind and timber. When I got into the stand of

trees, I noticed that it was a small patch about fifty yards wide and two hundred yards long, a thin patch with pockets of brush in it.

There were two major trails running lengthways through the trees, with deer and elk rubs along each trail. I moved cautiously along

the trail, looking and listening. About halfway through the timber patch, I heard a branch break, up the ridge from me. I figured the bucks had decided to find a less crowded hiding spot, so I decided to exit the patch of timber and look over the bare ridge again—nothing. I started back toward the pickup, walking parallel to the tree line. As I neared the end of the timber, I heard a noise to my left. I turned and there they stood in an opening about eight feet wide. The doe was furthest to the left, then a nice non-typical and then a typical buck. As they stared at me, it looked like nothing but horns across that opening. I already had an arrow nocked but couldn't draw without spooking them. The doe then moved into the timber and the two bucks turned and looked at her. I drew back. Just as I completed my draw, the non-typical buck turned broadside and stepped in front of the typical. I have always wanted a non-typical, so I released. I heard the thump of the arrow and watched the bucks burst in opposite directions. The buck I shot ran deeper into the timber and the typical burst out into the adjacent meadow directly in front of my father. When we found my buck, he was about fifty yards from where I had shot him. He had run back toward the road and died about fifteen yards above it. When people ask, "Where did you get him?" I tell them, "On No-tell-um Ridge."

(Final score: 236 7/8 P.Y.)

The Whitetail

by Gary Bertleson

Just after I had arrived home empty-handed on the evening of the first day of the 1983 deer season, I got a call from a hunting buddy. He said that he had missed a large mule deer buck out on the upper breaks of a large river drainage near our hometown and wanted to know if I would like to join him and another friend up there the next morning. I, of course, said, "No problem!"

By midmorning, we had not seen anything except does and fawns. So we decided to go back up on top to a large stand of heavy timber and try to drive something up off its bed. As I proceeded a couple of blocks or so into the heavy stuff I got onto a series of fresh tree rubs that appeared to have been made by deer.

As I moved slowly ahead through the thicket, looking carefully, I just about tripped over the hindquarters of a real large deer. Having been spotted, this trophy whitetail buck jumped up and then flagged off into the thicket. At about twenty yards, he cut across an old skid road. That was the break I needed. One shot through the chest from my model 700 .30-06 and the buck was down for good.

(Final score: 166 4/8 B.C.)

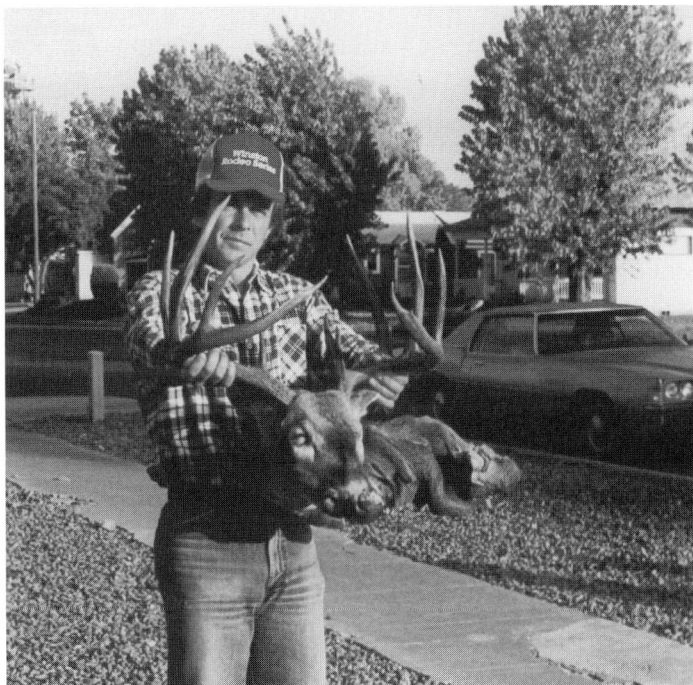

#7 Rocky Mountain Elk (Archery)

by Kenny Mills

My good friend Bill Hueckman and I went out after work on a Friday night to scout an area where I knew the elk were coming in. As we were getting close to the spot, a bull bugled below us, so we hurried to the waterhole. As we got closer we heard a bull bugle above us. All right, we were between them. First, six cows came in, and we could hear the bull coming toward us. His antlers were hitting in the poles. It was an exciting mo-ment. When he stepped out of the poles twenty-five yards away broadside, he laid his head back to bugle at the other bull. I drew my Martin bow back and made a good hit. He didn't go far and the whooping and hollering could be heard for miles.

Gary Madison of Prineville officially scored the bull. His comment was that I really should appreciate this caliber of bull because I'll be lucky to ever kill one this big again; this was a "once-in-a-lifetime bull." Well, twelve years and seven elk kills later, I am really starting to appreciate what he had to say.

(Final score: 353 0/8 P.Y.)

Bill Mattoon

by Pete Cornacchia

On a grey November day three years ago, Bill Mattoon hiked up through brush and timber in the hill southeast of Elkton and shot an elk. The slaying of the bull, a fine four-point, was no big thing and nothing new to the hunter. According to Game Commission figures, the Drain man was only one of 10,350 hunters who killed an elk in Oregon that fall.

But how many other than white-haired Bill Mattoon had seen eighty-one Novembers come around? And if there were others in that successful group who had reached four score, how many had gone out alone to do a job that wasn't easy back when heart and legs were strong half a century earlier?

Bill's son drove him to the end of a logging road that morning, but from there the old man wanted to go looking for elk on his own. He didn't want to be stuck on a stump in some saddle to wait while the young and the strong—meaning well, if not understanding—drove the elk to him.

In his attic were more than two dozen elk racks, most of them five-points or better, plus countless sets of deer antlers entwined in a huge pile. Nearly all those horns were from game he had brought down while hunting alone.

Ever since Bill was a kid, he had preferred to slip through the woods by himself. And that's the way he wanted it that morning—one more time, anyway.

So once again he trudged off through the wet patches of dead fern and young fir, picked his way past the stinging devil's club in the alder thickets along Brush Creek, and eased along quietly on the carpet of salal and sword fern beneath the second-growth timber.

He walked with the light wind in his face, so that the elk bedded somewhere up in the tangles of rhododendron wouldn't catch his scent above the pungent odors of the damp woods. So, too, that the musky odor of the big animals would waft strong to him when he was near them.

As the old hunter slipped along, looking closely for fresh sign, he must have recalled killing his first bull back in 1906, when he was twenty. He was hunting alone then, too. On Camp Creek, in the hill south of Scottsburg on the lower Umpqua. He packed the five-point out by himself.

The next year, after he had bought a beautiful .30-06 with box magazine, young Bill and five others at Drain decided to go after the real big bulls that were supposed to be in the upper Coos country to the south. They went the thirty-four miles to Scottsburg by team and wagon, crossed the Umpqua on the ferry, and rode their horses the rest of the way up over the divide and down into the Millicoma drainage.

They crossed that stream near Golden and Silver Falls, now a state park but primeval at that time, then climbed up into the rugged virgin country that several decades later would draw thousands of elk hunters each fall. That was before Weyerhaeuser came in to log off vast stands of timber and at the same time create ideal habitat for elk.

In 1907, however, the region had only a few elk and none of the many roads that now reach along almost every ridge. But up on those ridges and benches were supposed to be some awfully big bulls.

After helping set up their main camp, Bill and his brother headed out to hunt together and soon came across a single set of huge tracks larger than any they had ever seen before. Certain that this was a bull, they followed the tracks for several hours until night came.

They set a snag afire and dozed through the night, eager to resume the chase at daybreak. When it was barely light, they stashed their packsacks near the burning snag and started off. The woods were wet and the snag was away from the timber, so there was no concern about starting a big fire.

The tracks were followed through the morning and into afternoon. The elk was moving along at an easy pace, leaving scraped moss and freshly clipped or upturned broadleafs where it had fed. Twice they came to where the quarry had bedded down, each time on a point or knoll where it had a good view of its backtrack.

Then, as Bill was climbing up through a patch of high rhododendron, a huge dark head with massive antlers reared well above the brush not far ahead of him. The unbelievably big bull and the hunter gaped at each other for an instant, then Bill fired and the elk crashed to the ground.

Main beams of its sweeping antlers were as thick as a man's forearm. The ivory-tipped brow tines were as thick and almost as long as the main beams on many bulls, as you can see in the photo. Brow tines seldom have side points, but one of these did.

The hunters counted nine points on one side and eight on the other.

When the monster finally was dressed out and the thick hide was off, so that the meat would cool properly, Bill took the heart back to camp and told his partners he had killed a big blue grouse. But they knew that hooters didn't get that big.

Knowing that the meat wouldn't keep in the damp but warm weather through the several days before they would get home, they chopped some vine maple and got a good smoke going. Chunks and slabs of meat were hung on poles and cured right where the bull had dropped.

Bill was to kill many more big bulls, both Roosevelts in the coast range jungle and Rocky Mountains in the deep canyons of northeastern Oregon. Most times, he would hit a track and stay with it—sometimes for days—until he caught up with the unfortunate critter. He caught up with a good many cagey old six-points that way, but never again one so large as that monarch of the Millicoma in 1907.

Up there on Brush Creek three years ago, the eyes and the legs weren't what they used to be. Neither was the old .30-06, its stock worn shiny like driftwood and its barrel gleaming without the blueing lost so long ago. But when Bill Mattoon came upon that last set of fresh tracks that he would ever follow, the legs still had enough in them to overtake the luckless bull within an hour and the eyes were good enough that the battered aught-six could do its part. (Final score: 363 1/8 B.C.)

How I Found the Elk Horns

by Randy Ryerse

We were camped at Milk Springs in the Ochoco National Forest. My young son, about fourteen at the time, shot a mule deer buck, a nice three-point. We were at the top of the mountain (near Pisgah) in a box canyon. The deer stepped off the edge of the world. I followed the blood trail down into a swamp thicket. My son, Craig, stepped on a hip bone and said, "Hey, Dad, look at this." As I stepped on one of the ribs, the point hit me in the chest. We looked around and I saw the skull wedged between two small birch trees. It was massive. I soon found the deer and we dressed and cleaned him. It was a long trek back to camp where my mother and father were. It took the better part of four hours to get back to camp. I told my dad of the elk horns that we had seen, and he immediately said we had to go back and get them. We saw a State Trooper that night and told him of the find. He said that he would allow us to transport the horns under the "finder's" or "pick up" rule. Next morning, my son and I headed back down the canyon with an ax and a bow saw. It took us almost five and a half hours to get the horns out of that canyon and back to camp. We had to remove the front window of the fifth-wheel trailer to get the horns packed. They now hang in the Oregon Department of Fish and Wildlife Headquarters in Portland.

(Final score: 400 0/8 B.C.)

Bear

#1 Bear in Oregon—Rifle

Martin Pernoll, 21 10/16 B.C.,
Lake County, 1967

#1 Bear in Oregon—Archery

by Ray Cross

As I got my bait ready to pack to my baiting area, I remembered all of the bear sign at the bait. There were at least three good-sized bears coming into the bait. I'd decided to go in about 10:00 a.m. because most dominant bears feed off and on most of the daylight hours and don't get too far from the baiting area.

I'd been in the tree stand about one and a half hours when the first of the bears came in. It was a good-sized bear, and would have made Pope and Young with no trouble, but there was sign of a bigger bear in the area. By 2:00 p.m., three different bears had come in. At 2:15, the bear I wanted walked into the bait and started to feed. I eased to my feet, drew and released my arrow. The arrow hit—a good hit to the lungs. The bear charged into the brush. In seconds things were quiet. The retrieval of the bear was easy; there was a good blood trail. When I saw the bear lying there I knew I had something to be proud of. What a bear!

(Final score: 21 03/16 P.Y.)

Second Chance Bear
(#2 in Oregon—Archery)

by Brian Day

I spent three years hunting this bear with a 6″×8″ track. Each year, I couldn't even get a glimpse of this big bear until I had already given up and shot a smaller one. Then the next trip I would get to see the big one. One time he walked up the road almost right to the pickup before turning off into the brush, but I had already filled my tag.

This year, 1989, I thought I would try something different, and hunt the other side of the canyon. The first bear that showed up on the opening day of the season had a 5 3/4″ track and was even a different color than the other one I had been after, but it was definitely big enough for a trophy. I was nice and calm, and put an arrow right where I thought I should. The big bear roared and took off. I waited about fifteen minutes and was about to start looking for my fine trophy when I heard him growl. This went on for about an hour, till it got dark.

This made me think it would be just as fun to have help, so I went home and got my neighbor and bow-hunting buddy Steve Holte, and went back to look. No bear. No blood. So we followed his tracks to where he had been scratching around, but still found no blood. We went back to where I had shot him and found the arrow had bounced off and landed almost at the base of the tree I had been in. It was bent into an S shape.

To my surprise, the bear came back again the next day, and I got my hopes up again, but I still stayed away for a week. The next time I got in the stand the bear came in and I got the shakes. I got the shakes so bad I had to take the arrow off the rest and put it under my arm because it kept going clack, clack, clack on the bow. Then my jaw got to shaking so bad my teeth kept clacking together and I had to put my fingers in my mouth, even though the bear didn't seem to mind the noise. I was shaking so bad I was bouncing up and down in my chair. Then to my dismay, I got giant cramps in both legs from shaking so hard. I told myself this was supposed to be fun, but now it really hurt and there was nothing I could do about it. I kept telling myself to just settle down and shoot the bear, no big deal, but the harder I tried, the worse things got.

Finally, after about twenty minutes that seemed like hours, my body got so exhausted

from shaking that I quit bouncing enough to get an arrow off. This time I hit where I was supposed to.

I finally got a trophy, even if it wasn't the one I had originally been after. After sixty days, it scored 21 2/16 P.Y. points. I found that the first arrow had bounced off the bear's shoulder socket and the wound had all but disappeared. I sure felt lucky to get a second chance.

(Final score: 21 2/16 P.Y.)

Bear—Rifle
Minimum Score: 18 08/16

Final Score	Greatest Length	Greatest Width	Year	County	Hunter/Owner	Rank
21 10/16	13 05/16	8 05/16	1967	Lake	Martin V. Pernoll	1
21 04/16	12 12/16	8 08/16	1968	Curry	Joe Latimer	2
20 14/16	13 06/16	7 08/16	1985	Wallowa	Mark Moncreif	3
20 10/16	12 07/16	8 03/16	1993	Union	ODF&W	4
20 06/16	12 05/16	8 01/16	1980		Ken Moore	5
20 06/16	12 08/16	7 14/16	1964	Crook	Buck Flory/Bob Benson	5
20 05/16	12 04/16	8 01/16			Kerry Fann	7
20 05/16	12 08/16	7 13/16	1994	Umatilla	Richard C. Lebsock	7
20 04/16	12 05/16	7 15/16	1995	Wallowa	Curt Mattson	9
20 03/16	12 03/16	8 00/16	1991	Grant	Vern Freed	10
20 03/16	12 08/16	7 11/16	1995	Baker	Albert J. Wagner	10
20 00/16	12 06/16	7 10/16		Umatilla	Tim Fuzi	12
20 00/16	12 06/16	7 10/16	1988	Baker	Tim Moothart	12
20 00/16	12 09/16	7 07/16	1994	Jackson	Larry D. East, Jr.	12
19 15/16	12 09/16	7 06/16	1992	Umatilla	Kent Kilby/Kristi Kilby	15
19 14/16	12 04/16	7 10/16	1993	Curry	Terry McHorse	16
19 12/16	12 00/16	7 12/16	1984	Wallowa	Russ Rankin	17
19 12/16	12 01/16	7 11/16	1993	Union	Hugh Stephans	17
19 12/16	12 08/16	7 04/16	1994	Jackson	Dan Stanfield	17
19 11/16	12 03/16	7 08/16	1995	Grant	W.E. Berry	20
19 11/16	12 10/16	7 01/16	1993	Wallowa	Karl Penne	20
19 09/16	12 03/16	7 06/16	1990	Union	Bert DeVore	22
19 09/16	12 03/16	7 06/16	1995	Umatilla	Larry Ledbetter	22
19 07/16	11 14/16	7 09/16	1988	Union	Jerry Crossen	24
19 07/16	12 00/16	7 07/16	1993	Grant	Sandy Piazza	24
19 06/16	12 02/16	7 04/16	1994	Grant	Earl Lathrop	26
19 06/16	12 02/16	7 04/16	1991	Hood River	Michael G. Faulkender	26
19 04/16	12 01/16	7 03/16	1993	Grant	John Snyder	28
19 04/16	12 02/16	7 02/16	1994	Josephine	Dan Klicker	28
19 04/16	12 04/16	7 00/16	1986	Harney	Todd Higgins	28
19 04/16	12 05/16	6 15/16	1994	Wallowa	Mike Bennett	28
19 03/16	11 12/16	7 07/16	1994	Umatilla	Greg Turner	32
19 03/16	12 01/16	7 02/16	1993	Umatilla	Mick Kilby	32
19 02/16	11 14/16	7 04/16	1988	Grant	Kevin Maden	34
19 01/16	12 01/16	7 00/16	1980	Grant	Ken Moore	35
19 01/16	12 04/16	6 13/16	1995	Lincoln	Stephan M. Yerger. Jr.	35
19 00/16	11 12/16	7 04/16	1989	Harney	Jeff Riley	37
18 15/16	12 02/16	6 13/16	1995	Tillamook	Bill Henderson	38
18 14/16	11 14/16	7 00/16	1968	Douglas	Greg Vaughn	39
18 14/16	12 00/16	6 14/16		Union	Dale Kruse	39
18 14/16	12 01/16	6 13/16	1991	Union	Ron Allred	39
18 11/16	11 08/16	7 03/16	1994	Umatilla	Jeremy Garcia	42
18 09/16	11 06/16	7 03/16	1995	Union	Vernon Kelly	43
18 09/16	11 07/16	7 02/16	1992	Wallowa	Doug Tandy	43
18 09/16	11 10/16	6 15/16	1991	Umatilla	Javier Garcia	43
18 08/16	11 11/16	6 13/16	1995	Jackson	Martin Clark	46
18 08/16	11 12/16	6 12/16	1995	Wallowa	Angela Howell	46
18 08/16	11 15/16	6 09/16	1984	Morrow	Steve Lankford	46

Bear—Archery
Minimum Score: 18 00/16

Final Score	Greatest Length	Greatest Width	Year	County	Hunter/Owner	Rank
21 03/16	12 15/16	8 04/16	1989	Lane	Ray Cross	1
21 02/16	13 00/16	8 02/16	1989	Jackson	Brian Day	2
20 05/16	12 11/16	7 10/16	1994	Jackson	Mark Nouquier	3
19 12/16	12 04/16	7 08/16	1994	Umatilla	Tom Huebner	4
19 08/16	12 04/16	7 04/16	1990	Clackamas	Ben R. Cook	5
19 07/16	12 00/16	7 07/16	1982	Union	Bob Wondra	6
18 14/16	11 13/16	7 01/16	1974	Lincoln	Stanley D. Miles	7
18 09/16	11 09/16	7 00/16	1993	Jackson	Brian Day	8
18 08/16	12 00/16	6 08/16	1994	Lane	Gary Nyden	9
18 07/16	11 09/16	6 14/16	1983	Union	Scott Salsbery	10
18 06/16	11 09/16	6 13/16	1994	Umatilla	Javier Garcia	11
18 06/16	11 09/16	6 13/16	1993	Union	Justin Petty	12

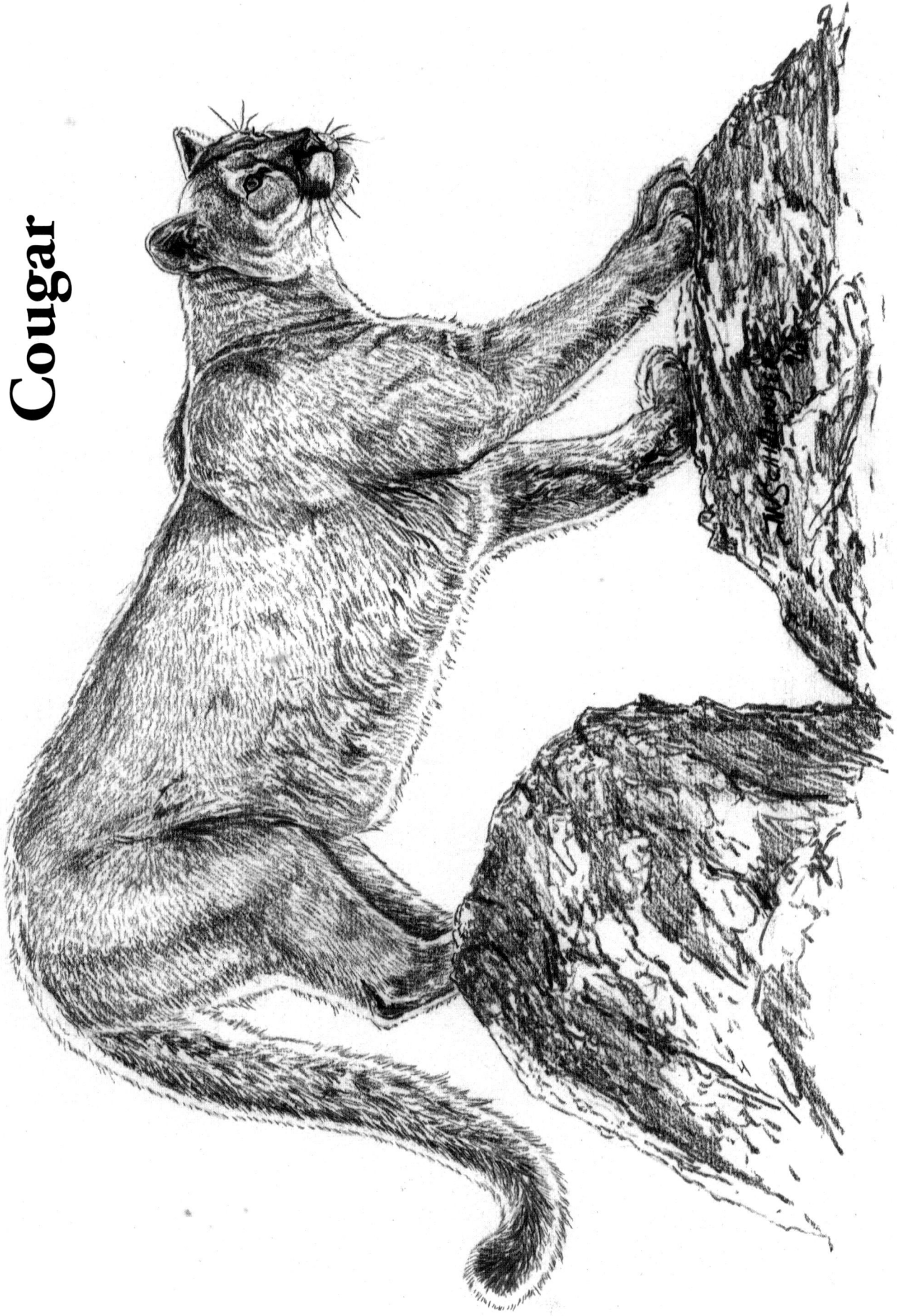

Cougar

Oregon State Record Cougar

by Mark Moncrief

I had just finished successfully guiding my last cougar hunter for the 1994 season. I had drawn a cougar tag myself and with just a few days remaining in the season, I decided to hunt an area where I had previously seen the tracks of a very large tom. On December 31, the last day of cougar season, I was taking some of my younger dogs for training. We started out low, below the snow line, and began working up the canyon. Before long the dogs had picked up a track. Judging by the way they were moving, it had to be a cougar. A lion will hunt the ridge tops and side-hill around the canyon, looking for deer or elk. A bobcat will stay down in the brush, hunting smaller game such as rabbits or birds.

Soon we were into the snow. The dogs continued to cold track the cougar until they were able to jump it. I followed on horseback as far as I could go, then walked in another two miles on foot to where the dogs had successfully treed the cougar. I have treed more than five hundred mountain lions, several that made the record book, since I started hunting with dogs sixteen years ago. I knew this was an extremely large tom.

Hunting with dogs, whether for lions, bobcats or bears, depends on the dogs, looking for the tracks, getting the tracks going with the hounds and staying with them until they tree. A tremendous amount of time and effort is put into the training of good dogs, and after spending countless hours covering miles and miles of some of the most rugged terrain in the country, you and your dog have become a team. Once you have successfully treed an animal you have to make a decision whether to take it or not.

The cougar I chose to take was measured by Sam McNeil at 15 14/16 B.C. and is currently the Oregon state record and fifth largest taken in North America.

(Final score: 15 14/16 B.C.)

Cougar—Rifle
Minimum Score: 14 00/16

Final Score	Greatest Length	Greatest Width	Year	County	Hunter/Owner	Rank
15 14/16	9 04/16	6 10/16	1992	Wallowa	Mark Moncrief	1
15 10/16	9 00/16	6 10/16	1993	Umatilla	Dan Laizure	2
15 10/16	9 03/16	6 07/16	1966	Union	Ron Lay	2
15 08/16	9 02/16	6 06/16	1992	Grant	Joe West	4
15 08/16	9 00/16	6 08/16	1987	Wallowa	Robin Dickenson	5
15 06/16	9 00/16	6 06/16		Umatilla	Oregon State Police	6
15 04/16	8 12/16	6 08/16	1989	Umatilla	Ernest Chrisman	7
15 04/16	8 15/16	6 05/16	1978	Wallowa	Greg Vaughn	7
15 04/16	8 13/16	6 07/16	1961	Union	Don Haefer	7
15 04/16	8 14/16	6 06/16	1981	Baker	Joe J. Lay	7
15 03/16	9 00/16	6 03/16		Jackson	Bill Martin	11
15 03/16	8 15/16	6 04/16	1993	Umatilla	Bob Walchi	11
15 03/16	9 00/16	6 03/16	1988	Wallowa	Larry Weems	11
15 00/16	8 13/16	6 03/16	1993	Wallowa	Dwayne Heikes	14
14 15/16	8 15/16	6 00/16	1989	Wallowa	Larry Weems	15
14 15/16	8 12/16	6 03/16	1992	Union	Armand Kerlec	15
14 13/16	8 10/16	6 03/16	1993	Union	Jerry Emmert	17
14 11/16	8 11/16	6 00/16	1994	Klamath	Mike Meeker	18
14 11/16	8 12/16	5 15/16	1990	Union	Curt Mattson	18
14 10/16	8 08/16	6 02/16	1992	Douglas	Craig Street	20
14 09/16	8 08/16	6 01/16	1993	Umatilla	Kristi Kilby	21
14 09/16	8 09/16	6 00/16	1990	Douglas	Craig Street	21
14 09/16	8 10/16	5 15/16	1992	Umatilla	Mick Kilby	21
14 08/16	8 08/16	6 00/16	1984	Linn	Shirley Andrews	24
14 07/16	8 05/16	6 02/16	1992	Union	Trent Hafer	25
14 05/16	8 07/16	5 14/16	1994	Union	Thomas Campbell	26
14 04/16	8 06/16	5 14/16	1988	Grant	Ken Moore	27

Cougar—Archery
Minimum Score: 13 08/16

Final Score	Greatest Length	Greatest Width	Year	County	Hunter/Owner	Rank
14 10/16	8 10/16	6 00/16	1989	Umatilla	Javier Garcia	1
14 06/16	8 11/16	5 11/16	1990	Josephine	Brian Day	2

Cougar—Black Powder
Minimum Score: 13 00/16

Final Score	Greatest Length	Greatest Width	Year	County	Hunter/Owner	Rank
14 01/16	8 02/16	5 15/16	1991	Linn	James A. Green	1
13 04/16	7 14/16	5 06/16	1990	Wallowa	Duane M. Bernard	2

Mountain Goat

Status and History of Mountain Goats in Oregon

Patrick E. Matthews, Assistant District Biologist,
Oregon Department of Fish and Wildlife

Victor L. Coggins, District Biologist,
Oregon Department of Fish and Wildlife

Abstract: *The status and history of mountain goats* (Oreamnos americanus) *in Oregon is reviewed. Recent archaeological evidence suggest goats occupied Hells Canyon prior to the influence of European settlement. Mountain goats were released in the Wallowa Mountains of northeast Oregon in 1950. The population status, influence of hunting, lack of genetic diversity and isolation of the Wallowa Mountain goat herd are discussed. Transplants to the Elkhorn Mountains of northeast Oregon and the Columbia River Gorge are reported.*

Indigenous mountain goat distribution has been described as rugged mountainous areas of western North America from southeastern Alaska to southcentral Washington, and from western Alberta as far south as central Idaho (Johnson 1977, Guenzel 1980, Wigal and Coggins 1982). Physical evidence has been lacking to establish the historical occurrence of goats in Oregon.

Mountain goats were not present in Oregon at the turn of the twentieth century (Bailey 1936); hence, goats have traditionally been considered an exotic species. In 1950, six goats were released in the Wallowa Mountains, and since that date subsequent transplants have occurred in the Wallowas, Elkhorn Mountains and Columbia Gorge. This article provides information on the historical occurrence of Rocky Mountain goats and a review of the current status of goat populations in Oregon.

Historic Evidence

Early literature reports mountain goat as an indigenous species in Oregon. Lewis and Clark describe the skins of mountain goat possessed by Indians along the Columbia River, and describe goats occurring "on the chain of mountains forming the commencement of the woody country on the coast, and passing the Columbia between the falls and the rapids" (Hosmer 1924: 180). Grant (1905) reported the mountain goat ranging as far south as Mount Jefferson, Oregon, based on the records he was able to obtain. However, Grant does not provide sources for his records. Bailey (1936) cites Richardson (1829), Townsend (1839), Suckley and Gibbs (1860), Grinnell and Fannin (1890), Hornaday (1906), and Miller (1924) reporting mountain goat as a species native to Oregon, but disagrees with these reports. Bailey questioned whether goats were ever native to Oregon since there were no authentic records of their occurrence in recent years. He admits that it is not improbable that in earlier times, goats may have occupied Mount Hood and perhaps other peaks in the Oregon Cascades, as well as the Wallowa Mountains in northeast Oregon, and the Seven Devils in Idaho. However, he suggests further evidence should be sought. Hall and Kelson (1959) describe goat distribution in North America, and include the north portion of the Cascade range in Oregon.

Diary entries by Henry H. Spalding describe a meeting with the Nez Perce Indians near Wallowa Lake, Oregon, in July 1839; "Joseph proposes a sport with goats" and "goes to a lick the goats frequent, to start them out," but does not find any (Drury 1958: 271). Horner (unpublished manuscript, Origin of Wallowa County Place Names, p. 120, Wallowa Library) describes a basin east of Joseph, Oregon, "named for a bunch of wild mountain goats that ranged there in the winter of the 1890s. Fred Herson killed the guard goat—they always have a guard on lookout. Their hair is different from that of the mountain sheep, also their horns grow up and back, different from the sheep." Both of these accounts have been questioned, since neither provides sufficient information differentiating between goats, bighorn sheep or pronghorns.

These reports of mountain goats occurring

in Oregon are based primarily on anecdotal accounts and have left managers with concerns as to their authenticity. However, archaeological evidence from the Bernard Creek Rock Shelter, along the Idaho side of Hells Canyon, indicates the presence of mountain goat remains in two excavation levels at that site (Randolph and Dahlstrom 1977). The goat remains (bones) were estimated to be 300–1000 years old (Reagan and Womack 1981). Since the goat remains were fragmented, it suggests their use as food rather than raw material for tools or religious objects (Reagan and Womack 1981). Based on this evidence, along with the current knowledge of prehistoric hunting and gathering activities, Reagan and Womack concluded goats were present in Hells Canyon 300–1000 years ago. In a later archaeological investigation on Camp Creek, Oregon side of Hells Canyon, goat remains were identified and radiocarbon dated from 500–1500 years before present (Leonhardy and Thompson 1991). Corless (1990) reported Weiser Indians hunting mountain goats in the Seven Devils Mountains, which coincides with these findings.

It has been argued that goats may have occurred in the Seven Devils Mountains on the Idaho side of Hells Canyon, but that the Snake River was a barrier to the goats; therefore, they were never indigenous on the Oregon side of Hells Canyon. This same argument has been proposed along the Columbia River separating the Washington and Oregon Cascades. We refute this argument. The Snake River would commonly freeze over during severe winters, prior to dams, and would have allowed goats easy access to either side of the Canyon. In addition, goats occur on adjacent canyon walls of large river corridors such as the Fraser in British Columbia (Macgregor 1977), and have been documented swimming across Kenai Lake, Alaska (Smith and Nichols 1984). This suggests that river corridors such as the Snake and probably the Columbia would not have been barriers to emigrating goats.

We conclude that early anecdotal reports and references, coupled with recent archaeological findings, demonstrate that mountain goats were indigenous to the northeast corner of Oregon and most likely portions of the Oregon Cascades. Goats probably disappeared from Oregon during or prior to European settlement in the early 1800s. The northeast corner of Oregon was isolated from European settlement by rugged terrain until the 1870s; however, European influence arrived much earlier, with Nez Perce Indians acquiring horses in the early 1700s. Improved mobility and firearms greatly changed local Indian culture which influenced tribal hunting impacts on native wildlife.

Status of Transplants

Wallowa Mountains

The Wallowa Mountains encompass an area of approximately 575 km^2 and are situated in the very northeast corner of Oregon. The area is characterized by U-shaped glaciated valleys, alpine basins, rugged precipitous terrain and sharp ridgetops. Elevation ranges from 1400–3000 m. Dense timber stands occur below 2287 m with Douglas fir (*Pseudotsuga menziesii*), white fir (*Abies concolor*), and western larch (*Larix occidentalis*) the most abundant tree species. Scattered timber stands occur above 2287 m with subalpine fir (*Abies lasiocarpa*) and white-bark pine (*Pinus albicaulis*) predominating. Forbs and grasses are the most abundant plant forms on high elevation ridgetops.

The Wallowa Mountain goat herd has originated from four separate releases (Table 1). One adult female died the day following the 1950 release. Of the thirty-three goats released in the 1980s, a minimum of six individuals, one male and five females, are known to have died within one year following the releases.

Survey Techniques
From 1962 through 1982, goats were counted and classified annually from fixed-wing aircraft during mid to late summer. Ground surveys oc-

Table 1 Mountain goat transplants to the Wallowa Mountains of Oregon

Release Location	Year	Number Released	Male	Female	Origin of Stock
Joseph Mt.	1950	5	3	2	Chopaka Mt., WA
Hurricane	1985	8	2	6	Olympic N.P., WA
Hurricane	1986	8	3	5	Misty Fiord, AK
Hurricane	1989	17	8	9	Olympic N.P., WA
Total		38	16	22	

casionally were incorporated with aerial surveys from 1983–1993. Ground surveys were conducted in areas of high goat use and helped provide a more thorough count in the area surveyed; however, ground surveys are more time consuming and have not been conducted with equal effort from year to year. Tracking of radio-collared individuals, from 1980s transplants, helped to locate animals during surveys and provide information on movements.

Population Status

The Wallowa Mountain goat population grew from the original transplant of five animals to a minimum population of twenty-nine animals by 1966 (Table 2). The population declined in the late 1960s and remained static through the 1980s, with aerial counts ranging from a low of ten to a high of thirty-two animals. The estimated population never exceeded forty-five animals during those years. Surveys from 1990–1993 indicated an increase with counts ranging from twenty-five to thirty-seven goats. The current population estimate is fifty-five animals.

Kid production was highest in 1966 with an adjusted kid ratio of sixty-one kids per one hundred adults (yearlings included with adults) (Table 2). Production decreased thereafter and remained static at low levels through the 1980s. From 1990–1993 kid production improved and remained stable with a mean kid ratio of thirty-three per one hundred adults.

Discussion

Hunting of mountain goats was initiated in 1965 and continued annually through 1968. A total of twenty-three tags were issued and twenty

animals, including thirteen males and seven females, were harvested (Table 3). During the corresponding time period, the number of goats observed on aerial surveys decreased to a low of ten animals. We believe that hunter harvest,

Table 2 Late summer mountain goat classification survey data for the Wallowa Mountains of Oregon

Year	Total Count	Adults[a]	Kids	Adjusted Kids/100 Adults
1962	12	8	4	50
1963	—	—	—	—
1964	26	18	8	44
1965	—	—	—	—
1966	29	18	11	61
1967	21	17	4	24
1968	11	9	2	22
1969	10	8	2	25
1970	17	12	5	42
1971	22	17	5	29
1972	18	17	1	6
1973	18	16	2	13
1974	15	13	2	15
1975	20	17	3	18
1976	19	17	2	12
1977	16	11	5	45
1978	22	18	4	22
1979	24	20	4	20
1980	31	23	8	33
1981	19	14	5	36
1982	15	13	2	15
1983	12	11	1	9
1984	10	8	2	25
1985	14	12	2	17
1986	—	—	—	—
1987	26	20	6	14
1988	8	8	0	0
1989	9	8	1	13
1990	31	23	8	35
1991	28	21	7	33
1992	25	19	6	32
1993	37	28	9	32
1994	51	38	13	34
1995	60	51	17	33
1996	73	47	26	55

[a]Includes subadults.

Table 3   Hunter harvest of mountain goats in the Wallowa Mountains, Oregon, 1965–68

Year	Tags Issued	Males	Females	Total
1965	5	4	1	5
1966	5	3	2	5
1967	5	3	2	5
1968	8	3	2	5
Total	23	13	7	20

particularly of adult females, was a major factor in the initial decline of this population. Similar relationships between hunter harvest and goat population declines have been reported (Macgregor 1977, Kuck 1977, Foster 1977, Bone 1978).

Although legal goat hunting has not been allowed since 1968, the population did not increase significantly until recently. There are various factors that may account for the lack of increase. Predation, avalanches and accidents are mortality factors which have been observed in this population. However, we do not believe them to be major factors limiting population growth.

Low kid production or survival in the Wallowa Mountains may be directly related to a lack of suitable winter range resulting in a winter nutritional deficiency (Vaughan 1975). We believe inbreeding may have been a major factor suppressing production. The effects of inbreeding in small populations have been discussed by Farnsworth (1978), Pettus (1982), and Nash (1982). In fifteen of sixteen species of captive wild ungulates, inbred young were significantly less likely to survive than non-inbred young (Ralls et al. 1979). Because the Wallowa goat population originated from a transplant of five individuals, of which only two were females, and

outbreeding has not been possible due to the isolation of these animals from any neighboring goat herds, we believe that a lack of gentic diversity through inbreeding may have been a major factor suppressing kid survival. In 1985, 1986 and 1989 supplemental goat releases provided genetic diversity to the Wallowa Mountains population. Individuals from the supplemental transplants have been observed utilizing the established goat ranges, as well as ranges previously unoccupied by goats. We believe the improvement in kid production and survival during the past four years was directly related to the supplemental releases. Survey information suggests that these releases provided the genetic diversity, along with the pioneering of new habitats, necessary to improve population production.

Elkhorn Mountains

The Elkhorn Mountains, approximately 126 km^2, lie just west of Baker City, Oregon. Elevation range from 1400–2770 m. The area is characterized by glaciated valleys and rugged alpine basins similar to the Wallowa Mountains.

From 1983–1986 a total of twenty-one goats were released in the Elkhorn Mountains (Table 4). Tracking of radio-collared individuals provided information on movements and establishment of herd ranges post release. In 1992, aerial surveys were initiated with fixed-wing aircraft to count and classify goats during late summer.

Total number of goats observed was lower in 1993 than in 1992 (Table 5); however, this was thought to be a result of observation error and not an actual decrease in population size. Kid production has been good (Table 5), and the

Table 4   Mountain goat transplants to the Elkhorn Mountains of Oregon

Release Location	Year	Number Released	Male	Female	Origin of Stock
Pine Cr.	1983	6	3	3	NF Clearwater, ID
Pine Cr.	1985	8	4	4	Olympic N.P., WA
Pine Cr.	1986	7	2	5	Misty Fiord, AK
Total		21	9	12	

Table 5 Elkhorn mountain goat release and inventory history

Year	Total	Un	Un AD	Yearling	Males	Females	Adults	Kids	Kid/100 Adult	Comments
1983	6				3	3	5	1		Release from NF Clearwater, ID
1985	8				4	4	8			Release from Olympic N.P., WA
1986	7				2	5	7		—	Release from Misty Fiord, AK
	21				9	12	20	1		**Total Release**
1987	12						9	3	33	Fixed Wing
1988	6						4	2	50	Fixed Wing
1991	15						11	4	36	Fixed Wing
1992	31						21	10	48	Fixed Wing
1993	25						15	10	67	Fixed Wing
1994	47						28	19	68	Fixed Wing
1995	26						20	6	30	Fixed Wing
1996	33						25	8	32	Fixed Wing (West, 8/19); warm & turbulent
1996	36						24	12	50	Fixed Wing (Humphreys, 8/29); warm, goats in shade
1996	47	3					35	9	26	Fixed Wing (West, 9/17); cool temps., goats in sun

Elkhorn Mountains goat population is believed to be growing.

Columbia River Gorge

Mountain goat habitat in the Columbia Gorge encompasses the northern extension of the Cascade Mountains in Oregon and lies within the Columbia Wilderness, Bull Run Watershed and the Mount Hood Wilderness. Elevations range from 670–3000 m. Lower elevation ranges are characterized by stands of Douglas fir and mountain hemlock (*Tsuga mertensiana*). Upper elevations consist of primarily alpine basins near the foothills of Mount Hood.

Since 1969, fifteen goats have been released in the Columbia Gorge (Table 6). Annual surveys specific to his goat herd have never been established. Miscellaneous observations of goats occurred from 1973–1990 and ranged from one to four individuals observed. Observations of two to four goats were reported occasionally from 1980–1985. However, since that time, observations have declined, with no goats reported since 1990.

Small transplant size, scattering of individual goats and paucity of male goats have been major concerns and possible explanations for the failure to establish goats in the Columbia Gorge.

Table 6 Mountain goat transplants to Tanner Butte in the Columbia River Gorge of Oregon

Year	Number Released	Male	Female	Origin of Stock
1969–71	8	2	6	Olympic N.P., WA
1975	6	2	4	Olympic N.P., WA
1976	1	1	—	Olympic N.P., WA
Total	15	5	10	

Summary

Archaeological findings presented in this manuscript demonstrate that mountain goats were indigenous to Hells Canyon prior to European settlement. Faunal remains now place goats within forty-eight km^2 of the existing Wallowa Mountains goat herd. We believe that goats also occurred in the Wallowa Mountains and probably other ranges in northeast Oregon, since rugged canyon corridors link the Wallowas to Hells Canyon. Wildlife managers typically have described the distribution of goats based on occurrence at the time of European exploration or settlement. Efforts to document the historical range of goats should continue through the identification of faunal remains recovered in archaeological excavations of human encampments and wood rat middens. We encourage wildlife managers to utilize archaeological information in conjunction with other sources of physical evidence to more accurately describe historical distribution of native wildlife. Restoration of mountain goats to native ranges should be continued, especially where priorities are to manage for ecological diversity.

The Wallowa Mountains goat population declined during the 1960s as a result of heavy hunter harvest. Legal hunter harvest was not allowed thereafter; however, the population level remained static with low kid production through the 1980s. We believe the lack of genetic diversity was a major factor affecting kid production and growth of this population. Recent supplemental goat transplants appear to have improved annual kid production, and the Wallowa Mountains goat herd currently is increasing.

The Elkhorn Mountains goat herd appears to be established. This goat herd continued to increase since the initial transplant in 1983 and has demonstrated good kid production in recent years.

Attempts to establish goats in the Columbia Gorge have not been successful. Currently there are no goats known to be alive in this area. Failure to establish goats in the Gorge may be due to small transplant size, lack of male goats and scattering of transplanted individuals.

Rocky Mountain Goat Hunting Seasons in the Wallowas (1965–1968)

The following reports were written by personnel of the Oregon Department of Fish and Wildlife.

The first Rocky Mountain Goat season was held from August 28–September 6, 1965, with five tags being issued. The following report was written by R.H. Stein.

Every hunter was successful in killing a goat. Four male goats and one female goat were taken. All five were killed on Hurwal ridge, in the area between Ice Lake and the head of Thorpe Creek, a tributary to Hurricane Creek. Every goat was on or near the top of the ridge when first fired on.

Mr. Ray Paul killed the first goat along Hurwal ridge. The animal rolled about two hundred yards down the slope on the Thorpe Creek side of the ridge. This animal was a male goat with horns measuring 7 1/2″ in length; its age was four years. Mr. Paul checked in at the Enterprise hatchery the morning of August 29 with only the horns and hide of the goat. He was issued a citation by Officer Harrison for wanton waste of game meat. Mr. Paul then returned to the site of the kill and packed the meat out. He checked back through the hatchery late that evening. The citation has not been dismissed as of this date.

Laimon Osis killed the second goat of the season a few minutes after Mr. Paul's kill. This goat was a three-year-old male with a right horn measurement of 8 1/2″ and a left horn measurement of 8 3/8″. Mr. Osis killed this goat in the same area as Mr. Paul's kill. The goat was packed out and returned to Enterprise the first day of the season. [See related story and final score on page 129.]

Sally Edinger killed the third goat about one hour after the second goat was killed. This animal also was a male goat, aged five years. The kill was made at the head of Thorpe Creek, on the east slope of Sacajawea Peak. The right horn measurement was 7″; the left horn was 5 1/4″, and had been broken in previous years. The animal was also very scarred-up, either from a fight or from falling. This animal was packed out the second day of the season. (Final score: 41 6/8 B.C.)

Dr. Ralph Ray bagged the fourth goat on August 30. This animal was killed on the slope of Hurwal ridge, north of Ice Lake. It too was a male goat, three years of age. The right horn measured 7 3/4″ and the left horn was 7 5/8″. Dr. Ray packed out the liver, lungs, heart and part of the lower intestine. The writer examined these parts and could find no sign of parasitism. The organs appeared very healthy in all respects.

Mr. Joseph P. Dolan bagged the final goat on September 2 in the same general area. This animal was a female goat with horn measurements as follows: right horn 7 1/8″, left horn 7″. This goat was three years of age.

The second season was held from September 24–30, 1966, with five tags being issued. The following report was written by Jack Melland.

The five goats, three billies and two nannies, were killed on Hurricane Divide. Four goats were killed on Saturday, September 24, and the last goat was taken on September 25.

Carl Hunter was the first hunter to check out with a goat. He killed a nanny with 8 1/2″ horns at the top of Slick Rock Creek. The age was not obtained. He observed one other goat. (Final score: 39 6/8 B.C.)

Robert Bartgers was the second man to check out. He killed a four-year-old billy above Francis Lake on Hurricane Divide. The horn length was 8″.

Lyle Hanscom was the third hunter to check out. He killed a four-year-old billy near Deadman Lake. The left horn was 7 5/8″ and the right horn 8″. Hanscom killed his goat on Sunday morning and checked in at the hatchery on Monday morning. He checked in with only the head and cape and stated he would not go back after the meat because the going was too tough. Officer Harrison cited him for wanton waste of game meat. Justice of the Peace McCubbin fined Hanscom $25. Hanscom saw one other goat.

William Whitmore checked out with the fourth goat. He killed a six-year-old billy with left horn 8 1/4″ long and right horn 8 3/4″. This goat was killed one mile south of Hawk Lake. This is the oldest and largest goat killed in the Wallowa Mountains.

Raymond Hunt was the last man to check out with a goat. He had a three-year-old nanny with right horn 7 3/8″ and left horn 7 1/2″ long. Mr. Hunt killed his goat the first day, near Fran-cis Lake, but it took until Wednesday to pack it out. He saw eight other goats.

The third season was held from September 23–27, 1967, with five tags being issued. The following report was written by Ronald Bartels.

Each of the five hunters was successful and three billies and two nannies were killed. Two billies and two nannies were killed in the Matterhorn, Hurwal Divide area, and one billy was taken from above La Gore Lake on the Hurricane Divide. The goats were in excellent condition and the quality of the pelts was good.

The first goat checked was killed by Richard C. Littleton on Sacajawea. The three-and-a-half-year-old billy weighed one hundred and four pounds field dressed, and measured 7 7/8″ on the right horn and 8″ on the left. This goat was packed out whole by Jack Hooker and the meat was spoiled. No citation was issued because Littleton claimed he was going to give the meat to friends, thus not wasting it.

V.W. Thornton killed a five-and-a-half-year-old nanny from the Hurricane Creek trail. The goat was using mountain mahogany thickets on the foot of Sacajawea. This goat also was brought out with the hide on and weighed 90 1/2 pounds. The horn measurements were 8 3/8″ for the right horn and 8 1/2″ for the left horn. Mr. Thornton was encouraged to skin and cape his goat here at the hatchery before traveling home to Newberg with it. The goat had been killed early in the morning of that same day and the meat was still in good condition. (Final score: 39 4/8 B.C.)

Mr. Rotl, from Roseburg, checked out on Tuesday, September 26, with a five-and-a-half-year-old billy. This goat was properly cared for and the meat was in good condition. Mr. Rotl hunted above La Gore Lake on the Hurricane Divide and his billy measured 8 1/2″ on both horns. This hunter reported seeing a very large trophy goat in the above area but was not able to approach it.

Dwight L. Hammack killed a five-and-a-half-year-old billy on the south face of Sacajawea.

His goat measured 7 1/2″ on the right horn (dubbed off) and 8 1/4″ on the left. Mr. Hammack did not bring the meat out and was advised to do so or be issued a citation for wanton waste. He was also packed and guided by Jack Hooker.

The fifth hunter checked out a nanny that was killed on the Matterhorn. This hunter checked out through La Grande.

The fourth and last season was held from September 28–October 2, 1968, with eight tags being issued. The following report was written by Ronald Bartels.

The hunters were well distributed over the area, with three at Francis Lake, two at Ice Lake, one at Echo Lake, one at Legore Mine and one on Pete's Point above the Polaris trail and south of Aneroid Lake. The weather was good during the season; the wind blew on the last day but did not bother the hunters because they had all checked out by that time.

There were no goats killed on the first day, but hunters reported seeing nine goats, five above Deadman Lake and two on the ridge west of Francis Lake. One of the hunters at Ice Lake saw a nanny and kid just south of Ice Lake. Francis Ives and I saw these same goats from the top of the Matterhorn, where we had climbed to look over the surrounding area. I also observed two adult goats and one kid across Hurricane Creek and above the Slick Rock basin.

Fred Schubert, Clackamas, shot a female goat that was aged at three-and-a-half years. The right horn was 6 1/2″ long and the left horn measured 6 1/16″. The reproductive tract and some stomach contents were collected from this animal. The kill was made on Sunday, September 29, on the Hurricane Divide (west side), near Deadman Lake.

Leo Wheadon, Aumsville, also killed a goat on Sunday. His animal was a four-and-a-half-

Oregon State Record
Dr. John Waterman, 45 6/8 B.C., 1968

year-old billy with horns that measured 7 3/4″ on the right horn and 7 7/8″ on the left. The animal was shot from the ridge to the west of Francis Lake.

Dean Van Nice, The Dalles, shot a one-and-a-half-year-old billy that measured 6″ on the right horn and 6 1/16″ on the left. Nice had scales with him and total weight was sixty-two pounds. With the entrails removed the goat weighed forty-two pounds. Samples of lungs, rumen and small and large intestines were collected.

Richard D. Wells, Hood River, was camped at Ice Lake and shot a six-and-a-half-year-old nanny on the bluff above the lake. The horn measurements were 7 15/16″ on the right horn and 8″ on the left. There was a kid with this nanny. Wells reported that the udder was dry.

Dr. John Waterman, Tualatin, killed a large billy on the ridge between Pete's Point and Aneroid Lake. The goat was at least twelve-and-a-half years old and was estimated by Waterman and his guide, Jack Hooker, to weigh approximately two hundred pounds, dead weight. The horns measured 8 3/8″ on the right and 8″ on the left. The skull was 13″ long and the basal circumference of the horns averaged about 5 1/4″, compared to 3 7/8″ for the nanny taken by Wells. This was the oldest recorded goat taken in this area and all the incisors were absent from the lower jaw. There was also an injury on the right eye that would have impaired vision. Waterman reported seeing a younger goat in the same area where he killed his goat. (Final score: 45 6/8 B.C.)

At the Top of Hurwal Divide

by Laimon Osis

I had the good fortune to be living in Wallowa County when Oregon's first mountain goat season was set, with five tags to be drawn. My good friend Tom Gaumer and I decided to apply and help each other if one of us lucked out. Tom was a veteran hunter, but I was a relative novice, only a year out of cob.

As luck would have it, I drew a tag.

Before the hunt, I scouted likely areas in the high Wallowas. I saw mountain goats way up high on Matterhorn, but I decided that a talus slope named Hurwal Divide would be more manageable. It stretched west and north from Ice Lake. Interestingly enough, on my way up the talus slope, I met a three-point buck on its way down the talus slope! The narrow spine of Hurwal Divide had a well-defined trail beaten in among the rocks. I also spotted a mountain goat, resting on the slope.

As promised, Tom helped me on the hunt and we made Ice Lake our base camp. On opening morning, we climbed Hurwal Divide, only to find another hunter ahead of us! We watched as he sneaked up on a goat that was resting on the talus slope below him. He shot. It was a clean kill, but the goat rolled and rolled down the slope. It was a challenging recovery for a single hunter.

Tom and I continued along the top of Hurwal Divide, not sure what to expect, when another goat came into view, this one heading uphill on the eastern side of the slope. My first shot was, in basketball parlance, an "airball," but the second bullet from my Winchester Model 70 found its mark, and my animal did not roll down the steep slope!

Tom and I field-dressed the animal, distributed the load between us and began our hike back to our camp. There we were met by Bob Stein and Vic Coggins of the Game Commission. They examined the goat and found it to be a two-and-a-half-year-old billy. All in all, a satisfactory hunt.

(Final score: 42 4/8 B.C.)

Official Scoring System for Oregon Big Game Trophies

Records of Oregon
Big Game

RECORD BOOK FOR OREGON

P.O. Box 759
Irrigon, OR 97844

ROCKY MOUNTAIN GOAT

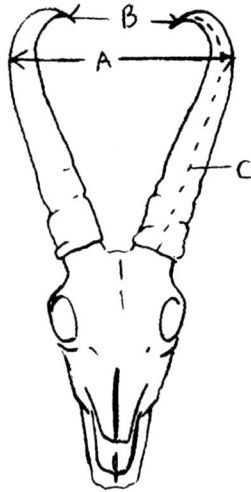

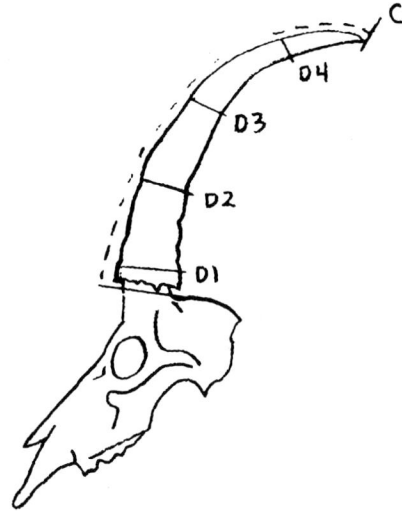

Species	Rifle	Archery	Muzzle
Rocky Mtn	All	All	All

				COLUMN 1	COLUMN 2	OLUMN 3
				Right Horn	Left Horn	Difference
A	Greatest Spread	6	3/8			
B	Tip to Tip Spread	6	1/8			
C	Length of Horn			8 2/8	8 0/8	.. 0 2/8
D-1	Circumference of Base			5 6/8	5 6/8	0 0/8
D-2	Circumference at First Quarter			4 3/8	4 3/8	0 0/8
D-3	Circumference at Second Quarter			3 0/8	3 0/8	0 0/8
D-4	Circumference at Third Quarter			1 6/8	1 6/8	0 0/8
		TOTALS		23 1/8	22 7/8	0 2/8

County where killed:	Wallowa	Date Killed:		**ADD**	**Column 1**	23 1/8
Hunter's First Name:	Dr. John	Last Name:	Waterman		**Column 2**	22 7/8
Owner's First Name:	Sarah	Last Name:	Jones		**Subtotal**	46 0/8
				Subtract Column 3		0 2/8
				FINAL SCORE		45 6/8

Rocky Mountain Goat—Rifle
Minimum Score: All

Final Score	Greatest Spread	Length of Horn		Base Circumference		First Quarter Circumference		Second Quarter Circumference		Third Quarter Circumference		Year	County	Hunter/Owner	Rank
		R	L	R	L	R	L	R	L	R	L				
45 6/8	6 3/8	8 2/8	8 0/8	5 6/8	5 6/8	4 3/8	4 3/8	3 0/8	3 0/8	1 6/8	1 6/8	1968	Wallowa	Dr. John Waterman/Sarah Jones	1
42 4/8	5 6/8	8 4/8	8 5/8	4 6/8	4 6/8	4 0/8	4 0/8	2 4/8	2 4/8	1 4/8	1 4/8	1965	Wallowa	Laimon Osis	2
41 6/8	5 0/8	7 0/8	7 0/8	5 0/8	5 0/8	4 2/8	4 2/8	3 0/8	3 0/8	1 6/8	1 5/8	1965	Wallowa	Sally Edinger	3
39 6/8	6 0/8	8 3/8	8 2/8	4 2/8	4 2/8	3 4/8	3 4/8	2 4/8	2 3/8	1 4/8	1 4/8	1966	Wallowa	Carl Hunter	4
39 4/8	7 6/8	8 4/8	8 6/8	4 1/8	4 2/8	3 3/8	3 3/8	2 2/8	2 3/8	1 4/8	1 5/8	1967	Wallowa	Virgil Thornton/Gwen Thornton	5

Bighorn Sheep

Rocky Mountain Bighorn Sheep—Rifle
Minimum Score: 165 0/8

Adjusted* Score	Final Score	Greatest Spread	Length of Horn R	Length of Horn L	Base Circumference R	Base Circumference L	First Quarter Circumference R	First Quarter Circumference L	Second Quarter Circumference R	Second Quarter Circumference L	Third Quarter Circumference R	Third Quarter Circumference L	Year	Age	County	Unit	Hunter/Owner	Rank
202 7/8	202 7/8	22 4/8	44 0/8	43 5/8	15 4/8	15 4/8	15 3/8	15 4/8	14 6/8	14 7/8	12 0/8	12 0/8	1986	14	Wallowa	Hurricane	ODF & W	1
200 6/8	200 6/8	24 2/8	44 6/8	43 0/8	16 4/8	16 4/8	15 3/8	15 6/8	14 3/8	14 4/8	10 2/8	10 2/8	1989	7	Wallowa	Joseph Cr.	Peter Bollinger	2
198 0/8	198 0/8	25 0/8	42 4/8	43 4/8	16 5/8	16 5/8	16 0/8	15 7/8	14 5/8	14 0/8	10 0/8	9 4/8	1988	9	Wallowa	Joseph Cr.	Todd Jaksick	3
192 0/8	192 0/8	24 2/8	43 3/8	42 7/8	15 5/8	15 6/8	14 7/8	14 6/8	13 4/8	14 0/8	9 0/8	9 6/8	1991	7	Wallowa	Joseph Cr.	H. James Tonkin	4
191 4/8	191 4/8	23 6/8	44 3/8	39 3/8	15 7/8	16 0/8	15 0/8	15 1/8	13 6/8	13 5/8	9 6/8	9 3/8	1987	10	Wallowa	Joseph Cr.	Sam Jaksick. Jr.	5
189 4/8	189 4/8		40 2/8	41 0/8	16 0/8	16 0/8	15 1/8	15 2/8	13 4/8	13 4/8	9 4/8	9 4/8	1996	6	Wallowa	Joseph Cr.	ODF & W	6
183 6/8	183 6/8	23 2/8	38 4/8	39 0/8	15 6/8	15 6/8	14 7/8	15 2/8	14 0/8	13 6/8	8 7/8	8 6/8	1992	8	Wallowa	Wenaha	Tom R. Croswell	7
183 1/8	183 1/8	21 2/8	39 3/8	39 4/8	15 4/8	15 5/8	15 0/8	15 0/8	13 2/8	13 1/8	8 6/8	8 4/8	1994	6	Wallowa	Joseph Cr.	Kenneth Kirsch	8
182 0/8	182 0/8	22 5/8	40 7/8	39 5/8	16 2/8	16 3/8	15 1/8	15 1/8	12 2/8	12 2/8	7 1/8	7 3/8	1988	5	Wallowa	Imnaha	Dale R. Dotson	9
181 3/8	181 3/8	22 6/8	38 5/8	40 2/8	14 5/8	14 7/8	14 3/8	14 6/8	13 1/8	13 3/8	9 2/8	9 1/8	1987	9	Wallowa	Imnaha	Michael L. Taylor	10
178 1/8	178 1/8	24 2/8	39 7/8	39 2/8	14 4/8	14 4/8	14 1/8	14 1/8	12 6/8	12 5/8	8 2/8	8 4/8	1994	6	Wallowa	Wenaha	Mark Richards	11
174 6/8	174 6/8	28 0/8	36 6/8	38 6/8	15 7/8	16 0/8	14 5/8	14 5/8	12 0/8	12 0/8	7 1/8	7 2/8	1992	6	Wallowa	Imnaha	Lenard Erickson	12
173 3/8	173 3/8	22 5/8	38 3/8	37 2/8	15 6/8	15 7/8	14 6/8	14 5/8	11 4/8	12 1/8	7 0/8	7 5/8	1995	6	Wallowa	Imnaha	Sam L. Wilkins, Jr.	13
172 1/8	172 1/8	20 0/8	35 6/8	34 3/8	15 3/8	15 0/8	14 2/8	14 1/8	15 5/8	12 5/8	7 7/8	8 3/8	1978	5	Wallowa	Hurricane	Dick K. Nusser	14
171 5/8	171 5/8	21 0/8	37 4/8	37 1/8	14 1/8	14 1/8	13 4/8	13 4/8	12 0/8	12 7/8	7 4/8	7 5/8	1992	5	Wallowa	Imnaha	Bud Zollman	15
169 6/8	169 6/8	20 3/8	35 0/8	34 2/8	15 4/8	15 4/8	14 6/8	14 4/8	12 3/8	12 5/8	7 7/8	8 2/8	1994	5	Wallowa	Snake	Jerry Donovan	16
168 4/8	165 6/8	20 4/8	35 0/8	35 6/8	14 2/8	14 5/8	13 3/8	13 0/8	12 1/8	11 7/8	8 3/8	9 4/8	1978	9	Wallowa	Hurricane	Dave Melville	17

*ADJUSTED SCORE = FINAL SCORE + SHRINKAGE

Official Scoring System for Oregon Big Game Trophies

Records of Oregon
Big Game

RECORD BOOK FOR OREGON

P.O. Box 759
Irrigon, OR 97844

SHEEP

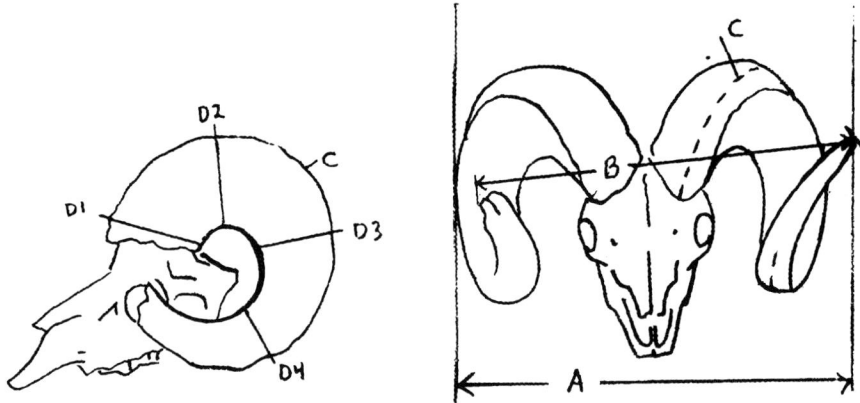

Species	Rifle	Archery	Muzzle
Rocky Mtn	165	140	136
California	145	140	140

				COLUMN 1	COLUMN 2	COLUMN 3
				Right Horn	Left Horn	Difference
A	Greatest Spread (Is often Tip to Tip Spread)		22 4/8			
B	Tip to Tip Spread		22 4/8			
C	Length of Horn			44 0/8	43 5/8	
D-1	Circumference of Base			15 4/8	15 4/8	0 0/8
D-2	Circumference at First Quarter			15 3/8	15 4/8	0 1/8
D-3	Circumference at Second Quarter			14 6/8	14 7/8	0 1/8
D-4	Circumference at Third Quarter			12 0/8	12 0/8	0 0/8
		TOTALS		101 5/8	101 4/8	0 2/8

County where killed: Wallowa	**Date Killed:** 10/86	**ADD**	**Column 1** 101 5/8
Hunter's Name:			**Column 2** 101 4/8
Owner's Name: ODF & W			**Subtotal** 203 1/8
			Subtract Column 3 0 2/8
			FINAL SCORE 202 7/8

SPOT
(currently owned by
Oregon Department of
Fish and Wildlife)

Rocky Mountain Bighorn Sheep

by Peter Bollinger

My hunt was finally going to begin for a bighorn sheep in Oregon. This day had come about by virtue of a conversation many months before with Mike Boyce of Animal Artistry Taxidermy in Reno, Nevada. Mike had mentioned that he had participated with two previous hunters in bighorn sheep hunts in Oregon and had seen some very large rams; in fact, they had taken two rams that were definitely trophy-sized. Mike mentioned that the permit was by bid and that it would be held at the annual convention dinner in Oregon. He also said that the hunting was complicated by the fact that the best hunting area, in his opinion, was on private land and that I would have to get permission from the owner of the property if I wanted to hunt in that area.

After many weeks of thought, investigation and effort, I was able to obtain a promise from the landowner that I could hunt on his property. I was convinced that there were bighorn rams in this area and that this was going to be my best opportunity to obtain a trophy-size bighorn and to complete my second grand slam.

I attended the dinner. There was one other bidder, but I was able to prevail and obtain the permit. No one in the room could have been more excited and happy than I. I could hardly wait until the season started. In fact, we did some scouting prior to the opening of the season and I saw a number of very good-size sheep. Some were in the high 180s to the low 190s. I was extremely enthusiastic. On our scouting trips we saw more bighorn rams than I have ever seen before.

Approximately two weeks later, the season began. In the interim, there had been a number of thunderstorms in the hunting area. When we arrived the day before the season began and did a little bit more scouting, we did not see any rams. The hunting area is a large canyon, so it is possible to see a fairly good-size area from vantage points. Mike Boyce and I were extremely surprised and somewhat discouraged because two weeks before we had seen many rams and now we were not seeing sign of any rams. Never-

happened to look back along the serpentine cattle path and saw the biggest ram I had ever seen in my life. There was no doubt in my mind that this was the ram we were looking for. It was

theless, we had a month to hunt, and so we went to sleep that night with a positive attitude.

The next day we commenced hunting at first light and hunted all day without seeing any rams, only a couple ewes and lambs. That evening over dinner in our camp, located in an old orchard at the top of the canyon, our thoughts and conversation were somewhat downbeat based upon the day's experience.

The second day dawned with a clear sky and it was going to be another warm day. Climbing down into the canyon was not too bad in the morning, but climbing out was a different story. We were walking along the cattle path, which was parallel to and about two-thirds of the way down from the canyon rim. We had been hunting for approximately three hours, when I

a long shot, but my only shot. Luckily, I was near a mound of dirt and could drop down and have a steady rest. The first shot was true. It stopped the sheep, who was rapidly moving out of sight in that classic prance of big rams. The shot was too far behind to be a killing shot, but the ram stopped against the canyon wall. I shot again and he fell off the canyon ledge down an embankment.

Mike stayed to watch while I went back along the path. The distance on a straight line was approximately five hundred yards, but on a serpentine path it took me fifteen to twenty minutes to get to where the ram was. He was there and he was mine—a ram to be proud of and to honor for the rest of my life.

(Final score: 200 6/8 B.C.)

State Record Sheep

by Red Iler

Here's how it works. First you draw the tag, next you do the research, then you go hunting. With tag in hand, I dialed the phone and Jack Palmer answered. His reputation as "Sheep Guru" had preceded him, and I was soon convinced he was authentic. Jack's information proved valuable and accurate.

The Upper Owyhee Unit (formerly Antelope Creek) had only recently opened up for sheep. Three years earlier, Jack had walked these rims and in his pocket was the first tag ever issued for this unit. He brought home a beautiful 169+ ram and the tale of another ram—which this story is about. His description of the one that got away would make any tag-holder dizzy and weak at the knees. His words were: "real heavy, droopy, wide and very symmetrical." I've learned over the years to be wary of seemingly exaggerated claims. We all know hunters who magnify everything at least twice. Usually, those who yell "Book 'er!" are the ones who don't know how to score. Jack was convinced the ram would go state record.

His brother, Orin, drew a tag the next season, so Jack and Orin hit the rims again. Sure enough, Jack found the ram in the canyon that he figured it would be in. The stalk put them within two hundred yards or so. The shot was nearly straight down and the ram was bedded. This canyon country can be a mile wide at the mouth, and then taper down to where the rims finally meet at the end—miles apart. Some spots are one hundred yards wide and one hundred yards deep. The basalt cliffs are nearly vertical for miles, with no way to get out from the bottom or down from the top. Orin's shot was on of these straight-down types that are known to produce consistent right-over-the-back results, and that's what happened. The ram jumped up and swapped ends. Not knowing which way to run, he stood there while running data through his computer. This gave Orin time for a second shot—all the while Jack was giving directions on what to do next. So, aiming lower, Orin touched another one off and killed the boulder in front of the barrel. The ram got his bearings and was gone in a flash—for the rest of the season. Jack remained confident this ram would go state record and now possibly be the first California bighorn to make the 180 minimum for Boone and Crockett. Orin later made a nice long shot on a great 165 head.

It was next season that I drew one of three tags for the Upper Owyhee Unit. Odds were 1.8% then. It's easy to lose friends when you hit the first time you apply after they've put in for years unnumbered. But as you'll discover, God showed me great favor from start to finish.

I did come out of it with one friend though, Carl. He had accompanied seven or eight others on sheep hunts over the years, as well as having done some Dall sheep guiding in Alaska. He's a savvy hunter as well as a walking ballistics table. Knowing him as I do, I could see Carl seemed to be rather skeptical of Jack's assessment of the big ram. He always reserved verbal judgment, but there remained that ever-present look—cocked head and raised eyebrow. The more I got to know Jack, the more I gained confidence in his judging ability. He never exaggerated the things we are all so prone to stretch. His integrity won me over. With me came my wife Vikki. She was more happy for me than excited about the actual hunt, I think. When I finally believed the ram was as good as he sounded, then Vik did too. She fueled the fire of one accord and from then on the ram was known as B&C—she's a woman of great faith.

Upper Owyhee Unit sits in the southeast corner of the state. It's big canyon country and only a fool would go in unprepared. It's got to be the most remote part of the state, and maybe of the whole country. Water is scarce, roads are only trails at best and there are no people anywhere. It's a great place for sheep. The unit borders Idaho and Nevada. The herd's gene pool comes from British Columbia, whcn sheep were reintroduced into the Owyhee County of Idaho in 1963. Several other introductions happened later. Now the herds are at capacity with an estimated herd size of fifteen hundred or so. I'm sure groups of sheep cross back and forth. The 1990 census for this unit was one hundred and fifteen sheep with a minimum of twenty rams.

From my home in Mt. Vernon, it's two hundred miles one way to the turn-off for the unit. We went down four times over a several-month period on various scouting trips. We'd usually spend two days spotting and hiking. The last scouting outing, Vik and I were gone for fourteen days. My Ford blew a head gasket about ten miles off the pavement, and that ate up four days. It's a long walk from nowhere to somewhere. We had ten days in the field before the opener.

Vik and I saw around twenty-five rams. A few were very good, 168–170, I'd guess. The season was October 12–21, but still the days were hot and dry. Most canyons had some water pooled up so we were finding small groups of rams here and there. We spotted, especially early and late, always up before dawn and walking back with flashlight. There were nights spent on the rims in hopes of finding B&C doing something that wasn't typical ram behavior. We hadn't seen him in the weeks of scouting and I began groping for answers. Maybe he was living in a cave and not feeding in the normal time slots like the other sheep. Or he just wasn't there—period. There are a number of big cats that live there and feed almost exclusively on sheep, or he could have just crossed a couple of canyons and moved to Idaho.

Vik remained confident through it all. She kept telling me God was going to do it for me and not to doubt because that's faith's biggest enemy. She was sure we'd find him. I guess I just hoped we would.

The season opened on Saturday, so Thursday night Carl showed up at a prearranged spot. I told him no B&C yet, but I had found a dandy 170-type that we named Chip. I would tag him in a heartbeat. He had a big chunk out of his right horn, right where a quarter measurement would be. I'd seen him three times in the last cou-

ple of months, and he was always within a mile or so from the last time. I felt sure I could get a crack at him if it came to it.

We had a pow-wow concerning what to do next. We had one day of scouting left. Vik wanted to stay and try for B&C one more time, Carl raised an eyebrow and I flipped a coin. So, Friday morning we all left camp going different directions. Vik became an accomplished sheep-spotter and I'd taught her what I knew about judging a head. It pretty much boiled down to "You'll know him when you see him." We got back together at camp during the heat of the day. No B&C, but Chip was seen bedded under a rim and there was a person standing right above him—apparently another tag-holder. Neither saw the other.

Antelope Creek lay north and west of us about five or six miles by air. Mostly, it's a nursery for ewes and lambs. I'd seen fifty or so in there a couple of weeks before, but no rams. They are usually separated this time of year, but the rut was coming on. I really do believe that God inspired me to finally make the decision to break camp and make for Antelope Creek before dark. Think about it—who among us would leave several good shooters and one very good one to go to an area known to be for "women only" in hopes of finding B&C hanging out in early rut? Vik said, "Yes!" Carl's head cocked and I started tearing down the tent. Five or six hours later, we pulled into Hawkins Basin and set up again, no tent this time, just cots and thousands of stars.

Saturday morning was absolutely beautiful. Vik stayed in camp because she was afraid she might interfere in a stalk. Carl and I headed out together and walked a while before getting to the canyon wall. We spotted for a while. The creek was running some and there was lots of green feed in the bottom, picture-perfect for sheep. I decided to cross over, so Carl stayed, and I headed down through the ledges and benches that would get me to the creek, and then up the other side through a narrow chute. We planned to hunt the canyon out together. I could look across canyon and spot under the rims on Carl's side, and he would do the same for me. I was about one-third of the way down and only ten minutes from my buddy when directly below me, on a sloping ledge maybe twenty-five yards wide, stood B&C. He was surrounded by a

dozen ewes with no other rams in sight. He was only about one hundred yards away. Nobody had seen me, even though I felt I'd taken one step too many. Then, an old ewe locked in on me and we both stood frozen in time. But she was looking into the sun and soon returned to business as usual.

The wind was from them to me. It was a perfect set up. If only I could keep it together. I kept saying to myself, "OK, this is it—here is what it's all about—don't blow it." I eased back a couple of feet and got out of my daypack. Then, with 10×, I eased over to take a real look. He looked just spectacular. So regal, so dominant, so at ease with his world around him. This picture remains one of my fondest memories.

Sheep fever is a powerful enemy. It's like you suddenly have the ability to screw up everything without even trying. Carl had to be there, was all I could think. So I backed off the ledge and headed back up the mountain. I could see Carl on the skyline. He was occupied with his spotting scope, and was oblivious to my waving arms and jumping up and down. So, I headed off for him as fast as I could go. Upon arrival, I told him what was up in ten words or less. Back down we went, nearly running the whole way.

We stopped and caught our breath. I lay on my back to calm down—it was really an exciting time. I remember closing my eyes and thanking God for the chance at B&C. We crawled over to the rim edge together and peeked over. The morning sun was shining on him and he gave us a perfect broadside look. He was beautiful. Sheep fever grabbed me again and I momentarily lost common sense. So, I asked Carl, "What do ya think?" He looked at me like I was from Mars. Finally, he said, "If it were my tag, I'd shoot right now—and don't forget your gun is sighted in high, and you are shooting downhill. Don't overshoot him." My .280 Remington Mountain Rifle was shooting 140 gr. Nosler Partition and was right on at three hundred yards—due to possible cross-canyon shooting. So, I put the gun in a perfect rest and at that exact time the ram pawed the ground a couple of times and then bedded down, looking the other way. I centered him in the scope, then dropped the cross hairs down to where his body line hit the ground.

Seeing him from the back simply magnified the mass of his horns. It was a time you would never forget. I said in a whisper, "In the name of Jesus, here we go." I was careful to concentrate on the cross hairs and the trigger squeeze. I hated the angle and knew I'd be around six inches high, but I had to take the shot. After the gun went off, I lost the sight picture from the recoil, but instantly chambered another round anyway. You guessed it—the bullet had struck high and entered the ram just behind the right shoulder, then run along the top of his shoulder blade, and come out a foot or so down the neck and into the ground, giving the impression of a clean miss. He was up and busting through the ewes like a linebacker. He was fifty yards or so from a corner in the rim that could put him out of sight and gone. I found him immediately in the scope and shot without too much care—just desperate to get some lead into him. The second shot was a definite right-over-the-back shot. It blew out a big chunk of rock from the rim and splattered him with fragments. I've never seen a more desperate pair—him on one end and me on the other. He was suicidal in his attempt to escape. With great leaping bounds, he would land recklessly in boulder slides. He was in the air more than on the ground. I'd chambered another and now all I had was a white rump patch that was nearly gone. I don't remember ever seeing his head or body on the last shot—just his white patch as he was going around and down. Carl kept yelling,

"Bring it down—you're overshootin' him!" That really helped calm me down. And it must've done some good, because the last shot ended with a thump, better known as a ham shot. The instant I shot, the ram was gone. I wasn't sure I'd even hit him, so I took off running up the rim to where I could see into the bend in the canyon. I couldn't believe I'd blown it so bad. I nearly threw up after the run to the top.

I sat and watched and tried to recover from the fever. After a few minutes of nothing, I slowly walked back along the rim to where I'd seen him last. A huge section of rock had fallen away from the canyon wall and created a maze of truck-sized boulders below me. It was there I saw his horns move. He was bedded down and trying to hide, but he got up and spun around when I saw him.

Carl showed up about then, and I lay down for a rest and waited just a minute before he showed again. We guessed the yardage at two hundred and twenty-five to two hundred and fifty. I held right on and squared him through the shoulders. Carl said, "It's about time!" I told him, "I wanted to get my money's worth—think he'll be as good as he looks when we get to him?" Carl cocked an eyebrow, and said, "He'll be better." We got on our packs and worked our way down to him. We just sat there and admired him, then did the pictures and caping and butchering. Then we taped him: 177 1/8—I thought we'd made a couple of mistakes, so we did it again. Same thing again: 176 5/8 after deductions, 176 Boone and Crockett.

Jack was right—he is a new state record. Carl was right, too—he is better than we thought. But Vik was right most of all—trust in God, because faith is the substance of things hoped for and the evidence of things not seen. This tag of a lifetime opened the door to an adventure of a lifetime. My hat's off to ya, B&C. Thanks for the memories.
(Final score: 176 0/8 B.C.)

Official Scoring System for Oregon Big Game Trophies

SHEEP

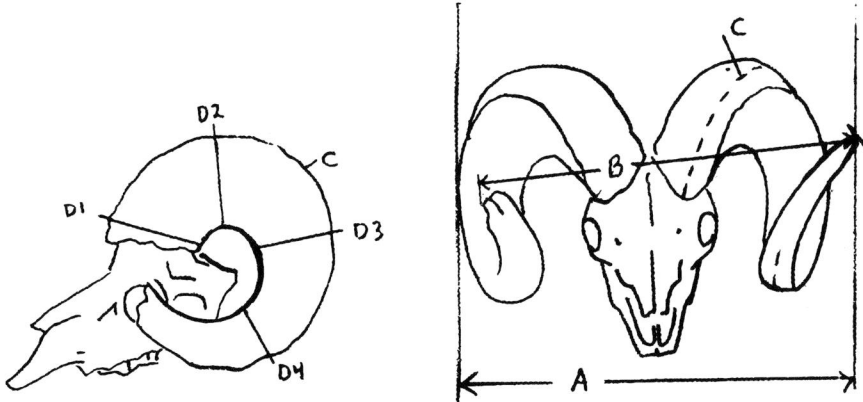

Species	Rifle	Archery	Muzzle
Rocky Mtn	165	140	136
California	145	140	140

				COLUMN 1	COLUMN 2	COLUMN 3
				Right Horn	Left Horn	Difference
A	Greatest Spread (Is often Tip to Tip Spread)	22	5/8			
B	Tip to Tip Spread	21	2/8			
C	Length of Horn			36 6/8	36 2/8	
D-1	Circumference of Base			15 0/8	15 1/8	0 1/8
D-2	Circumference at First Quarter			14 3/8	14 6/8	0 3/8
D-3	Circumference at Second Quarter			13 1/8	13 1/8	0 0/8
D-4	Circumference at Third Quarter			9 0/8	9 1/8	0 1/8
	TOTALS			88 2/8	88 3/8	0 5/8

County where killed: Harney	Date Killed: 10/12/91	ADD	Column 1	88 2/8
Hunter's Name: Red Iler			Column 2	88 3/8
Owner's Name: Red Iler			Subtotal	176 5/8
			Subtract Column 3	0 5/8
			FINAL SCORE	176 0/8

California Bighorn Sheep—Rifle
Minimum Score: 145 0/8

Adjusted* Score	Final Score	Greatest Spread	Length of Horn R	L	Base Circumference R	L	First Quarter Circumference R	L	Second Quarter Circumference R	L	Third Quarter Circumference R	L	Year	Age	County	Unit	Hunter/Owner	Rank
176 0/8	176 0/8	22 5/8	36 6/8	36 2/8	15 0/8	15 1/8	14 3/8	14 6/8	13 1/8	13 1/8	9 0/8	9 1/8	1991	7	Harney	Upper Owyhee	Red Iler	1
175 4/8	172 2/8	27 4/8	33 0/8	34 6/8	14 6/8	14 6/8	14 4/8	14 5/8	13 4/8	13 5/8	9 4/8	9 7/8	1988	10	Lake	Juniper	David Bruner	2
175 0/8	172 6/8	23 1/8	37 4/8	39 0/8	14 1/8	14 0/8	13 7/8	13 6/8	12 2/8	12 2/8	8 1/8	8 1/8	1987	9	Malheur	Leslie Gulch	Earl Buche	3
174 2/8	173 2/8	24 0/8	33 2/8	33 0/8	15 2/8	15 2/8	14 6/8	14 6/8	13 7/8	13 7/8	9 5/8	10 0/8	1994	10	Lake	Hart Mt.	Les Hawthorn	4
173 0/8	170 2/8	23 3/8	35 5/8	35 1/8	15 0/8	14 7/8	14 0/8	14 0/8	12 2/8	12 1/8	9 0/8	8 6/8	1984		Lake	Hart Mt.	Sherrain Glenn	5
171 7/8	171 7/8	27 4/8	37 0/8	38 1/8	14 4/8	14 4/8	14 2/8	14 2/8	12 0/8	12 0/8	7 5/8	7 7/8	1995		Lake	Hart Mt.	Jim Staats	6
170 5/8	167 7/8	23 5/8	34 2/8	34 1/8	14 4/8	14 6/8	14 2/8	14 4/8	12 3/8	12 6/8	8 6/8	8 5/8	1987	6	Harney	Steens Mt.'s	Douglas Vandehey	7
170 0/8	169 0/8	25 1/8	33 2/8	33 2/8	14 4/8	14 6/8	14 2/8	14 2/8	13 0/8	13 2/8	9 6/8	9 4/8	1993	9	Lake	Poker Jim	Vivan Flick	8
170 0/8	167 2/8	24 7/8	34 1/8	33 5/8	14 6/8	14 5/8	14 4/8	14 4/8	12 7/8	12 5/8	8 2/8	8 0/8	1984	7	Lake	Hart Mt.	Ted Carlson	8
169 2/8	168 2/8		33 6/8	33 6/8	14 2/8	14 0/8	13 7/8	13 7/8	13 0/8	13 2/8	9 4/8	9 4/8	1994	8	Lake	Hart Mt.	Robert Klink	10
168 6/8	166 0/8	24 4/8	33 6/8	33 6/8	15 0/8	14 5/8	14 4/8	14 3/8	12 2/8	12 4/8	8 0/8	8 4/8	1994	8	Lake	Hart Mt.	Stan Wickersham	11
168 5/8	165 7/8	27 1/8	33 5/8	36 4/8	14 4/8	14 6/8	14 1/8	14 1/8	12 1/8	11 6/8	7 7/8	7 4/8	1994	7	Lake	Poker Jim	Tyler Saunders	12
168 0/8	167 0/8		36 0/8	32 0/8	14 5/8	14 5/8	13 6/8	13 6/8	12 0/8	12 0/8	9 1/8	9 2/8	1992	9	Malheur	Upper Owyhee	Dakota Emerson	13
167 7/8	165 1/8	24 6/8	34 2/8	35 1/8	14 5/8	14 7/8	14 1/8	14 4/8	11 5/8	11 5/8	7 4/8	8 0/8	1988	9	Grant	Aldridge	Paul Westrup	14
167 6/8	165 0/8	26 4/8	32 4/8	32 0/8	14 3/8	14 1/8	13 5/8	13 7/8	13 0/8	13 0/8	9 4/8	9 6/8	1992	13	Lake	Steens Mt.'s	Bill Myers	15
167 2/8	164 4/8	23 3/8	34 0/8	32 6/8	14 5/8	15 0/8	14 1/8	14 3/8	12 0/8	11 7/8	8 0/8	7 6/8	1990	8	Lake	Hart Mt.	Ron Poole	16
167 0/8	167 4/8		32 4/8	33 0/8	15 2/8	15 3/8	14 5/8	14 6/8	13 0/8	12 6/8	8 7/8	8 3/8	1977	7	Harney	Steens Mt.'s	Robert Anthony	17
167 0/8	166 0/8	22 5/8	33 4/8	34 4/8	13 6/8	13 6/8	13 4/8	13 5/8	12 5/8	12 7/8	9 1/8	9 3/8		8	Harney	Iron Point	J.D. Gardner	17
166 7/8	166 7/8		34 4/8	33 5/8	14 5/8	14 3/8	14 0/8	14 0/8	12 4/8	12 4/8	8 4/8	8 7/8	1995		Lake	Hart Mt.	Linsey Ropp	19
166 5/8	166 5/8	23 4/8	32 0/8	36 1/8	14 0/8	14 0/8	13 4/8	14 2/8	13 0/8	13 4/8	8 6/8	10 3/8	1992	12	Lake	Hart Mt.	Dan Magee	20
166 5/8	163 7/8	25 3/8	31 3/8	38 0/8	14 7/8	14 7/8	13 7/8	14 0/8	11 4/8	12 0/8	7 0/8	7 6/8	1984		Lake	Hart Mt.	Gale Wall	20
166 2/8	163 4/8	24 2/8	35 3/8	35 3/8	13 6/8	14 4/8	13 2/8	13 1/8	11 4/8	11 5/8	8 0/8	8 0/8	1985	9	Harney	Steens Mt.'s	Patrick Wheeler	22
165 7/8	165 7/8	24 4/8	31 0/8	33 7/8	15 0/8	14 4/8	14 6/8	14 4/8	13 2/8	13 1/8	8 3/8	8 5/8	1995		Lake	Poker Jim	Dan Rousseau	23
165 6/8	163 0/8	22 0/8	36 0/8	35 2/8	13 4/8	13 4/8	13 1/8	13 0/8	11 3/8	11 3/8	8 3/8	8 0/8	1986	9	Grant	Aldridge	Steve McKern	24
165 3/8	162 5/8	26 6/8	32 4/8	35 7/8	13 6/8	14 2/8	13 4/8	14 0/8	11 7/8	11 7/8	8 1/8	8 0/8	1988	9	Harney	Pueblo Mt.	Gary Lawson	25
164 6/8	162 6/8	24 0/8	34 1/8	31 5/8	14 4/8	14 3/8	13 3/8	13 2/8	12 1/8	12 1/8	8 6/8	9 0/8	1992	9	Lake	Poker Jim	Vilas D. Ropp	26
164 6/8	162 0/8	24 0/8	32 5/8	33 3/8	14 4/8	14 3/8	14 2/8	14 3/8	12 2/8	12 1/8	7 2/8	7 6/8	1989	6	Grant	Aldridge	Doug Friske	26
164 0/8	164 4/8		37 2/8	33 2/8	14 2/8	14 2/8	13 4/8	13 4/8	12 1/8	11 6/8	8 4/8	7 4/8	1990	10	Malheur	Upper Owyhee	Orin Palmer	28
163 5/8	160 7/8	25 0/8	31 1/8	33 4/8	13 6/8	13 6/8	13 4/8	13 5/8	12 3/8	12 2/8	8 4/8	8 3/8	1992	10	Harney	Pueblo Mt.	Jim Oglesby	29
163 0/8	160 2/8		33 0/8	33 4/8	14 0/8	14 1/8	13 7/8	13 1/8	12 1/8	12 2/8	8 3/8	9 0/8	1990	9	Grant	Aldridge	Brad Browning	30
161 0/8	161 0/8	27 0/8	32 1/8	32 1/8	14 1/8	14 1/8	13 6/8	13 6/8	12 1/8	12 2/8	8 3/8	8 4/8	1993	7	Harney	Steens Mt.'s	Linda Phillips	31
160 1/8	157 3/8	21 2/8	30 4/8	34 5/8	13 0/8	13 0/8	12 6/8	12 3/8	12 0/8	11 7/8	8 7/8	9 2/8	1988	7	Harney	Steens Mt.'s	Randy Curtis	32
160 0/8	157 2/8	25 3/8	31 2/8	29 0/8	14 2/8	14 2/8	13 7/8	14 0/8	11 6/8	12 2/8	8 5/8	8 5/8	1988	6	Lake	Hart Mt.	Duane Bernard	33
159 4/8	158 4/8	25 6/8	31 6/8	32 4/8	13 6/8	13 4/8	13 4/8	13 4/8	11 6/8	11 5/8	8 2/8	8 3/8	1993	8	Harney	E. Beatty's Butte	Dwight Crump	34
159 4/8	157 4/8	23 2/8	33 4/8	35 4/8	14 3/8	14 5/8	13 3/8	13 4/8	10 6/8	10 4/8	6 0/8	6 0/8	1992	6	Grant	Aldridge	Craig Bozarth	34
158 4/8	155 6/8	24 4/8	30 4/8	33 4/8	13 3/8	13 5/8	13 2/8	13 2/8	11 2/8	11 2/8	8 0/8	8 3/8	1992	9	Harney	Pueblo Mt.	Pedro Zabala, Jr.	36
158 1/8	158 1/8	24 1/8	32 4/8	29 5/8	14 2/8	14 2/8	13 6/8	13 6/8	12 0/8	12 0/8	8 0/8	8 0/8	1995		Lake	Poker Jim	Steve Phillips	37
157 2/8	154 4/8	23 5/8	29 5/8	30 5/8	13 1/8	13 4/8	12 7/8	13 2/8	12 0/8	12 4/8	9 1/8	9 1/8	1986	6	Lake	Abert Rim	Heath W. Clark	38
155 7/8	153 1/8	23 6/8	34 2/8	31 5/8	13 5/8	13 6/8	13 2/8	13 0/8	11 0/8	10 4/8	7 0/8	6 4/8	1985	6	Lake	Poker Jim	Wayne Barry	39

Adjusted Score	Final Score	Greatest Spread	Length of Horn R	Length of Horn L	Base Circumference R	Base Circumference L	First Quarter Circumference R	First Quarter Circumference L	Second Quarter Circumference R	Second Quarter Circumference L	Third Quarter Circumference R	Third Quarter Circumference L	Year	Age	County	Unit	Hunter/Owner	Rank
155 1/8	155 1/8		29 4/8	30 7/8	14 0/8	14 0/8	13 3/8	13 2/8	11 7/8	11 7/8	8 2/8	8 2/8	1995		Lake	Hart Mt.	Robert Daniels	40
153 3/8	150 5/8	26 7/8	31 1/8	31 0/8	14 1/8	14 0/8	13 2/8	13 2/8	10 7/8	10 4/8	6 7/8	6 4/8	1983	4	Lake	Hart Mt.	Steve Mathers	41
152 4/8	150 4/8	25 0/8	29 0/8	34 0/8	13 3/8	13 3/8	12 7/8	12 6/8	11 0/8	10 7/8	7 2/8	6 6/8	1993	7	Lake	Hart Mt.	Robert George	42
152 2/8	152 2/8	23 7/8	30 6/8	34 4/8	13 0/8	13 3/8	12 4/8	12 7/8	11 1/8	10 7/8	7 2/8	7 1/8	1995		Harney	Steens Mt.'s	Ron Snively	43
151 1/8	149 3/8	24 0/8	31 6/8	30 7/8	13 4/8	13 4/8	12 5/8	12 7/8	10 5/8	10 6/8	6 5/8	7 0/8	1983	6	Harney	Steens Mt.'s	Ron Bozarth	44
150 6/8	148 0/8	26 2/8	32 2/8	29 2/8	13 7/8	13 7/8	13 1/8	13 1/8	10 2/8	10 2/8	6 0/8	6 1/8	1982	6	Lake	Abert Rim	Roy L. Knieriem	45
150 3/8	147 5/8		29 5/8	28 2/8	13 0/8	13 2/8	12 4/8	12 5/8	11 2/8	11 3/8	8 1/8	8 1/8	1990	9	Malheur	Upper Owyhee	Dave Boyd	46
150 0/8	147 5/8	24 0/8	29 0/8	29 2/8	13 5/8	13 6/8	14 0/8	13 2/8	10 7/8	11 1/8	6 6/8	7 1/8	1987		Harney	Steens Mt.'s	Shirlene Van Horn	47
149 5/8	147 2/8	21 4/8	27 1/8	30 2/8	13 1/8	12 6/8	12 7/8	12 5/8	11 4/8	11 4/8	8 0/8	7 7/8	1982	7	Malheur	Leslie Gulch	Rod Knieriem	48
146 7/8	144 6/8†	21 5/8	32 5/8	32 3/8	12 5/8	12 4/8	11 6/8	11 7/8	9 5/8	9 6/8	6 0/8	6 0/8	1995	6	Malheur	Upper Owyhee	Tim Hueckman	49

*ADJUSTED SCORE = FINAL SCORE + SHRINKAGE
†EWE

California Bighorn Sheep—Archery
Minimum Score: 140 0/8

Adjusted Score	Final Score	Greatest Spread	Length of Horn R	Length of Horn L	Base Circumference R	Base Circumference L	First Quarter Circumference R	First Quarter Circumference L	Second Quarter Circumference R	Second Quarter Circumference L	Third Quarter Circumference R	Third Quarter Circumference L	Year	Age	County	Unit	Hunter/Owner	Rank
175 2/8	175 2/8	25 2/8	35 2/8	33 0/8	15 4/8	15 2/8	0 0/8	0 0/8	0 0/8	0 0/8	0 0/8	0 0/8	1989	8	Lake	Hart Mt.	Stephen Herrara	1
164 1/8	161 3/8	25 4/8	34 5/8	33 0/8	13 4/8	13 2/8	13 0/8	12 6/8	12 1/8	12 1/8	8 6/8	8 6/8	1982	11	Harney	Steen Mt.'s	Jerry G. Rhodes	2
163 7/8	163 7/8	23 6/8	32 7/8	35 6/8	13 5/8	13 6/8	13 6/8	13 4/8	12 1/8	12 2/8	8 3/8	8 4/8	1992		Lake	Poker Jim	Robert T. Arnott	3

Pronghorn

My Antelope Story

by JoAnn Hathaway

We arrived at the spot near a waterhole where we had seen two bucks with very large horns when we were scouting. Although it was only 3:00 a.m., someone signaled from the hillside to indicate that that area was taken. I decided to go a half mile farther and work my way toward the backcountry behind the waterhole. This would put me in the area where the antelope had gone. As it became daylight I saw a nice buck. After I had watched it a bit, it came down past me, but I decided it didn't compare with the ones we had seen the day before. I moved on and after awhile stopped to snack and to watch. It wasn't long before the horns of a nice buck became visible just above the sky-line. I decided they were unusually wide and flat and would not score well. I had spread my jacket over the sage-brush to provide some shade. It attracted the does traveling with the buck and they came within ten feet of me. He came back and butted them to get them going. I confirmed my decision.

I decided to make my way toward where they had gone. I made my way to the only shade, a lone juniper tree. I was on a large, flat plateau that dropped off in all directions beyond. I calculated that the waterhole must be at a forty-five-degree angle to my right, and therefore I must be approaching my destination. I had not been there long when numerous antelope appeared. They were feeding at the edge of the plateau directly opposite me. As I watched I recognized the two big bucks from our scouting. I could see that one's horns were noticeably longer and the other's much heavier. I decided the heavier would score better. A strong wind was

blowing crosswise and the bucks were far enough off to make for a difficult shot. From behind my tree I watched them for more than an hour as they were feeding back and forth at the edge of the plateau. There was no way to move closer without scaring them away. Eventually I decided to attempt a shot. The herd ran off in the direction opposite to the waterhole. As I walked over to look at the area I realized that it was farther away than I had thought.

As I sat there, antelope returning from the waterhole came past me. My husband had heard the shot and came up to see what happened. He kept saying, "That is a good one," and I would answer, "Not like I saw." About 4:00 I heard a shot near the waterhole where the other hunter was. An hour later we decided to return to the car and come back tomorrow. Our route took us past the other hunter and his antelope, which I knew was neither of the ones I had seen.

The next day I chose a spot where I could cover antelope approaching the waterhole from either side. Several nice bucks came by, but I had become spoiled. At about 10:00 a.m. I recog-nized the heavy-horned buck from yesterday. He went into the waterhole and came toward me, out into the lake bed, with several does. I waited until I had a clear shot, took a steady rest and aimed for the heart. He dropped immediately and all the does surrounded him. Much to my dismay, he got up after a couple of minutes, but I had no opportunity for a second shot as there were too many does around him. There was a huge red circle near the heart. Before long, he headed back where he came from and out of range. As he reached the low ridge he was unable to keep up and the circle near his heart was more than a foot across. When I attained the ridge I could see that he was not with the herd as it approached the area where I had first seen them yesterday. From the saddle, we spied him where he had chosen a slightly downhill path and soon collapsed.

I will never forget the excitement at head-quarters when I took him (as required) on the refuge. Only then did I begin to realize what I had.

(Final score: 87 0/8 B.C.)

Official Scoring System for Oregon Big Game Trophies

PRONGHORN

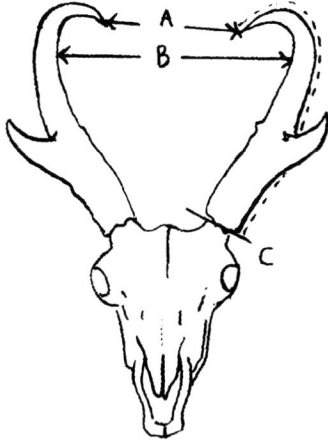

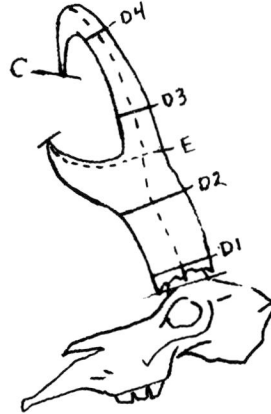

Species	Rifle	Archery	Muzzle
Pronghorn	76	64	63

			COLUMN 1	COLUMN 2	COLUMN 3
			Right Horn	Left Horn	Difference
A Tip to Tip Spread	8	0/8			
B Inside Spread of Main Beams	10	1/8			
C Length of Horn			19 4/8	19 5/8	0 1/8
D-1 Circumference of Base			7 0/8	6 6/8	0 2/8
D-2 Circumference at First Quarter			6 6/8	6 6/8	0 0/8
D-3 Circumference at Second Quarter			4 3/8	4 3/8	0 0/8
D-4 Circumference at Third Quarter			2 7/8	3 0/8	0 1/8
E Length of Prong			4 7/8	4 6/8	0 1/8
TOTALS			45 3/8	45 2/8	0 5/8

County where killed: Lake	Date Killed: 1942	**ADD**	Column 1	45 3/8
Hunter's First Name: E.C.	Last Name: Starr		Column 2	45 2/8
Owner's First Name:	Last Name:		Subtotal	90 5/8
			Subtract Column 3	0 5/8
			FINAL SCORE	90 0/8

Pronghorn—Rifle
Minimum Score: 76 0/8

Adjusted* Score	Final Score	Inside Spread	Length of Horn		Length of Prong		Base Circumference		First Quarter Circumference		Second Quarter Circumference		Third Quarter Circumference		Year	County	Hunter/Owner	Rank
			R	L	R	L	R	L	R	L	R	L	R	L				
90 0/8	90 0/8	10 1/8	19 4/8	19 5/8	4 7/8	4 6/8	7 0/8	6 6/8	6 6/8	6 6/8	4 3/8	4 3/8	2 7/8	3 0/8	1942	Lake	E.C. Starr	1
87 0/8	87 0/8	7 0/8	17 2/8	17 2/8	6 2/8	5 7/8	6 4/8	6 6/8	7 1/8	7 1/8	4 1/8	4 2/8	2 5/8	2 7/8	1976	Lake	JoAnn Hathaway	2
87 0/8	84 6/8	14 3/8	16 2/8	16 1/8	6 6/8	6 6/8	6 4/8	6 6/8	7 2/8	7 0/8	3 5/8	3 4/8	2 4/8	2 4/8	1980	Lake	Tim O'Leary	2
86 4/8	86 4/8	4 0/8	15 7/8	15 7/8	6 7/8	7 0/8	6 5/8	6 5/8	6 6/8	6 5/8	4 3/8	4 3/8	2 7/8	2 7/8	1976	Harney	James W. Greer	4
86 4/8	86 4/8	7 0/8	17 5/8	17 4/8	5 4/8	5 4/8	6 6/8	6 6/8	6 6/8	6 6/8	4 1/8	4 1/8	2 6/8	2 5/8	1991	Harney	Sam L. Wilkins, Jr.	4
86 2/8	84 0/8	12 0/8	16 4/8	16 4/8	6 4/8	6 5/8	6 4/8	6 4/8	6 4/8	6 4/8	3 4/8	3 5/8	2 4/8	2 5/8		Harney	Greg Atkeson	6
85 4/8	85 4/8	5 0/8	16 0/8	16 2/8	6 0/8	5 4/8	7 1/8	6 5/8	7 2/8	7 0/8	4 5/8	4 5/8	3 0/8	3 0/8	1990	Harney	Van G. Decker	7
85 4/8	85 4/8	1 0/8	16 3/8	16 1/8	6 5/8	6 4/8	6 6/8	6 7/8	7 1/8	7 0/8	3 7/8	3 7/8	2 4/8	2 4/8	1992	Harney	Jon McKnight	7
85 2/8	85 2/8	6 0/8	16 5/8	17 0/8	5 4/8	6 2/8	7 1/8	7 2/8	7 3/8	7 1/8	4 0/8	3 7/8	2 3/8	2 3/8	1992	Harney	Sharon L. Ganos	9
85 0/8	85 0/8	3 0/8	17 4/8	17 4/8	5 3/8	4 7/8	7 1/8	7 1/8	6 0/8	6 0/8	4 1/8	4 1/8	3 0/8	2 7/8	1991	Lake	Todd Hueckman	10
84 6/8	84 6/8	1 0/8	16 2/8	16 3/8	6 5/8	6 2/8	6 4/8	6 3/8	7 1/8	7 1/8	4 4/8	3 6/8	2 5/8	2 6/8	1980	Baker	Martin Vavra	11
84 4/8	84 4/8		17 0/8	17 4/8	5 2/8	5 2/8	7 0/8	6 7/8	6 6/8	6 6/8	4 3/8	4 0/8	2 5/8	2 3/8	1985	Deschutes	Rick Ward	12
84 2/8	84 2/8	5 0/8	16 7/8	16 6/8	5 6/8	6 0/8	6 5/8	6 3/8	7 0/8	6 6/8	3 6/8	4 1/8	2 6/8	2 6/8	1990	Harney	Douglas Modey	13
83 4/8	83 4/8	6 0/8	16 3/8	16 3/8	5 6/8	5 4/8	6 4/8	6 4/8	7 1/8	7 0/8	4 0/8	4 2/8	2 3/8	2 3/8	1995	Malheur	Tom D. Johnson	14
83 4/8	82 0/8		16 6/8	16 6/8	4 3/8	4 3/8	6 2/8	6 2/8	5 5/8	5 7/8	5 4/8	5 6/8	2 4/8	2 5/8	1994	Harney	Doug Tandy	14
83 0/8	80 6/8		16 0/8	16 0/8	6 0/8	5 3/8	6 3/8	6 3/8	6 1/8	6 2/8	3 6/8	3 6/8	2 6/8	2 6/8	1991	Baker	David Hunsaker	16
82 6/8	82 6/8	2 0/8	16 7/8	17 0/8	5 3/8	5 3/8	6 4/8	6 5/8	6 5/8	6 3/8	3 6/8	3 6/8	2 4/8	2 4/8	1990	Harney	Lowell E. Kropf	17
82 6/8	81 2/8		16 1/8	16 0/8	5 0/8	5 2/8	6 7/8	6 4/8	6 2/8	6 4/8	3 6/8	4 0/8	2 5/8	2 4/8	1994	Deschutes	George Terrill	17
82 6/8	81 2/8	6 0/8	15 1/8	15 2/8	6 0/8	6 2/8	7 0/8	7 0/8	6 2/8	6 4/8	3 6/8	3 6/8	2 4/8	2 4/8			Matt Fullerton	17
82 6/8	81 2/8	10 5/8	15 2/8	15 3/8	6 1/8	6 1/8	7 2/8	7 0/8	6 4/8	6 3/8	3 5/8	3 6/8	2 2/8	2 2/8	1993	Harney	Tim Wanichek	17
82 4/8	82 4/8		15 0/8	15 5/8	6 1/8	6 3/8	7 0/8	7 1/8	7 2/8	7 4/8	3 6/8	3 4/8	2 4/8	2 3/8	1990	Malheur	Mike Browning	21
82 2/8	82 2/8	1 0/8	17 3/8	17 3/8	5 4/8	5 2/8	5 6/8	5 7/8	6 2/8	6 2/8	4 0/8	4 1/8	2 4/8	2 4/8	1974	Lake	Jess Scott	22
82 2/8	82 2/8		14 4/8	15 4/8	6 6/8	6 6/8	6 5/8	6 5/8	6 6/8	6 5/8	3 2/8	3 4/8	2 2/8	2 3/8	1975	Lake	Carl Tracy	22
82 2/8	80 0/8		15 2/8	15 7/8	5 1/8	5 0/8	6 0/8	6 1/8	6 5/8	6 5/8	4 3/8	4 3/8	2 7/8	2 6/8	1973	Grant	Lawrence Wolfgram	22
82 0/8	82 0/8	5 0/8	17 1/8	17 1/8	4 1/8	4 1/8	6 2/8	6 2/8	6 3/8	6 2/8	4 2/8	4 2/8	3 1/8	3 0/8	1994	Harney	Errol Claire	25
81 6/8	81 6/8	7 0/8	16 1/8	16 1/8	5 0/8	4 6/8	6 3/8	6 3/8	6 2/8	6 2/8	3 7/8	3 7/8	2 4/8	2 4/8		Crook	Russell Rhoden	26
81 2/8	81 2/8	11 6/8	16 3/8	16 4/8	5 1/8	5 6/8	6 3/8	6 3/8	6 3/8	6 3/8	4 3/8	4 3/8	2 4/8	2 5/8	1941	Lake	A.C. Elliot	27
81 2/8	80 4/8	14 5/8	15 6/8	15 0/8	5 5/8	5 5/8	6 3/8	6 2/8	6 6/8	6 6/8	4 0/8	4 0/8	2 5/8	2 5/8	1995	Lake	Bill Howard	27
81 0/8	78 6/8	5 0/8	16 7/8	16 7/8	6 3/8	5 0/8	5 6/8	5 4/8	6 2/8	6 1/8	3 4/8	3 3/8	2 4/8	2 4/8	1990	Malheur	Doug Schlatter	29
80 6/8	80 6/8	4 0/8	15 2/8	15 2/8	4 6/8	4 4/8	6 1/8	6 1/8	6 0/8	6 0/8	5 6/8	5 7/8	2 5/8	2 6/8	1993	Baker	Gary Wright	30
80 4/8	78 2/8	10 0/8	15 6/8	15 6/8	5 2/8	5 4/8	6 0/8	5 6/8	6 1/8	6 0/8	3 6/8	3 6/8	2 7/8	3 0/8	08/87	Baker	Adam Brooks	31
80 2/8	80 2/8	13 0/8	16 1/8	16 2/8	3 3/8	3 7/8	6 2/8	6 2/8	6 3/8	5 7/8	5 6/8	5 5/8	2 5/8	2 4/8	1988	Baker	Patrick M. Bruce	32
80 2/8	80 2/8	5 0/8	16 6/8	16 6/8	5 2/8	5 0/8	6 2/8	6 2/8	6 2/8	6 0/8	3 5/8	3 7/8	2 2/8	2 2/8	1994	Harney	Betty R. Vandyke	32
80 2/8	78 4/8	5 0/8	17 2/8	17 0/8	4 6/8	5 0/8	6 0/8	6 0/8	6 0/8	6 0/8	3 3/8	3 2/8	2 7/8	2 7/8	1990	Crook	Fred Robertson	32
80 2/8	78 4/8	2 0/8	16 6/8	16 0/8	5 0/8	5 4/8	6 1/8	6 0/8	5 5/8	5 6/8	3 6/8	4 0/8	2 3/8	2 4/8	1983	Harney	J.D. Beahm	32
80 2/8	78 0/8	8 6/8	15 4/8	15 5/8	5 4/8	5 4/8	6 0/8	6 4/8	6 2/8	6 2/8	3 3/8	3 4/8	2 3/8	2 4/8	1990	Lake	Rex Heard	32
80 0/8	80 0/8	8 4/8	15 2/8	15 3/8	6 0/8	5 7/8	6 3/8	5 7/8	6 5/8	6 5/8	3 4/8	3 5/8	2 3/8	2 3/8	1993	Harney	Rusty Lindberg	37
80 0/8	77 6/8	6 0/8	17 2/8	17 1/8	5 7/8	4 5/8	6 0/8	6 6/8	6 0/8	5 5/8	3 3/8	3 2/8	2 2/8	2 2/8	1963	Malheur	Keith Steele	37
80 0/8	77 6/8	11 6/8	15 4/8	15 6/8	5 1/8	5 2/8	6 6/8	7 0/8	6 0/8	6 0/8	3 3/8	3 3/8	2 2/8	2 2/8	1981	Harney	Terry Edmonson	37
80 0/8	77 6/8	12 6/8	15 0/8	14 7/8	4 1/8	4 2/8	7 2/8	7 0/8	6 6/8	6 5/8	4 0/8	3 6/8	2 5/8	2 4/8	1992	Harney	Bert DeVore	37

Rank	Name	County	Year	C1	C2	C3	C4	C5	C6	C7	C8	C9	C10	C11	C12	C13	Final Score	Adjusted Score
41	Tony Schillinger	Harney	1960	2 2/8	2 2/8	3 5/8	3 5/8	7 6/8	7 2/8	6 0/8	6 0/8	5 3/8	5 3/8	14 5/8	14 6/8	12 1/8	78 2/8	79 6/8
41	Melvin L. Wills	Harney	1993	2 4/8	2 3/8	3 4/8	3 4/8	7 2/8	7 3/8	7 1/8	7 2/8	4 6/8	4 3/8	14 2/8	14 1/8	10 1/8	78 4/8	79 6/8
41	Timothy A. Hamar	Harney	1990	3 0/8	3 0/8	3 6/8	3 7/8	6 2/8	5 7/8	6 7/8	6 7/8	4 7/8	5 1/8	14 5/8	14 3/8	13 7/8	77 4/8	79 6/8
44	Russell Higgins	Harney	1992	2 4/8	2 2/8	3 4/8	3 4/8	6 7/8	6 7/8	6 3/8	6 2/8	5 7/8	5 4/8	16 0/8	14 0/8		77 2/8	79 4/8
44	Karen Pierce	Harney	1989	2 2/8	2 1/8	3 3/8	3 3/8	6 6/8	6 7/8	6 4/8	6 3/8	5 2/8	5 3/8	14 5/8	14 6/8	7 4/8	77 2/8	79 4/8
46	Larry Boydston	Crook	1980	2 2/8	2 4/8	3 2/8	3 2/8	5 6/8	5 6/8	6 0/8	6 2/8	5 0/8	4 7/8	16 4/8	16 6/8	10 1/8	77 0/8	79 2/8
46	Karen Gale	Lake	1979	2 5/8	2 4/8	3 5/8	3 6/8	6 2/8	6 1/8	6 2/8	6 2/8	5 0/8	5 0/8	15 0/8	15 3/8		77 0/8	79 2/8
48	Ed Salani	Harney	1975	2 5/8	2 1/8	3 5/8	3 5/8	5 6/8	5 7/8	6 2/8	6 2/8	4 4/8	4 6/8	16 0/8	16 0/8	13 5/8	76 6/8	79 0/8
48	Ken Moore	Grant	1978	2 2/8	2 3/8	3 2/8	3 2/8	6 5/8	6 1/8	5 6/8	6 0/8	5 5/8	6 1/8	16 2/8	15 4/8		76 6/8	79 0/8
48	Shirlene Vanhorn	Lake	1992	2 3/8	2 4/8	3 4/8	3 4/8	5 6/8	5 6/8	6 1/8	6 0/8	4 5/8	4 4/8	16 6/8	16 1/8		76 6/8	79 0/8
51	Bill DeVore	Harney	1982	4 0/8	4 0/8	5 4/8	5 3/8	5 5/8	5 7/8	4 4/8	4 5/8	2 6/8	2 6/8	16 3/8	16 1/8	17 5/8	76 6/8	79 0/8
51	Linda Hettinger	Harney	1990	2 4/8	2 3/8	3 6/8	3 5/8	6 0/8	5 7/8	6 0/8	6 1/8	5 4/8	5 2/8	15 5/8	16 0/8	0 0/8	76 4/8	78 6/8
51	Roger L. Whiteman	Harney	1988	2 3/8	2 4/8	3 4/8	3 4/8	5 6/8	5 7/8	6 2/8	6 2/8	4 7/8	4 7/8	15 5/8	15 2/8	10 1/8	76 4/8	78 6/8
51	Don Long	Harney	1983	2 3/8	2 4/8	3 4/8	3 4/8	6 2/8	6 2/8	6 3/8	6 1/8	5 0/8	4 7/8	15 4/8	15 1/8	6 1/8	76 4/8	78 6/8
55	Stan Wickersham	Lake	1994	2 4/8	2 3/8	3 2/8	3 2/8	5 4/8	6 2/8	6 5/8	6 3/8	4 7/8	4 6/8	15 7/8	15 1/8	13 3/8	76 4/8	78 6/8
55	Mary Salisbury	Harney	1989	2 3/8	2 2/8	2 7/8	3 0/8	5 7/8	6 1/8	5 5/8	5 6/8	6 1/8	6 0/8	16 2/8	15 7/8	7 5/8	77 0/8	78 4/8
57	Bob Cox	Lake	1995	2 3/8	2 4/8	3 5/8	3 5/8	6 2/8	6 3/8	6 2/8	6 2/8	4 2/8	4 5/8	16 4/8	16 2/8	10 5/8	77 4/8	78 4/8
57	Don Metcalf	Harney	1994	2 1/8	2 3/8	3 0/8	3 0/8	6 1/8	6 4/8	6 2/8	6 1/8	5 7/8	5 4/8	15 4/8	15 4/8	11 4/8	76 6/8	78 2/8
57	Mary A. TJomsland	Harney	1991	2 3/8	2 1/8	3 3/8	3 2/8	6 0/8	6 0/8	6 2/8	6 2/8	5 2/8	5 3/8	14 7/8	14 7/8	10 1/8	76 0/8	78 2/8
60	Mike Cochran	Harney	1994	2 4/8	2 3/8	3 5/8	3 4/8	6 4/8	6 3/8	6 2/8	6 4/8	4 2/8	4 2/8	15 6/8	16 0/8		77 2/8	78 2/8
60	Wayne Lemley	Lake	1995	2 3/8	2 4/8	3 4/8	3 4/8	5 6/8	5 6/8	5 4/8	5 6/8	5 3/8	5 3/8	16 2/8	14 5/8	9 4/8	76 4/8	78 0/8
60	Dan Bernards	Lake	1994	2 3/8	2 3/8	3 2/8	3 2/8	6 3/8	6 2/8	6 0/8	6 1/8	5 5/8	5 5/8	14 5/8	15 3/8		76 2/8	78 0/8
60	Norman Stephens	Lake	1990	2 4/8	2 4/8	2 7/8	2 7/8	6 3/8	6 2/8	5 7/8	6 0/8	5 6/8	5 3/8	15 1/8	15 6/8	12 3/8	75 6/8	78 0/8
64	David M. Morris	Wheeler	1991	2 3/8	2 3/8	3 3/8	3 3/8	5 6/8	5 6/8	6 0/8	6 0/8	5 4/8	5 4/8	15 6/8	15 4/8	2 0/8	77 6/8	78 0/8
64	Harold Orr	Crook	1968	2 4/8	2 4/8	3 4/8	3 4/8	5 4/8	5 4/8	6 2/8	6 2/8	4 4/8	4 4/8	15 4/8	15 4/8	9 4/8	75 4/8	77 6/8
66	John Snyder	Klamath	1989	2 3/8	2 5/8	3 6/8	3 6/8	6 2/8	6 2/8	6 1/8	6 1/8	5 3/8	5 7/8	14 0/8	14 0/8	13 3/8	75 2/8	77 4/8
67	Toby Mills	Lake	1994	2 2/8	2 3/8	3 4/8	3 4/8	6 2/8	6 2/8	6 1/8	6 2/8	5 6/8	5 4/8	14 1/8	14 1/8	14 1/8	75 4/8	77 0/8
67	Hugh Stephens	Baker	1989	2 5/8	2 3/8	3 3/8	3 2/8	6 0/8	6 0/8	5 6/8	5 6/8	5 3/8	5 2/8	15 1/8	15 1/8	12 4/8	74 6/8	77 0/8
69	George Pace	Lake	1995	2 4/8	2 3/8	3 6/8	3 3/8	6 2/8	6 2/8	6 1/8	6 1/8	5 5/8	5 5/8	14 6/8	14 7/8	5 0/8	76 0/8	76 6/8
69	Don Loansbury	Harney	1993	2 1/8	2 4/8	3 1/8	3 1/8	5 7/8	5 7/8	6 4/8	6 4/8	4 5/8	4 6/8	15 1/8	15 1/8	15 0/8	75 2/8	76 6/8
69	Ted Simmon		1994	2 6/8	2 0/8	4 2/8	4 1/8	7 1/8	7 0/8	6 5/8	6 5/8	3 7/8	3 6/8	14 1/8	14 2/8	2 0/8	75 2/8	76 6/8
73	Verlin Mills	Lake	1992	2 1/8	2 6/8	3 7/8	3 7/8	5 4/8	5 5/8	5 6/8	5 6/8	4 0/8	4 2/8	15 7/8	15 7/8	15 6/8	74 2/8	76 4/8
74	Jason Radinovich	Malheur	1990	2 2/8	2 1/8	3 0/8	3 0/8	6 1/8	6 1/8	6 5/8	6 3/8	4 5/8	5 1/8	14 4/8	14 4/8	12 6/8	74 0/8	76 2/8
74	Joseph Mawhin	Malheur	1975	2 6/8	2 2/8	3 6/8	3 6/8	5 6/8	5 4/8	6 4/8	6 4/8	4 5/8	4 5/8	14 6/8	14 3/8	5 0/8	74 0/8	76 2/8
76	Laney Davidson	Lake	1989	2 0/8	2 0/8	3 0/8	2 7/8	5 4/8	5 3/8	5 4/8	5 4/8	5 0/8	5 0/8	16 1/8	16 1/8	9 6/8	73 6/8	76 0/8

*ADJUSTED SCORE = FINAL SCORE + SHRINKAGE

Pronghorn—Archery
Minimum Score: 64 0/8

Adjusted* Score	Final Score	Inside Spread	Length of Horn R	L	Length of Prong R	L	Base Circumference R	L	First Quarter Circumference R	L	Second Quarter Circumference R	L	Third Quarter Circumference R	L	Year	County	Hunter/Owner	Rank
90 0/8	90 0/8	11 0/8	16 5/8	17 2/8	6 5/8	6 4/8	7 1/8	7 2/8	7 3/8	7 3/8	4 4/8	4 3/8	3 0/8	3 0/8	1994	Lake	Roger Clarno	1
80 6/8	80 6/8	9 4/8	15 3/8	15 6/8	4 4/8	4 4/8	7 4/8	7 3/8	6 6/8	6 6/8	3 7/8	4 0/8	2 4/8	2 5/8	1994	Lake	Brian Day	2
76 0/8	76 0/8	8 3/8	13 5/8	13 3/8	5 4/8	5 3/8	6 4/8	6 2/8	6 5/8	6 4/8	4 5/8	4 2/8	2 4/8	2 2/8	1993	Jefferson	Clinton J. Hall	3
75 6/8	75 6/8	12 4/8	15 2/8	15 3/8	4 4/8	4 4/8	6 1/8	6 1/8	5 7/8	5 7/8	3 7/8	3 6/8	2 4/8	2 3/8	1990	Harney	Gary Nyden	4
75 2/8	75 2/8	9 1/8	15 4/8	16 1/8	4 7/8	5 0/8	5 7/8	5 5/8	5 5/8	5 6/8	3 6/8	3 7/8	2 2/8	2 4/8	1990	Harney	Stanley Miles	5
74 4/8	73 0/8	6 6/8	13 4/8	13 1/8	5 0/8	4 7/8	6 2/8	6 1/8	6 2/8	6 1/8	3 6/8	3 6/8	2 4/8	2 4/8	1995	Lake	Greg Cole	6
73 4/8	73 4/8	10 4/8	14 1/8	14 7/8	5 4/8	5 1/8	6 2/8	6 0/8	6 1/8	5 6/8	3 3/8	3 3/8	2 3/8	2 4/8	1994	Harney	Patrick Wheeler	7
73 4/8	71 2/8	24 0/8	17 4/8	15 0/8	5 4/8	3 7/8	7 4/8	6 0/8	6 4/8	5 6/8	4 0/8	3 0/8	3 2/8	2 0/8	1993	Lane	Dennis Abeene	7
72 6/8	72 6/8	8 6/8	13 0/8	13 1/8	5 4/8	5 4/8	6 0/8	5 5/8	6 0/8	6 0/8	3 4/8	3 4/8	2 3/8	2 3/8	1984	Klamath	David M. Morris	9
72 2/8	70 0/8	12 5/8	14 6/8	14 6/8	5 2/8	4 3/8	6 0/8	5 6/8	5 6/8	5 3/8	2 7/8	3 0/8	2 0/8	2 2/8	1992	Harney	Greg Buhr	10
72 0/8	72 0/8	14 6/8	13 7/8	13 7/8	4 6/8	5 0/8	5 7/8	5 6/8	5 5/8	5 4/8	4 0/8	3 7/8	2 2/8	2 2/8	1991	Crook	Clinton J. Hall	11
68 2/8	68 2/8	12 7/8	13 0/8	12 7/8	4 6/8	4 1/8	6 0/8	6 0/8	6 0/8	5 5/8	3 2/8	3 2/8	2 2/8	2 2/8	1994	Lake	Mark Penninger	12

*ADJUSTED SCORE = FINAL + SHRINKAGE

Pronghorn—Black Powder
Minimum Score: 63 0/8

Adjusted* Score	Final Score	Inside Spread	Length of Horn R	L	Length of Prong R	L	Base Circumference R	L	First Quarter Circumference R	L	Second Quarter Circumference R	L	Third Quarter Circumference R	L	Year	County	Hunter/Owner	Rank
81 2/8	81 2/8	13 2/8	17 1/8	17 2/8	5 5/8	5 7/8	6 3/8	6 3/8	6 1/8	6 3/8	3 1/8	3 0/8	2 3/8	2 3/8	1995	Klamath	Jim Baley	1

*ADJUSTED SCORE = FINAL + SHRINKAGE

Official Scoring System for Oregon Big Game Trophies

Records of Oregon
Big Game

RECORD BOOK FOR OREGON

P.O. Box 759
Irrigon, OR 97844

PRONGHORN

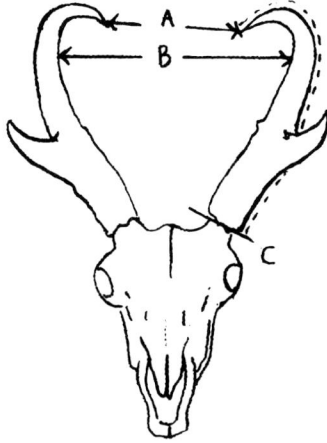

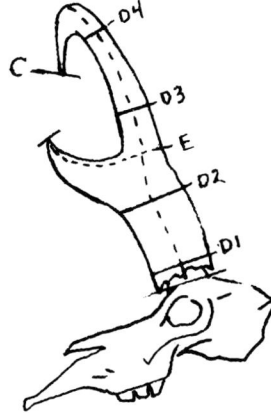

Species	Rifle	Archery	Muzzle
Pronghorn	76	64	63

			COLUMN 1	COLUMN 2	COLUMN 3
			Right Horn	Left Horn	Difference
A	Tip to Tip Spread	6 0/8			
B	**Inside Spread of Main Beams**	11 0/8			
C	Length of Horn		16 5/8	17 2/8	0 5/8
D-1	Circumference of Base		7 1/8	7 2/8	0 1/8
D-2	Circumference at First Quarter		7 3/8	7 3/8	0 0/8
D-3	Circumference at Second Quarter		4 4/8	4 3/8	0 1/8
D-4	Circumference at Third Quarter		3 0/8	3 0/8	0 0/8
E	Length of Prong		6 5/8	6 4/8	0 1/8
		TOTALS	45 2/8	45 6/8	1 0/8

County where killed: Lake Date Killed: 1994	**ADD**	Column 1	45 2/8
Hunter's First Name: Roger Last Name: Clarno		Column 2	45 6/8
Owner's First Name: Roger Last Name: Clarno		Subtotal	91 0/8
		Subtract Column 3	1 0/8
		FINAL SCORE	90 0/8

1995 Antelope Buck (#1 Black Powder)

by Jim Baley

After scouting the entire unit, I decided to hunt in one particular area where I had seen two real nice bucks plus several good bucks. I hunted these bucks for three days, never getting a chance to outsmart the larger of the two; "Old Loner" was always by himself in a remote area.

However, I did get the opportunity to pursue "Big Boy," the other large buck. He was with approximately twenty-five does and I found it extremely tough to get close to him. After four and a half hours of crawling, lying up and crawling some more in six- to twelve-inch brush and scab rock, I finally got him to the outside of the bedded herd. I guessed him to be one hundred and twenty to one hundred and thirty yards away, placed the sights just above the shoulder and shot, only to find out I had been hit with a horrible case of "yardage misjudgment." Bye-bye, Big Boy! I stepped the distance off at sixty-five yards. Discouraged, I headed home to curse myself and to let the prairie goats settle down.

When I returned later, I brought two good buddies, my seven-year-old son Jake and nine-year-old nephew Jesse. We arrived about 4 p.m. and started glassing. These boys were decked out in full camo gear including full face paint—I passed on the face color this time.

We glassed Old Loner's country first, but there were no sightings. I asked the boys if they wanted to walk another three-quarters of a mile to the next glassing area. "You bet! Let's go!" was their response. We then walked up to a big flat rock and sat down, looking like three pigeons on a highwire. From there we began to glass. Then Jesse gave me a big elbow in the ribs and said, "Hey, Hey, look!" I looked up to see six does and a buck coming in our direction. However, as I spotted them, they spotted us and stopped.

I didn't recognize the buck as one I had seen, and when he turned his head, I saw the long horns coming more forward out of the skull and then upwards. There wasn't much time to think. I raised the 50 caliber to my shoulder, remem-

bered my previous overshot on Big Boy, placed the peep on the buck's lower body behind the shoulders and let loose. While the smoke was clearing and I was reloading, the boys said that the buck was running funny. I looked to see that the does were running with level heads, but the buck was bobbing his head up and down, no blood at all. Jesse and Jake looked to me and said, "You would have gotten him if your face was painted." Darkness fell upon us and we started on our long drive back home.

In the morning the boys stayed home, but I had to go back and look again. I walked into the area and started searching for blood, bone or antelope, but there was nothing to be seen. I kept walking in the direction that we had last seen the antelope heading. Then a racket came from under a juniper tree I was nearing. It was the buck. I had hit him in the left lower leg and shot his foot off. Now the chase was on. If he had had four good legs, I would never have caught him. Three and a half hours and three miles later, he finally stopped long enough and close enough for a shot. I found a good rock for a rest and aimed where I wanted to hit him. He went down.

It had to be the face paint I had put on at 4 a.m. on the drive over. I wish the boys had come along to help with their buck.
(Final score: 81 2/8 B.C.)

Blacktail Deer

The Columbian Blacktailed Deer in Oregon

by H.R. Sturgis, Jr.

The Columbian blacktailed deer, *Odocoileus hemionus columbianus*, is one of seven subspecies of mule deer found in North America, and is the only blacktailed deer occurring in Oregon. A similar subspecies, the Sitka blacktailed deer, *O. h. sitkensis*, inhabits southeastern Alaska and the north coast of British Columbia. The name "blacktailed deer" originated with early explorers of the West, who first gave the name to the animal we know now as the Rocky Mountain mule deer, conveniently differentiating the animal from the whitetailed deer of the East. (The name "mule deer" derives from "mule-eared deer," another term coined by early explorers.) For the purpose of this discussion, the writer will, to the probable dismay of wildlife scientists worldwide, use the convenient and widely accepted "blacktail."

The ranges of the blacktail and the Rocky Mountain mule deer meet essentially only along the summit of the Cascade Mountains, and the likelihood of observing the two together in most blacktail range is remote. In western Oregon the blacktail and the whitetail occur together, however, in the Umpqua valley near Roseburg and along the lower Columbia River in Clatsop and Columbia counties. Reports of whitetails in areas outside their known western Oregon ranges are relatively common, but most of these reports actually involve blacktail bucks bearing three-point antlers resembling those of the whitetail, single points growing from a main beam. There is very little difference between the two points growing from a main beam in the whitetail and a forward fork and single rear tine in the three-point blacktail. There are more reliable identifying characteristics.

The facial features in the whitetail are similar in both sexes, featuring a white ring at the nose and white eye-rings. Blacktails lack the distinctive eye-rings. Also, in their winter pelage, blacktail bucks have a dark cap above the eyes, and between the muzzle and the eyes the face is whitish, becoming almost pure white in older bucks. The ears of the whitetail are short. The tail of the whitetail is longer and wider than that of the blacktail, light brown on the upper surface, and fringed with white. In contrast, the tail of the blacktail is dark brownish-black, shading to pure black near the tip. The metatarsal glands, which lie under those tufts of hair on the outside of the hind leg halfway between the hock and foot, differ in length, measuring less than 1.65 inches in the whitetail, and more than 2.75 inches in the blacktail.

Blacktails are distributed throughout western Oregon west of the summit of the Cascade Mountains, and east nearly to Klamath Falls in the southern part of the state. They live in abundance where cover is adequate in the Willamette, Umpqua and Rogue valleys, and are permanent residents within the city limits of all of western Oregon's major population centers.

Many deer that summer at higher elevations in the Cascades exhibit a combination of blacktail and mule deer characteristics that causes many observers to consider them "hybrids," an intergrade between the typical blacktail and the Rocky Mountain mule deer. The principal feature identifying these deer is a black stripe running the length of a tail that is otherwise more mule deer than blacktail in appearance. According to Oregon Department of Fish and Wildlife biologists, this characteristic is confined to deer of the Cascades and is seen only rarely on stragglers in winter ranges further east. It is seldom seen in the southern Cascades, where the typical blacktail is found throughout.

Blacktails in the Coast Range are essentially not migratory, occupying the same range the year around, with short movements to lower elevations in some areas to avoid the occasional deep snowfall. In the Cascades, there is a predictable annual movement west to lower elevations with the coming of winter snow. These are relatively short movements of a few miles in most areas, a major exception being in extreme southern

Oregon, where biologists report movements of up to forty-five miles from summer to winter range. The so-called hybrids of the high Cascades typically migrate to lower elevations on the east slope.

Blacktails are adapted to virtually every terrestrial habitat in the western portion of the state. They are creatures of disturbed environments, most numerous on forest land where wildfires or timber harvests have created openings that produce abundant forage, in major riparian areas and woodlots in farmland within the large interior valleys and along foothill edges where there is interfingering of forest and farmland.

Blacktails prefer to feed year round on green leafy material, when available. Throughout much of western Oregon, grasses, herbaceous plants and the leaves and tender twigs of trailing blackberry, red huckleberry, salal, thimbleberry, salmonberry and vine maple make up most of the annual diet. Acorns, wedgeleaf ceanothus and blueblossom are important foods in the southern portion of their range, where vegetation types differ from the rest of the west side.

Private and public forest lands have provided the access and habitat that have been the backbone of deer hunting through the years. Logging or fire provides a fertile, open site that will produce abundant forage for several years, contributing to rapid increases in deer numbers and providing good hunting. But such a habitat and the good hunting that goes with it are temporary. Conifer regeneration occupies the land within a few years and soon shades out all low-growing vegetation, creating an environment with virtually no capacity to support deer. Thus, the pattern of deer habitat on forest land continuously changes, following timber harvest and the occasional fire.

Breeding in blacktails can happen from late October to early December, but much of the breeding is done around the third week of November, according to reproductive studies. After a gestation period averaging one hundred and ninety-eight days, fawns are born any time from April through July, with the peak of fawning oc-

curring during the first week of June. Fawns born of healthy does weigh about seven pounds. Following a severe winter, fawns may weigh as little as five to six pounds at birth and face an uphill struggle to survive the first several weeks of life. The sex ratio at birth is about forty-six percent females to fifty-four percent males; this preponderance of males is found in other members of the deer family, as well. This early imbalance tips before long to favor the female, however, for males in deer population have a shorter life expectancy than females.

Blacktail does normally breed for the first time at about sixteen months of age and bear a single fawn at age two. For the rest of their breeding lives, does tend to bear twins each spring. Triplets are occasionally seen.

The spring fawn crop will average somewhat more than one fawn for every breeding doe, as the number of first-time breeders bearing only a single fawn is relatively high in a normal population. Loss of fawns due to natural factors is high, however, and it is likely that no more than forty to fifty percent of fawns born will survive to the age of one. So, while a deer herd tends to increase by as much as thirty-five percent each spring, the many factors that act on wild populations, such as accidents, predation, parasites, disease, malnutrition and hunting, combine during the year to limit this potential increase.

Age determinations for six hundred deer taken by hunters in the Alsea management unit during 1984 and 1985 hunting seasons revealed that eighty percent of the deer taken were younger than four years of age. With the exception of one doe that had lived to age twenty, the remaining twenty percent ranged in age from four to twelve years. Only thirteen of the six hundred animals had lived to age ten or older. Obviously the blacktail is a short-lived animal.

Where the habitat is favorable, blacktail numbers can be surprisingly high, but the abundant cover typical of blacktail country and their nocturnal behavior make estimating their true numbers difficult. In the course of a study of blacktails done by the Oregon Department of Fish and Wildlife in the Tillamook burn during the late 1950s, a three-hundred-and-forty-acre deer-proof enclosure was constructed in Cedar Creek, a tributary of Wilson River. The habitat was relatively open, post-burn vegetation, rich in forage plants preferred by deer. Following completion of the fence, it was learned that forty-seven deer had been enclosed. No effort had been made during

The body size and antler growth achieved by blacktails varies greatly throughout their range. Although two world-record heads were taken in the Coast Range, it is nevertheless probably safe to state that the west slope of the Cascades produces bucks of larger average body size and antler growth. The mountainous area from Crater Lake south to the California line is well known for

Fifteen-month-old buck: 205 pounds liveweight

construction either to trap deer or haze them out of the enclosure, and it seems reasonable to assume that the number of deer enclosed represented the naturally occurring population density, that is, about eighty-eight deer per square mile. In a similar situation in Coos County, within an enclosure of more than four hundred acres constructed as part of a study of Roosevelt elk, the deer density was at least forty per square mile. During the 1970 hunting season on Oregon State University's MacDonald Forest near Corvallis, six hundred and eight deer were taken from an area approximately twenty miles square, about thirty deer *harvested* per square mile.

large bucks that grow exceptional antlers, although one is likely to find a better-than-average buck almost anywhere in the Cascades.

Body size and antler growth are largely determined by the access to adequate year-round nutrition. A study designed to develop supplementary rations for deer during emergency winters, conducted during the 1970s by an Oregon State University researcher, produced convincing evidence of this. The deer used in the feeding trials had been taken from the wild as fawns by well-meaning citizens and were collected at the E.E. Wilson wildlife area near Corvallis. Since the deer were taken at random as "abandoned" fawns from many different areas of northwest Oregon, it seems safe to assume that there was little possibility of bias toward unusual antler growth in the group chosen for the experiment. The deer were fed nutritionally complete diets through their first winter and to midsummer of their second year, when the project ended and the deer were released into the wild. At about fifteen months of age, six of the bucks carried small three- or four-point antlers. A typical yearling buck in the wild in the Coast Range will bear spikes three to five inches long. Another buck used in this study is shown in the accompanying photograph (see page 157). This buck weighed two hundred and five pounds live weight at age one, twice as heavy as one would expect a wild yearling buck taken in the fall to be. The antlers grown by this buck at fifteen months of age are of a size one would expect to see on a three- to five-year-old buck in the wild.

No Other Way

by Dennis King

In late October of 1970, my hunting companion Charley Spencer and I were doing some spotting scope work between rainstorms in the Little Applegate drainage of southwestern Oregon, when we spotted a lone blacktail buck on an open ridgetop a thousand yards almost straight up. After fighting the brush for nearly two hours, we finally reached the edge of the clearing but could not find the deer. After some searching we discovered he had vacated the area via a deer trail a couple of ridges beyond the ridge we took to get up to the clearing.

We repeated this same scenario three days later, after spotting him from exactly the same place as before. Another two hours struggling up the steep, brushy route brought us to his tracks, which were again going down that same ridge.

The pressure was on as we brainstormed ways to get close enough to get a shot. After a good night's rest we decided to attack the ridge at daylight the next morning, hoping the deer would be in exactly the same place as before.

Dawn brought a "frog strangler" of a rainstorm in which you could only see for a couple hundred yards. The plan was for Charley to go up exactly as we had done before, while I opted to try the "escape trail" ridge. After fighting brush for an hour, I finally found a deer trail going up toward the clearing. The only problem was, deer are one half the height we are and when the trail went under manzanita brush I had to get down on my hands and knees and crawl. Needless to say, in a short time I was a miserable wet muddy mess!

Still a couple hundred yards from the clearing, I again encountered one of these crawl-on-your-hands-and-knees tunnels. After crawling for twenty to thirty feet I heard a shot that sounded really close. Assuming that it was Charley, and that he might have gotten the buck, I stood up in the only place I could and breathed a sigh of relief. Then the brush started popping uphill from me! Crouching back down and looking up the tunnel, I heard more brush break. Suddenly a deer was barreling down the trail directly at me! I couldn't get the rifle to my shoulder because of the confining brush, so I more or less sighted down the barrel as he went by at five or ten feet. The .30-06 went off and he was gone. I could hear him going for quite a while so I was afraid I had missed him completely or, worse, hit him badly. I was feeling kind of sick about the whole thing when Charley yelled at me from ahead in the clearing. I went on up to him and we stood for a while discussing the situation. Evidently Charley had gotten close enough to the deer to see him through the rain and mist. He took an offhand shot at him as the buck was moving off and about to enter the brush. At the sound of the shot the deer took off and almost immediately Charley heard me shoot.

We both slipped and slid down through the deer tunnels to where I had shot. Following the muddy, splayed tracks was very easy and within

a few yards I found a pretty good smear of blood on a dead manzanita tree. A little further more blood, then more, more and all of a sudden there he was!

After some congratulations and back slapping, we stood there wondering how we were going to get him and ourselves out of this jungle. About three hours later we were standing in the road with Mr. Buck in tow.

Back at my shop we pulled him inside and started cleaning the mud, blood and gore off of both him and us. This was the first time we slowed down long enough to actually take a good look at the deer. He was extra large for a blacktail and in proportion the antlers didn't appear abnormally large.

Looking back after a quarter century of trying to outwit blacktails, it seems to me we had some extraordinary luck that day. Over the course of all these years, out of several hundred attempts to outwit large blacktail deer, I won four or five; the deer won all the rest. But then I guess we really wouldn't have it any other way. (Final score: 171 7/8 B.C.)

Official Scoring System for Oregon Big Game Trophies

TYPICAL
MULE AND BLACKTAIL DEER

DETAIL OF POINT MEASUREMENT

Abnormal Points	
Right Antler	Left Antler
0 0/8	0 0/8
0 0/8	0 0/8
0 0/8	0 0/8
0 0/8	0 0/8
0 0/8	0 0/8
0 0/8	0 0/8
0 0/8	0 0/8
0 0/8	0 0/8
0 0/8	0 0/8
0 0/8	0 0/8
Subtotals 0 0/8	0 0/8
Total to E	0 0/8

Species	Rifle	Archery	Muzzle	Shed	Archery - Velvet
Mule Deer	160	145	146	70	145
Columbia Blacktail	115	90	110	50	90
Cascade Blacktail	115	90	110	50	90
Northwest Blacktail	115	90	110	50	90

					COLUMN 1	COLUMN 2	COLUMN 3	COLUMN 4
					Spread Credit	Right Antler	Left Antler	Difference
A	Number of Points on Right Antler	5	Number of Points on Left Antler	5				
B	Tip to Tip Spread	8 0/8	C Greatest Spread	22 5/8				
D	Inside Spread of Main Beam	20 5/8	(Credit may be equal to but not exceed longer antler)	20 5/8				
E	Total of Length of Abnormal Points							0 0/8
F	Length of Main Beam					26 4/8	26 4/8	0 0/8
G-1	Length of First Point, if present					2 6/8	2 4/8	0 2/8
G-2	Length of Second Point					14 2/8	13 0/8	1 2/8
G-3	Length of Third Point, if present					8 5/8	8 0/8	0 5/8
G-4	Length of Fourth Point, if present					11 2/8	9 7/8	1 3/8
H-1	Circumference at smallest place between burr and first point					4 5/8	4 6/8	0 1/8
H-2	Circumference at smallest place between first and second point					4 0/8	4 0/8	0 0/8
H-3	Circumference at smallest place between main beam and 3rd pt					3 3/8	3 2/8	0 1/8
H-4	Circumference at smallest place between second and fourth points					4 0/8	3 7/8	0 1/8
				TOTALS	20 5/8	79 3/8	75 6/8	3 7/8

County where killed: Jackson	**Date Killed:** 10/70	**Column 1**	20 5/8
Hunter's Name: Dennis King	**ADD**	**Column 2**	79 3/8
Owner's Name: Dennis King		**Column 3**	75 6/8
		Subtotal	175 6/8
		Subtract Column 4	3 7/8
		FINAL SCORE	**171 7/8**

Typical Columbian Blacktail—Rifle
Minimum Score: 115 0/8

Final Score	Gross Typical	Net Typical	Abnormal Points	Greatest Spread	Inside Spread	Main Beam R	Main Beam L	Number of Points R	Number of Points L	First Circumference R	First Circumference L	Year	County	Hunter/Owner	Rank
171 7/8	175 6/8	171 7/8	0/8	22 5/8	20 5/8	26 4/8	26 4/8	5	5	4 5/8	4 6/8	1970	Jackson	Dennis King	1
170 0/8	174 1/8	170 0/8	0/8	22 4/8	20 2/8	23 2/8	24 0/8	5	5	4 3/8	4 3/8	1989	Jackson	Wayne Despain	2
169 5/8	172 7/8	169 5/8	0/8		18 7/8	24 2/8	23 6/8	5	5	4 6/8	4 6/8	1953	Jackson	Fred Bean/Riley Bean	3
169 0/8	173 3/8	169 0/8	0/8	25 6/8	23 4/8	25 1/8	24 0/8	5	5	5 5/8	5 4/8	1956	Jackson	Fred Bean	4
167 0/8	169 3/8	167 0/8	0/8	20 7/8	19 0/8	24 1/8	24 4/8	5	5	4 6/8	4 7/8	1940	Jackson	Fred Bean	5
163 6/8	167 1/8	163 6/8	0/8	22 3/8	18 0/8	22 3/8	21 4/8	5	5	5 0/8	5 0/8	1984	Jackson	Don Spence	6
159 5/8	183 5/8	179 3/8	19 6/8	25 4/8	20 7/8	23 6/8	24 6/8	11	12	5 1/8	5 2/8	1900	Jackson	James Ball/Robert Suttles	7
159 2/8	162 0/8	159 2/8	0/8	24 4/8	19 4/8	22 4/8	22 7/8	5	5	4 4/8	4 4/8	1979	Josephine	Wayne Despain	8
157 2/8	160 3/8	157 2/8	0/8	23 0/8	19 4/8	21 6/8	20 5/8	5	5	4 5/8	4 5/8	1946	Josephine	Fred Bean/Riley Bean	9
157 1/8	169 5/8	164 7/8	7 6/8	24 7/8	20 7/8	22 1/8	23 1/8	7	6	4 5/8	4 5/8	1947	Jackson	Fred Bean	10
150 4/8	159 7/8	153 6/8	3 2/8	21 6/8	19 4/8	24 5/8	24 0/8	6	6	4 3/8	4 5/8	1982	Jackson	Sonny Loomis	11
149 7/8	162 6/8	154 0/8	4 1/8		20 6/8	22 0/8	24 1/8	6	5	4 6/8	4 6/8	1973	Jackson	Fred Bean/Riley Bean	12
149 6/8	156 3/8	149 6/8	0/8	25 0/8	21 2/8	21 4/8	22 4/8	5	4	4 4/8	4 6/8	1960	Josephine	Fred Bean	13
149 2/8	159 5/8	151 3/8	2 1/8	20 6/8	17 5/8	22 6/8	22 4/8	6	6	4 4/8	4 4/8	1986	Polk	John Williams	14
148 3/8	161 3/8	157 4/8	9 1/8	20 7/8	16 4/8	21 7/8	23 0/8	6	7	5 4/8	5 3/8	1989	Douglas	Andy Adams	15
148 0/8	152 3/8	148 0/8	0/8	20 4/8	17 4/8	21 7/8	20 0/8	5	5	3 6/8	3 5/8	1981	Douglas	Joe Adams	16
147 1/8	153 1/8	149 5/8	2 4/8	19 6/8	17 3/8	22 0/8	21 2/8	5	4	4 5/8	4 7/8	1995	Jackson	Robert J. Rhodes	17
145 3/8	150 1/8	145 3/8	0/8	20 2/8	18 1/8	22 5/8	23 4/8	5	4	3 5/8	3 6/8	1993	Douglas	Paul Goodson/Daren Jones	18
144 7/8	160 5/8	146 0/8	11 1/8	24 0/8	21 0/8	25 4/8	25 0/8	6	4	5 1/8	5 0/8	1971	Jackson	Riley Bean	19
144 5/8	148 4/8	144 5/8	0/8	20 6/8	17 1/8	21 7/8	21 6/8	5	5	4 0/8	4 0/8	1974	Josephine	Bob Wolfe	20
144 3/8	148 0/8	144 3/8	0/8	19 4/8	17 7/8	22 2/8	22 3/8	5	5	4 6/8	4 5/8	1994	Douglas	Daren Jones	21
144 3/8	148 6/8	144 3/8	0/8	20 4/8	18 3/8	22 4/8	21 4/8	5	5	4 0/8	4 1/8	1991	Jackson	Layne Bettingfield	21
144 3/8	149 3/8	144 3/8	0/8	21 5/8	16 7/8	19 3/8	18 5/8	5	5	4 2/8	4 2/8	1995	Yamhill	Robert Brown	21
144 2/8	151 4/8	148 2/8	4 0/8	26 2/8	20 3/8	20 2/8	19 6/8	6	5	3 6/8	3 6/8	1975	Josephine	Clinton Moore	24
143 7/8	151 6/8	148 4/8	4 5/8	21 4/8	17 6/8	20 6/8	20 6/8	6	6	5 2/8	5 0/8	1992	Douglas	Daren Jones	25
143 2/8	158 0/8	143 2/8	0/8	19 5/8	17 0/8	25 0/8	23 0/8	5	3	4 6/8	4 4/8	1941	Jackson	Fred Bean	26
143 2/8	146 2/8	143 2/8	0/8	22 0/8	18 6/8	20 2/8	20 4/8	5	5	4 5/8	4 5/8	1972	Jackson	Riley Bean	26
143 1/8	148 3/8	144 2/8	1 1/8	18 3/8	15 0/8	19 0/8	19 1/8	6	5	5 0/8	5 0/8	1976	Jackson	Max Adams	28
143 0/8	145 0/8	143 0/8	0/8	20 4/8	18 0/8	22 3/8	22 3/8	4	4	4 2/8	4 2/8	1956	Josephine	Riley Bean	29
142 2/8	149 3/8	142 2/8	0/8	23 1/8	19 2/8	22 4/8	22 1/8	5	5	4 1/8	4 2/8	1992	Jackson	Gary Gooden	30
142 1/8	144 7/8	142 1/8	0/8	19 4/8	16 3/8	21 3/8	21 3/8	5	5	4 4/8	4 3/8		Lane	Bill Jordan	31
141 3/8	144 6/8	141 3/8	0/8	19 3/8	17 5/8	22 4/8	22 3/8	5	5	4 4/8	4 4/8	1989	Douglas	Dave Milton	32
141 2/8	150 0/8	147 0/8	5 6/8	22 3/8	19 0/8	20 1/8	20 3/8	5	7	4 6/8	5 2/8		Douglas	Bill Whitlatch	33
141 2/8	143 7/8	141 2/8	0/8	18 4/8	16 0/8	22 0/8	21 2/8	5	5	3 6/8	3 7/8	1993	Douglas	Jeff Moore	33
140 2/8	154 0/8	146 1/8	5 7/8	23 5/8	19 7/8	22 6/8	23 0/8	6	6	4 7/8	5 0/8	1936	Josephine	Fred Bean	35
140 2/8	145 7/8	140 2/8	0/8	23 2/8	19 0/8	21 6/8	20 6/8	5	5	4 0/8	4 0/8	1986	Jackson	Doug McKinley	35
140 0/8	143 0/8	140 0/8	0/8	21 0/8	17 6/8	23 1/8	24 1/8	4	4	4 0/8	4 0/8	1967	Jackson	Riley Bean	37
140 0/8	143 1/8	140 0/8	0/8	22 0/8	19 0/8	20 5/8	21 3/8	5	5	5 0/8	4 7/8	1991	Linn	Dan Magee	37
139 4/8	154 6/8	146 0/8	6 4/8	29 6/8	19 4/8	20 7/8	22 3/8	6	7	4 7/8	4 5/8	1985	Jackson	Everett Music	39
139 3/8	141 4/8	139 3/8	0/8	21 0/8	19 1/8	23 0/8	23 0/8	4	4	4 5/8	4 7/8	1963	Douglas	Kid Harvey/Ed Harvey	40

Typical Columbian Blacktail—Rifle (continued)

Final Score	Gross Typical	Net Typical	Abnormal Points	Greatest Spread	Inside Spread	Main Beam R	Main Beam L	Number of Points R	Number of Points L	First Circumference R	First Circumference L	Year	County	Hunter/Owner	Rank
139 1/8	142 5/8	139 1/8	0 0/8	20 0/8	16 1/8	21 0/8	21 5/8	5	5	4 1/8	4 1/8	1993	Jackson	Gary Godden	41
139 0/8	156 3/8	147 5/8	8 5/8	23 2/8	19 5/8	23 5/8	23 0/8	6	7	4 7/8	4 7/8	1974	Jackson	Fred Bean/Riley Bean	42
138 3/8	141 3/8	138 3/8	0 0/8	20 4/8	18 5/8	21 0/8	21 7/8	5	5	4 3/8	4 5/8	1980	Douglas	Doug Dozhier	43
138 0/8	139 7/8	138 0/8	0 0/8	21 4/8	19 4/8	19 7/8	20 3/8	4	4	4 4/8	4 7/8	1992	Jackson	Chris Bandle	44
138 0/8	145 6/8	139 7/8	1 7/8	19 5/8	16 7/8	19 6/8	19 6/8	5	6	4 6/8	4 5/8	1948	Douglas	Will H. Brown	44
137 5/8	144 5/8	137 5/8	0 0/8	23 2/8	21 3/8	22 2/8	21 5/8	4	5	4 0/8	4 3/8	1959	Jackson	Donald L. Phillips, Jr.	46
137 3/8	143 7/8	137 3/8	0 0/8	17 2/8	15 1/8	21 0/8	21 3/8	5	5	4 2/8	4 2/8	1995	Jackson	Steve Hoffman	47
137 2/8	141 2/8	137 2/8	0 0/8	19 5/8	17 4/8	22 1/8	23 2/8	4	4	4 7/8	5 0/8	1995	Linn	Dan Magee	48
137 1/8	140 5/8	137 1/8	0 0/8	22 2/8	19 3/8	19 5/8	19 3/8	5	5	4 4/8	4 4/8	1992	Douglas	Eric Long	49
136 6/8	145 1/8	136 6/8	0 0/8	16 2/8	14 4/8	22 3/8	22 3/8	5	5	4 4/8	4 1/8	1981	Polk	Phil Kiebs	50
136 4/8	140 5/8	136 4/8	0 0/8	20 6/8	18 6/8	19 4/8	19 4/8	5	5	4 3/8	4 3/8	1970	Josephine	Richard Berry	51
136 2/8	141 7/8	136 2/8	0 0/8	22 0/8	17 4/8	20 5/8	18 5/8	5	5	3 6/8	3 5/8	1995	Douglas	Bob T. Jomsland	52
136 2/8	142 2/8	138 4/8	2 2/8	22 5/8	16 2/8	19 5/8	20 1/8	6	6	4 0/8	3 7/8	1974	Jackson	Dick France	52
135 6/8	141 1/8	137 7/8	2 1/8	17 1/8	14 5/8	21 3/8	21 0/8	5	6	3 7/8	4 0/8	1994	Linn	Brady Potter	54
135 4/8	143 5/8	137 4/8	1 6/8	21 6/8	16 4/8	18 4/8	19 1/8	5	6	5 2/8	5 3/8	1977	Linn	Joel B. Care	54
135 4/8	140 2/8	135 4/8	0 0/8	19 5/8	16 0/8	18 1/8	19 4/8	5	5	4 4/8	4 2/8	1995	Douglas	Nick Parker	56
135 3/8	142 0/8	135 3/8	0 0/8	19 6/8	15 3/8	18 7/8	16 2/8	5	5	3 6/8	3 7/8	1956	Josephine	Fred Bean	57
135 3/8	142 4/8	135 3/8	0 0/8	20 1/8	17 3/8	21 7/8	22 6/8	5	5	4 2/8	4 3/8	1980	Linn	Kelly Spencer/Myrrle Spencer	57
135 2/8	146 4/8	136 4/8	1 2/8	16 6/8	14 6/8	23 1/8	22 5/8	4	5	4 5/8	4 3/8	1990	Linn	David Oleman	59
135 1/8	147 1/8	140 0/8	4 7/8	21 4/8	16 4/8	19 6/8	17 5/8	5	7	4 0/8	3 7/8	1959	Jackson	Fred Bean	60
134 4/8	140 0/8	137 5/8	3 1/8	23 4/8	17 7/8	22 3/8	22 1/8	4	5	4 1/8	4 0/8	1982	Jackson	Richard Wright	61
133 7/8	146 0/8	143 0/8	9 1/8	20 0/8	15 2/8	20 0/8	20 4/8	6	6	4 0/8	4 1/8	1969	Douglas	Jeffery J. Muttens	62
133 7/8	135 0/8	133 7/8	0 0/8	18 4/8	16 3/8	21 7/8	21 7/8	4	4	4 7/8	5 0/8	1985	Lane	Delbert Bates	62
133 4/8	137 6/8	133 4/8	0 0/8	19 3/8	15 6/8	19 3/8	20 1/8	5	5	4 5/8	4 4/8	1962	Lane	Bill Jordan	64
133 3/8	143 5/8	134 5/8	1 2/8	19 1/8	15 5/8	20 5/8	22 2/8	5	5	5 1/8	5 0/8	1986	Lane	Sid Hammer	65
133 0/8	136 1/8	133 0/8	0 0/8	22 1/8	20 7/8	20 4/8	19 3/8	4	4	4 7/8	4 6/8	1970	Jackson	Riley Bean	66
132 4/8	143 3/8	134 6/8	2 2/8	17 1/8	15 0/8	21 0/8	20 6/8	5	5	4 1/8	3 6/8	1975	Jackson	Allen Sedey	67
132 3/8	139 4/8	135 7/8	3 4/8	20 6/8	18 1/8	22 0/8	21 5/8	6	5	4 2/8	4 1/8	1970	Jackson	Riley Bean	68
132 3/8	133 7/8	132 3/8	0 0/8	20 6/8	18 5/8	21 2/8	21 3/8	4	4	5 0/8	4 7/8	1991	Clackamas	Jonahs Jennings	68
132 3/8	136 0/8	132 3/8	0 0/8	18 4/8	15 5/8	18 3/8	17 5/8	5	5	4 4/8	4 3/8	1993	Douglas	Michael Scott	68
132 1/8	145 0/8	140 0/8	7 7/8	17 1/8	14 0/8	20 3/8	20 6/8	8	7	4 4/8	4 6/8	1995	Marion	Rick Schmitz	71
131 7/8	137 2/8	133 2/8	1 3/8	20 6/8	18 0/8	23 0/8	23 0/8	3	5	4 5/8	4 3/8	1982	Jackson	Alvin Thompson/Leroy Thompson	72
131 5/8	146 5/8	136 0/8	4 3/8	21 4/8	19 4/8	20 0/8	22 1/8	6	5	4 2/8	4 2/8	1978	Lane	James L. Awbrey	73
131 1/8	136 2/8	131 1/8	0 0/8	15 1/8	12 3/8	20 7/8	20 6/8	6	5	5 0/8	4 5/8	1991	Lane	David L. Spriggs	74
131 1/8	132 6/8	131 1/8	0 0/8	20 4/8	18 5/8	21 0/8	21 2/8	4	4	5 0/8	4 7/8	1991	Clackamas	Jonahs F. Jennings	74
131 0/8	133 7/8	131 0/8	0 0/8	17 2/8	15 2/8	18 3/8	19 0/8	5	5	4 6/8	4 2/8	1966	Lane	Bill Jordan	76
131 0/8	146 2/8	139 0/8	8 0/8	16 5/8	15 0/8	23 2/8	21 7/8	6	7	4 5/8	4 5/8	1992	Benton	Bruce W. O'Key	76
131 0/8	141 3/8	135 0/8	4 0/8	15 6/8	12 6/8	18 2/8	19 3/8	6	6	4 2/8	4 2/8	1995	Benton	Marion Coffman	76
130 7/8	135 7/8	130 7/8	0 0/8	16 3/8	14 5/8	20 6/8	21 1/8	5	4	4 0/8	4 0/8	1965	Clackamas	Peter Ferrero	79
130 4/8	135 6/8	130 4/8	0 0/8	20 3/8	18 6/8	21 3/8	21 5/8	4	5	3 7/8	4 0/8	1993	Jackson	Cukirt Keller	80
130 3/8	136 6/8	132 0/8	1 5/8	21 5/8	19 4/8	23 4/8	23 3/8	4	6	4 4/8	4 5/8	1994	Linn	Kevin Morehead	81
130 3/8	141 0/8	136 2/8	5 7/8	25 4/8	18 6/8	22 2/8	22 2/8	5	6	4 2/8	4 4/8	1969	Jackson	R.W. Burkhart/Ed Burkhart	81

	Name	County	Year											
83	Matt Brown	Douglas	1995	4 1/8	4 1/8	5	5	19 4/8	19 6/8	15 3/8	18 4/8	0/8	130 1/8	131 5/8
84	Ben Simpson	Douglas	1959	3 3/8	3 7/8	5	5	21 1/8	21 3/8	17 3/8	19 3/8	0/8	129 7/8	134 7/8
85	Riley Bean	Jackson	1968	4 5/8	4 0/8	4	5	20 5/8	19 6/8	19 4/8	20 6/8	0/8	129 6/8	139 3/8
85	Bret Jeppsen	Linn	1976	4 2/8	4 2/8	4	4	22 4/8	20 3/8	16 6/8	19 1/8	0/8	129 6/8	134 5/8
85	Anthony DeSantis	Marion	1994	3 7/8	3 4/8	5	5	22 0/8	21 6/8	17 6/8	19 1/8	2 5/8	129 6/8	134 0/8
88	Donald Clark	Lane	1984	4 0/8	4 4/8	5	6	20 0/8	18 6/8	14 3/8	18 4/8	2 0/8	132 1/8	137 1/8
88	Nick Begrin	Linn	1994	4 4/8	4 3/8	7	5	19 7/8	20 2/8	16 4/8	19 0/8	0/8	131 4/8	135 1/8
90	Lester Gilpatrick	Douglas	1985	4 1/8	4 1/8	5	5	20 4/8	20 4/8	14 2/8	16 0/8	0/8	129 0/8	131 5/8
91	Fred Bean/Riley Bean	Jackson	1971	3 2/8	4 0/8	4	5	20 6/8	20 1/8	19 2/8	21 0/8	0/8	128 6/8	136 6/8
92	Mike Pratt	Josephine	1995	3 4/8	3 3/8	4	4	19 6/8	21 3/8	15 5/8	18 2/8	0/8	128 5/8	132 7/8
93	Fred Bean/Riley Bean	Jackson	1955	4 6/8	4 4/8	5	3	22 0/8	25 0/8	22 2/8	24 4/8	0/8	128 4/8	147 0/8
93	Kevin Morehead	Linn	1989	5 0/8	4 3/8	5	5	18 2/8	18 3/8	15 0/8	18 3/8	0/8	128 4/8	130 6/8
95	Chuck Jarvis	Douglas	1994	4 3/8	4 4/8	4	4	21 5/8	21 2/8	17 7/8	19 5/8	0/8	128 3/8	131 1/8
96	John Howe	Lane	1995	4 4/8	4 2/8	5	5	21 5/8	21 0/8	15 0/8	17 0/8	0/8	128 0/8	131 1/8
97	Rick Baker	Douglas	1991	4 3/8	4 1/8	5	5	18 7/8	17 7/8	17 0/8	17 4/8	0/8	127 6/8	132 0/8
97	Dean Trent	Marion	1993	4 3/8	4 1/8	4	5	22 1/8	20 6/8	16 6/8	17 2/8	9 2/8	127 6/8	131 0/8
99	Bill Matthews	Douglas	1975	4 1/8	4 1/8	7	6	20 6/8	20 6/8	14 5/8	20 0/8	0/8	136 7/8	140 0/8
100	Roy Simpson	Douglas	1990	3 7/8	3 6/8	5	5	18 2/8	18 0/8	13 6/8	16 0/8	3 0/8	127 4/8	129 7/8
101	Mike Pratt	Josephine	1994	4 1/8	4 0/8	5	6	17 6/8	18 1/8	15 2/8	18 3/8	0/8	130 2/8	133 7/8
102	Ric Farm	Linn	1995	3 5/8	3 5/8	5	5	19 0/8	17 5/8	15 1/8		0/8	127 1/8	132 1/8
104	Mike Crudele	Linn	1994	4 3/8	4 3/8	5	5	20 5/8	19 4/8	16 5/8	19 4/8	0/8	127 1/8	130 7/8
104	Warren Frazier	Jackson		4 1/8	4 2/8	4	4	20 4/8	20 0/8	14 0/8	16 4/8	0/8	127 0/8	129 3/8
106	Rex Heard	Douglas	1976	4 2/8	4 1/8	5	5	19 5/8	18 7/8	15 2/8	17 6/8	0/8	127 0/8	130 6/8
106	Greg Vaughn	Douglas	1993	4 4/8	4 4/8	5	5	18 7/8	18 6/8	14 4/8	16 3/8	0/8	126 6/8	129 3/8
108	Dave Hammond	Jackson	1994	4 2/8	4 4/8	6	6	22 3/8	21 4/8	20 3/8	22 4/8	6 3/8	133 1/8	144 7/8
108	Marcus B. Hecker	Lane	1992	4 0/8	4 0/8	5	5	19 0/8	18 1/8	14 5/8	17 1/8	0/8	126 3/8	129 2/8
110	Judy Hill	Douglas	1993	4 1/8	3 7/8	5	5	19 5/8	19 3/8	15 7/8		0/8	126 3/8	134 4/8
110	Fred Bean	Josephine	1938	4 4/8	4 2/8	2	2	25 0/8	25 2/8	20 0/8	22 2/8	0/8	126 0/8	127 4/8
110	Dave Thomas	Josephine	1993	4 0/8	4 0/8	5	5	19 3/8	20 5/8	17 6/8	19 2/8	0/8	126 0/8	131 0/8
113	Mark Johnston	Coos	1991	3 4/8	3 4/8	5	4	20 7/8	19 2/8	14 0/8		2 6/8	126 0/8	132 1/8
113	Rich Plattner	Linn	1960	4 4/8	4 4/8	4	5	21 6/8	21 5/8	16 2/8	18 3/8	0/8	125 4/8	132 1/8
115	Wade Hogg	Douglas	1992	3 7/8	3 6/8	6	6	19 6/8	20 6/8	14 5/8	18 3/8	3 5/8	129 1/8	136 3/8
116	Jeff Canessa	Benton	1994	4 2/8	4 2/8	5	5	18 4/8	18 3/8	15 7/8	19 1/8	2 1/8	125 3/8	131 4/8
117	Robbie Parker	Douglas	1988	3 6/8	3 7/8	6	5	20 2/8	20 2/8	16 1/8	17 4/8	0/8	127 1/8	129 6/8
118	Fred Rask	Clackamas	1962	4 0/8	4 2/8	5	5	20 0/8	19 7/8	14 7/8	17 1/8	2 5/8	124 7/8	129 6/8
119	John Marble	Linn	1994	4 3/8	4 3/8	6	6	21 2/8	21 2/8	16 1/8	18 2/8	0/8	124 6/8	133 3/8
120	Wyatt Dunham	Douglas	1992	4 2/8	4 2/8	5	5	19 4/8	18 4/8	12 2/8	14 4/8	0/8	124 4/8	126 7/8
121	Fred Bean	Jackson	1942	4 1/8	4 1/8	5	5	17 1/8	19 6/8	24 0/8	27 4/8	2 6/8	124 2/8	134 1/8
121	Dennis Blackford	Linn	1994	4 4/8	4 3/8	4	5	20 4/8	19 5/8	18 7/8	21 0/8	0/8	123 7/8	126 1/8
123	Jana Jarvis	Douglas	1994	4 1/8	4 4/8	5	5	19 3/8	20 1/8	14 3/8	17 0/8	7 0/8	123 7/8	136 7/8
124	Gregg L. Munson	Lane	1967	4 1/8	4 1/8	7	5	19 0/8	18 3/8	12 4/8	13 7/8	0/8	123 4/8	126 5/8
124	Jim Cook	Yamhill	1995	4 2/8	4 4/8	5	5	18 6/8	18 5/8	14 5/8	17 4/8	0/8	123 3/8	127 2/8
126	Jerry Barber/Mike Mordell	Marion		4 1/8	4 1/8	6	5	20 0/8	19 4/8	14 5/8	16 4/8	1 0/8	124 3/8	129 3/8
127	Roland Morehead	Linn	1975	4 5/8	4 2/8	5	5	20 4/8	20 2/8	17 1/8	19 1/8	0/8	123 1/8	126 4/8
128	Marlin Pose	Douglas	1995	3 5/8	3 6/8	5	5	19 0/8	19 0/8	18 4/8	21 2/8	0/8	123 0/8	127 0/8
129	Brett Klages	Marion	1995	3 7/8	3 7/8	4	5	19 3/8	21 0/8	14 5/8	16 4/8	0/8	122 5/8	129 7/8
129	Sotero Llamas	Marion	1994	4 4/8	4 4/8	5	5	19 4/8	18 6/8	16 4/8	18 6/8	0/8	122 2/8	130 6/8

Typical Columbian Blacktail—Rifle (continued)

Final Score	Gross Typical	Net Typical	Abnormal Points	Greatest Spread	Inside Spread	Main Beam R	Main Beam L	Number of Points R	Number of Points L	First Circumference R	First Circumference L	Year	County	Hunter/Owner	Rank
122 0/8	125 4/8	122 0/8	0 0/8	16 6/8	14 6/8	19 1/8	19 6/8	5	5	4 0/8	4 0/8	1983	Linn	Mike Lowery	130
121 3/8	127 6/8	121 3/8	0 0/8	19 7/8	18 1/8	20 2/8	21 0/8	4	5	4 0/8	4 4/8	1966	Clackamas	Steve Rask	131
121 2/8	125 4/8	121 2/8	0 0/8	18 4/8	15 6/8	19 6/8	19 6/8	5	4	3 7/8	3 2/8	1993	Jackson	Linden C. Longbrake	132
120 7/8	143 3/8	132 1/8	11 2/8	20 0/8	17 5/8	23 2/8	20 4/8	6	10	4 7/8	5 2/8	1988	Coos	Keith W. Arnold	133
120 6/8	128 1/8	120 6/8	0 0/8	20 5/8	18 4/8	22 0/8	20 1/8	4	4	3 6/8	3 4/8	1964	Polk	Zack R. Smith, Sr./ Terry W. Smith	134
120 2/8	123 2/8	120 2/8	0 0/8	19 4/8	17 6/8	20 3/8	20 0/8	4	4	3 5/8	3 4/8	1983	Douglas	Steve Gausnell	135
119 7/8	124 5/8	122 5/8	2 6/8	15 7/8	13 7/8	18 6/8	19 1/8	4	5	4 3/8	4 2/8	1989	Linn	Mike Lowrey	136
119 7/8	123 6/8	119 7/8	0 0/8	17 0/8	14 7/8	18 5/8	19 0/8	5	5	4 5/8	4 7/8	1987	Linn	Dennis Steinborn	136
119 6/8	123 5/8	119 6/8	0 0/8	17 2/8	15 0/8	20 2/8	20 3/8	4	4	4 0/8	3 7/8	1981	Linn	Clarence Hubb	138
119 5/8	126 1/8	119 5/8	0 0/8	19 3/8	18 7/8	19 4/8	19 1/8	5	5	3 4/8	3 4/8	1992	Jackson	Bill Whitlatch	139
119 2/8	126 7/8	119 2/8	0 0/8	19 6/8	16 2/8	18 4/8	18 0/8	5	4	3 7/8	3 3/8	1981	Multnomah	John Ray	140
119 2/8	122 2/8	119 2/8	0 0/8		15 0/8	18 6/8	18 6/8	5	5	4 2/8	4 2/8	1992	Multnomah	Randy Miller	140
119 0/8	125 0/8	119 0/8	0 0/8	15 3/8	13 0/8	18 4/8	19 0/8	4	5	4 0/8	4 3/8	1960	Benton	Don R. Pillar	142
118 6/8	122 1/8	118 6/8	0 0/8	18 6/8	17 2/8	20 3/8	21 0/8	4	5	4 0/8	4 2/8	1986	Yamhill	Bryan Burnham	143
118 6/8	131 3/8	122 2/8	3 4/8	19 2/8	17 0/8	21 6/8	22 0/8	5	4	4 3/8	4 2/8	1987	Douglas	Terry Floyd	143
118 6/8	125 0/8	118 6/8	0 0/8	14 0/8	12 2/8	17 4/8	16 2/8	4	4	3 5/8	3 6/8	1961	Lane	Eric Olsen	143
118 5/8	123 6/8	118 5/8	0 0/8	18 5/8	16 5/8	18 4/8	18 2/8	4	4	3 4/8	3 5/8	1990	Jackson	Fred Bean	146
118 4/8	132 7/8	124 7/8	6 3/8	17 4/8	15 1/8	23 0/8	22 5/8	5	6	4 6/8	4 4/8	1990	Jackson	Rick Sequeira	147
118 2/8	123 0/8	118 2/8	0 0/8	17 7/8	14 6/8	17 6/8	17 6/8	4	5	3 6/8	3 6/8	1989	Marion	Randy Woolcott	148
118 2/8	129 4/8	118 2/8	0 0/8	21 4/8	18 6/8	21 2/8	21 5/8	4	5	3 7/8	3 6/8	1983	Douglas	Wade Hogg	148
118 0/8	120 7/8	118 0/8	0 0/8	15 5/8	13 6/8	17 2/8	17 3/8	5	5	3 7/8	4 2/8	1990	Polk	Harry R. Carson	150
117 5/8	124 0/8	117 5/8	0 0/8	18 3/8	15 7/8	18 1/8	18 1/8	5	4	4 1/8	4 2/8	1993	Lane	James Howe	151
117 2/8	122 3/8	117 2/8	0 0/8	17 3/8	15 6/8	20 1/8	19 5/8	4	5	4 4/8	4 3/8	1990	Lane	Eric Olsen	152
116 6/8	119 3/8	116 6/8	0 0/8	17 6/8	15 2/8	18 6/8	18 4/8	5	5	3 6/8	4 1/8	1975	Linn	Ronald Lee Atkins	153
116 6/8	119 5/8	116 6/8	0 0/8	19 0/8	16 2/8	20 5/8	20 5/8	4	4	4 3/8	4 0/8	1994	Lane	Doug Morehead	153
116 3/8	120 0/8	116 3/8	0 0/8	17 1/8	14 7/8	18 0/8	16 6/8	5	5	4 6/8	4 6/8	1995	Lane	Bill Cutshall	155
116 2/8	122 0/8	116 2/8	0 0/8	19 0/8	17 2/8	19 2/8	18 6/8	4	4	3 5/8	3 6/8	1989	Lane	Raul Rodriguez, Jr.	156
116 1/8	125 3/8	116 1/8	0 0/8	21 3/8	18 5/8	22 2/8	20 7/8	4	5	3 2/8	4 2/8	1979	Jackson	Donald L. Phillips, Jr.	157
116 1/8	123 4/8	116 1/8	0 0/8	18 0/8	15 7/8	19 2/8	19 2/8	4	5	4 1/8	4 2/8	1972	Benton	John Wheland	157
115 6/8	119 5/8	115 6/8	0 0/8	17 2/8	15 4/8	19 6/8	20 1/8	5	5	4 6/8	4 7/8	1985	Linn	Doug Morehead	159
115 6/8	117 4/8	115 6/8	0 0/8	18 4/8	16 4/8	19 4/8	20 0/8	4	4	4 1/8	4 0/8	1980	Douglas	Wyatt Dunham	159
115 5/8	120 5/8	115 5/8	0 0/8	14 2/8	12 1/8	17 4/8	18 3/8	5	4	4 3/8	4 1/8	1993	Lane	Lloyd Dykstra	161
115 4/8	128 4/8	123 0/8	7 4/8	20 0/8	17 4/8	20 4/8	20 4/8	7	8	4 0/8	4 0/8	1950	Josephine	Fred Bean	162
115 4/8	125 6/8	115 4/8	0 0/8	17 4/8	14 2/8	18 7/8	16 7/8	5	5	3 6/8	3 6/8	1994	Yamhill	Colin Hilton	162
115 3/8	120 2/8	115 3/8	0 0/8	19 5/8	18 1/8	18 4/8	18 7/8	4	4	3 7/8	4 0/8	1994	Jackson	Larry Justin	164
115 0/8	126 6/8	115 0/8	0 0/8	20 1/8	17 6/8	20 1/8	19 7/8	5	5	4 2/8	4 6/8	1992	Linn	Chad Flack	165

Typical Columbian Blacktail—Archery
Minimum Score: 90 0/8

Final Score	Gros. Typical	Net Typical	Abnormal Points	Greatest Spread	Inside Spread	Main Beam R	Main Beam L	Number of Points R	Number of Points L	First Circumference R	First Circumference L	Year	County	Hunter/Owner	Rank
172 3/8	188 5/8	180 3/8	8 0/8	22 7/8	19 7/8	25 6/8	26 4/8	8	7	6 7/8	6 3/8	1995	Jackson	Randy Allen	1
166 2/8	174 2/8	166 2/8	0 0/8	21 2/8	17 2/8	23 4/8	24 0/8	5	5	4 5/8	4 6/8	1991	Jackson	David Baird	2
141 3/8	145 5/8	141 3/8	0 0/8	17 5/8	15 3/8	20 2/8	20 2/8	5	5	4 4/8	4 3/8		Linn	Mike Brady/Shirley Andrews	3
139 5/8	144 2/8	141 1/8	1 4/8	20 6/8	17 3/8	20 4/8	21 1/8	5	6	4 2/8	4 3/8	1987	Lane	John Hill	4
139 2/8	141 4/8	139 2/8	0 0/8	19 0/8	16 6/8	21 5/8	22 1/8	5	5	4 0/8	4 0/8	1993	Josephine	Michael Parks	5
137 0/8	141 5/8	138 1/8	1 1/8	19 0/8	15 7/8	21 1/8	21 2/8	4	5	4 4/8	4 0/8	1985	Linn	Charlie Endicott	6
133 1/8	137 1/8	133 1/8	0 0/8	19 6/8	15 3/8	18 7/8	17 6/8	5	5	4 6/8	4 5/8	1990	Lane	Matt Dodson	7
131 3/8	136 1/8	131 3/8	0 0/8	19 3/8	17 3/8	20 1/8	20 2/8	5	5	4 1/8	4 1/8	1988	Douglas	Kenneth A. French	8
130 7/8	138 0/8	132 1/8	1 2/8	19 7/8	17 1/8	21 0/8	19 0/8	5	6	4 6/8	4 6/8	1993	Marion	Loren E. McLaughlin	9
128 5/8	136 7/8	128 5/8	0 0/8	19 4/8	17 7/8	22 6/8	23 3/8	4	5	4 2/8	4 2/8	1995	Josephine	Lee Darrow	10
126 5/8	130 2/8	126 5/8	0 0/8	18 1/8	13 7/8	18 2/8	17 4/8	5	5	3 6/8	3 5/8	1989	Douglas	Kenneth A. French	11
123 1/8	127 5/8	123 1/8	0 0/8	18 4/8	14 3/8	19 7/8	19 7/8	5	5	3 4/8	3 4/8	1995		Tarrant Jason	12
122 5/8	126 7/8	122 5/8	0 0/8	17 4/8	15 1/8	19 2/8	19 5/8	4	4	3 6/8	3 6/8	1993	Linn	Mark Penninger	13
113 6/8	115 7/8	113 6/8	0 0/8	18 2/8	15 4/8	19 6/8	19 6/8	3	3	3 7/8	4 0/8	1992	Douglas	Mike Oglesby	14
112 3/8	125 2/8	117 0/8	4 5/8	16 0/8	13 6/8	17 4/8	19 2/8	4	5	4 2/8	4 2/8	1980	Douglas	Kenneth A. French	15
112 1/8	114 0/8	112 1/8	0 0/8	16 1/8	13 3/8	17 1/8	17 4/8	5	5	3 5/8	3 5/8	1986	Benton	Gary Nyden	16
111 5/8	113 1/8	111 5/8	0 0/8	16 1/8	14 1/8	18 1/8	18 4/8	5	5	3 7/8	4 0/8	1994	Lane	Gary Nyden	17
111 2/8	115 4/8	111 2/8	0 0/8	17 4/8	15 2/8	19 0/8	18 6/8	4	3	4 4/8	4 1/8		Linn	Mike Brady/Shirley Andrews	18
109 0/8	113 7/8	109 0/8	0 0/8	12 0/8	9 1/8	18 1/8	17 7/8	3	5	3 3/8	4 0/8	1983	Douglas	Kenneth A. French	19
104 1/8	108 6/8	104 1/8	0 0/8	15 4/8	13 3/8	15 4/8	15 6/8	5	5	4 1/8	4 0/8	1988	Clackamas	Ben Cook	20
103 0/8	105 7/8	103 0/8	0 0/8	18 2/8	16 6/8	18 6/8	18 7/8	3	4	3 2/8	3 4/8	1994	Josephine	Brian Day	21
101 1/8	109 0/8	101 1/8	0 0/8	10 1/8	12 1/8	17 2/8	17 6/8	4	4	3 6/8	3 6/8	1985	Douglas	Kenneth A. French	22
98 6/8	110 7/8	98 6/8	0 0/8	18 4/8	16 6/8	17 6/8	16 5/8	4	4	3 2/8	3 3/8	1994	Clackamas	Jon Mattson	23
96 6/8	102 4/8	96 6/8	0 0/8	16 1/8	13 6/8	16 2/8	16 3/8	5	4	3 6/8	3 2/8	1995	Lane	James Howe	24
92 0/8	94 4/8	92 0/8	0 0/8	15 4/8	15 2/8	14 6/8	15 0/8	4	4	3 0/8	2 7/8	1992	Douglas	Kenneth A. French	25

Typical Columbian Blacktail—Archery (Velvet)
Minimum Score: 90 0/8

Final Score	Gros. Typical	Net Typical	Abnormal Points	Greatest Spread	Inside Spread	Main Beam R	Main Beam L	Number of Points R	Number of Points L	First Circumference R	First Circumference L	Year	County	Hunter/Owner	Rank
120 0/8	134 4/8	127 6/8	7 6/8	16 6/8	13 2/8	19 0/8	18 3/8	5	6	5 1/8	4 6/8	1990	Jackson	Scott Thompson	1

Typical Columbian Blacktail—Black Powder
Minimum Score: 110 0/8

Final Score	Gross Typical	Net Typical	Abnormal Points	Greatest Spread	Inside Spread	Main Beam R	Main Beam L	Number of Points R	Number of Points L	First Circumference R	First Circumference L	Year	County	Hunter/Owner	Rank
159 2/8	166 4/8	162 0/8	2 6/8	21 5/8	18 2/8	21 7/8	20 7/8	5	6	4 3/8	4 3/8	1988	Jackson	Jeff E. Sedey	1
148 5/8	151 5/8	148 5/8	0 0/8	22 7/8	19 3/8	22 6/8	22 4/8	5	5	4 6/8	4 4/8	1995	Josephine	Mike Gilmore	2
143 3/8	148 2/8	143 3/8	0 0/8	19 5/8	16 5/8	21 3/8	20 6/8	5	5	5 0/8	5 1/8	1984	Josephine	Mike Gilmore	3
135 6/8	138 4/8	135 6/8	0 0/8	19 4/8	16 0/8	18 1/8	18 2/8	5	5	4 2/8	4 2/8	1988	Jackson	Frank R. Haynes	4
135 0/8	141 6/8	135 0/8	0 0/8	16 7/8	13 6/8	18 7/8	19 1/8	5	5	4 6/8	4 3/8	1987	Lane	Ken Dunham	5
112 6/8	134 0/8	126 4/8	13 6/8	21 0/8	16 4/8	19 3/8	18 4/8	5	8	4 4/8	4 4/8		Douglas	Delbert Applegrath	6

Typical Columbian Blacktail—Shed Antlers
Minimum Score: 50 0/8

Final Score	Subtotal	Abnormal Points	Main Beam	First Point	Second Point	Third Point	Fourth Point	First Circumference	Right/Left	Year	County	Owner's Name	Rank
78 7/8	78 7/8	0 0/8	23 0/8	3 4/8	13 1/8	9 5/8	10 4/8	7 0/8	Left		Jackson	Steve Holte	1
74 1/8	74 1/8	0 0/8	24 1/8	2 2/8	11 3/8	10 0/8	9 6/8	4 1/8	Left		Jackson	Steve Holte	2
73 0/8	73 0/8	0 0/8	21 4/8	2 6/8	11 4/8	9 3/8	10 0/8	5 3/8	Left		Jackson	Max Adams	3
71 5/8	71 5/8	0 0/8	23 2/8	2 4/8	12 4/8	9 6/8	8 0/8	4 2/8	Left		Jackson	Steve Holte	4
71 1/8	71 1/8	0 0/8	23 2/8	2 4/8	12 0/8	7 3/8	10 6/8	4 1/8	Right		Jackson	Steve Holte	5
70 7/8	70 7/8	0 0/8	22 6/8	2 6/8	11 1/8	9 7/8	9 2/8	4 3/8	Right		Jackson	Steve Holte	6
70 1/8	70 1/8	0 0/8	22 2/8	2 2/8	12 2/8	8 5/8	9 6/8	4 2/8	Right		Jackson	Steve Holte	7
70 0/8	70 0/8	0 0/8	22 2/8	2 7/8	11 3/8	6 1/8	8 6/8	5 3/8	Right		Jackson	Steve Holte	8
69 4/8	69 4/8	0 0/8	23 2/8	2 1/8	12 1/8	8 5/8	8 4/8	4 0/8	Left		Jackson	Steve Holte	9
69 3/8	69 3/8	0 0/8	23 2/8	2 5/8	10 6/8	8 5/8	8 4/8	4 4/8	Right		Jackson	Steve Holte	10
68 7/8	68 7/8	0 0/8	22 0/8	1 5/8	13 1/8	9 6/8	8 6/8	4 0/8	Right		Jackson	Mike Benton	11
68 4/8	68 4/8	0 0/8	21 4/8	1 4/8	11 2/8	8 6/8	10 2/8	4 2/8	Right		Jackson	Steve Holte	12
68 0/8	68 0/8	0 0/8	20 0/8	2 0/8	11 3/8	9 0/8	9 1/8	5 0/8	Left		Jackson	Steve Holte	13
67 7/8	67 7/8	0 0/8	22 2/8	1 7/8	12 0/8	7 6/8	8 5/8	4 0/8	Right		Jackson	Steve Holte	14
67 3/8	67 3/8	0 0/8	21 1/8	2 4/8	7 7/8	9 6/8	9 2/8	5 0/8	Right		Jackson	Al Garcia	15
67 1/8	67 1/8	0 0/8	21 4/8	0 0/8	14 6/8	8 5/8	9 2/8	3 3/8	Left		Jackson	Mike Benton	16
66 3/8	66 3/8	0 0/8	21 2/8	2 0/8	12 4/8	7 0/8	9 5/8	3 7/8	Right		Jackson	Al Garcia	17
66 0/8	66 0/8	0 0/8	24 3/8	2 4/8	13 2/8	8 7/8	0 0/8	5 2/8	Left		Jackson	Steve Holte	18
65 0/8	65 0/8	0 0/8	21 4/8	1 3/8	12 4/8	8 3/8	7 2/8	4 0/8	Right		Jackson	Matt Holte	19
64 5/8	64 5/8	0 0/8	24 4/8	1 2/8	13 7/8	8 1/8	0 0/8	5 5/8	Right		Jackson	Steve Holte	20
64 4/8	64 4/8	0 0/8	23 4/8	0 0/8	14 6/8	8 4/8	4 1/8	4 0/8	Left		Jackson	Matt Holte	21

Non-Typical Columbian Blacktail—Rifle

Minimum Score: 145 0/8

Final Score	Gross Typical	Net Typical	Abnormal Points	Greatest Spread	Inside Spread	Main Beam R	Main Beam L	Number of Points R	Number of Points L	First Circumference R	First Circumference L	Year	County	Hunter/Owner	Rank
202 1/8	178 7/8	173 2/8	28 7/8	26 4/8	22 2/8	21 7/8	22 0/8	8	14	5 4/8	5 4/8	1935	Josephine	Fred Bean/Riley Bean	1
199 1/8	183 5/8	179 3/8	19 6/8	25 4/8	20 7/8	23 6/8	24 6/8	10	12	5 1/8	5 2/8	1904		James Ball/Robert Surtles	2
194 7/8	172 4/8	167 0/8	27 7/8	23 1/8	19 6/8	25 6/8	24 0/8	11	10	4 5/8	4 5/8	1907	Jackson	R.B. Baker/Donald C. Baker	3
187 7/8	162 6/8	158 2/8	30 5/8	25 5/8	19 0/8	22 6/8	22 6/8	7	9	4 4/8	4 3/8	1976	Jackson	Riley Bean	4
185 7/8	153 2/8	146 6/8	39 1/8	27 4/8	23 2/8	22 4/8	22 6/8	8	12	5 2/8	5 5/8	1978	Polk	Frank Foldi/Steve Crossley	5
175 2/8	160 4/8	156 6/8	18 4/8	24 0/8	22 2/8	22 6/8	24 1/8	11	9	5 1/8	5 1/8	1950	Jackson	Fred Bean/Riley Bean	6
174 4/8	143 4/8	135 1/8	39 3/8	23 7/8	16 3/8	23 1/8	21 6/8	8	8	4 1/8	4 3/8	1970	Clackamas	Ron Searls	7
174 1/8	140 0/8	137 5/8	36 4/8	27 0/8	23 3/8	23 1/8	23 3/8	6	6	4 3/8	4 3/8	1964	Jackson	Darrell Leek	8
172 7/8	161 2/8	156 4/8	16 3/8	22 2/8	17 6/8	22 7/8	23 0/8	7	6	4 7/8	4 6/8	1952	Jackson	Doug Lewis	9
172 5/8	169 5/8	164 7/8	7 6/8	24 7/8	20 7/8	22 1/8	23 1/8	7	6	4 5/8	4 5/8	1947	Jackson	Fred Bean	10
169 2/8	153 6/8	147 4/8	21 6/8	20 5/8	18 2/8	23 6/8	23 5/8	6	9	5 0/8	4 6/8	1993	Jackson	Doug Storey	11
165 0/8	159 2/8	155 4/8	9 4/8	26 2/8	17 6/8	22 4/8	23 0/8	6	6	5 0/8	5 1/8	1954	Jackson	Riley Bean	12
163 3/8	159 0/8	155 3/8	8 0/8	18 3/8	14 7/8	22 2/8	22 6/8	6	6	4 4/8	4 5/8		Jackson	Max Adams	13
163 0/8	158 2/8	154 6/8	8 2/8	23 6/8	20 2/8	21 2/8	19 7/8	10	5	4 4/8	4 5/8	1985	Jackson	Ray Foulon	14
162 1/8	152 4/8	148 0/8	14 1/8	26 0/8	16 4/8	20 4/8	20 0/8	9	6	5 2/8	5 2/8	1948	Jackson	Fred Bean/Riley Bean	15
157 0/8	152 0/8	147 1/8	9 7/8	24 4/8	18 3/8	23 5/8	23 1/8	7	7	3 6/8	3 7/8	1984	Douglas	Bill Ratledge	16
157 0/8	159 7/8	153 6/8	3 2/8	21 6/8	19 4/8	24 5/8	24 0/8	6	6	4 3/8	4 5/8	1982	Jackson	Sonny Loomis	16
156 2/8	156 3/8	147 5/8	8 5/8	23 2/8	19 5/8	23 5/8	23 0/8	6	7	4 7/8	4 7/8	1974	Jackson	Fred Bean/Riley Bean	18
155 6/8	139 7/8	134 6/8	21 0/8	16 1/8	11 0/8	18 6/8	18 5/8	9	12	4 6/8	4 7/8	1988	Douglas	James Crudele	19
154 6/8	146 4/8	143 5/8	11 1/8	24 5/8	21 1/8	23 0/8	23 1/8	9	5	4 7/8	4 7/8		Jackson	Larry Shele	20
152 6/8	150 0/8	147 0/8	5 6/8	22 3/8	19 0/8	20 1/8	20 3/8	5	7	4 6/8	5 2/8		Jackson	Bill Whitlatch	21
152 1/8	146 0/8	143 0/8	9 1/8	20 0/8	15 2/8	20 0/8	20 4/8	6	6	4 0/8	4 1/8	1969	Douglas	Jeffery J. Murtens	22
151 6/8	138 7/8	135 5/8	16 1/8	18 7/8	15 7/8	21 1/8	21 3/8	6	9	4 2/8	4 2/8	1995		Rick Baker	23
150 2/8	139 2/8	133 0/8	17 2/8	23 1/8	22 0/8	19 6/8	20 2/8	9	10	4 4/8	4 3/8	1966	Jackson	Riley Bean	24
147 7/8	145 0/8	140 0/8	7 7/8	17 1/8	14 0/8	20 3/8	20 6/8	8	7	4 4/8	4 6/8	1995	Marion	Rick Schmitz	25
147 0/8	146 2/8	139 0/8	8 0/8	16 5/8	15 0/8	23 2/8	21 7/8	6	7	4 5/8	4 5/8	1992	Benton	Bruce W. O'Key	26
146 1/8	140 0/8	136 7/8	9 2/8	20 0/8	14 5/8	20 6/8	20 6/8	7	6	4 1/8	4 1/8	1975	Douglas	Bill Matthews	27
145 0/8	135 2/8	130 0/8	15 0/8	18 6/8	14 4/8	19 2/8	20 1/8	9	6	4 6/8	4 4/8	1961	Douglas	Floyd W. Ross/Kitty Ross Grauf	28

Non-Typical Columbian Blacktail—Archery
Minimum Score: 110 0/8

Final Score	Gross Typical	Net Typical	Abnormal Points	Greatest Spread	Inside Spread	Main Beam R	Main Beam L	Number of Points R	Number of Points L	First Circumference R	First Circumference L	Year	County	Hunter/Owner	Rank
194 4/8	171 3/8	162 7/8	31 5/8	24 4/8	19 1/8	23 3/8	23 4/8	10	8	5 6/8	6 0/8	1988	Jackson	James Decker	1
188 3/8	188 3/8	180 3/8	8 0/8	22 7/8	19 7/8	25 6/8	26 4/8	8	7	6 7/8	6 3/8	1995	Jackson	Randy Allen	2
160 6/8	158 3/8	154 3/8	6 3/8	24 6/8	19 7/8	21 2/8	21 4/8	7	7	4 4/8	4 7/8	1982	Jackson	Ray Foulon	3
147 5/8	139 6/8	135 7/8	11 6/8	22 1/8	17 5/8	21 4/8	22 4/8	7	5	4 7/8	4 7/8	1985	Jackson	Chuck Coleman	4
136 1/8	130 1/8	125 2/8	10 7/8	0 0/8	15 0/8	20 2/8	21 0/8	5	7	3 6/8	4 1/8	1994	Linn	Mike Brady/Shirley Andrews	5

Non-Typical Columbian Blacktail—Shed Antlers
Minimum Score: 60 0/8

Final Score	Subtotal	Abnormal Points	Main Beam	First Point	Second Point	Third Point	Fourth Point	First Circumference	Right/Left	Year	County	Owner's Name	Rank
102 5/8	70 6/8	31 7/8	19 6/8	4 1/8	10 6/8	9 4/8	8 0/8	4 7/8	Left		Jackson	Al Garcia	1
96 7/8	74 0/8	22 7/8	23 4/8	4 5/8	13 6/8	7 0/8	6 6/8	4 5/8	Right	1893	Jackson	Purl Bean	2
89 5/8	70 2/8	19 3/8	25 0/8	1 0/8	13 1/8	6 2/8	7 7/8	5 2/8	Left		Jackson	Cody Rambo	3
89 2/8	72 7/8	16 3/8	20 4/8	4 0/8	11 4/8	8 1/8	10 0/8	5 0/8	Right		Jackson	Al Garcia	4
80 7/8	73 0/8	7 7/8	21 6/8	4 1/8	11 4/8	8 7/8	8 5/8	5 4/8	Left		Jackson	Max Adams	5
80 6/8	76 6/8	4 0/8	21 4/8	4 2/8	13 0/8	9 5/8	11 2/8	5 2/8	Left		Jackson	Steve Holte	6
80 3/8	72 6/8	7 5/8	21 6/8	3 5/8	12 1/8	9 0/8	9 4/8	5 5/8	Right		Jackson	Max Adams	7
79 6/8	70 1/8	9 5/8	23 4/8	3 6/8	12 7/8	6 0/8	7 0/8	5 3/8	Right		Jackson	Cody Rambo	8
76 2/8	64 5/8	11 5/8	19 7/8	2 2/8	11 0/8	8 5/8	8 0/8	4 3/8	Right		Jackson	Matt Holte	9
76 1/8	72 1/8	4 0/8	21 6/8	4 0/8	11 7/8	7 6/8	9 2/8	5 2/8	Right		Jackson	Max Adams	10
71 6/8	69 6/8	2 0/8	22 6/8	2 0/8	13 5/8	8 0/8	4 3/8	5 4/8	Left		Jackson	Steve Holte	11
65 0/8	55 5/8	9 3/8	20 2/8	1 4/8	8 1/8	3 0/8	7 7/8	4 3/8	Right	1994	Tillamook	Dan Hartzman	12
60 1/8	60 1/8	0 0/8	18 7/8	2 1/8	11 5/8	7 5/8	6 0/8	4 1/8	Right			Chad Flack	13

Official Scoring System for Oregon Big Game Trophies

Records of Oregon
Big Game

RECORD BOOK FOR OREGON

P.O. Box 759
Irrigon, OR 97844

TYPICAL
MULE AND BLACKTAIL DEER

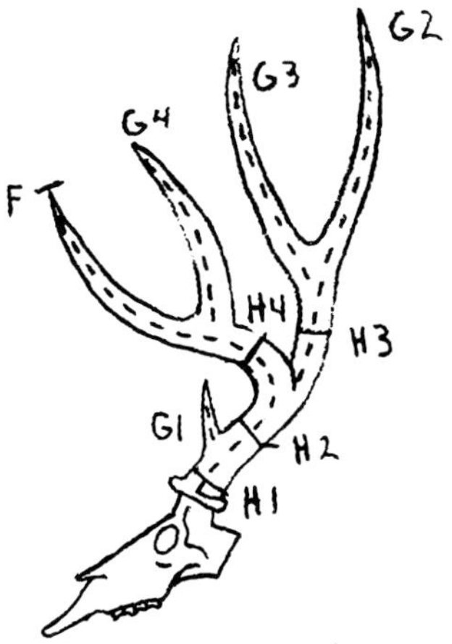

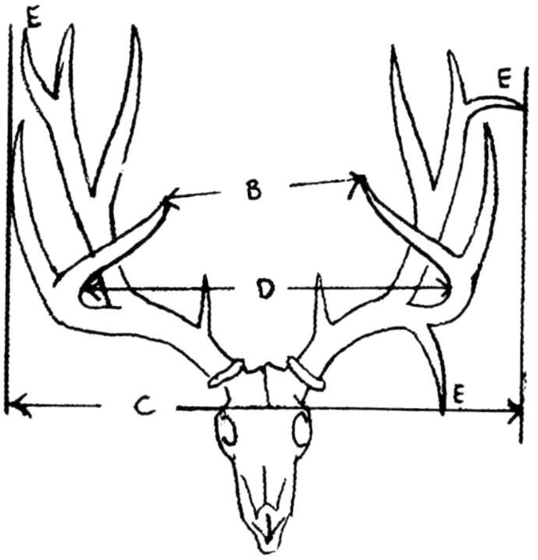

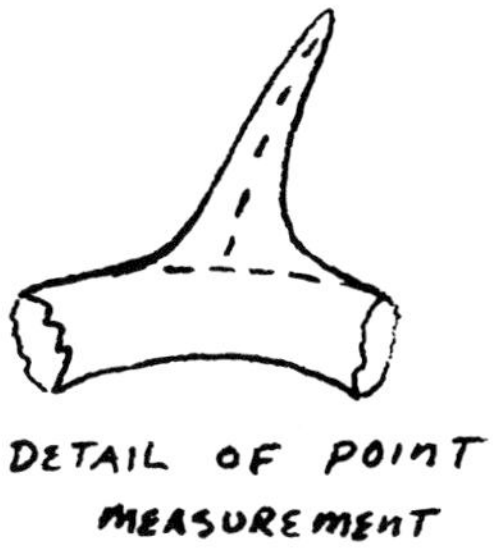

DETAIL OF POINT MEASUREMENT

Species	Rifle	Archery	Muzzle	Shed	Archery - Velvet
Mule Deer	160	145	146	70	145
Columbia Blacktail	115	90	110	50	90
Cascade Blacktail	115	90	110	50	90
Northwest Blacktail	115	90	110	50	90

Abnormal Points

Right Antler		Left Antler	
2	0/8	2	0/8
1	2/8	1	3/8
1	3/8	0	0/8
0	0/8	0	0/8
0	0/8	0	0/8
0	0/8	0	0/8
0	0/8	0	0/8
0	0/8	0	0/8
0	0/8	0	0/8
0	0/8	0	0/8
Subtotals 4	5/8	3	3/8
Total to E		8	0/8

					COLUMN 1	COLUMN 2		COLUMN 3		COLUMN 4	
A	Number of Points on Right Antler	8	Number of Points on Left Antler	7	Spread Credit	Right Antler		Left Antler		Difference	
B	Tip to Tip Spread	15 2/8	C Greatest Spread	22 7/8							
D	Inside Spread of Main Beam	19 7/8	(Credit may be equal to but not exceed longer antler)	19 7/8							
E	Total of Length of Abnormal Points									8	0/8
F	Length of Main Beam					25	6/8	26	4/8	0	6/8
G-1	Length of First Point, if present					3	5/8	3	2/8	0	3/8
G-2	Length of Second Point					14	1/8	15	4/8	1	3/8
G-3	Length of Third Point, if present					10	7/8	7	5/8	3	2/8
G-4	Length of Fourth Point, if present					11	4/8	10	3/8	1	1/8
H-1	Circumference at smallest place between burr and first point					6	7/8	6	3/8	0	4/8
H-2	Circumference at smallest place between first and second point					5	2/8	4	7/8	0	3/8
H-3	Circumference at smallest place between main beam and 3rd pt					4	0/8	3	6/8	0	2/8
H-4	Circumference at smallest place between second and fourth points					4	1/8	4	1/8	0	0/8
			TOTALS		19 7/8	86	1/8	82	3/8	16	0/8

County where killed: Jackson	**Date Killed:** 11/25/95	**ADD**	Column 1	19	7/8
Hunter's Name: Randy Allen			Column 2	86	1/8
Owner's Name: Randy Allen			Column 3	82	3/8
			Subtotal	188	3/8
			Subtract Column 4	16	0/8
			FINAL SCORE	172	3/8

New Pope and Young Record?

by Chris Neufeld

It was May 24, 1995. The day began much like any other day. The pounding got louder. His heartbeat quickened and the unexpected happened. Randy Allen, a 43-year-old building contractor from Klamath Falls, Oregon, suffered an incredible heart attack. Only an immediately available team of skilled surgeons could perform the triple-bypass surgery needed to save his life.

It was November 25, 1995. The day began much like any other day. The pounding got louder. His heart beat quickened and the unexpected happened.

With Oregon's Columbian blacktail season coming to a close, Randy Allen made his mind up to take the next legal buck that he saw. Randy has taken several trophy game animals throughout Oregon and many would easily score high in the Pope and Young records. Randy had spent ten days chasing the elusive blacktail and had seen nearly one hundred bucks and does during the season. However, none of this was on his mind at 10:30 a.m. as he spotted a beautiful forked-horn blacktail within range.

Between Randy and this subspecies of the western mule deer was a mixed bag of fir and oak trees and an assortment of incredibly thick underbrush. The landscape was gently sloping and the temperature hovered around forty degrees. Randy was hunting in the Jackson County unit of southwestern Oregon, a unit known for record class blacktail deer.

Directly in front of him was a dandy forked-horn and with the season rapidly coming to a close,

Randy made the decision to take the buck. As Randy rounded a thicket in an attempt to improve his position for a shot on the forked-horn buck, he could not believe what stood before his eyes. The senses kicked in, taking advantage of a slight breeze pushing against his face and he thought the wind was perfect.

In a smooth, many times rehearsed, poetic motion, he raised his left arm holding his Blue Mountain Predator. He nocked his XX78 2315 SuperSlam tipped with an 85 grain Thunderhead. He estimated the distance to be twenty-five yards. He had done this before in twenty-five years of bowhunting, yet he had never seen such

a buck! It was perfectly broadside and within reach. He brought the bow smoothly to full draw.

His estimation of the distance was perfect and so was the shot. A single arrow slipped through the top of the heart and Randy stood still, watching, as the incredible buck made a short but nonetheless spectacular last ditch effort to escape. A forty-yard tracking job was over and Randy Allen had set a Pope and Young record. Or should we say pending record. Until officially scored by three independent certified scorers for Pope and Young and an awards banquet to take place later this year, nothing is, as they say, "concrete." The current record was arrowed in 1969 by B.J. Shurtleff. Mr. Shurtleff killed his record buck in Marion County, Oregon.

The Columbian blacktail is a species that frequents the coastal ranges of northern California, Oregon and Washington. Archery seasons for these prized deer run late in the year and give archers the chance to hunt prior to and during the rut.

The 1995 season now past, his ticker working beautifully, Randy is looking forward to the 1996 season and hunting with his new Blue Mountain RazorBack. His gear, his heart and his desire all strong, Randy is focusing on the 1996 spring Oregon black bear hunt. After all, it's something to do until the blacktail season opens. (Final score: 172 3/8 P.Y.)

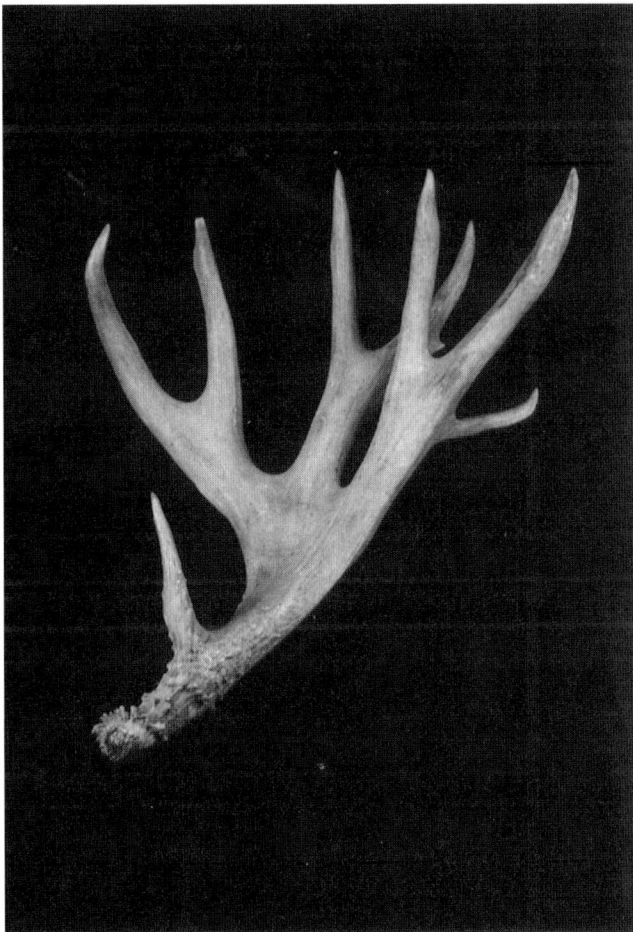

Shed antlers (non-typical),
found by Purl Bean, 96 7/8 B.C., Jackson County,
1893

Official Scoring System for Oregon Big Game Trophies

Records of Oregon
Big Game

RECORD BOOK FOR OREGON

P.O. Box 759
Irrigon, OR 97844

TYPICAL
MULE AND BLACKTAIL DEER

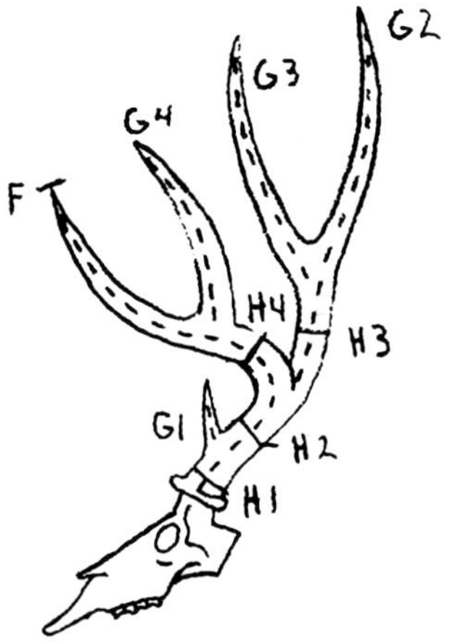

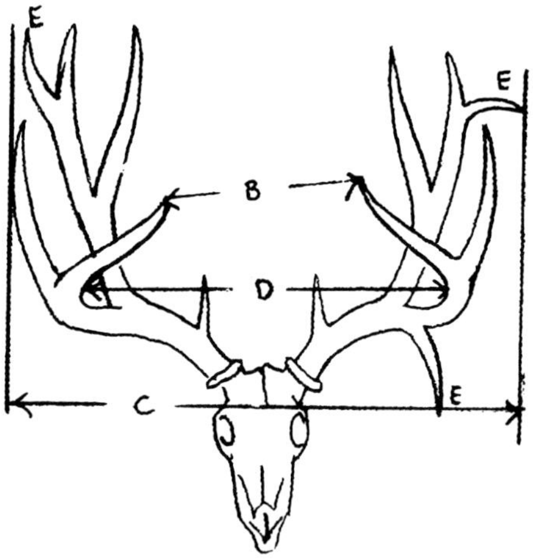

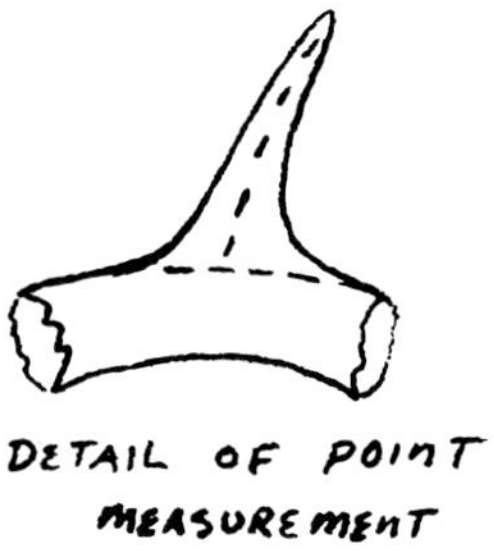

DETAIL OF POINT MEASUREMENT

Abnormal Points	
Right Antler	Left Antler
0 0/8	2 6/8
0 0/8	0 0/8
0 0/8	0 0/8
0 0/8	0 0/8
0 0/8	0 0/8
0 0/8	0 0/8
0 0/8	0 0/8
0 0/8	0 0/8
0 0/8	0 0/8
0 0/8	0 0/8
Subtotals 0 0/8	2 6/8
Total to E	2 6/8

Species	Rifle	Archery	Muzzle	Shed	Archery - Velvet
Mule Deer	160	145	146	70	145
Columbia Blacktail	115	90	110	50	90
Cascade Blacktail	115	90	110	50	90
Northwest Blacktail	115	90	110	50	90

					COLUMN 1	COLUMN 2	COLUMN 3	COLUMN 4
					Spread Credit	Right Antler	Left Antler	Difference
A	Number of Points on Right Antler	5	Number of Points on Left Antler	6				
B	Tip to Tip Spread	13 2/8	C Greatest Spread	21 5/8				
D	Inside Spread of Main Beam	18 2/8	(Credit may be equal to but not exceed longer antler)	18 2/8				
E	Total of Length of Abnormal Points							2 6/8
F	Length of Main Beam					21 7/8	20 7/8	1 0/8
G-1	Length of First Point, if present					2 4/8	2 6/8	0 2/8
G-2	Length of Second Point					13 2/8	15 4/8	2 2/8
G-3	Length of Third Point, if present					10 4/8	9 7/8	0 5/8
G-4	Length of Fourth Point, if present					9 3/8	9 5/8	0 2/8
H-1	Circumference at smallest place between burr and first point					4 3/8	4 3/8	0 0/8
H-2	Circumference at smallest place between first and second point					4 2/8	4 2/8	0 0/8
H-3	Circumference at smallest place between main beam and 3rd pt					3 3/8	3 3/8	0 0/8
H-4	Circumference at smallest place between second and fourth points					4 1/8	4 0/8	0 1/8
				TOTALS	18 2/8	73 5/8	74 5/8	7 2/8

County where killed:	Jacksonville	Date Killed:	11/29/88		Column 1	18 2/8
Hunter's Name:	Jeff E.	Sedey		ADD	Column 2	73 5/8
Owner's Name:	Jeff E.	Sedey			Column 3	74 5/8
					Subtotal	166 4/8
					Subtract Column 4	7 2/8
					FINAL SCORE	159 2/8

A Special Buck

by Jeff Sedey

My older brother Allen and I have been hunting together since we were in our early teens. In the beginning, our competitiveness may have been sibling rivalry. But in 1988, with us in our thirties, it was more in jest and good spirit. We always want good for each other. Sometimes, I'll lie and tell him how I want him to shoot the big one. He tells me the same thing; only he's a better liar because I always believe him.

That morning I was pretty excited. We had hunted with muzzle loaders in the Applegate unit of southern Oregon before. We had even gone out a few times earlier in the week, but passed on a couple of bucks because we had time yet to look for bigger ones. But today was the day when I had decided I would shoot any legal buck, because my time was running out. There were only two days to go. As usual, Allen and I were up before dawn, with coffee in our mugs and thermos and a quick breakfast out of the way. Ready to go, I loaded up the Ford Bronco with our gear.

When we were in our youth, we lived in the Griffin Creek area southwest of Medford, where the hills from Anderson Butte meet the valley. I now live in Portland, but Anderson Butte is only a forty-five-minute drive from my brother's house in Medford. We spent the morning hunting the ridges and valleys with names that only we know—Buck Point, Big Valley, Bear Gap—named so because we don't know the real names or they don't have one.

We had seen deer at the head of Big Valley. The road rounds the valley near the top, so Allen and I decided to have me "still" hunt a few hundred yards below the road through the oaks and pine. He would sneak into the woods and wait, hoping for any deer that I pushed ahead of me to pass by his stand. He knows where to go, and I usually just do as he says. Within five minutes after dropping into the timber I was following a path that parallels the road. Probably fifty yards below the road on a side slope that tailed out into gentler woods with sparse underbrush, I began moving slowly along the path. I walked maybe ten or fifteen yards and stopped for a few minutes. Using this technique, I have surprised a few deer in their beds. But more often, I find them moving and feeding, and, hopefully, see them before they see me. With little time invested in the hunt yet, I saw my first deer. I crouched down and they started passing within about forty yards of me, parallel to the path I was on. It was a perfect setup. They trotted into my area, but stopped and began to walk. I don't recall how many deer came through, four or five, maybe. All I know is that standing in front of me at that moment was a young three-point. He may have been a four-point, but I'll never know. I lowered the barrel of my Thompson Center, Hawkins 50 caliber with a roundball at the ready as he stepped into the clearing, zeroed in on the chest about at the level of the heart and fired away. I don't know what I hit, but it wasn't deer. He stood there and looked at me, as though he was curious but not concerned. And why should he be? I had missed. Now it was his turn to trot off and join the others. I found that it was hard for me to reload the black powder rifle when I was shaking from excitement. Jeez! And all I could do was watch them disappear. "I must have blown a hole in the sky over him," I thought to myself.

Allen, as it turns out, was to have a better day. Later that morning, he bagged a nice three-point with a shot between the eyes. He said that's all he could see. The deer must have thought Allen couldn't see even that much because it was in a thicket about twenty yards away and down a steep hill from him. After I had caught up to him and his deer, we finished packing the buck out to the nearest road and brought the truck around to it. We drove to a nearby stream and ate lunch while we talked about what to do next. Allen talked me into trying at least one more hunt while he skinned his buck.

We went back to the Listening Tree Trail area and tried another hunt in the early afternoon. I hiked quite a ways and saw nothing. I was pretty tired, not to mention disappointed that we were still out there in the woods, instead of home taking care of our kills. I returned to the truck to find Al waiting. He had cleaned up, washing in the stream after taking care of his deer. We were tired, but we still had time to find a spot to shoot my rifle and see where it was hitting. In this country it doesn't take too long to find a spur off the main road that isn't used for travel. We found a safe site, unloaded the gear and prepared to touch off a few rounds. An old milk carton with water in it should be some fun to shoot at. I laid over a log for a good rest and peered down the barrel at the unsuspecting carton sitting on the bank of an inside corner. Blam! Complete miss—over the top again. I couldn't believe I was that bad. So I tried Allen's Thompson Center, Cherokee 45 caliber with a roundball. Blam, splat! Beautiful. We reloaded both rifles and then Allen shot mine to see for himself if it was off.

Since we had one deer to take home and hang, Al and I decided that we would leave and that I would try one more time the next day. All of the gear was packed away, rifles in the rack and two tired boys were ready to go. We were still on the dirt road headed for the main road, and had traveled maybe a mile or two, when we rounded a corner. There, about fifty yards ahead of us, was a magnificent buck kind of trotting across the road, headed for the hill above. Allen hit the brakes and I hit neutral. "Oh my God!" was all I could say. The hill was not steep but gradually rose away from us. It was littered with brush and openings. I had noticed that the buck had a limp and was not in a hurry to get out of there. I, however, sat frozen to my seat wondering what to do, until Allen practically pushed me out the door with the 45 caliber and a percussion cap in my hands. I managed to get the cap on and then headed for the roadside. I couldn't see him. I jumped off the road, crossed a dirt pile about ten yards wide, and headed for a better view. I was sure he was around and worked my way toward the hill he had seemed to be headed for. Allen watched from the road behind, trying to see the deer himself. I peeked around a small fir and spotted the buck behind a small patch of brush. He saw me and turned to leave. Just as he came out from behind the brush, I pulled down on him and pulled the trigger. A huge plume of blue smoke billowed out and suddenly I couldn't see the deer. I had no idea if I had hit him or missed him. Allen ran up to me and tossed me a quick reload kit for the rifle. I popped the top and proceeded to pour all of the powder down the barrel of the rifle. Unfortunately, I also poured the percussion cap down the barrel. I looked at Allen and told him what I'd done. I was so nervous! I knew I had a good shot at a monster whose points were as high and wide as I have ever seen, and it was taking its toll on me. Allen mumbled something about me dumping out the barrel and tossed me another quick load kit. Then he took off to see if he could find some sign of blood to trail. He said he had seen the hit, a dimple in the skin right behind the front leg in the heart area, as the bullet struck. I shook bad as I tried to get only the powder down the barrel this time. I managed that and started preparing the roundball to place in the barrel when Allen called out that he had found the deer—dead!

I ran over to where he was, maybe forty yards away under some thick firs. There lay the finest blacktail buck I had ever seen. It had been a perfect hit in the heart and lung area. His antlers were covered with a little dirt from his fall, but there was no hiding the fact that he was one of the finest of his kind and deserved the respect reserved for his age and wisdom. The buck had apparently been in a fight. Although the skin had not been punctured, he had a puncture wound in the rib cage muscle and a broken rib, most likely from another buck's antler tip. His own antlers, five points on one side and six on the other, were scraped but beautiful. Allen and I had just had one of the most successful deer hunts of our careers, and knew as we drove home that in the back of the truck was a very special buck.

(Final score: 159 2/8 B.C.)

Official Scoring System for Oregon Big Game Trophies

Records of Oregon Big Game

RECORD BOOK FOR OREGON

P.O. Box 759
Irrigon, OR 97844

NON-TYPICAL
MULE AND BLACKTAIL DEER

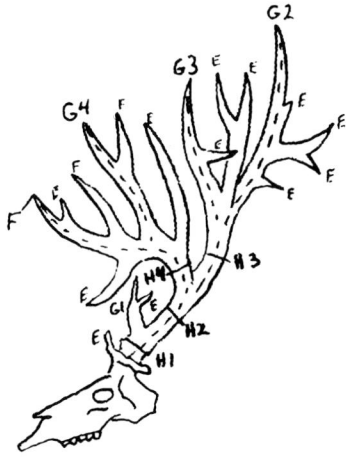

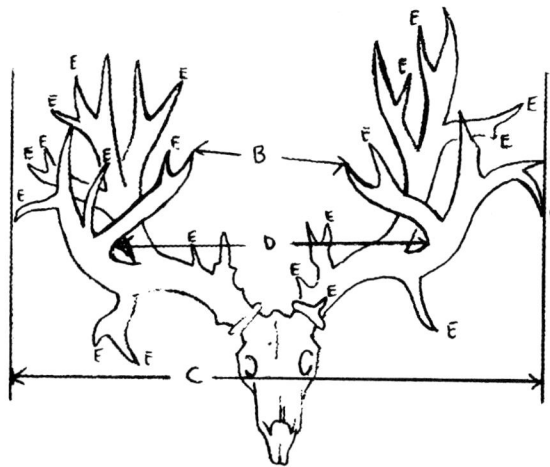

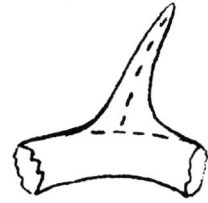

DETAIL OF POINT MEASUREMENT

Abnormal Points	
Right Antler	Left Antler
2 5/8	3 4/8
3 3/8	3 5/8
1 2/8	2 4/8
0 0/8	3 5/8
0 0/8	2 2/8
0 0/8	2 2/8
0 0/8	1 7/8
0 0/8	1 0/8
0 0/8	1 0/8
0 0/8	0 0/8

Species	Rifle	Archery	Muzzle	Shed	Archery-Velvet		
Mule Deer	200	160	175	85	160		
Columbia Blacktail	145	110	115	60	110		
Cascade Blacktail	145	110	115	60	110	**Subtotals**	7 2/8	21 5/8
Northwest Blacktail	145	110	115	60	110	**Total to E**	28 7/8

					COLUMN 1	COLUMN 2	COLUMN 3	COLUMN 4
					Spread Credit	Right Antler	Left Antler	Difference
A	Number of Points on Right Antler	8	Number of Points on Left Antler	14				
B	Tip to Tip Spread	15 5/8	**C** Greatest Spread	26 4/8				
D	Inside Spread of Main Beam	22 2/8	(Credit may be equal to but not exceed longer antler)	22 0/8				
E	Total of Length of Abnormal Points			28 7/8				
F	Length of Main Beam					21 7/8	22 0/8	0 1/8
G-1	Length of First Point, if present					2 1/8	2 4/8	0 3/8
G-2	Length of Second Point					11 3/8	13 5/8	2 2/8
G-3	Length of Third Point, if present					10 2/8	10 2/8	0 0/8
G-4	Length of Fourth Point, if present					10 3/8	12 0/8	1 5/8
H-1	Circumference at smallest place between Burr and First point					5 4/8	5 4/8	0 0/8
H-2	Circumference at smallest place between First and Second points					5 0/8	4 7/8	0 1/8
H-3	Circumference at smallest place between Main Beam and Third point					5 0/8	4 2/8	0 6/8
H-4	Circumference at smallest place between Second and Fourth points					5 3/8	5 0/8	0 3/8
	TOTALS				28 7/8	22 0/8	76 7/8	80 0/8	5 5/8

County where killed: Josephine	**Date Killed:** 1935		
Hunter's Name: Fred Bean		**ADD**	**Column 1**	22 0/8
Owner's Name: Riley Bean			**Column 2**	76 7/8
			Column 3	80 0/8
			Subtotal	178 7/8
			Subtract Column 4	5 5/8
			Result	173 2/8
			Add Line E Total	28 7/8
			FINAL SCORE	202 1/8

Official Scoring System for Oregon Big Game Trophies

Records of Oregon Big Game	RECORD BOOK FOR OREGON	P.O. Box 759 Irrigon, OR 97844

NON-TYPICAL
MULE AND BLACKTAIL DEER

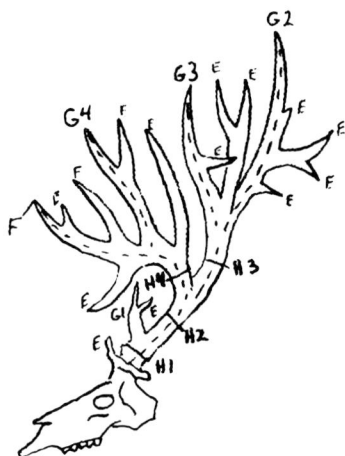

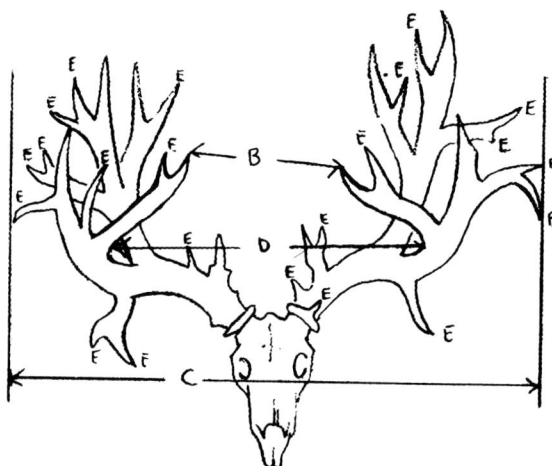

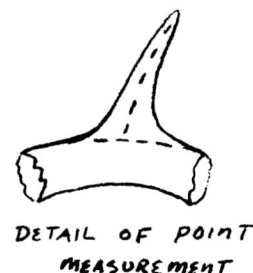

DETAIL OF POINT MEASUREMENT

Abnormal Points

Right Antler		Left Antler	
3	2/8	5	3/8
2	2/8	1	5/8
6	7/8	1	4/8
0	0/8	1	1/8
0	0/8	9	5/8
0	0/8	0	0/8
0	0/8	0	0/8
0	0/8	0	0/8
0	0/8	0	0/8
0	0/8	0	0/8

Species	Rifle	Archery	Muzzle	Shed	Archery-Velvet
Mule Deer	200	160	175	85	160
Columbia Blacktail	145	110	115	60	110
Cascade Blacktail	145	110	115	60	110
Northwest Blacktail	145	110	115	60	110

	Subtotals	12	3/8	19	2/8
	Total to E			31	5/8

				COLUMN 1 Spread Credit	COLUMN 2 Right Antler	COLUMN 3 Left Antler	COLUMN 4 Difference
A	Number of Points on Right Antler	10	Number of Points on Left Antler	8			
B	Tip to Tip Spread	17 6/8	**C** Greatest Spread	24 4/8			
D	Inside Spread of Main Beam	19 1/8	(Credit may be equal to but not exceed longer antler)	19 1/8			
E	Total of Length of Abnormal Points			31 5/8			
F	Length of Main Beam				23 3/8	23 4/8	0 1/8
G-1	Length of First Point, if present				5 0/8	4 4/8	0 4/8
G-2	Length of Second Point				13 2/8	13 4/8	0 2/8
G-3	Length of Third Point, if present				8 5/8	7 6/8	0 7/8
G-4	Length of Fourth Point, if present				9 0/8	3 2/8	5 6/8
H-1	Circumference at smallest place between Burr and First point				5 6/8	6 0/8	0 2/8
H-2	Circumference at smallest place between First and Second points				4 7/8	4 7/8	0 0/8
H-3	Circumference at smallest place between Main Beam and Third point				4 6/8	4 5/8	0 1/8
H-4	Circumference at smallest place between Second and Fourth points				5 1/8	4 4/8	0 5/8
	TOTALS			31 5/8	19 0/8	79 6/8	72 4/8	8 4/8

County where killed: Jackson	Date Killed: 12/04/88	ADD	Column 1	19	0/8
Hunter's Name: James Decker			Column 2	79	6/8
Owner's Name: James Decker			Column 3	72	4/8
			Subtotal	171	2/8
			Subtract Column 4	8	4/8
			Result	162	6/8
			Add Line E Total	31	5/8
			FINAL SCORE	194	3/8

Official Scoring System for Oregon Big Game Trophies

TYPICAL
MULE AND BLACKTAIL DEER

DETAIL OF POINT MEASUREMENT

Abnormal Points

	Right Antler		Left Antler	
	0	0/8	3	2/8
	0	0/8	0	0/8
	0	0/8	0	0/8
	0	0/8	0	0/8
	0	0/8	0	0/8
	0	0/8	0	0/8
	0	0/8	0	0/8
	0	0/8	0	0/8
	0	0/8	0	0/8
	0	0/8	0	0/8
Subtotals	0	0/8	3	2/8
Total to E			3	2/8

Species	Rifle	Archery	Muzzle	Shed	Archery - Velvet
Mule Deer	160	145	146	70	145
Columbia Blacktail	115	90	110	50	90
Cascade Blacktail	115	90	110	50	90
Northwest Blacktail	115	90	110	50	90

					COLUMN 1	COLUMN 2	COLUMN 3	COLUMN 4
A	Number of Points on Right Antler	4	Number of Points on Left Antler	5	Spread Credit	Right Antler	Left Antler	Difference
B	Tip to Tip Spread	18 4/8	C Greatest Spread	26 0/8				
D	Inside Spread of Main Beam	23 4/8	(Credit may be equal to but not exceed longer antler)	23 4/8				
E	Total of Length of Abnormal Points							3 2/8
F	Length of Main Beam					24 2/8	24 6/8	0 4/8
G-1	Length of First Point, if present					0 0/8	0 0/8	0 0/8
G-2	Length of Second Point					20 2/8	18 4/8	1 6/8
G-3	Length of Third Point, if present					11 4/8	9 4/8	2 0/8
G-4	Length of Fourth Point, if present					8 1/8	8 1/8	0 0/8
H-1	Circumference at smallest place between burr and first point					5 2/8	4 7/8	0 3/8
H-2	Circumference at smallest place between first and second point					5 2/8	4 7/8	0 3/8
H-3	Circumference at smallest place between main beam and 3rd pt					4 0/8	3 6/8	0 2/8
H-4	Circumference at smallest place between second and fourth points					3 5/8	3 5/8	0 0/8
				TOTALS	23 4/8	82 2/8	78 0/8	8 4/8

County where killed: Jackson	Date Killed: 1963		Column 1	23 4/8
Hunter's Name:		ADD	Column 2	82 2/8
Owner's Name: Frank Norton			Column 3	78 0/8
			Subtotal	183 6/8
			Subtract Column 4	8 4/8
			FINAL SCORE	175 2/8

Typical Cascade Blacktail—Rifle
Minimum Score: 115 0/8

Final Score Typical	Gross Typical	Net Typical	Abnormal Points	Greatest Spread	Inside Spread	Main Beam R	L	Number of Points R	L	First Circumference R	L	Year	County	Hunter/Owner	Rank
175 2/8	183 6/8	178 4/8	3 2/8	26 0/8	23 4/8	24 2/8	24 6/8	4	5	5 2/8	4 7/8	1963	Jackson	Frank Norton	1
174 7/8	178 6/8	174 7/8	0 0/8		27 4/8	23 3/8	23 0/8	0	0	4 7/8	5 1/8	1947	Deschutes	Arthur Dahlgren	2
172 3/8	181 2/8	174 7/8	2 4/8	25 3/8	22 3/8	26 3/8	26 6/8	5	5	4 6/8	5 0/8	1981	Klamath	Bob Vinson	3
163 7/8	167 2/8	163 7/8	0 0/8	22 0/8	19 7/8	23 2/8	22 5/8	5	5	5 6/8	5 5/8	1983	Jackson	Dave McCollum	4
163 6/8	168 1/8	165 2/8	1 4/8	21 4/8	18 0/8	24 3/8	24 5/8	6	5	4 4/8	4 7/8	1985	Lane	Kevin Gardner	5
158 2/8	164 7/3	161 4/8	3 2/8		23 7/8	23 2/8	23 6/8	7	5	4 6/8	4 6/8	1956	Lane	Carl Boyd/Alan McKinney	6
157 1/8	160 2/3	157 1/8	0 0/8	21 5/8	18 3/8	22 3/8	22 6/8	5	5	5 0/8	5 1/8	1978	Clackamas	Dick Loomis	7
155 4/8	159 1/3	155 4/8	0 0/8	18 0/8	15 6/8	21 4/8	22 4/8	5	5	4 6/8	4 6/8	1987	Klamath	Benjamin Brooks/Loren Brooks	8
152 5/8	159 0/3	153 6/8	1 1/8	23 3/8	21 2/8	20 1/8	22 2/8	5	6	5 3/8	5 2/8	1994	Hood River	Lloyd Frasier	9
152 4/8	157 6/3	152 4/8	0 0/8	21 3/8	19 2/8	24 4/8	25 7/8	4	4	5 2/8	5 2/8	1952	Wasco	Robert Sendlinger	10
151 6/8	154 1/3	151 6/8	0 0/8	22 4/8	19 6/8	22 2/8	22 4/8	5	5	4 3/8	4 5/8	1978	Jackson	Darrell Leek	11
147 0/8	150 5/3	147 0/8	0 0/8	20 3/8	17 2/8	23 0/8	21 4/8	5	5	4 4/8	4 4/8	1966	Douglas	Red Linson	12
146 5/8	155 0/3	149 1/8	2 4/8	17 4/8	15 3/8	23 4/8	23 7/8	6	5	4 3/8	4 4/8	1995	Jackson	Scott Fitzgerald	13
146 3/8	160 2/3	155 0/8	8 5/8	25 1/8	23 7/8	22 6/8	21 7/8	6	6	5 0/8	5 3/8	1995	Jackson	Don Ward	14
146 1/8	152 6/3	147 7/8	1 6/8	19 0/8	16 3/8	20 4/8	20 3/8	6	5	4 3/8	4 6/8			Eric Kendall	15
146 0/8	150 1/8	146 0/8	0 0/8	21 1/8	19 6/8	22 1/8	22 2/8	5	5	5 1/8	5 2/8	1963	Hood River	Billy O. Andrews/Gordon Andrews	16
145 2/8	153 4/8	145 2/8	0 0/8	21 0/8	17 0/8	21 2/8	19 4/8	5	5	4 3/8	4 4/8	1995	Douglas	Kevin Parazoo	17
143 0/8	154 0/8	146 1/8	3 1/8	23 4/8	18 5/8	22 0/8	22 1/8	6	5	4 1/8	4 2/8	1992	Linn	Sharon Heath	18
140 6/8	144 1/8	140 6/8	0 0/8	20 0/8	18 2/8	21 3/8	20 6/8	5	5	4 1/8	4 0/8	1982	Douglas	Paul Olsen	19
140 5/8	144 3/8	140 5/8	0 0/8		19 1/8	21 1/8	22 1/8	5	5	4 0/8	4 3/8	1992	Douglas	Brian Riley	20
140 2/8	147 0/8	140 2/8	0 0/8	24 6/8	21 4/8	23 0/8	22 1/8	4	5	4 2/8	4 0/8		Hood River	Tarquin Waggoner	21
138 6/8	142 5/8	140 0/8	1 2/8	18 4/8	16 4/8	21 5/8	21 6/8	6	5	3 7/8	3 7/8	1995	Clackamas	Gary McDonald	22
138 4/8	145 2/8	138 4/8	0 0/8	19 1/8	16 4/8	21 0/8	21 2/8	5	4	4 4/8	4 5/8	1980	Jackson	Dan Stanfield	23
137 4/8	140 3/8	138 6/8	1 2/8	21 0/8	18 4/8	22 0/8	22 2/8	4	5	4 1/8	4 2/8	1978	Douglas	Earnest Thomas	24
137 3/8	143 1/8	137 3/8	0 0/8	18 1/8	16 1/8	20 3/8	19 4/8	5	5	4 5/8	4 3/8	1993	Jefferson	Bob Frazier	25
137 0/8	146 5/8	137 0/8	0 0/8	22 7/8	18 2/8	21 7/8	20 6/8	5	5	4 1/8	4 0/8	1992	Jackson	Milt Smith	26
136 1/8	144 5/8	140 6/8	4 5/8	19 5/8	15 0/8	18 7/8	20 4/8	6	5	3 5/8	3 7/8	1980	Douglas	Mike Oglesby	27
134 1/8	143 6/8	139 6/8	5 5/8	18 2/8	16 0/8	19 2/8	18 4/8	6	6	4 0/8	4 0/8	1978	Douglas	Bob Gatlin	28
133 7/8	140 6/8	135 2/8	1 3/8	21 4/8	19 4/8	23 5/8	23 6/8	6	4	4 5/8	4 3/8	1987		Marvin Morey	29
132 7/8	151 7/8	146 5/8	13 6/8	28 1/8	19 7/8	20 6/8	20 4/8	7	7	4 2/8	4 1/8	1983	Linn	Daniel Magee	30
132 6/8	138 1/8	132 6/8	0 0/8	19 4/8	13 2/8	20 0/8	20 4/8	5	4	3 6/8	3 5/8	1976	Douglas	Ron Phillips	31
131 4/8	135 4/8	131 4/8	0 0/8	18 6/8	16 0/8	19 5/8	21 1/8	5	5	4 6/8	5 2/8	1974	Jackson	Leroy Thompson	32
130 7/8	136 4/8	130 7/8	0 0/8	19 3/8	15 5/8	20 4/8	20 1/8	5	4	3 6/8	3 4/8	1992	Douglas	Jeff Heil	33
130 5/8	140 6/8	135 3/8	4 6/8	18 5/8	16 1/8	21 6/8	20 5/8	6	5	3 6/8	3 6/8	1990	Douglas	Toby Mills	34
129 4/8	134 1/8	129 4/8	0 0/8	23 2/8	20 2/8	19 3/8	20 7/8	5	5	4 2/8	4 3/8	1985	Lane	Dale Banton	35
126 5/8	131 4/8	126 5/8	0 0/8	17 4/8	15 5/8	21 2/8	20 5/8	4	4	4 0/8	3 6/8	1984	Clackamas	Larry J. Griffin	36
126 1/8	129 1/8	126 1/8	0 0/8	19 0/8	16 5/8	19 4/8	18 6/8	5	5	4 2/8	4 3/8		Jackson	Dwight Crump	37
124 5/8	128 2/8	124 5/8	0 0/8	18 6/8	16 5/8	20 5/8	20 0/8	5	5	4 1/8	4 1/8	1981	Jackson	Larry Damon	38
124 1/8	127 1/8	124 1/8	0 0/8	16 6/8	14 3/8	17 7/8	19 1/8	5	5	3 4/8	3 5/8	1987	Douglas	Don Ring	39

Final Score	Gross Typical	Net Typical	Abnormal Points	Greatest Spread	Inside Spread	Main Beam R	Main Beam L	Points R	Points L	First Circ. R	First Circ. L	Year	County	Hunter/Owner	Rank
123 6/8	127 2/8	123 6/8	0 0/8	18 1/8	14 4/8	18 0/8	17 2/8	5	5	3 7/8	4 0/8	1995	Klamath	Timothy J. Tirill	40
120 0/8	125 3/8	122 0/8	0 0/8	21 4/8	16 6/8	18 1/8	19 0/8	5	5	3 6/8	3 6/8	1988	Douglas	Wayne C. Smith	41
120 2/8	121 3/8	120 2/8	0 0/8	20 1/8	17 4/8	20 4/8	19 7/8	4	4	4 5/8	4 4/8		Jackson	Dwight Crump	42
116 0/8	124 5/8	116 0/8	0 0/8	18 3/8	16 0/8	18 1/8	18 4/8	5	4	4 2/8	4 1/8		Jackson	Dwight Crump	43
115 7/8	119 0/8	115 7/8	0 0/8	17 1/8	14 7/8	17 6/8	18 5/8	4	4	3 4/8	3 4/8	1988	Douglas	Don Ring	44

Typical Cascade Blacktail—Archery
Minimum Score: 90 0/8

Final Score	Gross Typical	Net Typical	Abnormal Points	Greatest Spread	Inside Spread	Main Beam R	Main Beam L	Points R	Points L	First Circ. R	First Circ. L	Year	County	Hunter/Owner	Rank
172 2/8	0 0/8	0 0/8	0 0/8	22 6/8	20 4/8	26 3/8	25 7/8	7	7	0 0/8	0 0/8	1969	Marion	B.G. Schurtleff	1
150 7/8	162 3/8	150 7/8	0 0/8	24 0/8	20 3/8	24 3/8	23 5/8	4	5	4 4/8	4 4/8	1993	Douglas	Jimmy Brown	2
150 0/8	152 7/8	150 0/8	0 0/8	18 5/8	16 6/8	24 1/8	23 7/8	5	5	4 6/8	4 5/8	1983	Jackson	Ray Foulon	3
143 0/8	145 7/8	143 0/8	0 0/8	22 3/8	19 6/8	20 4/8	19 7/8	5	5	3 6/8	3 5/8	1995	Lane	Michael Tanner	4
137 1/8	141 0/8	137 1/8	0 0/8	19 6/8	17 3/8	19 7/8	18 7/8	5	5	4 4/8	4 6/8	1991	Jackson	Scott Thompson	5
132 3/8	144 0/8	141 0/8	8 5/8	23 1/8	19 6/8	21 5/8	20 6/8	5	8	4 0/8	4 0/8	1995	Jackson	Brian Hammer	6
123 5/8	130 4/8	123 5/8	0 0/8	19 4/8	17 3/8	20 7/8	20 7/8	5	5	4 4/8	4 5/8	1995	Douglas	Glen St. Onge	7
120 2/8	126 6/8	124 3/8	4 1/8	17 6/8	14 1/8	17 1/8	17 0/8	5	6	4 0/8	4 0/8	1993	Jackson	Greg Valencia	8

Typical Cascade Blacktail—Black Powder
Minimum Score: 110 0/8

Final Score	Gross Typical	Net Typical	Abnormal Points	Greatest Spread	Inside Spread	Main Beam R	Main Beam L	Points R	Points L	First Circ. R	First Circ. L	Year	County	Hunter/Owner	Rank
137 7/8	142 0/8	137 7/8	0 0/8	22 6/8	17 7/8	20 3/8	20 6/8	5	5	4 2/8	4 1/8	1982	Douglas	Ernest Thomas	1
128 3/8	130 1/8	128 3/8	0 0/8	17 0/8	15 1/8	20 0/8	19 4/8	4	4	4 0/8	4 0/8	1992	Lane	Murray Leslie	2
123 3/8	127 3/8	124 3/8	1 0/8	16 1/8	14 1/8	20 3/8	20 1/8	5	6	4 2/8	4 2/8	1995	Douglas	Shannon Strong	3
116 5/8	124 4/8	117 6/8	1 1/8	19 4/8	17 0/8	19 6/8	19 6/8	5	6	4 7/8	4 7/8	1988	Lane	Murray Leslie	4

Typical Cascade Blacktail—Shed Antlers
Minimum Score: 50 0/8

Final Score	Subtotal	Abnormal Points	Main Beam	First Point	Second Point	Third Point	Fourth Point	First Circumference	Right/Left	Year	County	Owner's Name	Rank
77 1/8	77 1/8	0 0/8	21 4/8	2 6/8	15 5/8	11 5/8	9 7/8	4 3/8	Right		Jackson	Randy Peyton	1
72 5/8	72 5/8	0 0/8	22 0/8	3 6/8	10 4/8	9 0/8	9 7/8	5 3/8	Left		Jackson	Randy Peyton	2
69 7/8	71 2/8	1 3/8	21 1/8	3 5/8	11 5/8	8 2/8	9 4/8	5 3/8	Right	1990	Jackson	Randy Peyton	3
51 7/8	56 4/8	4 5/8	18 0/8	0 0/8	10 7/8	5 3/8	7 0/8	4 2/8	Right		Linn	Mike Lowery	4

Non-Typical Cascade Blacktail—Rifle
Minimum Score: 145 0/8

Final Score	Gross Typical	Net Typical	Abnormal Points	Greatest Spread	Inside Spread	Main Beam R	Main Beam L	Number of Points R	Number of Points L	First Circumference R	First Circumference L	Year	County	Hunter/Owner	Rank
235 6/8	173 7/3	168 4/8	67 2/8	22 1/8	17 6/8	23 6/8	25 1/8	14	15	6 2/8	5 6/8	1991	Jackson	Ed Burkhart	1
220 2/8	170 4/3	162 0/8	58 2/8	31 0/8	20 0/8	24 2/8	22 6/8	8	12	4 6/8	4 4/8		Jackson	Leroy Cox	2
213 7/8	176 0/3	170 1/8	43 6/8	27 5/8	20 7/8	22 4/8	24 0/8	11	10	4 4/8	4 0/8	1990	Jackson	Jason Hinkle	3
199 5/8	160 6/3	157 1/8	42 4/8	25 2/8	18 7/8	21 6/8	21 6/8	13	10	4 2/8	4 2/8	1978	Jackson	Bill Penhall	4
185 3/8	158 6/3	145 1/8	40 2/8		20 1/8	22 0/8	19 2/8	9	12	5 1/8	5 5/8	1952	Jackson	Max Hull	5
176 7/8	169 4/3	164 4/8	12 3/8	18 5/8	16 4/8	24 1/8	24 3/8	8	7	5 6/8	5 3/8	1946	Jackson	Larry Konkel/John Hinkle	6
167 7/8	160 7/3	156 5/8	11 2/8	22 0/8	18 5/8	21 1/8	22 4/8	6	6	4 3/8	4 4/8	1978	Jackson	Tom Sutton	7
160 3/8	151 7/3	146 5/8	13 6/8	28 1/8	19 7/8	20 6/8	20 4/8	7	7	4 2/8	4 1/8	1983	Linn	Daniel Magee	8
159 3/8	148 2/3	140 7/8	18 4/8	25 2/8	23 1/8	22 6/8	24 0/8	8	6	5 1/8	5 2/8	1994	Jefferson	Tony Mitchell	9
145 3/8	143 6/3	149 6/8	5 5/8	18 2/8	16 0/8	19 2/8	18 4/8	6	6	4 0/8	4 0/8	1978	Douglas	Bob Gatlin	10

Non-Typical Cascade Blacktail—Archery
Minimum Score: 110 0/8

Final Score	Gross Typical	Net Typical	Abnormal Points	Greatest Spread	Inside Spread	Main Beam R	Main Beam L	Number of Points R	Number of Points L	First Circumference R	First Circumference L	Year	County	Hunter/Owner	Rank
153 6/8	149 4/3	145 6/8	8 0/8	23 0/8	16 2/8	20 7/8	20 4/8	7	6	4 2/8	4 2/8	1992	Klamath	Glen Gregory	1
140 5/8	132 6/3	127 0/8	13 5/8	19 5/8	17 2/8	18 3/8	16 0/8	7	6	3 4/8	3 3/8	1991	Klamath	Bill Martin	2

Non-Typical Cascade Blacktail—Shed Antlers
Minimum Score: 60 0/8

Final Score	Subtotal	Abnormal Points	Main Beam	First Point	Second Point	Third Point	Fourth Point	First Circumference	Right/Left	Year	County	Owner's Name	Rank
72 5/8	71 2/8	1 3/8	21 1/8	3 5/8	11 5/8	8 2/8	9 4/8	5 3/8	Right		Jackson	Randy Peyton	1
61 1/8	56 4/8	4 5/8	18 0/8	0 0/8	10 7/8	5 3/8	7 0/8	4 2/8	Right		Linn	Mike Lowery	2

Official Scoring System for Oregon Big Game Trophies

Records of Oregon Big Game

RECORD BOOK FOR OREGON

P.O. Box 759
Irrigon, OR 97844

TYPICAL
MULE AND BLACKTAIL DEER

DETAIL OF POINT MEASUREMENT

Abnormal Points			
Right Antler		Left Antler	
0	0/8	0	0/8
0	0/8	0	0/8
0	0/8	0	0/8
0	0/8	0	0/8
0	0/8	0	0/8
0	0/8	0	0/8
0	0/8	0	0/8
0	0/8	0	0/8
0	0/8	0	0/8
0	0/8	0	0/8

Species	Rifle	Archery	Muzzle	Shed	Archery - Velvet
Mule Deer	160	145	146	70	145
Columbia Blacktail	115	90	110	50	90
Cascade Blacktail	115	90	110	50	90
Northwest Blacktail	115	90	110	50	90

	Subtotals	0 0/8	0 0/8
	Total to E		0 0/8

		COLUMN 1	COLUMN 2	COLUMN 3	COLUMN 4
		Spread Credit	Right Antler	Left Antler	Difference
A	Number of Points on Right Antler: 4 — Number of Points on Left Antler: 5				
B	Tip to Tip Spread: 11 7/8 **C** Greatest Spread: 24 0/8				
D	Inside Spread of Main Beam: 20 3/8 (Credit may be equal to but not exceed longer antler): 20 3/8	20 3/8			
E	Total of Length of Abnormal Points				0 0/8
F	Length of Main Beam		24 3/8	23 5/8	0 6/8
G-1	Length of First Point, if present		1 7/8	1 5/8	0 2/8
G-2	Length of Second Point		14 3/8	13 6/8	0 5/8
G-3	Length of Third Point, if present		0 0/8	9 1/8	9 1/8
G-4	Length of Fourth Point, if present		10 5/8	10 1/8	0 4/8
H-1	Circumference at smallest place between burr and first point		4 4/8	4 4/8	0 0/8
H-2	Circumference at smallest place between first and second point		4 0/8	4 0/8	0 0/8
H-3	Circumference at smallest place between main beam and 3rd pt		3 4/8	3 4/8	0 0/8
H-4	Circumference at smallest place between second and fourth points		4 3/8	4 1/8	0 2/8
	TOTALS	20 3/8	67 5/8	74 3/8	11 4/8

County where killed:	Douglas	Date Killed:	1993		Column 1	20	3/8
Hunter's Name:	Jimmy	Brown		**ADD**	Column 2	67	5/8
Owner's Name:	Jimmy	Brown			Column 3	74	3/8
					Subtotal	162	3/8
					Subtract Column 4	11	4/8
					FINAL SCORE	**150**	**7/8**

Official Scoring System for Oregon Big Game Trophies

TYPICAL
MULE AND BLACKTAIL DEER

DETAIL OF POINT MEASUREMENT

Abnormal Points	
Right Antler	Left Antler
0 0/8	0 0/8
0 0/8	0 0/8
0 0/8	0 0/8
0 0/8	0 0/8
0 0/8	0 0/8
0 0/8	0 0/8
0 0/8	0 0/8
0 0/8	0 0/8
0 0/8	0 0/8
0 0/8	0 0/8
Subtotals 0 0/8	0 0/8
Total to E	0 0/8

Species	Rifle	Archery	Muzzle	Shed	Archery - Velvet
Mule Deer	160	145	146	70	145
Columbia Blacktail	115	90	110	50	90
Cascade Blacktail	115	90	110	50	90
Northwest Blacktail	115	90	110	50	90

					COLUMN 1	COLUMN 2	COLUMN 3	COLUMN 4
A	Number of Points on Right Antler	5	Number of Points on Left Antler	5	Spread Credit	Right Antler	Left Antler	Difference
B	Tip to Tip Spread	12 2/8	C Greatest Spread	22 6/8				
D	Inside Spread of Main Beam	17 7/8	(Credit may be equal to but not exceed longer antler)	17 7/8				
E	Total of Length of Abnormal Points							0 0/8
F	Length of Main Beam					20 3/8	20 6/8	0 3/8
G-1	Length of First Point, if present					3 0/8	3 5/8	0 5/8
G-2	Length of Second Point					11 2/8	10 5/8	0 5/8
G-3	Length of Third Point, if present					6 0/8	5 0/8	1 0/8
G-4	Length of Fourth Point, if present					6 3/8	7 5/8	1 2/8
H-1	Circumference at smallest place between burr and first point					4 2/8	4 1/8	0 1/8
H-2	Circumference at smallest place between first and second point					3 6/8	3 6/8	0 0/8
H-3	Circumference at smallest place between main beam and 3rd pt					3 2/8	3 2/8	0 0/8
H-4	Circumference at smallest place between second and fourth points					3 4/8	3 5/8	0 1/8
			TOTALS		17 7/8	61 6/8	62 3/8	4 1/8

County where killed:	Douglas	Date Killed:	11/82			
Hunter's Name:	Ernest	Thomas		ADD	Column 1	17 7/8
Owner's Name:	Ernest	Thomas			Column 2	61 6/8
					Column 3	62 3/8
					Subtotal	142 0/8
					Subtract Column 4	4 1/8
					FINAL SCORE	137 7/8

Official Scoring System for Oregon Big Game Trophies

**Records of Oregon
Big Game**

RECORD BOOK FOR OREGON

P.O. Box 759
Irrigon, OR 97844

NON-TYPICAL
MULE AND BLACKTAIL DEER

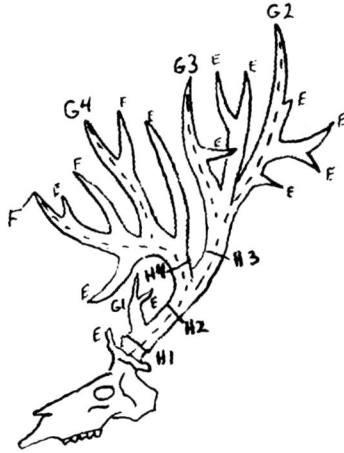

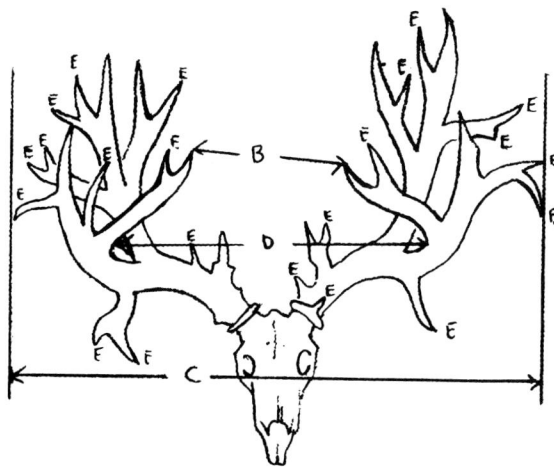

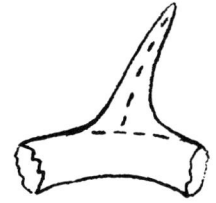

DETAIL OF POINT MEASUREMENT

Abnormal Points	
Right Antler	Left Antler
8 4/8	10 0/8
2 6/8	12 7/8
1 2/8	1 3/8
4 1/8	1 4/8
3 3/8	3 4/8
2 0/8	2 2/8
4 0/8	3 0/8
3 6/8	2 0/8
1 0/8	0 0/8
0 0/8	0 0/8

Species	Rifle	Archery	Muzzle	Shed	Archery-Velvet
Mule Deer	200	160	175	85	160
Columbia Blacktail	145	110	115	60	110
Cascade Blacktail	145	110	115	60	110
Northwest Blacktail	145	110	115	60	110

	Subtotals	30 6/8	36 4/8
	Total to E		67 2/8

						COLUMN 1	COLUMN 2	COLUMN 3	COLUMN 4
A	Number of Points on Right Antler	14		Number of Points on Left Antler	15	Spread Credit	Right Antler	Left Antler	Difference
B	Tip to Tip Spread	9 4/8	C	Greatest Spread	22 1/8				
D	Inside Spread of Main Beam	17 6/8		(Credit may be equal to but not exceed longer antler)		17 6/8			
E	Total of Length of Abnormal Points				67 2/8				
F	Length of Main Beam						23 6/8	25 1/8	1 3/8
G-1	Length of First Point, if present						4 2/8	4 4/8	0 2/8
G-2	Length of Second Point						13 4/8	14 0/8	0 4/8
G-3	Length of Third Point, if present						5 4/8	5 0/8	0 4/8
G-4	Length of Fourth Point, if present						12 0/8	10 6/8	1 2/8
H-1	Circumference at smallest place between Burr and First point						6 2/8	5 6/8	0 4/8
H-2	Circumference at smallest place between First and Second points						4 6/8	4 3/8	0 3/8
H-3	Circumference at smallest place between Main Beam and Third point						3 6/8	3 2/8	0 4/8
H-4	Circumference at smallest place between Second and Fourth points						4 7/8	4 6/8	0 1/8
	TOTALS					67 2/8	17 0/8	78 5/8	77 4/8	5 3/8

County where killed: Jackson Date Killed: 1991
Hunter's Name: Ed Burkhart
Owner's Name: Ed Burkhart

ADD	Column 1	17 0/8
	Column 2	78 5/8
	Column 3	77 4/8
	Subtotal	173 1/8
	Subtract Column 4	5 3/8
	Result	167 6/8
	Add Line E Total	67 2/8
	FINAL SCORE	235 0/8

Official Scoring System for Oregon Big Game Trophies

Records of Oregon
Big Game

RECORD BOOK FOR OREGON

P.O. Box 759
Irrigon, OR 97844

NON-TYPICAL
MULE AND BLACKTAIL DEER

DETAIL OF POINT MEASUREMENT

Abnormal Points

Right Antler		Left Antler	
2	0/8	2	4/8
3	4/8	0	0/8
0	0/8	0	0/8
0	0/8	0	0/8
0	0/8	0	0/8
0	0/8	0	0/8
0	0/8	0	0/8
0	0/8	0	0/8
0	0/8	0	0/8
0	0/8	0	0/8
Subtotals 5	4/8	2	4/8
Total to E		8	0/8

Species	Rifle	Archery	Muzzle	Shed	Archery-Velvet
Mule Deer	200	160	175	85	160
Columbia Blacktail	145	110	115	60	110
Cascade Blacktail	145	110	115	60	110
Northwest Blacktail	145	110	115	60	110

					COLUMN 1	COLUMN 2	COLUMN 3	COLUMN 4
					Spread Credit	Right Antler	Left Antler	Difference
A	Number of Points on Right Antler	7	Number of Points on Left Antler	6				
B	Tip to Tip Spread	11 7/8	C Greatest Spread	23 0/8				
D	Inside Spread of Main Beam	16 2/8	(Credit may be equal to but not exceed longer antler)	16 2/8				
E	Total of Length of Abnormal Points			8 0/8				
F	Length of Main Beam					20 7/8	20 4/8	0 3/8
G-1	Length of First Point, if present					2 0/8	2 0/8	0 0/8
G-2	Length of Second Point					13 0/8	13 4/8	0 4/8
G-3	Length of Third Point, if present					7 6/8	7 0/8	0 6/8
G-4	Length of Fourth Point, if present					7 6/8	8 6/8	1 0/8
H-1	Circumference at smallest place between Burr and First point					4 2/8	4 2/8	0 0/8
H-2	Circumference at smallest place between First and Second points					3 6/8	3 6/8	0 0/8
H-3	Circumference at smallest place between Main Beam and Third point					3 2/8	3 6/8	0 4/8
H-4	Circumference at smallest place between Second and Fourth points					3 7/8	3 2/8	0 5/8
	TOTALS				8 0/8	16 0/8	66 4/8	66 6/8	3 6/8

County where killed: Klamath	Date Killed: 11/92		Column 1	16 0/8
Hunter's Name: Glen Gregory		**ADD**	Column 2	66 4/8
Owner's Name: Glen Gregory			Column 3	66 6/8
			Subtotal	149 2/8
			Subtract Column 4	3 6/8
			Result	145 4/8
			Add Line E Total	8 0/8
			FINAL SCORE	**153 4/8**

Typical Northwest Blacktail—Rifle
Minimum Score: 115 0/8

Final Score	Gross Typical	Net Typical	Abnormal Points	Greatest Spread	Inside Spread	Main Beam R	Main Beam L	Number of Points R	Number of Points L	First Circumference R	First Circumference L	Year	County	Hunter/Owner	Rank
135 0/8	136 7/8	135 0/8	0 0/8	22 3/8	17 4/8	20 7/8	21 0/8	5	5	4 0/8	3 7/8	1995	Lincoln	Bill H. Henderson	1
133 5/8	143 2/8	136 0/8	2 3/8	17 5/8	15 0/8	21 1/8	19 5/8	6	5	4 6/8	4 7/8	1952	Columbia	Duane Bernard	2
133 4/8	149 0/8	141 7/8	8 3/8	18 4/8	15 7/8	22 2/8	21 5/8	7	7	4 5/8	4 4/8	1994	Lincoln	Glen Silbernagel	3
133 2/8	137 1/8	133 2/8	0 0/8	22 4/8	19 4/8	20 4/8	21 6/8	5	5	4 1/8	4 3/8	1985	Lincoln	David Oleman	4
132 1/8	137 3/8	132 1/8	0 0/8	20 4/8	18 3/8	20 4/8	20 2/8	5	5	4 4/8	4 3/8	1990	Tillamook	Robert Brown	5
131 7/8	136 0/8	131 7/8	0 0/8	19 4/8	16 7/8	21 2/8	21 3/8	5	5	4 4/8	4 5/8	1962	Clatsop	Hal Hankel	6
126 3/8	134 6/8	126 3/8	0 0/8	19 0/8	17 3/8	20 7/8	16 4/8	4	4	4 0/8	4 4/8	1971	Columbia	Rusty Lindberg	7
126 2/8	128 5/8	126 2/8	0 0/8		15 4/8	20 6/8	20 2/8	4	4	3 7/8	3 5/8	1995	Columbia	Tom Jones	8
124 7/8	129 2/8	126 5/8	1 6/8	17 4/8	14 7/8	19 1/8	19 4/8	5	6	3 6/8	4 0/8	1981	Lincoln	Sam Settlemire/Terry W. Smith	9
124 3/8	131 0/8	124 3/8	0 0/8	16 6/8	14 7/8	20 4/8	20 3/8	4	5	4 1/8	4 2/8	1983	Tillamook	Jerry Roberts	10
124 2/8	132 2/8	127 3/8	3 1/8	16 4/8	14 5/8	20 4/8	20 6/8	6	5	4 3/8	4 3/8	1969	Clatsop	Robert L. Brown	11
122 6/8	126 3/8	122 6/8	0 0/8	20 2/8	17 2/8	20 7/8	21 3/8	3	4	4 5/8	4 4/8	1995	Clatsop	Ryan Rusley	12
122 3/8	128 5/8	122 3/8	0 0/8	17 4/8	15 5/8	21 3/8	21 2/8	4	4	4 3/8	4 3/8	1990	Columbia	Kelly P. Dering/Michael Dering	13
121 7/8	126 2/8	121 7/8	0 0/8	18 0/8	16 3/8	19 6/8	19 6/8	4	4	4 2/8	4 2/8	1992	Columbia	Daniel J. Bernard	14
121 5/8	127 5/8	121 5/8	0 0/8		16 1/8	20 0/8	19 5/8	4	4	3 7/8	3 7/8	1995	Clatsop	Steve McLeod	15
120 2/8	125 7/8	120 2/8	0 0/8	18 4/8	16 4/8	21 4/8	21 4/8	4	5	3 6/8	4 0/8	1977	Clatsop	Steven Berglund	16
119 2/8	123 7/8	119 2/8	0 0/8	20 6/8	19 0/8	20 5/8	20 0/8	4	5	3 4/8	3 7/8	1990	Lincoln	David Oleman	17
119 0/8	122 0/8	119 0/8	0 0/8	15 4/8	13 4/8	18 1/8	18 1/8	5	5	4 4/8	4 3/8	1970	Clatsop	Robert L. Brown	18
118 6/8	122 1/8	118 6/8	0 0/8	16 0/8	14 4/8	19 2/8	19 6/8	5	5	4 2/8	4 2/8	1992	Lincoln	Terry Smith	19
118 1/8	129 2/8	125 6/8	7 5/8	18 4/8	16 4/8	18 4/8	18 6/8	6	7	4 3/8	4 3/8	1992	Tillamook	Rick Herron	20
169 3/8*	173 0/8	169 3/8	0 0/8	20 4/8	16 7/8	22 5/8	22 1/8	5	5	5 4/8	5 2/8		Tillamook	Arrice L. Day	
172 5/8*	176 7/8	174 2/8	1 5/8	24 2/8	21 0/8	23 6/8	23 1/8	5	5	4 7/8	4 6/8	1919	Washington	Fred Wolford/Swede French	

*To be ranked in the top ten, entries must also qualify for Boone and Crockett.

Typical Northwest Blacktail—Archery
Minimum Score: 90 0/8

Final Score	Gross Typical	Net Typical	Abnormal Points	Greatest Spread	Inside Spread	Main Beam R	Main Beam L	Number of Points R	Number of Points L	First Circumference R	First Circumference L	Year	County	Hunter/Owner	Rank
118 4/8	122 3/8	118 4/8	0 0/8	16 0/8	14 4/8	20 0/8	20 3/8	4	4	3 5/8	3 2/8	1992	Lincoln	Terry Smith/Larry Smith	1
100 1/8	102 0/8	100 1/8	0 0/8	15 7/8	13 3/8	16 7/8	16 7/8	4	4	3 4/8	3 5/8	1994	Lincoln	Terry W. Smith	2
91 7/8	95 4/8	91 7/8	0 0/8	14 5/8	12 7/8	15 4/8	14 4/8	4	4	3 2/8	3 5/8	1995	Lincoln	John Boydston, Jr.	3

Non-Typical Northwest Blacktail—Rifle
Minimum Score: 145 0/8

Final Score	Gross Typical	Net Typical	Abnormal Points	Greatest Spread	Inside Spread	Main Beam R	Main Beam L	Number of Points R	Number of Points L	First Circumference R	First Circumference L	Year	County	Hunter/Owner	Rank
152 6/8	128 1/8	123 0/8	29 6/8	19 0/8	13 4/8	18 5/8	19 1/8	11	9	5 0/8	5 0/8	1952	Columbia	Ray Anicker	1
150 2/8	149 0/8	141 7/8	8 3/8	18 4/8	15 7/8	22 2/8	21 5/8	7	7	4 5/8	4 4/8	1994	Lincoln	Glen Silbernagel	2
138 2/8	124 7/8	116 1/8	22 1/8	15 6/8	12 7/8	18 7/8	17 6/8	6	5	5 0/8	4 6/8	1948	Columbia	Bill Eckland/Brad Eckland	3

Mule Deer

Top 25 Mule Deer
Sorted by Gross Typical Score

Gross Typical	Final Score	Net Typical	Abnormal Points	Greatest Spread	Inside Spread	Main Beam R	Main Beam L	Number of Points R	Number of Points L	First Circumference R	First Circumference L	Year	County	Hunter/Owner	Rank
219 1/8	197 6/8	212 7/8	15 1/8	35 0/8	27 5/8	31 4/8	31 1/8	7	12	5 0/8	5 1/8	1968	Lake	Bill King	1
215 4/8	321 1/8	209 5/8	111 4/8	34 2/8	26 5/8	28 1/8	25 4/8	17	25	6 7/8	6 7/8	1925	Umatilla	Albert Peterson/David Ayars	2
215 1/8	187 2/8	209 6/8	22 4/8	27 4/8	25 2/8	29 2/8	29 1/8	7	11	5 5/8	5 4/8	1929	Grant	Dolly Williams/Ed Heid	3
215 0/8	224 3/8	208 2/8	16 1/8	33 6/8	28 7/8	28 4/8	27 4/8	7	6	6 0/8	5 5/8	1995	Malheur	William T. Monson	4
214 0/8	183 6/8	208 2/8	24 4/8	40 0/8	29 0/8	26 2/8	27 4/8	8	9	5 0/8	5 0/8	1952	Harney	The Gun Room	5
213 7/8	236 6/8	207 2/8	29 4/8	39 3/8	34 0/8	30 0/8	29 4/8	9	11	5 5/8	5 7/8	1977	Klamath	George Hessler/Elvis Tillman	6
213 5/8	189 0/8	209 2/8	20 2/8	35 0/8	27 4/8	26 2/8	27 7/8	7	7	6 0/8	5 4/8	1943	Crook	Harry Sederance/Ned Sederance	7
212 4/8	228 5/8	197 6/8	30 7/8	27 0/8	22 6/8	25 2/8	24 6/8	10	11	5 0/8	5 4/8	1935	Grant	Cliff Mulcare/Mike Mulcare	8
212 1/8	223 5/8	210 3/8	13 2/8	35 4/8	26 3/8	27 6/8	28 3/8	8	6	5 1/8	5 1/8	1962	Jefferson	Harvey Rhoades	9
211 7/8	211 6/8	205 4/8	6 2/8	31 0/8	26 0/8	25 2/8	26 4/8	7	5	6 4/8	6 4/8	1975	Lake	Dan Callaghan	10
211 0/8	256 4/8	207 6/8	48 6/8	32 5/8	22 0/8	28 3/8	28 4/8	10	9	5 1/8	5 1/8	1988	Baker	Thomas Rosseau	11
210 5/8	239 5/8	204 1/8	35 4/8	35 0/8	30 4/8	27 5/8	26 6/8	9	10	6 3/8	6 0/8	1927	Harney	Culver Page/Glen Shelley	12
210 0/8	216 7/8	207 0/8	9 7/8	35 0/8	29 4/8	26 2/8	26 6/8	6	7	5 0/8	5 0/8	1948	Wheeler	Fran Cherry/Lorraine Cherry	13
209 6/8	232 0/8	203 5/8	28 3/8	33 6/8	25 1/8	27 5/8	27 5/8	8	8	4 7/8	4 7/8	1995	Sherman	Wendell Clodfelter	14
209 1/8	238 7/8	198 4/8	40 3/8	34 5/8	27 0/8	26 6/8	24 0/8	10	9	5 4/8	6 0/8	1920	Klamath	Harley Hall	15
208 6/8	203 0/8	205 4/8	2 4/8	31 7/8	26 0/8	27 5/8	27 4/8	5	7	6 6/8	6 6/8	1994	Harney	Doug White	16
208 6/8	236 4/8	200 5/8	35 7/8	30 5/8	18 1/8	24 0/8	24 4/8	14	10	5 0/8	5 0/8	1995	Union	Logan Girrard	16
208 5/8	214 5/8	202 7/8	11 6/8	30 6/8	20 5/8	31 1/8	31 1/8	6	8	5 3/8	5 4/8	1960	Grant	Gary Engle	18
207 3/8	208 4/8	201 4/8	7 0/8	31 0/8	26 0/8	27 2/8	27 2/8	6	5	5 2/8	5 4/8	1982	Grant	Joe D. Brooks	19
207 3/8	208 2/8	199 1/8	9 1/8	31 0/8	22 1/8	24 4/8	26 5/8	5	7	5 4/8	5 3/8	1930	Harney	Roy Heinz/Gary Arntz	19
207 0/8	270 5/8	200 0/8	70 5/8	37 0/8	27 6/8	29 3/8	28 4/8	17	16	5 7/8	5 7/8	1962	Grant	C.F. Cheney/Carl Christen	21
207 0/8	202 4/8	197 3/8	5 1/8	31 0/8	24 1/8	26 6/8	27 0/8	6	5	5 4/8	5 0/8	1959	Wallowa	Gene Roberts	21
206 6/8	187 5/8	195 2/8	7 5/8	37 0/8	30 4/8	29 4/8	28 2/8	7	7	5 5/8	5 7/8	1981	Crook	Clark Onsley	23
206 3/8	233 7/8	200 6/8	33 1/8	32 0/8	29 3/8	28 2/8	28 4/8	10	8	5 3/8	5 3/8	1991	Lake	Carl Tracy	24
206 2/8	199 3/8	201 5/8	2 2/8	27 1/8	24 1/8	26 4/8	28 4/8	7	5	5 1/8	5 2/8	1995	Harney	John Echanis	25

Top 25 Mule Deer
Sorted by Net Typical Score

Net Typical	Final Score	Gross Typical	Abnormal Points	Greatest Spread	Inside Spread	Main Beam R	Main Beam L	Number of Points R	Number of Points L	First Circumference R	First Circumference L	Year	County	Hunter/Owner	Rank
217 0/8	209 4/8	219 1/8	8 3/8	30 1/8	28 0/8	28 7/8	29 6/8	6	8	5 7/8	5 7/8	1920	Wallowa	John C. Evans/Stan Neitling	1
212 7/8	197 6/8	219 1/8	15 1/8	35 0/8	27 5/8	31 4/8	31 1/8	7	12	5 0/8	5 1/8	1968	Lake	Bill King	2
210 3/8	223 5/8	212 1/8	13 2/8	35 4/8	26 3/8	27 6/8	28 3/8	8	6	5 1/8	5 1/8	1962	Jefferson	Harvey Rhoades	3
209 6/8	232 2/8	215 1/8	22 4/8	27 4/8	25 2/8	29 2/8	29 1/8	7	11	5 5/8	5 4/8	1929	Grant	Dolly Williams/Ed Heid	4
209 5/8	321 1/8	215 4/8	111 4/8	34 2/8	26 5/8	28 1/8	25 4/8	17	25	6 7/8	6 7/8	1925	Umatilla	Albert Peterson/David Ayars	5
209 2/8	189 0/8	213 5/8	20 2/8	35 0/8	27 4/8	26 2/8	27 7/8	7	7	6 0/8	5 4/8	1943	Crook	Harry Sederance/Ned Sederance	6
208 2/8	232 6/8	214 0/8	24 4/8	40 0/8	29 0/8	26 2/8	27 4/8	8	9	5 0/8	5 0/8	1952	Harney	The Gun Room	7
208 2/8	224 3/8	215 0/8	16 1/8	33 6/8	28 7/8	28 4/8	27 4/8	7	6	6 0/8	5 5/8	1995	Malheur	William T. Monson	7

Top 25 Mule Deer Sorted by Net Typical Score (continued)

Net Typical	Final Score	Gross Typical	Abnormal Points	Greatest Spread	Inside Spread	Main Beam R	Main Beam L	Points R	Points L	First Circ R	First Circ L	Year	County	Hunter/Owner	Rank
207 6/8	256 4/8	211 0/8	48 6/8	32 5/8	22 0/8	28 3/8	28 4/8	10	9	5 1/8	5 1/8	1988	Baker	Thomas Rosseau	9
207 2/8	236 6/8	213 7/8	29 4/8	39 3/8	34 0/8	30 0/8	29 4/8	9	11	5 5/8	5 7/8	1977	Klamath	George Hessler/Elvis Tillman	10
207 0/8	216 7/8	210 0/8	9 7/8	35 0/8	29 4/8	26 2/8	26 6/8	6	7	5 0/8	5 0/8	1948	Wheeler	Fran Cherry/Lorraine Cherry	11
205 4/8	203 0/8	208 6/8	2 4/8	31 7/8	26 0/8	27 5/8	27 4/8	5	7	6 6/8	6 6/8	1994	Harney	Doug White	12
205 4/8	211 6/8	211 7/8	6 2/8	31 0/8	26 0/8	25 2/8	26 4/8	7	5	6 4/8	6 4/8	1975	Lake	Dan Callaghan	12
204 1/8	239 5/8	210 5/8	35 4/8	35 0/8	30 4/8	27 5/8	26 6/8	9	10	6 3/8	6 0/8	1927	Harney	Culver Page/Glen Shelley	14
203 5/8	232 0/8	209 6/8	28 3/8	33 6/8	25 1/8	27 5/8	27 5/8	8	8	4 7/8	4 7/8	1995	Sherman	Wendell Clodfelter	15
202 7/8	214 5/8	208 5/8	11 6/8	30 6/8	20 5/8	31 1/8	31 1/8	6	8	5 3/8	5 4/8	1960	Grant	Gary Engle	16
202 2/8	229 3/8	205 7/8	27 1/8	32 4/8	26 6/8	25 4/8	26 2/8	11	9	6 2/8	6 2/8			Joseph Hardware	17
201 7/8	197 7/8	205 6/8	4 0/8	28 1/8	24 1/8	27 0/8	27 4/8	6	6	4 4/8	4 4/8	1995		Leah O. Robertson	18
201 5/8	201 5/8	206 0/8	0 0/8	29 3/8	24 3/8	26 2/8	27 3/8	5	5	5 4/8	5 4/8	1988	Baker	Terry Williams	19
201 5/8	199 3/8	206 2/8	2 2/8	27 1/8	24 1/8	26 4/8	28 4/8	7	5	5 1/8	5 2/8	1995	Harney	John Echanis	19
201 4/8	208 4/8	207 3/8	7 0/8	31 0/8	26 0/8	27 2/8	27 2/8	6	5	5 2/8	5 4/8	1982	Grant	Joe D. Brooks	21
200 7/8	195 7/8	204 6/8	5 0/8	36 1/8	30 2/8	29 7/8	29 7/8	6	7	5 1/8	5 5/8	1990	Crook	Hop Jackson	22
200 6/8	233 7/8	206 3/8	33 1/8	32 0/8	29 3/8	28 2/8	28 4/8	10	8	5 3/8	5 3/8	1991	Lake	Carl Tracy	23
200 5/8	236 4/8	208 6/8	35 7/8	30 5/8	18 1/8	24 0/8	24 4/8	14	10	5 0/8	5 0/8	1995	Union	Logan Girrard	24
200 1/8	176 5/8	205 1/8	23 4/8	39 0/8	35 0/8	29 1/8	29 1/8	9	6	5 7/8	5 0/8	1995	Lake	Nolan Greiner	25

Top 25 Non-Typical Mule Deer Regardless of Kill Method

Final Score	Gross Typical	Net Typical	Abnormal Points	Greatest Spread	Inside Spread	Main Beam R	Main Beam L	Points R	Points L	First Circ R	First Circ L	Year	County	Hunter/Owner	Rank
321 1/8	215 4/8	209 5/8	111 4/8	34 2/8	26 5/8	28 1/8	25 4/8	17	25	6 7/8	6 7/8	1925	Umatilla	Albert Peterson/David Ayars	1
297 7/8	206 0/8	198 5/8	99 2/8	39 6/8	35 6/8	29 1/8	27 5/8	20	18	5 4/8	5 3/8	1971	Malheur	Bradley Barclay	2
283 7/8	193 5/8	190 7/8	93 0/8	30 3/8	23 3/8	25 4/8	26 2/8	17	17	6 1/8	6 1/8	1965	Harney	Ken Pruitt/Alan Hogan	3
270 5/8	207 0/8	200 0/8	70 5/8	37 0/8	27 6/8	29 3/8	28 4/8	17	16	5 7/8	5 7/8	1962	Grant	C.F. Cheney/Carl Christen	4
268 5/8	162 0/8	155 2/8	113 3/8	38 7/8	27 0/8	24 2/8	22 7/8	14	15	6 0/8	6 3/8	1941	Grant	Lige Davis/Coy Johnston	5
256 4/8	211 0/8	207 6/8	48 6/8	32 5/8	22 0/8	28 3/8	28 4/8	10	9	5 1/8	5 1/8	1988	Baker	Thomas Rosseau	6
252 2/8	198 0/8	196 1/8	56 1/8		25 3/8	25 3/8	25 0/8	13	12	5 0/8	5 0/8			S Centwise Sporting Good	7
250 6/8	173 1/8	168 1/8	82 5/8	34 0/8	20 1/8	23 1/8	22 4/8	17	13	5 4/8	5 4/8	1993	Grant	Stoney E. Gienger	8
248 4/8	195 3/8	186 2/8	62 2/8	34 2/8	20 4/8	29 2/8	27 3/8	15	16	5 2/8	5 3/8	1964	Baker	Duane Hutton/Dwayne Wright	9
246 3/8	203 5/8	198 0/8	48 3/8	33 4/8	24 6/8	24 6/8	24 2/8	11	15	4 6/8	5 0/8	1934	Grant	Clyde Stormer/Mckern's Texaco	10
244 3/8	176 3/8	171 6/8	72 5/8	34 1/8	20 4/8	21 7/8	21 7/8	14	13	4 7/8	5 0/8	1984	Deschutes	M.S. Wattier	11
242 5/8	194 1/8	186 7/8	55 6/8	28 3/8	21 7/8	24 2/8	24 4/8	10	9	4 6/8	4 6/8	1960	Deschutes	Buck D. Matson/Sandy Mergel	12
242 2/8	187 7/8	184 2/8	58 0/8	36 5/8	32 7/8	26 4/8	25 7/8	9	13	6 3/8	6 2/8	1960	Union	Ralph Hardy/Jan Roulet	13
240 2/8	197 4/8	186 3/8	53 7/8	33 5/8	23 1/8	28 4/8	26 4/8	9	8	5 1/8	4 5/8	1995	Crook	Charles H. Kies	14
239 5/8	210 5/8	204 1/8	35 4/8	35 0/8	30 4/8	27 5/8	26 6/8	9	10	6 3/8	6 0/8	1927	Harney	Culver Page/Glen Shelley	15
239 3/8	202 7/8	197 4/8	41 7/8	40 2/8	29 0/8	28 2/8	30 2/8	12	12	6 0/8	6 1/8	1968	Lake	Nolan Greiner	16
238 7/8	178 2/8	167 1/8	71 6/8	25 6/8	16 7/8	22 1/8	23 4/8	22	13	6 1/8	4 3/8	1968	Umatilla	Ray Paynes/Mike Lawkford	17
238 7/8	209 1/8	198 4/8	40 3/8	34 5/8	27 0/8	26 6/8	24 0/8	10	9	5 4/8	6 0/8	1920	Klamath	Harley Hall	17

Rank	Final Score	Gross Typical	Net Typical	Abnormal Points	Greatest Spread	Inside Spread	Main Beam R	Main Beam L	Number of Points R	Number of Points L	First Circumference R	First Circumference L	Year	County	Hunter/Owner
19	237 0/8	180 2/8	170 3/8	66 5/8	30 4/8	20 3/8	26 4/8	24 4/8	15	13	6 1/8	6 1/8	1926	Morrow	W.O. Bayless/John Howton
20	236 6/8	213 7/8	207 2/8	29 4/8	39 3/8	34 0/8	30 0/8	29 4/8	9	11	5 5/8	5 7/8	1977	Klamath	George Hessler/Elvis Tillman
21	236 4/8	208 6/8	200 5/8	35 7/8	30 5/8	18 1/8	24 0/8	24 4/8	14	10	5 0/8	5 0/8	1995	Union	Logan Girrard
22	233 7/8	206 3/8	200 6/8	33 1/8	32 0/8	29 3/8	28 2/8	28 4/8	10	8	5 3/8	5 3/8	1991	Lake	Carl Tracy
23	232 6/8	214 0/8	208 2/8	24 4/8	40 0/8	29 0/8	26 2/8	27 4/8	8	9	5 0/8	5 0/8	1952	Harney	The Gun Room
24	232 2/8	215 1/8	209 6/8	22 4/8	27 4/8	25 2/8	29 2/8	29 1/8	7	11	5 5/8	5 4/8	1929	Grant	Dolly Williams/Ed Heid
25	232 0/8	209 6/8	203 5/8	28 3/8	33 6/8	25 1/8	27 5/8	27 5/8	8	8	4 7/8	4 7/8	1995	Sherman	Wendell Clodfelter

Top 25 Typical Mule Deer Regardless of Kill Method

Rank	Final Score	Gross Typical	Net Typical	Abnormal Points	Greatest Spread	Inside Spread	Main Beam R	Main Beam L	Number of Points R	Number of Points L	First Circumference R	First Circumference L	Year	County	Hunter/Owner
1	209 4/8		217 0/8	8 3/8	30 1/8	28 0/8	28 7/8	29 6/8	6	8	5 7/8	5 7/8	1920	Wallowa	John C. Evans/Stan Neitling
2	203 0/8	208 6/8	205 4/8	2 4/8	31 7/8	26 0/8	27 5/8	27 4/8	5	7	6 6/8	6 6/8	1994	Harney	Doug White
3	201 5/8	206 0/8	201 5/8	0 0/8	29 3/8	24 3/8	26 2/8	27 3/8	5	5	5 4/8	5 4/8	1988	Baker	Terry Williams
4	199 6/8	204 3/8	199 6/8	0 0/8	27 2/8	20 0/8	26 5/8	27 0/8	4	4	5 4/8	5 3/8	1995	Harney	Chris Schweizer
5	199 3/8	206 2/8	201 5/8	2 2/8	27 1/8	24 1/8	26 4/8	28 4/8	7	5	5 1/8	5 2/8	1995	Harney	John Echanis
6	199 2/8	211 7/8	205 4/8	6 2/8	31 0/8	26 0/8	25 2/8	26 4/8	7	5	6 4/8	6 4/8	1975	Lake	Don Callaghan
7	197 7/8	205 6/8	201 7/8	4 0/8	28 1/8	24 1/8	27 0/8	27 4/8	6	6	4 4/8	4 4/8	1995		Leah O. Robertson
8	197 6/8	219 1/8	212 7/8	15 1/8	35 0/8	27 5/8	31 4/8	31 1/8	7	12	5 0/8	5 1/8	1968	Lake	Bill King
9	197 1/8	212 1/8	210 3/8	13 2/8	35 4/8	26 3/8	27 6/8	28 3/8	8	6	5 1/8	5 1/8	1962	Jefferson	Harvey Rhoades
9	197 1/8	210 0/8	207 0/8	9 7/8	35 0/8	29 4/8	26 2/8	26 6/8	0	0	5 0/8	5 0/8	1948	Wheeler	Fran Cherry/Lorraine Cherry
11	196 5/8	201 5/8	196 5/8	0 0/8	26 6/8	21 3/8	25 0/8	26 3/8	5	5	5 1/8	5 1/8		Grant	Joey Wood
12	195 7/8	204 6/8	200 7/8	5 0/8	36 1/8	30 2/8	29 7/8	29 7/8	6	7	5 1/8	5 5/8	1990	Crook	Hop Jackson
13	194 4/8	207 3/8	201 4/8	7 0/8	31 0/8	26 0/8	27 2/8	27 2/8	0	0	5 2/8	5 4/8	1982	Grant	Joe Brooks
14	194 2/8	199 3/8	194 2/8	0 0/8	28 0/8	22 2/8	26 6/8	28 3/8	5	5	4 6/8	4 6/8	1973	Umatilla	Walter Williams/Robert Mawhin
15	193 0/8	199 5/8	193 0/8	0 0/8	27 4/8	23 0/8	26 7/8	24 1/8	5	5	5 4/8	5 4/8	1978	Malheur	LeRoy Zollo/Nick Spiropolos
16	192 6/8	201 6/8	194 7/8	2 1/8	32 0/8	28 3/8	26 4/8	27 5/8	5	6	5 3/8	5 2/8	1936	Lake	Lee Freeman/Sam Myers
17	192 3/8	195 1/8	192 3/8	0 0/8	26 2/8	24 5/8	24 6/8	25 2/8	5	5	5 3/8	5 4/8	1960	Klamath	Lynn Casey Jones
18	192 2/8	201 5/8	196 6/8	4 4/8	30 3/8	24 2/8	26 4/8	27 5/8	6	4	5 5/8	5 5/8	1994	Harney	Glen Dobson
18	192 2/8	207 0/8	197 3/8	5 1/8	31 0/8	24 1/8	26 6/8	27 0/8	6	5	5 4/8	5 0/8	1959	Wallowa	Gene Roberts
20	192 1/8	215 0/8	208 2/8	16 1/8	33 6/8	28 7/8	28 4/8	27 4/8	7	6	6 0/8	5 5/8	1995	Malheur	William T. Monson
21	192 0/8	193 4/8	192 0/8	0 0/8	28 0/8	23 0/8	26 3/8	26 4/8	5	5	4 0/8	4 1/8	1975	Grant	Martin Hettinga
22	191 6/8	199 5/8	193 4/8	1 6/8	31 3/8	24 2/8	25 6/8	27 3/8	5	6	4 2/8	4 1/8	1981	Grant	Malcolm Cameron
23	191 3/8	194 5/8	193 3/8	2 0/8	26 6/8	23 5/8	26 5/8	27 2/8	6	5	5 4/8	5 4/8		Grant	LaVern Starbuck
24	191 2/8	202 0/8	197 7/8	6 5/8	34 0/8	28 5/8	26 0/8	26 3/8	7	6	5 5/8	5 6/8	1969	Malheur	Ron Daniel
25	191 1/8	208 5/8	202 7/8	11 6/8	30 6/8	20 5/8	31 1/8	31 1/8	6	8	5 3/8	5 4/8	1960	Grant	Gary Engle

Top 25 Mule Deer
Sorted by Greatest Spread

Rank	Hunter/Owner	County	Year	First Circumference R	First Circumference L	Number of Points R	Number of Points L	Main Beam R	Main Beam L	Inside Spread	Abnormal Points	Net Typical	Gross Typical	Final Score	Greatest Spread
1	Larry Powell	Crook	1995	6 0/8	6 0/8	9	8	27 0/8	26 6/8	24 3/8	28 4/8	197 7/8	206 1/8	226 3/8	42 0/8
2	Nolan Greiner	Lake		6 0/8	6 1/8	12	12	28 2/8	30 2/8	29 0/8	41 7/8	197 4/8	202 7/8	239 3/8	40 2/8
3	Jack Smith	Grant	1973	5 2/8	6 0/8	6	11	25 6/8	25 0/8	25 6/8	37 3/8	173 6/8	177 5/8	211 1/8	40 1/8
4	The Gun Room	Harney	1952	5 0/8	5 0/8	8	9	26 2/8	27 4/8	29 0/8	24 4/8	208 2/8	214 0/8	232 6/8	40 0/8
4	Frank McCullough/ The Bowman Museum	Crook		6 0/8	6 2/8	10	9	28 1/8	25 4/8	24 2/8	26 4/8	185 2/8	192 6/8	211 6/8	40 0/8
6	Bradley Barclay	Malheur	1971	5 4/8	5 3/8	20	18	29 1/8	27 5/8	35 6/8	99 2/8	198 5/8	206 0/8	297 7/8	39 6/8
7	George Hessler/Elvis Tillman	Klamath	1977	5 5/8	5 7/8	9	11	30 0/8	29 4/8	34 0/8	29 4/8	207 2/8	213 7/8	236 6/8	39 3/8
8	Dick Haney	Deschutes	1979	5 2/8	5 4/8	13	10	24 3/8	25 0/8	26 1/8	44 4/8	176 6/8	184 7/8	221 2/8	39 2/8
9	Nolan Greiner	Lake		5 7/8	5 0/8	9	6	29 1/8	29 1/8	35 0/8	23 4/8	200 1/8	205 1/8	223 5/8	39 0/8
10	Lige Davis/Coy Johnston	Grant	1941	6 0/8	6 3/8	14	15	24 2/8	22 7/8	27 0/8	113 3/8	155 2/8	162 0/8	268 5/8	38 7/8
11	Harold Aycock/Jacquelyn Smith	Baker	1937	4 2/8	4 2/8	5	5	25 4/8	25 7/8	31 0/8	0 0/8	181 7/8	184 7/8	181 7/8	38 1/8
12	Karen Kelvin/The Gun Room	Harney		4 7/8	5 0/8	8	8	24 0/8	25 0/8	25 7/8	23 4/8	176 4/8	181 2/8	200 0/8	38 0/8
13	Grant Saunders	Union	1958	5 1/8	5 0/8	9	8	26 4/8	25 5/8	26 3/8	32 3/8	176 1/8	185 2/8	208 4/8	37 6/8
14	Clark Onsley	Crook	1981	5 5/8	5 7/8	7	7	29 4/8	28 2/8	30 4/8	7 5/8	195 2/8	206 6/8	187 5/8	37 0/8
14	C.F. Cheney/Carl Christen	Grant	1962	5 7/8	5 7/8	17	16	29 3/8	28 4/8	27 6/8	70 5/8	200 0/8	207 0/8	270 5/8	37 0/8
14	Michael Barden	Jefferson	1993	5 2/8	5 0/8	11	13	24 2/8	26 0/8	24 5/8	58 6/8	162 3/8	171 6/8	221 1/8	37 0/8
18	Charles Wetzel	Lake	1967	4 0/8	4 0/8	9	10	24 6/8	25 4/8	23 7/8	27 5/8	183 5/8	187 2/8	211 2/8	36 6/8
18	Bud Dullian	Lake		4 4/8	4 4/8	10	11	24 3/8	23 5/8	19 1/8	61 7/8	155 5/8	161 1/8	217 4/8	36 6/8
19	Ralph Hardy/Jan Roulet	Union	1960	6 3/8	6 2/8	9	13	26 4/8	25 7/8	32 7/8	58 0/8	184 2/8	187 7/8	242 2/8	36 5/8
20	Mark Rhoden	Crook	1992	4 3/8	4 0/8	5	4	24 5/8	24 1/8	28 6/8	0 0/8	160 5/8	166 1/8	160 5/8	36 4/8
20	Nolan Greiner	Lake		5 5/8	5 6/8	8	7	26 3/8	27 5/8	28 4/8	10 2/8	191 7/8	199 7/8	202 1/8	36 4/8
22	Hop Jackson	Crook	1990	5 1/8	5 5/8	6	7	29 7/8	29 7/8	30 2/8	5 0/8	200 7/8	204 6/8	195 7/8	36 1/8
23	David M. Morris	Grant	1985	4 7/8	5 0/8	5	6	25 5/8	24 5/8	23 0/8	3 2/8	179 0/8	180 7/8	175 6/8	36 0/8
23	Ron DeRoest	Baker	1965	5 3/8	5 4/8	7	7	26 0/8	23 3/8	24 6/8	19 6/8	187 0/8	198 0/8	167 2/8	36 0/8
25	Harvey Rhoades	Jefferson	1962	5 1/8	5 1/8	8	6	27 6/8	28 3/8	26 3/8	13 2/8	210 3/8	212 1/8	197 1/8	35 4/8

Oregon State Record—Rifle (typical)
John C. Evans, 209 4/8 B.C.,
Wallowa County, 1920

Oregon State Record—Archery (typical)
Hop Jackson, 195 7/8 P.Y.,
Crook County, 1990

Official Scoring System for Oregon Big Game Trophies

TYPICAL
MULE AND BLACKTAIL DEER

DETAIL OF POINT MEASUREMENT

Abnormal Points	
Right Antler	Left Antler
1 6/8	1 7/8
0 0/8	1 3/8
0 0/8	0 0/8
0 0/8	0 0/8
0 0/8	0 0/8
0 0/8	0 0/8
0 0/8	0 0/8
0 0/8	0 0/8
0 0/8	0 0/8
0 0/8	0 0/8

Species	Rifle	Archery	Muzzle	Shed	Archery - Velvet
Mule Deer	160	145	146	70	145
Columbia Blacktail	115	90	110	50	90
Cascade Blacktail	115	90	110	50	90
Northwest Blacktail	115	90	110	50	90

		Subtotals	1 6/8	3 2/8
		Total to E		5 0/8

					COLUMN 1	COLUMN 2	COLUMN 3	COLUMN 4
A	Number of Points on Right Antler	6	Number of Points on Left Antler	7	Spread Credit	Right Antler	Left Antler	Difference
B	Tip to Tip Spread	24 0/8	C Greatest Spread	36 1/8				
D	Inside Spread of Main Beam	30 2/8	(Credit may be equal to but not exceed longer antler)		29 7/8			
E	Total of Length of Abnormal Points							5 0/8
F	Length of Main Beam					29 7/8	29 7/8	0 0/8
G-1	Length of First Point, if present					4 1/8	4 1/8	0 0/8
G-2	Length of Second Point					16 1/8	16 2/8	0 1/8
G-3	Length of Third Point, if present					7 7/8	8 7/8	1 0/8
G-4	Length of Fourth Point, if present					10 3/8	12 1/8	1 6/8
H-1	Circumference at smallest place between burr and first point					5 1/8	5 5/8	0 4/8
H-2	Circumference at smallest place between first and second point					4 2/8	4 4/8	0 2/8
H-3	Circumference at smallest place between main beam and 3rd pt					3 4/8	3 5/8	0 1/8
H-4	Circumference at smallest place between second and fourth points					4 2/8	4 3/8	0 1/8
				TOTALS	29 7/8	85 4/8	89 3/8	8 7/8

County where killed:	Crook	Date Killed:	09/07/90		Column 1	29 7/8
Hunter's Name:	Hop	Jackson		ADD	Column 2	85 4/8
Owner's Name:	Hop	Jackson			Column 3	89 3/8
					Subtotal	204 6/8
					Subtract Column 4	8 7/8
					FINAL SCORE	195 7/8

Official Scoring System for Oregon Big Game Trophies

Records of Oregon
Big Game

RECORD BOOK FOR OREGON

P.O. Box 759
Irrigon, OR 97844

TYPICAL
MULE AND BLACKTAIL DEER

DETAIL OF POINT MEASUREMENT

Abnormal Points	
Right Antler	*Left Antler*
0 0/8	0 0/8
0 0/8	0 0/8
0 0/8	0 0/8
0 0/8	0 0/8
0 0/8	0 0/8
0 0/8	0 0/8
0 0/8	0 0/8
0 0/8	0 0/8
0 0/8	0 0/8
0 0/8	0 0/8

Species	Rifle	Archery	Muzzle	Shed	Archery - Velvet
Mule Deer	160	145	146	70	145
Columbia Blacktail	115	90	110	50	90
Cascade Blacktail	115	90	110	50	90
Northwest Blacktail	115	90	110	50	90

						Subtotals	0 0/8	0 0/8
						Total to E		0 0/8

		COLUMN 1	COLUMN 2	COLUMN 3	COLUMN 4
		Spread Credit	Right Antler	Left Antler	Difference
A	Number of Points on Right Antler	5	Number of Points on Left Antler	5			
B	Tip to Tip Spread	22 1/8	C Greatest Spread	31 0/8			
D	Inside Spread of Main Beam	24 4/8	(Credit may be equal to but not exceed longer antler)	24 4/8			
E	Total of Length of Abnormal Points					0 0/8
F	Length of Main Beam			26 2/8	25 3/8	0 7/8
G-1	Length of First Point, if present			2 6/8	2 6/8	0 0/8
G-2	Length of Second Point			10 3/8	13 5/8	3 2/8
G-3	Length of Third Point, if present			10 4/8	13 7/8	3 3/8
G-4	Length of Fourth Point, if present			13 4/8	11 6/8	1 6/8
H-1	Circumference at smallest place between burr and first point			4 4/8	4 6/8	0 2/8
H-2	Circumference at smallest place between first and second point			4 2/8	4 3/8	0 1/8
H-3	Circumference at smallest place between main beam and 3rd pt			3 7/8	4 2/8	0 3/8
H-4	Circumference at smallest place between second and fourth points			4 6/8	4 6/8	0 0/8
	TOTALS	24 4/8	80 6/8	85 4/8	10 0/8

County where killed: Harney	**Date Killed:**	Column 1	24 4/8
Hunter's Name: Patrick Hagon	**ADD**	Column 2	80 6/8
Owner's Name: Patrick Hagon		Column 3	85 4/8
		Subtotal	190 6/8
		Subtract Column 4	10 0/8
		FINAL SCORE	**180 6/8**

Official Scoring System for Oregon Big Game Trophies

Records of Oregon
Big Game

RECORD BOOK FOR OREGON

P.O. Box 759
Irrigon, OR 97844

TYPICAL
MULE AND BLACKTAIL DEER

DETAIL OF POINT MEASUREMENT

Species	Rifle	Archery	Muzzle	Shed	Archery - Velvet
Mule Deer	160	145	146	70	145
Columbia Blacktail	115	90	110	50	90
Cascade Blacktail	115	90	110	50	90
Northwest Blacktail	115	90	110	50	90

Abnormal Points		
Right Antler	Left Antler	
0 0/8	1 4/8	
0 0/8	1 0/8	
0 0/8	0 0/8	
0 0/8	0 0/8	
0 0/8	0 0/8	
0 0/8	0 0/8	
0 0/8	0 0/8	
0 0/8	0 0/8	
0 0/8	0 0/8	
0 0/8	0 0/8	
Subtotals 0 0/8	2 4/8	
Total to E	2 4/8	

						COLUMN 1 Spread Credit	COLUMN 2 Right Antler	COLUMN 3 Left Antler	COLUMN 4 Difference
A	Number of Points on Right Antler		5	Number of Points on Left Antler	7				
B	Tip to Tip Spread	21 1/8	C	Greatest Spread	31 7/8				
D	Inside Spread of Main Beam	26 0/8	(Credit may be equal to but not exceed longer antler)		26 0/8				
E	Total of Length of Abnormal Points								2 4/8
F	Length of Main Beam						27 5/8	27 4/8	0 1/8
G-1	Length of First Point, if present						3 0/8	3 0/8	0 0/8
G-2	Length of Second Point						18 1/8	17 5/8	0 4/8
G-3	Length of Third Point, if present						7 6/8	9 3/8	1 5/8
G-4	Length of Fourth Point, if present						13 0/8	12 3/8	0 5/8
H-1	Circumference at smallest place between burr and first point						6 6/8	6 6/8	0 0/8
H-2	Circumference at smallest place between first and second point						5 6/8	5 6/8	0 0/8
H-3	Circumference at smallest place between main beam and 3rd pt						4 2/8	4 1/8	0 1/8
H-4	Circumference at smallest place between second and fourth points						5 1/8	4 7/8	0 2/8
				TOTALS		26 0/8	91 3/8	91 3/8	5 6/8

County where killed:	Harney	Date Killed:	11/26/94		Column 1	26 0/8
Hunter's Name:	Doug	White		**ADD**	Column 2	91 3/8
Owner's Name:	Doug	White			Column 3	91 3/8
					Subtotal	208 6/8
					Subtract Column 4	5 6/8
					FINAL SCORE	203 0/8

State Record Mule Deer (Black Powder)

by Doug White

We had just finished a great breakfast of pancakes, eggs and bacon cooked by John Powell, the father of one of the other hunters in my hunting party. John came along to be head camp wrangler and make sure we got out and hunted every day on a full stomach (Thanks, John!).

It was finally opening morning. It had been snowing all night. As I worked my way up the ridge, it was just getting light enough to see. About eighty yards in front of me was a buck that I guessed to be about 31″ wide, but he had small back forks. I couldn't see the bottom half of his horns because of the high sagebrush he was in. I never would have guessed that his bases would be so big.

The muzzle-loader mule deer hunt that I had drawn was to start November 26, 1994, and run for a week. I and the other three people that I had drawn this tag with (Larry Powell, Dave Noble and Bruce Hawkins) had decided we would leave on Wednesday (November 23), the day before Thanksgiving, and spend a couple of days scouting. Since there were only fifteen tags issued for this hunt, we didn't want to get in a hurry and shoot the first buck we saw. We had seen plenty of nice bucks in the two days that we had to scout. This was only the second year that the Oregon Department of Fish and Wildlife (ODFW) had issued tags for this hunt. This was to be a trophy desert mule deer hunt on their winter range, according to ODFW.

Back to the buck in the sage. I backed off and left the buck and went looking for a buck I had seen earlier that week that I guessed would go about 34″ wide with large forks in the front and back. After hunting all morning and seeing plenty of bucks but nothing that compared with the buck I had seen that morning, I decided to go take a better look at the 4×4 I had seen at first light. Maybe I could get a better look at him.

On the way back over to the ridge where I had last seen the buck that morning, I ran into two of my hunting partners, Bruce and Dave. After telling them about the buck I had seen, they were both interested in taking a look at the buck, so the three of us went to look for him.

We sat in some rim rocks overlooking the ridge and glassed for about forty-five minutes. We didn't see anything and decided to hike down

to the main road. On the way down, Bruce looked off to our left and asked me what I thought of that buck. There, standing on the top of the ridge we had just been glassing, was the same buck I had seen that morning. There was no mistaking his back forks. Bruce and Dave had both said that if we saw the buck and he was over 30″ that they would take him. Bruce was to get the first shot; then Dave. If something happened, I was to get the next shot, if it got to that. But I didn't think that it would and I still wasn't sure, if it did get to me, that I even wanted this buck. Well, that's when the buck turned and walked out of the sagebrush directly at us and that's when I got my first look at the bottom half of his horns—the bases were huge! The bases were so heavy that it looked like he would fall over because of the weight. Well, I've never been known for being the brightest person in the world, so it looked like one of my friends was going to get to kill this exceptional buck.

Well, the hunting gods must have been smiling on me because Bruce got into position

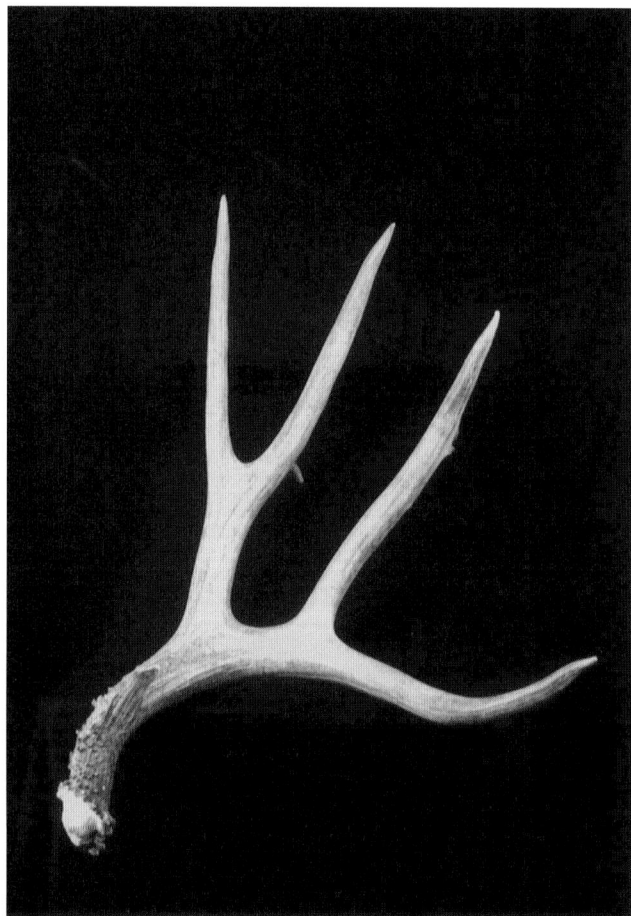

and the buck turned, quartering away. Bruce shot and the buck ran off up the ridge, shaking his head. Dave and I ran up the ridge to cut the buck off. The buck stopped and was still shaking his head. We figured Bruce must have hit him in the horns some place. Dave pulled down on him and shot. He must have shot high because the buck just ran off a short distance and started walking up the ridge as if nothing had happened. Like I said, the hunting gods must have been smiling on me, or this buck and me were meant to be together, because Bruce and Dave are both great shots. Anyway, I moved up the ridge until I had a clear view of him. He was quartering away and walking. I sat down and waited for him to stop. When he did, I took my shot. He ran about fifteen yards and went down.

The three of us went over to take a closer look at the buck I had just shot. We still couldn't believe how massive his horns were. It turned out that Bruce's shot had indeed hit the horns and put a groove in one of the eye guards. My shot had gone through just behind the left shoulder and come out through the right shoulder.

I was using a Thompson 54 caliber Hawkins rifle to take my buck that net-scored 203 after the official drying period. It gross-scored over 206, but some of the burrs at the bases were deductions because they were over an inch long. His outside spread was 31 7/8 after the drying period.

Before the hunt was over, all four of us had taken nice bucks. Larry Powell killed a dandy 4×4 with a 28° spread the next evening and on the last day we were to hunt, Bruce took a nice 4×4 and Dave took a really nice 3×3 that turned out to have the biggest body of all the four bucks.
(Final score: 203 0/8 B.C.)

Oregon State Record—Shed Antlers (typical)
Wennie Powell, 94 0/8 B.C.,
Grant County

196

Typical Mule Deer—Rifle
Minimum Score: 160 0/8

Final Score	Gross Typical	Net Typical	Abnormal Points	Greatest Spread	Inside Spread	Main Beam R	Main Beam L	Number of Points R	Number of Points L	First Circumference R	First Circumference L	Year	County	Hunter/Owner	Rank
209 4/8	0 0/8	217 0/8	8 3/8	30 1/8	28 0/8	28 7/8	29 6/8	6	8	5 7/8	5 7/8	1920	Wallowa	John C. Evans/Stan Neitling	1
201 5/8	206 0/8	201 5/8	0 0/8	29 3/8	24 3/8	26 2/8	27 3/8	5	5	5 4/8	5 4/8	1988	Baker	Terry Williams	2
199 6/8	204 3/8	199 6/8	0 0/8	27 2/8	20 0/8	26 5/8	27 0/8	4	4	5 4/8	5 3/8	1995	Harney	Chris Schweizer	3
193 3/8	206 2/8	201 5/8	2 2/8	27 1/8	24 1/8	26 4/8	28 4/8	7	5	5 1/8	5 2/8	1995	Harney	John Echanis	4
199 2/8	211 7/8	205 4/8	6 2/8	31 0/8	26 0/8	25 2/8	26 4/8	7	5	6 4/8	6 4/8	1975	Lake	Don Callaghan	5
177 7/8	205 6/8	201 7/8	4 0/8	28 1/8	24 1/8	27 0/8	27 4/8	6	6	4 4/8	4 4/8	1995	Lake	Leah O. Robertson	6
197 6/8	219 1/8	212 7/8	15 1/8	35 0/8	27 5/8	31 4/8	31 1/8	7	12	5 0/8	5 1/8	1968	Lake	Bill King	7
197 1/8	212 1/8	210 3/8	13 2/8	35 4/8	26 3/8	27 6/8	28 3/8	8	6	5 1/8	5 1/8	1962	Jefferson	Harvey Rhoades	8
197 1/8	210 0/8	207 0/8	9 7/8	35 0/8	29 4/8	26 2/8	26 6/8	6	6	5 0/8	5 0/8	1948	Wheeler	Fran Cherry/Lorraine Cherry	8
196 5/8	201 5/8	196 5/8	0 0/8	26 6/8	21 3/8	25 0/8	26 3/8	5	5	5 1/8	5 1/8		Grant	Joey Wood	10
194 4/8	207 3/8	201 4/8	7 0/8	31 0/8	26 0/8	27 2/8	27 2/8	7	5	5 2/8	5 4/8	1982	Grant	Joe Brooks	11
194 2/8	199 3/8	194 2/8	0 0/8	28 0/8	22 2/8	26 6/8	28 3/8	5	5	4 6/8	4 6/8	1973	Umatilla	Walter Williams/Robert Mawhin	12
193 0/8	199 5/8	193 0/8	0 0/8	27 4/8	23 0/8	26 7/8	24 1/8	5	5	5 4/8	5 4/8	1978	Malheur	LeRoy Zollo/Nick Spiropolos	13
192 6/8	201 6/8	194 7/8	2 1/8	32 0/8	28 3/8	26 4/8	27 5/8	5	6	5 3/8	5 2/8	1936	Lake	Lee Freeman/Sam Myers	14
192 3/8	195 1/8	192 3/8	0 0/8	26 2/8	24 5/8	24 6/8	25 2/8	5	5	5 3/8	5 4/8	1960	Klamath	Lynn Casey Jones	15
192 2/8	201 5/8	196 6/8	4 4/8	30 3/8	24 2/8	26 4/8	27 5/8	6	4	5 5/8	5 5/8	1994	Harney	Glen Dobson	16
192 2/8	207 0/8	197 3/8	5 1/8	31 0/8	24 1/8	26 6/8	27 0/8	6	5	5 4/8	5 0/8	1959	Wallowa	Gene Roberts	16
192 1/8	215 0/8	208 2/8	16 1/8	33 6/8	28 7/8	28 4/8	27 4/8	7	6	6 0/8	5 5/8	1995	Malheur	William T. Monson	18
192 0/8	193 4/8	192 0/8	0 0/8	28 0/8	23 0/8	26 3/8	26 4/8	5	5	4 0/8	4 1/8		Grant	Martin Hettinga	19
191 6/8	199 5/8	193 4/8	1 6/8	31 3/8	24 2/8	25 6/8	27 3/8	6	6	4 2/8	4 1/8	1975	Grant	Malcolm Cameron	20
191 3/8	194 5/8	193 3/8	2 0/8	26 6/8	23 5/8	26 5/8	27 2/8	6	5	5 4/8	5 4/8	1981	Grant	LaVern Starbuck	21
191 2/8	202 0/8	197 7/8	6 5/8	34 0/8	28 5/8	26 0/8	26 3/8	7	6	5 5/8	5 6/8	1969	Malheur	Ron Daniel	22
191 1/8	208 5/8	202 7/8	11 6/8	30 6/8	20 5/8	31 1/8	31 1/8	6	8	5 3/8	5 4/8	1960	Grant	Gary Engle	23
190 3/8	197 3/8	194 1/8	3 6/8	29 7/8	26 1/8	25 5/8	25 2/8	5	5	4 6/8	4 5/8	1995	Deschutes	Ron Robinson, Jr.	24
190 2/8	201 1/8	190 2/8	0 0/8	32 0/8	27 2/8	27 2/8	27 6/8	4	4	4 7/8	5 0/8	1949		Don Alexander	25
190 2/8	193 4/8	190 1/8	0 0/8	25 3/8	21 4/8	25 4/8	26 4/8	5	5	4 6/8	4 4/8	1995	Union	Nancy Yancey	25
190 1/8	195 1/8	190 1/8	0 0/8	29 0/8	26 5/8	27 5/8	27 1/8	5	5	5 0/8	5 0/8	1983	Harney	Glen Saelly	27
190 0/8	207 3/8	199 1/8	9 1/8	31 0/8	22 1/8	24 4/8	26 5/8	5	7	5 4/8	5 3/8	1930	Harney	Roy Heinz	28
189 5/8	196 5/8	191 2/8	1 5/8	28 1/8	23 4/8	26 0/8	25 2/8	10	8	5 6/8	6 1/8	1984	Lake	Carl Tracy	29
189 2/8	197 1/8	189 2/8	0 0/8	29 5/8	25 4/8	24 6/8	24 6/8	5	5	4 2/8	4 3/8	1971	Baker	Ron Wright	30
189 0/8	213 5/8	209 2/8	20 2/8	35 0/8	27 4/8	26 2/8	27 7/8	7	7	6 0/8	5 4/8	1943	Crook	Harry Sederance/Ned Sederance	31
189 0/8	196 4/8	192 1/8	3 1/8	24 2/8	24 3/8	26 6/8	27 1/8	6	5	4 6/8	4 5/8	1992	Grant	Linda Hettinga	31
188 6/8	196 4/8	192 4/8	3 6/8		23 0/8	25 0/8	25 4/8	6	6	5 0/8	5 1/8	1994	Grant	Chad Holiday	33
188 6/8	203 0/8	196 2/8	7 4/8	27 6/8	24 2/8	24 4/8	25 5/8	6	7	6 2/8	6 5/8	1945	Baker	Steve Grant	33
188 5/8	194 4/8	190 3/8	1 6/8	25 4/8	22 5/8	26 0/8	27 2/8	5	6	4 7/8	4 7/8	1980	Grant	Larry Powell	35
188 3/8	192 6/8	188 3/8	0 0/8	30 0/8	24 1/8	26 1/8	24 6/8	5	5	4 6/8	4 6/8	1968	Wallowa	Craig Klug	36
188 2/8	196 5/8	188 2/8	0 0/8	31 0/8	24 4/8	26 4/8	27 5/8	5	5	4 7/8	5 2/8	1971	Deschutes	Tom Garcia	37
188 1/8	197 5/8	192 5/8	4 4/8	31 0/8	27 6/8	27 5/8	27 5/8	6	6	4 7/8	5 0/8	1995	Crook	Charles Dix	38
188 0/8	196 1/8	190 3/8	2 3/8	23 4/8	20 1/8	25 1/8	24 3/8	5	6	5 0/8	5 1/8	1995	Harney	Randy Hurd	39
187 7/8	190 6/8	187 7/8	0 0/8	31 3/8	27 2/8	26 1/8	26 1/8	5	5	4 7/8	5 3/8	1972	Lake	Richard Nelson	40

Typical Mule Deer—Rifle (continued)

Final Score	Gross Typical	Net Typical	Abnormal Points	Greatest Spread	Inside Spread	Main Beam R	Main Beam L	Number of Points R	Number of Points L	First Circumference R	First Circumference L	Year	County	Hunter/Owner	Rank
187 6/8	190 4/8	187 6/8	0 0/8	29 0/8	25 0/8	25 2/8	25 1/8	4	4	5 2/8	5 2/8	1935	Gilliam	Roger White	41
187 6/8	200 3/8	194 3/8	6 5/8	27 0/8	21 1/8	25 2/8	23 0/8	7	6	5 5/8	5 6/8	1988	Crook	Mike Burcham	41
187 5/8	206 6/8	195 2/8	7 5/8	37 0/8	30 4/8	29 4/8	28 2/8	7	7	5 5/8	5 7/8	1981	Crook	Clark Onsley	43
187 5/8	194 2/8	188 5/8	1 0/8	26 6/8	25 1/8	25 4/8	24 6/8	5	6	5 4/8	5 6/8	1986	Harney	Tim Wells	43
187 4/8	198 5/8	192 2/8	4 6/8	28 0/8	22 4/8	26 3/8	26 2/8	6	6	6 0/8	5 6/8		Wallowa	Dale Dotson	45
187 3/8	190 5/8	187 3/8	0 0/8		21 7/8	23 7/8	23 6/8	5	5	5 3/8	5 4/8	1972	Lake	Steven Berglund	46
187 2/8	215 1/8	209 6/8	22 4/8	27 4/8	25 2/8	29 2/8	29 1/8	7	11	5 5/8	5 4/8	1929	Grant	Dolly Williams/Ed Heid	47
187 2/8	200 3/8	194 1/8	6 7/8	30 4/8	27 1/8	25 1/8	26 3/8	6	7	4 6/8	4 6/8	1978	Wallowa	Mike Norton	47
186 6/8	201 7/8	197 2/8	10 4/8	25 0/8	21 2/8	25 5/8	24 6/8	9	8	5 6/8	6 1/8	1958	Grant	W.V. Masson	49
186 2/8	194 3/8	189 4/8	3 2/8	25 4/8	18 0/8	24 0/8	22 7/8	6	6	5 5/8	5 2/8	1986	Grant	Leslie Brady	50
186 1/8	193 0/8	190 0/8	3 7/8	25 0/8	22 2/8	26 5/8	27 0/8	6	6	5 4/8	5 2/8	1945	Lake	Mark Fogelquist/Dave Fogelquist	51
185 4/8	195 1/8	192 0/8	6 4/8	31 2/8	23 6/8	25 4/8	25 4/8	6	6	4 6/8	4 7/8	1979	Lake	Ed Carlton	52
185 2/8	190 3/8	188 2/8	3 0/8	30 5/8	21 4/8	24 7/8	25 2/8	6	5	4 2/8	4 2/8	1957	Baker	Byrl Landers	53
185 1/8	191 4/8	187 3/8	2 2/8	30 4/8	26 2/8	24 7/8	24 4/8	5	6	5 1/8	4 7/8	1992	Grant	Lawrence Wolfgram	54
185 0/8	190 5/8	185 0/8	0 0/8	27 0/8	23 0/8	25 4/8	27 3/8	5	5	4 6/8	5 0/8	1948	Wallowa	Paul Yost	55
185 0/8	191 7/8	188 2/8	3 2/8	30 2/8	21 6/8	25 7/8	25 4/8	6	5	5 0/8	5 0/8	1995	Grant	Gary Bucklein	55
184 7/8	196 0/8	192 0/8	7 1/8	27 0/8	22 0/8	27 0/8	26 2/8	5	7	4 7/8	5 0/8	1995	Baker	Travis Duby	57
184 7/8	190 7/8	186 5/8	1 6/8	26 4/8	24 1/8	25 2/8	25 3/8	6	5	5 0/8	5 0/8	1995	Harney	Bob Woodside	57
184 7/8	191 5/8	184 7/8	0 0/8	30 0/8	23 3/8	24 0/8	23 0/8	5	5	5 4/8	5 3/8	1981	Crook	Larry Powell	57
184 5/8	191 1/8	188 1/8	3 4/8	32 0/8	24 1/8	24 1/8	24 5/8	6	5	4 7/8	5 0/8	1953	Wallowa	Grant Warnock	60
184 5/8	188 2/8	184 5/8	0 0/8	29 3/8	19 7/8	24 4/8	24 2/8	5	5	4 7/8	5 0/8		Grant	Mark Mosely	60
184 4/8	194 3/8	190 7/8	6 3/8	32 0/8	21 7/8	26 0/8	26 1/8	7	6	6 1/8	6 4/8	1980	Wallowa	Keith W. Arnold	62
184 4/8	187 2/8	184 4/8	0 0/8	22 6/8	22 6/8	23 6/8	23 4/8	5	5	4 6/8	4 6/8	1992	Grant	Tony Cop	62
184 3/8	189 6/8	184 3/8	0 0/8	26 6/8	20 7/8	25 3/8	25 4/8	4	5	4 0/8	4 1/8	1964	Baker	Walter Buchanon/Eldon Deardorff	64
184 2/8	190 6/8	184 2/8	0 0/8	29 1/8	24 6/8	23 4/8	24 4/8	5	5	5 3/8	5 1/8	1986	Harney	Kevin Yekel	65
184 1/8	201 0/8	195 6/8	11 5/8	24 5/8	19 6/8	26 6/8	26 6/8	9	7	4 7/8	4 6/8	1990	Wallowa	Brad Smith	66
184 1/8	189 1/8	185 3/8	1 2/8	35 2/8	27 5/8	24 2/8	26 1/8	5	6	4 5/8	4 6/8	1976	Baker	Grant Saunders	66
184 0/8	190 0/8	185 6/8	1 6/8	26 5/8	21 6/8	23 5/8	23 2/8	5	6	5 2/8	5 1/8	1994	Harney	Jake Peasley	68
183 7/8	186 6/8	183 7/8	0 0/8	25 0/8	22 2/8	19 2/8	19 3/8	4	4	4 2/8	4 2/8	1991	Baker	Chris Blacker	69
183 6/8	187 0/8	183 6/8	0 0/8	25 0/8	24 2/8	28 2/8	27 6/8	4	4	5 2/8	5 6/8	1995	Umatilla	Bob McLean	70
183 6/8	214 0/8	208 2/8	24 4/8	40 0/8	29 0/8	26 2/8	27 4/8	8	9	5 0/8	5 0/8	1952	Harney	The Gun Room	70
183 6/8	189 3/8	183 6/8	0 0/8	26 0/8	22 0/8	23 4/8	23 5/8	5	5	5 2/8	5 3/8	1994	Umatilla	Glynn Simms	70
183 5/8	186 7/8	183 5/8	0 0/8		20 1/8	24 6/8	24 7/8	5	5	4 4/8	4 4/8	1970	Malheur	Don Pillar	73
183 3/8	188 0/8	183 3/8	0 0/8	26 6/8	24 5/8	24 7/8	24 3/8	5	5	4 6/8	4 5/8	1966	Wallowa	Delwyn Zollman/Joseph Hardware	74
183 0/8	187 5/8	183 0/8	0 0/8	27 0/8	22 4/8	27 6/8	28 1/8	5	5	5 0/8	5 0/8	1980	Baker	Joe Spellman	75
183 0/8	203 4/8	198 5/8	15 5/8	34 0/8	25 1/8	27 1/8	25 6/8	7	7	5 1/8	5 3/8	1933	Grant	Clifton Lemons	75
183 0/8	190 2/8	183 0/8	0 0/8	35 0/8	27 2/8	26 0/8	24 5/8	5	5	5 5/8	5 4/8	1958		Marshall Swearinger/The Tumalo Restaurant	75
182 7/8	193 6/8	191 2/8	8 3/8	29 7/8	23 6/8	26 2/8	26 5/8	7	7	4 7/8	5 0/8	1960	Baker	Johnny Sparrow/Mark Fox	78
182 6/8	187 6/8	182 6/8	0 0/8	23 4/8	20 2/8	21 4/8	22 1/8	5	5	5 2/8	5 7/8	1980	Crook	Ross Loveland	79
182 4/8	192 6/8	182 4/8	0 0/8	30 4/8	26 2/8	24 5/8	28 2/8	5	5	5 6/8	5 5/8	1960	Baker	Joe Mahoney/Tim Mahoney	80
182 3/8	187 7/8	182 3/8	0 0/8	23 0/8	19 3/8	24 3/8	23 6/8	5	5	4 5/8	4 5/8	1990	Baker	Lyle Steens	81
182 2/8	186 1/8	182 2/8	0 0/8	30 0/8	26 0/8	26 4/8	25 2/8	5	5	4 3/8	4 3/8	1972	Grant	Mark Powell	82

#	Name	County	Year											
83	Larry Wolfgram	Grant	1972	4 7/8	4 7/8	5	4	25 1/8	26 2/8	28 5/8	1 1/8	183 2/8	188 6/8	182 1/8
83	David M. Morris	Grant	1986	4 2/8	4 1/8	6	7	24 4/8	24 0/8	34 0/8	7 7/8	190 0/8	195 3/8	182 1/8
85	Todd Turner	Wallowa	1976	4 3/8	4 3/8	5	5	23 4/8	23 0/8	26 5/8	0 0/8	182 0/8	184 0/8	182 0/8
85	Greg Roberts	Grant	1994	4 5/8	4 5/8	5	5	23 2/8	21 2/8	27 3/8	0 0/8	182 0/8	186 2/8	182 0/8
87	Terry Pennington		1971	4 5/8	4 7/8	5	5	22 1/8	25 4/8	30 2/8	3 5/8	185 4/8	190 6/8	181 7/8
87	Harold Aycock/Jacquelyn Smith	Baker	1937	4 2/8	4 2/8	5	5	25 4/8	25 6/8	38 1/8	0 0/8	181 7/8	184 7/8	181 7/8
87	Weldon S. Hugh Banks/Kyle Jones	Crook	1948	4 6/8	4 4/8	4	4	25 1/8	26 0/8	26 0/8	0 0/8	183 0/8	183 0/8	181 7/8
90	Justin Bradley	Grant	1995	4 3/8	4 2/8	5	5	24 6/8	20 6/8	24 0/8	0 0/8	181 6/8	188 4/8	181 6/8
90	Thomas Bowers	Crook	1995	5 1/8	5 0/8	5	5	23 0/8	23 0/8	25 1/8	0 0/8	181 6/8	185 5/8	181 6/8
92	Nolan Greiner	Lake		5 6/8	5 5/8	7	8	27 5/8	28 4/8	36 4/8	10 2/8	191 7/8	199 7/8	181 5/8
92	Tim Smith	Wallowa	1995	4 3/8	4 3/8	5	5	23 5/8	22 5/8	27 1/8	0 0/8	181 5/8	185 1/8	181 5/8
94	Will H. Brown	Union	1952	4 5/8	4 4/8	5	4	22 1/8	20 6/8	25 1/8	0 0/8	181 4/8	186 2/8	181 4/8
95	Ruddy Presley	Harney	1986	4 7/8	5 0/8	9	5	23 4/8	22 1/8	30 0/8	2 2/8	183 5/8	189 5/8	181 3/8
96	Donald Yarbrough	Harney	1995	5 7/8	5 5/8	5	6	27 0/8	24 5/8	29 0/8	12 6/8	193 7/8	198 1/8	181 1/8
96	Terry Simpson	Umatilla	1994	4 6/8	5 1/8	7	5	25 2/8	26 0/8	26 0/8	9 3/8	190 4/8	193 1/8	181 1/8
96	John Mercer			5 3/8	5 2/8	5	6	24 2/8	26 0/8	26 0/8	0 0/8	181 1/8	189 1/8	181 1/8
99	Don Brummer/Jerry Brummer	Crook	1948	5 0/8	5 0/8	5	5	26 3/8	27 0/8	27 0/8	0 0/8	181 0/8	183 2/8	181 0/8
100	Wade Evans	Grant	1995	5 2/8	5 3/8	5	5	28 1/8	28 6/8	28 6/8	0 0/8	180 7/8	189 0/8	180 7/8
101	D.G. Dahlgren/Darrell Dahlgren	Grant	1974	6 2/8	6 0/8	8	8	26 6/8	27 6/8	33 2/8	17 0/8	197 5/8	201 0/8	180 5/8
102	Joe L. Gaylord	Umatilla	1995	4 2/8	4 3/8	9	6	26 5/8	27 0/8	28 3/8	11 6/8	192 1/8	195 5/8	180 3/8
102	Dennis Branin	Lake	1980	4 6/8	4 6/8	6	6	26 1/8	24 5/8	31 6/8	4 0/8	184 3/8	190 7/8	180 3/8
102	Marilyn Anderson	Wallowa		5 0/8	4 7/8	7	7	22 4/8	23 4/8	31 5/8	6 5/8	187 0/8	191 4/8	180 3/8
105	Carl Cox/Heath Prince		1960	4 2/8	4 0/8	5	6	25 0/8	21 2/8	24 5/8	3 2/8	183 4/8	188 1/8	180 2/8
106	John McWhorter	Lake	1983	5 1/8	5 0/8	7	6	25 0/8	25 2/8	29 2/8	6 1/8	186 0/8	192 3/8	179 7/8
106	Steve Harris	Lake	1986	5 6/8	5 7/8	5	5	24 7/8	25 1/8	29 0/8	0 0/8	179 7/8	183 6/8	179 7/8
106	Elmer Faulk		1960	5 4/8	5 6/8	7	8	24 0/8	18 3/8	30 0/8	13 0/8	192 7/8	199 4/8	179 7/8
109	Platt Talbott/Joseph Hardware	Wallowa	1995	5 2/8	5 0/8	6	7	25 4/8	21 6/8	25 6/8	5 7/8	185 4/8	188 5/8	179 5/8
110	Robert Zavodsky, Jr.	Wallowa	1979	4 4/8	4 5/8	5	5	24 6/8	21 0/8	23 3/8	0 0/8	179 4/8	182 2/8	179 4/8
110	Lawrence Wolfgram	Grant	1986	4 6/8	5 3/8	5	5	24 2/8	23 0/8	25 6/8	0 0/8	179 4/8	185 5/8	179 4/8
112	Richard Christenson	Umatilla	1947	4 6/8	4 4/8	6	6	26 7/8	26 1/8	28 4/8	2 2/8	181 5/8	194 3/8	179 3/8
113	Leon Mawlin	Wallowa		4 4/8	5 0/8	5	5	24 4/8	23 1/8	27 0/8	0 0/8	179 1/8	187 5/8	179 1/8
114	Ray Moles	Grant	1972	4 5/8	4 3/8	6	5	25 6/8	22 7/8	27 4/8	2 6/8	185 2/8	185 2/8	178 7/8
115	Edger J. Parker	Deschutes	1967	5 0/8	5 0/8	6	6	27 4/8	26 6/8	28 0/8	0 0/8	187 2/8	187 2/8	178 6/8
115	Ray Smith/Cecil Smith	Jefferson	1985	4 6/8	4 3/8	5	5	26 0/8	26 0/8	32 3/8	0 0/8	186 0/8	186 0/8	178 6/8
115	Daniel McGee		1995	4 5/8	4 6/8	5	5	25 0/8	25 2/8	25 7/8	0 0/8	183 5/8	183 5/8	178 6/8
115	Byron Richardson	Crook	1984	4 4/8	4 4/8	6	5	25 2/8	24 2/8	24 5/8	2 6/8	181 4/8	186 3/8	178 6/8
115	Chris Blacker		1981	4 4/8	4 4/8	5	5	24 0/8	24 0/8	23 3/8	0 0/8	178 6/8	183 4/8	178 6/8
120	Brad Eckland	Grant	1983	5 0/8	5 4/8	7	7	27 2/8	26 3/8	28 3/8	5 5/8	184 1/8	193 0/8	178 4/8
120	Mark Bagett	Grant	1993	4 1/8	4 1/8	6	6	23 6/8	27 0/8	27 0/8	6 2/8	184 6/8	186 3/8	178 4/8
122	Ed Pugh	Jefferson	1994	4 3/8	4 4/8	5	5	25 4/8	23 4/8	23 4/8	0 0/8	178 3/8	184 0/8	178 3/8
123	Fred Dulley	Lake	1988	4 6/8	4 6/8	6	7	27 1/8	24 3/8	33 2/8	12 1/8	190 3/8	195 2/8	178 2/8
123	Lynn Comini	Grant	1955	4 7/8	4 7/8	5	5	25 2/8	22 4/8	25 2/8	0 0/8	178 2/8	181 1/8	178 2/8
123	Ione Berry/Duane Berry	Wallowa	1995	4 5/8	4 6/8	5	5	24 5/8	25 2/8	29 2/8	2 3/8	180 5/8	183 3/8	178 2/8
123	Joe Edwards	Lake	1970	5 0/8	5 0/8	6	5	24 1/8	24 5/8	25 3/8	0 0/8	178 2/8	181 7/8	178 2/8
123	Gary Girrard/Martin Girrard	Union	1984	4 5/8	4 4/8	5	5	23 5/8	23 6/8	29 0/8	0 0/8	178 2/8	179 4/8	178 2/8
123	Jerry Lambeth	Grant		4 7/8	4 7/8	5	5	21 6/8	23 4/8	22 2/8	0 0/8	178 2/8	181 6/8	178 2/8

Typical Mule Deer—Rifle (continued)

Final Score	Gross Typical	Net Typical	Abnormal Points	Greatest Spread	Inside Spread	Main Beam		Number of Points		First Circumference		Year	County	Hunter/Owner	Rank
						R	L	R	L	R	L				
178 1/8	186 3/8	184 1/8	6 0/8	27 7/8	22 7/8	26 1/8	26 0/8	5	6	4 4/8	4 5/8	1991	Grant	Ronald Yockim	129
178 1/8	185 1/8	178 1/8	0 0/8	26 7/8	22 7/8	25 1/8	25 4/8	5	5	4 3/8	4 5/8	1969	Grant	Ray Moles	129
178 0/8	185 4/8	182 5/8	4 5/8	30 6/8	22 7/8	24 0/8	24 0/8	6	6	4 3/8	4 6/8	1981	Umatilla	Rick Etter	131
177 7/8	196 5/8	192 3/8	14 4/8	29 1/8	23 7/8	26 1/8	25 5/8	9	6	4 7/8	5 1/8	1959	Deschutes	Bryan Barnes	132
177 7/8	182 4/8	177 7/8	0 0/8	27 6/8	21 5/8	22 6/8	24 6/8	5	5	4 2/8	4 2/8	1986	Union	Jim Willis	132
177 6/8	183 7/8	177 6/8	0 0/8	25 3/8	22 0/8	23 4/8	24 3/8	5	5	4 7/8	4 7/8	1992		Ted Kratz	134
177 3/8	194 0/8	179 5/8	2 2/8	27 5/8	25 3/8	27 3/8	27 6/8	5	5	5 2/8	5 1/8	1994	Klamath	Ed Peterson	135
177 3/8	200 2/8	190 6/8	13 3/8	32 0/8	26 2/8	26 0/8	26 3/8	7	9	4 4/8	4 5/8	1933	Wallowa	Alfred Zollman/Joseph Hardware	135
177 3/8	181 3/8	177 3/8	0 0/8	26 0/8	21 3/8	22 5/8	23 4/8	5	5	4 5/8	4 6/8	1928	Jefferson	Otis Pauls/Lee Rhoden	135
177 3/8	180 4/8	177 3/8	0 0/8	23 0/8	17 7/8	20 6/8	22 0/8	5	5	5 2/8	5 2/8	1948	Umatilla	Vernon Case	135
177 2/8	190 3/8	187 4/8	10 2/8	26 2/8	21 6/8	26 6/8	27 0/8	6	5	5 0/8	5 2/8	1995	Jefferson	Ed Pugh	139
177 2/8	192 7/8	188 5/8	11 3/8	26 0/8	21 1/8	23 6/8	24 0/8	9	7	5 4/8	5 5/8			Joey Wood	139
177 2/8	178 3/8	177 2/8	0 0/8	28 0/8	23 2/8	23 0/8	23 3/8	5	5	4 7/8	4 7/8	1985	Grant	Ken Moore	139
177 1/8	188 0/8	183 2/8	6 1/8	34 0/8	24 4/8	24 4/8	25 0/8	7	6	4 4/8	4 4/8	1990	Grant	Jerry Lambeth	142
177 1/8	181 5/8	179 3/8	2 2/8	23 7/8	20 7/8	23 3/8	24 0/8	5	6	4 5/8	4 3/8	1995	Grant	Monte Davidson	142
177 0/8	183 0/8	177 0/8	0 0/8	31 0/8	23 2/8	24 3/8	25 4/8	5	5	5 0/8	5 0/8	1971	Lake	Maury Anderson	144
176 7/8	187 4/8	176 7/8	0 0/8	24 0/8	21 5/8	24 2/8	24 2/8	5	4	5 1/8	5 2/8	1950	Gilliam	John Maddock/John Irzyk	145
176 5/8	205 1/8	200 1/8	23 4/8	39 0/8	35 0/8	29 1/8	29 1/8	9	6	5 7/8	5 0/8		Lake	Nolan Greiner	146
176 5/8	183 7/8	178 3/8	1 6/8	25 2/8	20 5/8	25 5/8	24 1/8	5	6	4 4/8	4 2/8	1992	Wallowa	John Kirzmiller	146
176 4/8	191 1/8	182 2/8	5 6/8	28 3/8	24 0/8	26 6/8	26 2/8	7	6	5 6/8	5 6/8	1948	Umatilla	Lon Etter	148
176 4/8	180 7/8	176 4/8	0 0/8	27 4/8	24 0/8	25 7/8	25 7/8	4	4	4 4/8	4 5/8	1967	Baker	Nick Spiropolos	148
176 4/8	182 4/8	178 4/8	2 0/8	22 4/8	19 6/8	23 1/8	24 1/8	6	5	5 2/8	5 2/8	1995	Crook	Ron Bozarth	148
176 4/8	179 7/8	176 4/8	0 0/8	26 1/8	18 6/8	23 4/8	22 4/8	5	5	4 6/8	4 6/8	1969	Grant	Bob Williams	148
176 4/8	180 6/8	176 4/8	0 0/8	28 4/8	21 4/8	22 2/8	22 7/8	5	5	4 2/8	4 4/8	1994	Union	Kevin Robins	148
176 3/8	182 4/8	176 3/8	0 0/8	25 6/8	21 3/8	25 3/8	25 7/8	4	5	5 2/8	5 2/8	1928	Jefferson	Otis Pauls/Lee Rhoden	153
176 2/8	191 5/8	178 5/8	2 3/8	22 4/8	18 3/8	27 6/8	26 4/8	5	6	6 1/8	6 1/8	1972	Grant	David Oliver	154
176 2/8	187 2/8	177 6/8	1 4/8	27 2/8	22 6/8	25 6/8	26 5/8	6	5	5 1/8	4 7/8	1934	Deschutes	H.L. Young/Carm Anderson	154
176 2/8	179 2/8	176 2/8	0 0/8	28 2/8	24 2/8	23 5/8	23 6/8	4	4	4 4/8	4 3/8	1995	Lake	Roy Hillmick/Roy Hillmick	154
176 2/8	181 5/8	176 2/8	0 0/8	25 3/8	22 0/8	23 0/8	24 3/8	5	5	5 2/8	5 2/8	1974	Grant	Lawrence Wolfgram	154
176 2/8	178 4/8	176 2/8	0 0/8	24 6/8	21 2/8	23 5/8	23 4/8	5	5	4 6/8	4 6/8	1993	Crook	Brian Thompson	154
176 1/8	197 0/8	190 7/8	14 6/8	33 5/8	26 5/8	27 6/8	26 1/8	9	7	5 6/8	5 3/8	1951		Marshal Snearinger/ The Tumalo Restaurant	159
176 0/8	181 0/8	176 0/8	0 0/8	31 4/8	29 7/8	26 6/8	26 5/8	5	5	5 1/8	5 2/8	1994	Baker	Ron Bruce	160
175 7/8	181 4/8	177 1/8	1 2/8	25 3/8	23 5/8	25 0/8	24 4/8	6	5	4 5/8	4 4/8	1982	Harney	Mike Ferrera	161
175 7/8	182 6/8	175 7/8	0 0/8	25 2/8	20 5/8	24 1/8	25 1/8	4	5	5 3/8	5 4/8	1992	Crook	Kim Glaspie	161
175 6/8	180 1/8	175 6/8	0 0/8	25 6/8	22 4/8	26 1/8	26 0/8	5	5	4 5/8	4 5/8	1980	Deschutes	Greg Thomas	163
175 6/8	180 7/8	179 0/8	3 2/8	36 0/8	23 0/8	25 5/8	24 5/8	5	6	4 7/8	5 0/8	1985	Grant	David M. Morris	163
175 6/8	180 0/8	175 6/8	0 0/8	27 2/8	24 6/8	24 7/8	24 6/8	5	5	4 6/8	5 2/8	1988	Morrow	Jerry D. Donovan	163
175 6/8	180 3/8	175 6/8	0 0/8	26 5/8	22 0/8	24 0/8	23 6/8	5	5	5 2/8	5 3/8	1994	Baker	Robert Glover	163
175 6/8	189 2/8	183 7/8	8 1/8	24 0/8	22 5/8	23 4/8	24 0/8	7	6	6 0/8	5 3/8	1977	Umatilla	Opal Swiesberger/Craig Erickson	163
175 6/8	179 3/8	175 6/8	0 0/8	25 6/8	21 2/8	21 6/8	22 2/8	5	5	4 6/8	4 7/8	1993	Wallowa	James A. Bickmaier	163
175 3/8	186 4/8	180 5/8	5 2/8	35 0/8	25 0/8	23 0/8	24 1/8	5	6	4 6/8	5 0/8	1994	Harney	Tim Van DeGrift	169
175 3/8	181 2/8	178 0/8	2 5/8	28 0/8	21 6/8	22 7/8	22 6/8	5	6	4 6/8	4 6/8	1994	Baker	Milo Gross	169

175 2/8	209 5/8	203 5/8	28 3/8	33 6/8	25 1/8	27 5/8	27 5/8	8	8	4 7/8	4 7/8	1995	Sherman	Wendell Clodfelter	171
175 2/8	189 5/8	185 3/8	10 1/8	35 4/8	23 7/8	26 1/8	25 6/8	7	6	4 6/8	4 2/8	1988	Jefferson	Rodney Smith	171
175 2/8	179 3/8	175 2/8	0 0/8	29 7/8	25 0/8	24 3/8	25 0/8	5	5	4 3/8	4 3/8	1994	Deschutes	Dick Sapler	171
175 2/8	188 3/8	183 2/8	8 0/8		24 2/8	24 4/8	24 2/8	6	6	5 0/8	5 0/8	1989	Umatilla	David Powell	171
175 2/8	183 0/8	179 0/8	3 6/8	25 0/8	19 4/8	23 2/8	22 5/8	6	5	4 7/8	5 0/8	1930	Umatilla	Duane DeGrofft	171
175 1/8	205 7/8	202 2/8	27 1/8	32 4/8	26 6/8	25 4/8	26 2/8	11	9	6 2/8	6 2/8			Joseph Hardware	176
175 1/8	186 3/8	178 4/8	3 3/8	22 3/8	18 4/8	21 2/8	23 5/8	4	4	5 1/8	5 2/8	1993	Jefferson	Ron Phifer	176
174 7/8	182 2/8	178 7/8	4 0/8	28 3/8	26 5/8	24 0/8	24 3/8	5	6	4 6/8	4 7/8	1983	Malheur	Ben Simpson	178
174 6/8	183 4/8	176 2/8	1 4/8	29 4/8	23 2/8	25 1/8	25 5/8	6	5	4 7/8	5 0/8	1987	Baker	Mark Sieckman	179
174 6/8	183 2/8	174 6/8	0 0/8	30 1/8	22 6/8	25 0/8	24 3/8	5	5	5 0/8	5 0/8	1977	Grant	Ken Moore	179
174 6/8	183 5/8	174 6/8	0 0/8	25 4/8	23 2/8	23 1/8	25 2/8	4	5	5 2/8	5 2/8	1975	Malheur	Ray Moles	179
174 6/8	187 0/8	184 6/8	10 0/8	29 5/8	24 3/8	24 0/8	23 7/8	6	8	4 6/8	4 5/8	1976	Wallowa	Dave Melville	179
174 6/8	180 [illegible]/8	174 6/8	0 0/8	25 4/8	20 4/8	23 4/8	23 6/8	5	5	4 6/8	4 7/8	1994	Grant	Daniel Smith	179
174 6/8	180 [illegible]/8	174 6/8	0 0/8	24 4/8	22 4/8	23 4/8	23 4/8	5	5	5 4/8	5 4/8	1975	Grant	John Howell	179
174 6/8	178 7/8	174 6/8	0 0/8	25 2/8	21 6/8	23 0/8	22 4/8	5	5	4 1/8	4 2/8			Mike Lowenstein	179
174 5/8	189 2/8	177 6/8	3 1/8	31 6/8	24 6/8	26 2/8	24 5/8	5	5	4 3/8	4 5/8	1994	Lake	Gerald Bushnell	186
174 4/8	189 [illegible]/8	182 4/8	8 0/8	21 4/8	18 4/8	24 0/8	21 0/8	4	5	4 6/8	4 6/8	1936	Wallowa	Kirk Beith/Joseph Hardware	187
174 3/8	180 4/8	174 3/8	0 0/8	25 6/8	21 5/8	24 4/8	25 5/8	5	5	4 4/8	4 6/8	1944	Grant	Murray Leslie	188
174 3/8	183 0/8	177 5/8	3 2/8	23 0/8	19 7/8	23 2/8	24 3/8	5	6	4 3/8	4 4/8	1989	Baker	Vi Seever	188
174 2/8	178 0/8	175 4/8	1 2/8	25 6/8	21 0/8	24 7/8	24 6/8	5	6	5 0/8	4 7/8	1991	Umatilla	Clifford Widel	190
174 2/8	182 6/8	174 2/8	0 0/8	25 0/8	21 0/8	23 4/8	24 0/8	5	5	4 6/8	4 4/8	1995	Baker	Donald McLean	190
174 2/8	178 1/8	174 2/8	0 0/8	26 5/8	21 0/8	23 0/8	22 4/8	5	5	4 3/8	4 5/8	1985	Lake	Richard Drexelius	190
174 1/8	180 7/8	177 1/8	3 0/8	30 7/8	25 7/8	24 3/8	24 1/8	5	5	5 1/8	5 2/8	1967	Gilliam	Fred Reed	193
174 1/8	175 0/8	174 1/8	0 0/8	28 7/8	22 5/8	23 3/8	23 5/8	5	5	3 7/8	3 5/8	1984	Harney	Denny Presley	193
174 0/8	178 3/8	174 0/8	0 0/8	27 2/8	21 4/8	21 6/8	23 6/8	4	4	4 2/8	4 3/8	1952	Wallowa	Wayne Marks	195
173 6/8	181 0/8	173 6/8	0 0/8	23 4/8	21 4/8	23 4/8	24 4/8	5	5	4 7/8	4 6/8	1993	Harney	Kevin Radinovich	196
173 6/8	175 0/8	173 6/8	0 0/8	33 0/8	26 7/8	23 6/8	23 6/8	5	5	5 0/8	4 7/8	1962	Grant	Donald Brown	196
173 5/8	176 2/8	173 5/8	0 0/8	30 6/8	24 5/8	24 2/8	24 3/8	5	5	4 4/8	4 4/8	1995	Malheur	Michael McCafferety	198
173 3/8	182 3/8	179 5/8	6 2/8	24 4/8	19 1/8	23 5/8	23 0/8	5	7	4 3/8	4 5/8	1994	Umatilla	Dawn Sims	199
173 2/8	177 5/8	173 2/8	0 0/8	28 2/8	25 0/8	25 6/8	24 2/8	5	5	4 4/8	4 4/8	1935	Wallowa	Leon Mawhin	200
173 1/8	193 7/8	186 7/8	13 6/8	31 0/8	22 5/8	26 4/8	26 5/8	5	7	5 4/8	5 5/8	1977	Baker	Kerry Bratcher	201
173 1/8	180 2/8	173 1/8	0 0/8	29 2/8	24 7/8	26 0/8	24 7/8	4	4	5 0/8	5 0/8	1987	Wallowa	Gerald Arbogast	201
173 1/8	177 6/8	173 1/8	0 0/8	27 4/8	25 4/8	25 1/8	24 3/8	5	5	4 5/8	4 4/8	1984	Malheur	C.J. Munroe	201
173 1/8	176 7/8	173 1/8	0 0/8	28 7/8	23 7/8	24 2/8	24 6/8	4	4	4 0/8	4 0/8	1986	Klamath	Jim Brown	201
173 0/8	179 4/8	174 3/8	1 3/8	30 7/8	27 3/8	23 5/8	25 5/8	5	6	5 0/8	4 7/8	1992	Baker	Michael Van Allen	205
173 0/8	177 1/8	173 0/8	0 0/8	26 0/8	20 4/8	24 1/8	23 0/8	5	5	4 4/8	4 4/8	1957	Grant	Lola DeRosier	205
172 6/8	187 7/8	181 6/8	9 0/8		30 0/8	25 4/8	24 7/8	6	6	5 4/8	5 6/8	1995	Deschutes	Betty Dodge	207
172 5/8	176 6/8	172 5/8	0 0/8	24 3/8	20 3/8	23 6/8	23 0/8	5	5	4 3/8	4 3/8	1962	Umatilla	Mick Kilby	208
172 4/8	177 4/8	172 4/8	0 0/8	25 4/8	21 0/8	24 6/8	23 3/8	5	5	5 2/8	5 4/8	1962	Lake	Carm Anderson	209
172 3/8	174 7/8	172 3/8	0 0/8		22 3/8	24 0/8	23 7/8	5	5	5 0/8	5 0/8	1993	Morrow	Judy Barber	210
172 1/8	176 3/8	174 1/8	2 0/8	26 0/8	22 7/8	24 5/8	25 5/8	6	6	4 5/8	4 4/8	1953	Crook	Boyd W. Care/Joel B. Care	211
172 1/8	176 5/8	174 4/8	2 3/8	22 4/8	18 0/8	22 6/8	22 7/8	6	5	5 3/8	5 3/8	1991	Union	Ken Hessel	211
172 0/8	181 0/8	173 2/8	1 2/8	26 5/8	24 2/8	27 2/8	26 6/8	6	5	5 0/8	5 0/8	1989	Wheeler	Lee Rhoden	213
172 0/8	192 0/8	184 5/8	12 5/8	30 4/8	23 3/8	25 4/8	26 2/8	7	7	5 6/8	5 6/8		Grant	Joey Wood	213
171 7/8	174 3/8	171 7/8	0 0/8	32 1/8	25 7/8	24 4/8	24 5/8	5	5	4 3/8	4 2/8	1968	Klamath	Jim Rogers/Evan Wright	215
171 6/8	179 6/8	174 6/8	3 0/8	25 0/8	19 6/8	22 3/8	24 5/8	6	5	4 4/8	4 4/8	1980	Harney	Jim Wells	216

Typical Mule Deer—Rifle (continued)

Final Score	Gross Typical	Net Typical	Abnormal Points	Greatest Spread	Inside Spread	Main Beam R	Main Beam L	Number of Points R	Number of Points L	First Circumference R	First Circumference L	Year	County	Hunter/Owner	Rank
171 5/8	177 1/8	171 5/8	0 0/8	24 5/8	21 7/8	23 5/8	24 4/8	5	5	4 3/8	4 5/8		Umatilla	Ron Polley	217
171 5/8	173 0/8	171 5/8	0 0/8	20 2/8	17 7/8	23 6/8	23 4/8	4	4	4 7/8	4 6/8	1994	Crook	Monte Burch	217
171 5/8	175 1/8	171 5/8	0 0/8		20 3/8	23 3/8	23 3/8	5	5	4 5/8	4 5/8	1978	Grant	Mark Bagett	217
171 4/8	173 7/8	171 4/8	0 0/8	27 1/8	20 2/8	23 4/8	23 2/8	4	4	5 0/8	5 0/8	1978	Wallowa	Russell Shirley	220
171 3/8	176 0/8	171 3/8	0 0/8	30 1/8	27 2/8	26 0/8	26 3/8	5	5	4 7/8	4 6/8	1982	Lake	Betty Morris/Ken Sankey	221
171 3/8	179 4/8	172 3/8	1 0/8	28 6/8	22 7/8	26 4/8	25 5/8	5	6	5 2/8	5 1/8	1968		Walt Jesse	221
171 3/8	186 7/8	171 3/8	0 0/8	31 5/8	27 4/8	25 7/8	25 7/8	4	5	5 6/8	5 4/8	1986	Grant	Ken Moore	221
171 3/8	183 4/8	173 7/8	2 4/8	29 2/8	22 1/8	25 0/8	25 4/8	4	6	5 1/8	5 1/8	1952	Crook	Don Edwards	221
171 3/8	175 0/8	171 3/8	0 0/8	21 3/8	17 3/8	24 6/8	23 7/8	5	5	5 1/8	5 1/8	1957	Wallowa	Fred Pearson/Rusty Lindberg	221
171 3/8	185 0/8	178 0/8	6 5/8	23 7/8	20 0/8	22 4/8	23 6/8	6	5	4 4/8	5 0/8		Grant	Ron Early/Ernie Smith	221
171 1/8	174 2/8	171 1/8	0 0/8	25 4/8	23 3/8	24 0/8	24 6/8	5	5	4 2/8	4 2/8	1980	Harney	Terry Presley	227
171 1/8	173 6/8	171 1/8	0 0/8	28 0/8	21 3/8	23 7/8	24 2/8	5	5	4 1/8	4 0/8	1979	Umatilla	Cliff Widel	227
171 0/8	176 4/8	171 0/8	0 0/8	24 2/8	20 0/8	20 5/8	21 3/8	5	5	4 6/8	4 6/8	1946	Wallowa	Paul Yost	229
170 7/8	182 2/8	170 7/8	0 0/8	28 4/8	26 7/8	25 0/8	26 5/8	5	6	5 0/8	4 7/8	1989	Harney	Sara Wheland	230
170 7/8	176 7/8	172 4/8	1 5/8	31 0/8	27 5/8	24 4/8	25 0/8	5	6	4 4/8	4 4/8	1958	Grant	Wayne Simmons	230
170 7/8	181 3/8	174 6/8	3 7/8	24 6/8	20 6/8	24 0/8	25 1/8	7	4	4 4/8	4 5/8	1991	Umatilla	Gary Graybeal	230
170 6/8	173 5/8	170 6/8	0 0/8	28 1/8	25 2/8	26 5/8	26 2/8	4	4	5 4/8	5 4/8	1985	Klamath	Jim Shelton	233
170 6/8	179 3/8	170 6/8	0 0/8	25 2/8	22 2/8	26 2/8	24 6/8	4	5	4 0/8	4 0/8	1968	Deschutes	Dick Sadler	233
170 6/8	175 0/8	170 6/8	0 0/8	22 4/8	17 6/8	22 6/8	22 6/8	5	6	4 0/8	4 1/8	1990	Umatilla	Guy Patterson	233
170 5/8	181 0/8	176 2/8	5 5/8	28 0/8	21 0/8	26 1/8	26 4/8	6	6	5 2/8	5 3/8	1963	Harney	Louis W. LaMotte/Zelma LaMotte	236
170 5/8	176 7/8	170 5/8	0 0/8	30 6/8	24 0/8	23 5/8	22 3/8	5	5	4 5/8	4 4/8	1967	Deschutes	Milton LaFranchie	236
170 2/8	179 1/8	175 5/8	5 3/8	24 3/8	20 7/8	23 4/8	23 4/8	6	6	4 5/8	4 4/8		Lake	Nolan Geiner	238
170 1/8	173 7/8	170 1/8	0 0/8	27 6/8	21 3/8	25 3/8	25 4/8	5	5	5 1/8	5 0/8	1994	Umatilla	Larry Young/Mike Brown	239
170 1/8	173 6/8	170 1/8	0 0/8	27 6/8	18 3/8	24 6/8	24 4/8	5	5	4 0/8	4 1/8	1981	Grant	Trent Wright	239
170 0/8	179 4/8	173 0/8	3 0/8	27 4/8	26 2/8	25 0/8	24 4/8	6	5	4 7/8	4 4/8	1966	Grant	Gary Miller	241
170 0/8	174 7/8	170 0/8	0 0/8	26 2/8	23 6/8	25 2/8	24 2/8	5	4	4 5/8	4 5/8	1950	Grant	Robert Morris/Merle Morris	241
170 0/8	176 6/8	170 0/8	0 0/8	23 0/8	17 6/8	23 4/8	21 6/8	5	5	4 4/8	4 6/8	1994	Grant	Bob Wolfe	241
169 7/8	190 1/8	179 2/8	9 3/8		20 2/8	25 0/8	26 6/8	6	5	4 4/8	4 2/8	1976	Crook	Lee Rhoden	244
169 4/8	193 1/8	187 4/8	18 0/8	20 4/8	20 4/8	24 2/8	25 2/8	7	9	4 2/8	4 2/8	1993	Umatilla	John Wagner	245
169 3/8	191 2/8	182 7/8	13 4/8	30 4/8	25 1/8	27 6/8	26 4/8	6	7	5 2/8	5 3/8	1994	Wheeler	Clay Woodward	246
169 3/8	173 2/8	169 3/8	0 0/8	29 2/8	23 1/8	26 1/8	25 6/8	4	5	4 7/8	5 0/8	1974	Lake	Floyd Jacobs	246
169 2/8	173 0/8	169 2/8	0 0/8	26 6/8	21 4/8	23 2/8	23 4/8	5	5	4 5/8	4 4/8	1964	Grant	Ray Moles	248
169 0/8	172 1/8	169 0/8	0 0/8	23 3/8	20 6/8	24 4/8	24 0/8	4	4	4 4/8	4 5/8	1958	Grant	Ransom W. Brown/Gary Lee Brown	249
169 0/8	173 2/8	170 6/8	1 6/8	27 2/8	23 7/8	22 4/8	22 4/8	5	6	5 6/8	5 6/8	1995	Malheur	Bruce Lawson	249
168 7/8	186 2/8	168 7/8	0 0/8	34 0/8	32 2/8	29 3/8	28 0/8	4	5	5 2/8	5 4/8	1953	Gilliam	Fred Reed	251
168 7/8	173 4/8	168 7/8	0 0/8	22 7/8	22 7/8	24 6/8	23 5/8	4	5	4 6/8	4 0/8	1982	Grant	Andrew Radinovich	251
168 6/8	182 7/8	177 6/8	9 0/8	26 0/8	21 6/8	23 0/8	23 7/8	8	7	4 6/8	4 6/8	1961	Union	Bill Peacock	253
168 6/8	172 2/8	168 6/8	0 0/8	23 3/8	21 0/8	22 4/8	23 3/8	5	5	4 1/8	4 0/8	1987	Union	Bill Alexander	253
168 4/8	194 1/8	184 3/8	15 7/8	32 2/8	23 5/8	27 1/8	26 0/8	7	7	5 0/8	5 1/8	1989	Harney	Scott Ritner	255
168 4/8	198 0/8	190 0/8	21 4/8	28 3/8	26 2/8	26 0/8	25 4/8	6	6	5 3/8	5 4/8	1984	Harney	Paul Okita	255
168 3/8	174 7/8	168 3/8	0 0/8	29 0/8	26 4/8	24 1/8	22 7/8	4	4	4 1/8	4 1/8		Grant	Joey Wood	257

Rank	Name	County	Year	1	2	3	4	5	6	7	8	9	10	11	Net Score
257	Lee Johnson	Umatilla	1977	4 4/8	4 4/8	5	5	23 2/8	23 2/8	20 1/8	24 5/8	0 0/8	168 3/8	169 5/8	168 3/8
259	Steve Lankford	Morrow	1982	5 1/8	4 7/8	7	8	23 4/8	24 0/8	20 0/8	25 0/8	7 0/8	175 2/8	181 1/8	168 2/8
259	Daryl Scheckla	Wallowa	1978	4 4/8	4 2/8	4	5	23 1/8	23 6/8	24 6/8	29 2/8	0 0/8	168 2/8	176 2/8	168 2/8
259	Delwyn Zollman/Joseph Hardware	Wallowa	1966	4 5/8	4 5/8	5	5	21 3/8	23 6/8	20 2/8	26 6/8	0 0/8	168 2/8	172 7/8	168 2/8
262	Guy Patterson	Umatilla	1991	4 6/8	4 6/8	5	5	22 0/8	23 6/8	18 2/8	21 1/8	0 0/8	167 6/8	171 2/8	167 6/8
263	Ken Green	Harney	1989	4 6/8	4 6/8	5	8	24 1/8	23 1/8	22 1/8	29 6/8	6 4/8	174 1/8	177 7/8	167 5/8
263	Tim Mahoney	Baker	1990	4 5/8	4 6/8	5	6	23 1/8	22 6/8	17 4/8	23 0/8	8 3/8	176 0/8	181 7/8	167 5/8
265	Mike Norton	Wallowa	1991	4 6/8	4 6/8	6	5	22 3/8	23 1/8	20 4/8	23 1/8	3 2/8	170 6/8	173 2/8	167 4/8
266	Allen Van Dyke	Deschutes	1992	4 4/8	4 4/8	5	5	27 7/8	26 1/8	23 1/8	25 6/8	0 0/8	167 3/8	173 2/8	167 3/8
266	Dick Faulk/Don Brown	Malheur	1950	5 1/8	5 2/8	6	8	26 3/8	27 0/8	22 0/8	29 3/8	22 1/8	189 4/8	197 1/8	167 3/8
266	Earl D. Rist	Baker	1988	5 7/8	5 6/8	5	5	25 4/8	25 0/8	23 3/8	25 4/8	0 0/8	167 3/8	175 3/8	167 3/8
266	Ben Weinke	Umatilla	1987	4 3/8	4 3/8	5	5	24 7/8	24 3/8	24 1/8	27 6/8	0 0/8	167 3/8	172 2/8	167 3/8
271	Toscia Meyer	Lake	1981	4 7/8	4 5/8	5	6	24 7/8	22 0/8	21 4/8	24 2/8	6 3/8	173 6/8	180 2/8	167 3/8
271	Ray Thomason	Deschutes	1995	5 1/8	5 7/8	8	9	27 4/8	27 0/8	25 7/8	31 0/8	13 5/8	180 7/8	185 6/8	167 3/8
271	Ron DeRoest	Baker	1965	5 4/8	5 3/8	7	7	23 3/8	26 0/8	24 6/8	36 0/8	19 6/8	187 0/8	198 0/8	167 2/8
271	Ken/Dan Moore	Grant	1994	4 4/8	4 2/8	5	5	22 6/8	24 7/8	19 6/8	22 2/8	0 0/8	167 2/8	171 2/8	167 2/8
271	Margaret Deardorff	Baker	1993	4 7/8	4 7/8	5	5	23 3/8	23 1/8	23 0/8	27 0/8	0 0/8	167 2/8	175 6/8	167 2/8
276	Kevin Polley	Grant	1988	4 3/8	4 4/8	5	5	22 5/8	23 0/8	20 0/8	24 1/8	0 0/8	167 2/8	170 7/8	167 2/8
277	Chester Elliot	Union	1962	4 6/8	4 4/8	6	5	22 6/8	23 6/8	20 1/8	28 1/8	1 6/8	168 7/8	173 4/8	167 1/8
277	Merle Morris	Grant	1995	4 6/8	5 1/8	5	5	24 0/8	24 1/8	20 6/8	24 0/8	0 0/8	167 0/8	172 3/8	167 0/8
277	Jerry D. Donovan	Harney	1995	4 4/8	4 4/8	6	6	23 0/8	23 0/8	19 3/8	25 0/8	8 5/8	175 5/8	178 1/8	167 0/8
280	J. Russel Genevieve	Umatilla	1978	5 1/8	4 7/8	5	6	19 0/8	20 4/8	20 5/8	25 6/8	1 6/8	168 6/8	174 0/8	167 0/8
280	John Spencer	Umatilla	1976	5 6/8	5 7/8	7	5	24 5/8	23 5/8	21 0/8	32 2/8	6 7/8	173 6/8	182 7/8	166 7/8
280	Delwyn Zollman/Joseph Hardware	Wallowa		4 6/8	4 6/8	6	9	23 6/8	23 4/8	22 0/8	33 4/8	10 7/8	177 6/8	182 2/8	166 7/8
282	Don Moody	Harney	1963	5 4/8	5 3/8	8	9	27 0/8	26 3/8	22 6/8	31 0/8	19 7/8	186 2/8	190 7/8	166 3/8
282	Ransom Brown/Gary Lee Brown	Grant	1962	5 0/8	5 0/8	6	5	25 4/8	25 7/8	22 7/8	28 0/8	1 6/8	168 1/8	176 2/8	166 3/8
284	Mike Garrett	Lake	1977	4 5/8	4 4/8	5	5	23 6/8	24 0/8	22 2/8	27 4/8	0 0/8	166 2/8	169 1/8	166 2/8
284	Alton Mitchell	Crook	1978	4 3/8	4 4/8	5	4	22 3/8	25 1/8	24 6/8	29 2/8	0 0/8	166 2/8	175 6/8	166 2/8
286	Jim Mayhew	Wasco	1990	5 4/8	5 3/8	5	5	24 4/8	26 0/8	23 5/8	26 5/8	0 0/8	166 1/8	171 7/8	166 1/8
286	Jim Grosjacques	Union	1987	4 7/8	4 5/8	5	5	24 0/8	25 0/8	20 1/8	25 5/8	6 3/8	166 1/8	172 1/8	166 1/8
286	Benjamin K. Weinke	Umatilla	1995	5 2/8	5 2/8	5	6	22 4/8	22 5/8	20 6/8	30 0/8	8 5/8	172 4/8	177 2/8	166 0/8
289	Glen Dobson	Harney	1976	5 3/8	5 3/8	5	7	24 3/8	25 6/8	25 1/8	24 2/8	4 1/8	174 5/8	181 0/8	166 0/8
289	Scott Latranchi	Deschutes	1976	4 6/8	4 5/8	6	6	25 0/8	23 6/8	21 5/8	30 0/8	0 0/8	170 1/8	176 6/8	166 0/8
289	Jerry Brummer	Crook	1992	4 1/8	4 0/8	4	4	24 5/8	23 3/8	23 2/8	23 2/8	1 1/8	166 0/8	169 5/8	166 0/8
292	Dale Victor	Wallowa	1940	4 2/8	4 3/8	5	6	23 6/8	23 4/8	16 4/8	25 7/8	0 0/8	167 0/8	172 1/8	165 7/8
292	Howard Scheckla/Daryl Scheckla	Crook	1946	5 0/8	5 0/8	5	5	23 3/8	21 5/8	22 3/8	25 0/8	0 0/8	165 7/8	171 5/8	165 7/8
294	Robert Zavodsky, Sr.	Wallowa		3 5/8	3 5/8	5	5	23 2/8	19 2/8	17 4/8	25 0/8	0 0/8	165 6/8	171 2/8	165 6/8
295	Ray Moles	Grant	1968	4 7/8	4 7/8	4	4	24 3/8	23 2/8	21 3/8	28 0/8	0 0/8	165 5/8	174 2/8	165 5/8
296	Russ Rhoden	Wheeler	1995	4 3/8	4 3/8	6	7	28 6/8	26 4/8	26 4/8	26 4/8	11 2/8	176 4/8	181 0/8	165 2/8
296	Russell Dotson	Umatilla	1962	4 7/8	5 0/8	7	5	23 1/8	24 7/8	21 7/8	21 7/8	5 7/8	171 1/8	178 3/8	165 2/8
298	Fred Reed/Bob Reed	Gilliam	1950	5 0/8	5 0/8	3	3	27 4/8	28 0/8	30 6/8	33 5/8	8 4/8	173 4/8	179 0/8	165 0/8
298	Jack DeRosier	Grant	1980	5 7/8	5 7/8	4	4	26 2/8	28 1/8	22 4/8	26 4/8	0 0/8	165 0/8	170 6/8	165 0/8
300	Stan Rychuck/David Rychlick	Umatilla	1960	5 2/8	5 2/8	6	6	25 5/8	25 5/8	23 6/8	21 7/8	6 3/8	171 2/8	178 1/8	164 7/8
300	David Davies	Deschutes	1994	4 7/8	4 5/8	5	5	23 1/8	23 0/8	25 0/8	31 0/8	0 0/8	164 7/8	168 1/8	164 7/8

Typical Mule Deer—Rifle (continued)

Final Score	Gross Typical	Net Typical	Abnormal Points	Greatest Spread	Inside Spread	Main Beam		Number of Points		First Circumference		Year	County	Hunter/Owner	Rank
						R	L	R	L	R	L				
164 6/8	189 0/8	184 0/8	19 2/8	31 0/8	22 0/8	24 2/8	25 3/8	7	9	5 0/8	5 0/8	1991	Harney	Greg Quart	302
164 5/8	169 5/8	164 5/8	0 0/8	29 0/8	21 5/8	23 7/8	23 6/8	5	5	4 6/8	4 6/8	1960	Umatilla	Chet Schiewe	303
164 4/8	172 0/8	164 4/8	0 0/8	33 6/8	26 2/8	27 5/8	25 0/8	3	3	4 6/8	4 4/8	1995	Harney	Jeff Riley	304
164 4/8	173 5/8	168 2/8	3 6/8	31 7/8	27 3/8	23 3/8	23 4/8	5	8	5 0/8	5 4/8	1986	Deschutes	Dennis Brown	304
164 4/8	178 3/8	173 1/8	8 5/8	22 2/8	17 7/8	22 2/8	21 7/8	7	6	5 4/8	5 3/8	1995	Umatilla	Jerry Johnson	304
164 3/8	184 4/8	179 4/8	15 1/8	23 3/8	20 6/8	27 5/8	26 5/8	7	7	5 4/8	5 4/8	1992	Deschutes	Rodney Moss	307
164 1/8	172 3/8	164 1/8	0 0/8	24 2/8	18 3/8	24 4/8	22 2/8	5	5	4 5/8	4 7/8	1983	Lake	David Van Dyke	308
164 0/8	167 6/8	164 0/8	0 0/8	17 1/8	15 2/8	23 2/8	21 4/8	5	5	4 3/8	4 1/8	1995	Malheur	Don Pillar	309
163 5/8	172 6/8	163 5/8	0 0/8	27 1/8	23 1/8	25 4/8	25 1/8	5	4	5 0/8	5 0/8	1989		Don Stroeber	310
163 5/8	171 4/8	163 5/8	0 0/8	29 0/8	21 3/8	24 6/8	25 0/8	4	4	4 2/8	4 2/8	1984	Wallowa	Dale Dotson	310
163 5/8	177 3/8	167 4/8	3 7/8		21 6/8	25 4/8	23 0/8	4	6	5 1/8	5 3/8	1994	Union	Dirk E. Martin	310
163 5/8	167 3/8	163 5/8	0 0/8	22 2/8	20 7/8	23 2/8	23 7/8	5	5	4 3/8	4 3/8	1978	Crook	Wade Sallee	310
163 3/8	188 6/8	171 2/8	7 7/8	27 3/8	20 0/8	23 5/8	25 5/8	5	7	4 4/8	4 5/8	1991	Union	Ed Kruse	314
163 3/8	170 0/8	164 4/8	1 1/8	26 0/8	25 7/8	23 0/8	22 3/8	5	6	4 7/8	5 0/8	1977	Umatilla	David Rychlick	314
163 3/8	181 6/8	176 3/8	13 0/8	27 5/8	19 3/8	22 1/8	21 1/8	7	6	4 2/8	4 1/8	1967	Umatilla	Walter Gaylord/Dale Gaylord	314
163 1/8	164 6/8	163 1/8	0 0/8	25 2/8	25 3/8	27 0/8	27 1/8	3	3	0 0/8	0 0/8	1986	Grant	G. Kent Hettinga	317
163 1/8	172 3/8	163 1/8	0 0/8		23 2/8	22 5/8	22 3/8	5	5	4 1/8	4 1/8	1995	Deschutes	Gilbert L. Daniels	317
163 0/8	198 1/8	181 6/8	18 6/8		22 2/8	23 4/8	26 1/8	9	8	5 2/8	5 2/8	1991	Grant	Tony Gardner	319
163 0/8	170 1/8	163 0/8	0 0/8	27 1/8	22 6/8	23 3/8	23 5/8	5	5	4 5/8	4 5/8	1991	Crook	Roger Lutter	319
163 0/8	174 0/8	163 0/8	0 0/8	29 2/8	25 5/8	21 3/8	24 4/8	5	5	4 2/8	4 2/8	1965	Wallowa	John Groupe	319
163 0/8	179 4/8	177 0/8	14 0/8	22 0/8	18 4/8	22 4/8	21 6/8	9	6	4 5/8	4 2/8	1949	Wallowa	Leon Mawlin	319
162 7/8	172 7/8	167 1/8	4 2/8	29 0/8	27 1/8	22 6/8	24 1/8	7	6	5 5/8	5 6/8	1993	Klamath	Ted Carlson	323
162 6/8	181 2/8	178 2/8	15 4/8	20 4/8	16 4/8	22 3/8	22 6/8	7	6	4 7/8	5 0/8	1969	Grant	Dean Tewell	324
162 6/8	172 1/8	165 6/8	3 0/8	30 6/8	19 6/8	21 4/8	23 0/8	5	7	5 0/8	4 7/8	1948	Union	Bill Marcum	324
162 6/8	166 5/8	162 6/8	0 0/8	26 4/8	23 2/8	21 2/8	21 4/8	5	5	4 3/8	4 4/8	1964	Grant	Ted Smith	324
162 4/8	164 3/8	162 4/8	0 0/8	26 5/8	22 2/8	26 3/8	26 6/8	4	4	4 1/8	4 0/8	1990	Deschutes	Gilbert Daniels/Cecil Smith	327
162 4/8	172 1/8	162 4/8	0 0/8	24 4/8	21 2/8	24 3/8	24 3/8	5	5	5 1/8	5 5/8	1980	Crook	Clark Owsley	327
162 4/8	170 6/8	163 6/8	1 2/8	28 2/8	22 6/8	23 4/8	23 7/8	5	6	4 7/8	4 6/8	1947	Baker	Ballard Brooks/Adam Brooks	327
162 3/8	172 6/8	162 3/8	0 0/8	25 4/8	20 1/8	23 0/8	23 0/8	5	5	4 2/8	4 2/8	1993	Wallowa	Duane O'Brien	330
162 3/8	167 6/8	162 3/8	0 0/8	22 1/8	20 1/8	22 2/8	21 6/8	5	5	4 7/8	5 1/8	1979	Umatilla	Charles Clark	330
162 3/8	167 4/8	162 3/8	0 0/8	21 1/8	17 7/8	22 2/8	21 5/8	5	5	5 0/8	5 2/8	1964	Umatilla	Bill Martin	330
162 2/8	174 2/8	169 2/8	7 0/8	29 0/8	27 4/8	23 0/8	21 4/8	6	7	4 3/8	4 6/8	1994	Umatilla	Rodney Cox	333
162 1/8	163 4/8	162 1/8	0 0/8	31 7/8	26 7/8	22 7/8	22 5/8	5	5	4 7/8	4 5/8	1976		Loren Brooks	334
161 7/8	173 0/8	165 1/8	3 2/8	23 0/8	19 5/8	21 3/8	23 2/8	6	6	4 5/8	4 7/8	1969	Grant	Ken Moore	335
161 6/8	175 1/8	169 0/8	7 2/8	23 2/8	20 4/8	26 0/8	25 2/8	4	6	5 5/8	5 5/8		Crook	Ross Loveland	336
161 6/8	174 4/8	169 3/8	7 5/8	25 1/8	22 3/8	23 6/8	25 0/8	8	6	4 5/8	4 7/8	1992	Deschutes	Steve Dunn	336
161 6/8	163 3/8	161 6/8	0 0/8	23 5/8	19 0/8	22 3/8	22 2/8	4	4	4 1/8	4 1/8	1995	Wallowa	Chuck Simpson	336
161 6/8	164 7/8	161 6/8	0 0/8	22 0/8	16 4/8	21 4/8	20 5/8	5	5	4 1/8	4 2/8	1969	Baker	Earlin S. Bennett	336
161 6/8	165 2/8	161 6/8	0 0/8	24 2/8	19 3/8	19 0/8	19 2/8	5	5	4 7/8	4 7/8	1994	Umatilla	Gordon Wright	336
161 5/8	174 1/8	169 0/8	7 3/8	27 4/8	26 7/8	25 0/8	26 6/8	6	7	5 4/8	5 6/8	1990	Lake	Matt Bostwick	341
161 5/8	170 3/8	161 5/8	0 0/8		20 3/8	26 2/8	24 6/8	4	4	4 4/8	4 4/8	1992		Steve Mayfield	341
161 1/8	180 3/8	169 5/8	8 4/8	24 4/8	19 1/8	25 1/8	25 4/8	6	6	5 1/8	5 0/8	1979	Grant	Wayne Barry	343
161 0/8	174 2/8	169 2/8	8 2/8		22 2/8	25 4/8	26 4/8	6	6	5 2/8	5 0/8	1992	Deschutes	Paul Nordstrom	344

Final Score	Gross Typical	Net Typical	Abnormal Points	Greatest Spread	Inside Spread	Main Beam R	Main Beam L	No. Points R	No. Points L	First Circ. R	First Circ. L	Year	County	Hunter/Owner	Rank
161 0/8	166 0/8	161 0/8	0 0/8	26 1/8	23 2/8	23 0/8	23 2/8	5	5	5 2/8	5 4/8	1986	Deschutes	Walt Weber	344
160 7/8	162 7/8	160 7/8	0 0/8	26 4/8	23 0/8	22 4/8	22 5/8	5	5	4 6/8	4 5/8	1995	Wallowa	Russell Shirley	346
160 7/8	163 6/8	160 7/8	0 0/8	28 4/8	19 3/8	21 5/8	22 5/8	5	5	4 5/8	4 5/8	1968	Lake	Edgar Parker	346
160 5/8	166 1/8	160 5/8	0 0/8	36 4/8	28 6/8	24 5/8	24 1/8	5	4	4 3/8	4 0/8	1992	Crook	Mark Rhoden	348
160 5/8	171 4/8	166 0/8	5 3/8	29 6/8	25 2/8	26 0/8	24 2/8	5	6	4 5/8	4 7/8	1980	Umatilla	Ed McLaren	348
160 5/8	184 0/8	176 0/8	15 3/8	33 1/8	22 6/8	24 7/8	25 0/8	6	6	4 2/8	4 2/8	1987	Wallowa	Charlie Warnock	348
160 4/8	162 2/8	160 4/8	0 0/8	28 4/8	24 3/8	24 0/8	23 6/8	5	5	4 3/8	4 2/8	1962	Baker	Leonard Nemel	351
160 2/8	166 4/8	160 2/8	0 0/8	21 0/8	20 0/8	20 0/8	20 2/8	5	5	4 4/8	4 5/8	1995	Umatilla	Walter Gaylord/Dale Gaylord	352
160 2/8	174 1/8	165 2/8	5 0/8	20 3/8	18 4/8	23 0/8	24 5/8	5	5	4 2/8	4 6/8	1976	Umatilla	Pat Flint	352
160 1/8	172 5/8	167 2/8	7 1/8	20 4/8	18 4/8	22 5/8	22 2/8	6	6	4 7/8	5 1/8	1983	Harney	Tony Huisman	354
160 1/8	180 2/8	173 6/8	13 5/8	24 2/8	25 4/8	26 3/8	26 3/8	7	8	5 3/8	5 2/8	1993	Crook	Rob DeWitt	354
160 1/8	173 6/8	164 0/8	3 7/8	24 4/8	21 6/8	24 2/8	22 3/8	5	6	5 1/8	5 4/8	1994	Union	Dick Martin	354
160 0/8	173 7/8	165 2/8	5 2/8	29 0/8	25 0/8	25 3/8	26 0/8	6	7	5 2/8	5 3/8	1983	Grant	John Spencer	357
160 0/8	162 4/8	160 0/8	0 0/8	25 1/8	19 2/8	21 4/8	21 7/8	5	5	4 4/8	4 5/8	1980	Linn	Mary Cook	357

Typical Mule Deer—Archery
Minimum Score: 145 0/8

Final Score	Gross Typical	Net Typical	Abnormal Points	Greatest Spread	Inside Spread	Main Beam R	Main Beam L	No. Points R	No. Points L	First Circ. R	First Circ. L	Year	County	Hunter/Owner	Rank
195 7/8	204 6/8	200 7/8	5 0/8	36 1/8	30 2/8	29 7/8	29 7/8	6	7	5 1/8	5 5/8	1990	Crook	Hop Jackson	1
188 2/8	197 6/8	192 0/8	3 6/8	29 0/8	22 6/8	26 6/8	24 6/8	7	5	5 2/8	5 3/8	1994	Grant	David M. Morris	2
178 5/8	184 5/8	178 5/8	0 0/8	27 4/8	20 5/8	22 2/8	24 1/8	5	5	5 1/8	4 7/8	1986	Malheur	Ben Simpson	3
178 3/8	181 7/8	178 3/8	0 0/8	25 4/8	19 7/8	25 1/8	25 1/8	5	5	5 0/8	5 0/8	1994	Union	Bob Stables	4
177 1/8	183 2/8	177 1/8	0 0/8	26 6/8	22 7/8	23 1/8	23 1/8	5	5	5 4/8	5 4/8	1991	Harney	Robert Reed	5
176 4/8	180 6/8	176 4/8	0 0/8	28 4/8	21 4/8	22 2/8	22 7/8	5	6	4 2/8	4 4/8	1994	Union	Keven S. Robins	6
175 3/8	183 2/8	177 5/8	2 2/8	29 4/8	24 1/8	24 6/8	24 3/8	4	6	4 6/8	5 0/8	1992	Harney	Patrick E. Wheeler	7
174 2/8	178 0/8	175 4/8	1 2/8	25 6/8	21 0/8	24 7/8	24 6/8	5	6	5 0/8	4 7/8	1991	Umatilla	Clifford W. Widel	8
172 4/8	176 4/8	173 7/8	1 3/8	27 4/8	19 1/8	22 4/8	22 1/8	5	6	4 4/8	4 5/8	1995	Deschutes	Nate York/Lyle Stratton	9
171 7/8	178 1/8	171 7/8	0 0/8		26 4/8	24 0/8	25 1/8	5	5	4 5/8	4 6/8	1988	Deschutes	Jim Smeroglio	10
167 3/8	170 5/8	167 3/8	0 0/8	32 1/8	22 1/8	23 6/8	24 2/8	5	5	4 7/8	4 5/8	1995	Umatilla	Stephen Larimer	11
166 6/8	169 6/8	166 6/8	0 0/8	23 5/8	20 0/8	22 2/8	22 3/8	4	4	4 5/8	4 4/8	1959	Union	Lloyd V. Christensen	12
166 1/8	172 5/8	166 1/8	0 0/8	25 3/8	22 5/8	23 5/8	22 0/8	5	5	5 0/8	5 0/8	1992	Harney	Brian Blaylock	13
163 5/8	174 5/8	165 2/8	1 5/8	26 0/8	23 2/8	24 3/8	24 2/8	5	5	4 4/8	4 4/8	1986	Grant	Jeff Whitacker	14
162 4/8	169 2/8	163 6/8	1 2/8	24 0/8	20 2/8	24 6/8	24 0/8	5	6	4 3/8	4 3/8	1993	Grant	David M. Morris	15
159 4/8	166 0/8	161 3/8	1 7/8	25 2/8	22 0/8	21 7/8	21 1/8	5	6	5 1/8	5 2/8	1993	Deschutes	Bill Hueckman	16
159 2/8	166 1/8	159 2/8	0 0/8	26 2/8	20 4/8	21 2/8	20 7/8	4	4	4 6/8	4 6/8	1925	Deschutes	Hop Jackson	17
155 5/8	160 7/8	155 5/8	0 0/8	27 2/8	24 4/8	23 2/8	23 5/8	5	5	4 6/8	4 6/8	1993	Deschutes	Jason Jaschke	18
155 3/8	168 2/8	155 3/8	0 0/8	25 6/8	22 7/8	25 7/8	26 0/8	3	5	4 1/8	4 4/8	1995	Jefferson	Steve Stratton	19
154 6/8	160 4/8	154 6/8	0 0/8	24 4/8	20 0/8	21 5/8	20 6/8	5	4	4 1/8	4 1/8	1995	Jefferson	Rod Gibson	20
154 1/8	161 0/8	155 3/8	1 2/8	20 6/8	18 1/8	19 6/8	20 5/8	5	6	4 5/8	4 5/8	1993	Jefferson	Doris T. Campbell	21
153 6/8	161 2/8	153 6/8	0 0/8	22 1/8	18 2/8	19 1/8	20 5/8	5	5	6 0/8	6 0/8	1960	Jefferson	Lloyd V. Christensen	22
153 2/8	159 7/8	153 2/8	0 0/8	29 2/8	18 2/8	21 4/8	18 4/8	4	4	3 5/8	3 4/8	1992	Grant	David M. Morris	23
150 4/8	155 4/8	150 4/8	0 0/8	23 3/8	20 0/8	19 3/8	20 6/8	5	5	4 4/8	4 3/8	1995	Crook	David Jonnenburg	24
150 2/8	156 2/8	150 2/8	0 0/8	20 0/8	18 0/8	23 0/8	20 5/8	5	5	4 4/8	4 6/8	1995	Jefferson	Richard Reynolds	25

Typical Mule Deer—Archery (continued)

Final Score	Gross Typical	Net Typical	Abnormal Points	Greatest Spread	Inside Spread	Main Beam R	Main Beam L	Number of Points R	Number of Points L	First Circumference R	First Circumference L	Year	County	Hunter/Owner	Rank
148 5/8	160 1/8	154 5/8	6 0/8	25 0/8	23 1/8	21 7/8	21 3/8	5	7	4 7/8	4 7/8	1990	Harney	Patrick E. Wheeler	26
148 4/8	151 1/8	148 4/8	0 0/8	23 7/8	20 2/8	20 7/8	22 2/8	5	5	4 2/8	4 4/8	1993	Harney	Douglas Modey	27
147 4/8	162 5/8	147 4/8	0 0/8	24 7/8	20 2/8	24 2/8	22 2/8	4	5	5 2/8	5 2/8	1985	Harney	Gary D. Nyden	28
146 0/8	153 1/8	146 0/8	0 0/8	27 0/8	25 0/8	24 3/8	24 6/8	4	5	4 2/8	4 3/8	1994	Jefferson	Mike Towell	29

Typical Mule Deer—Black Powder
Minimum Score: 146 0/8

Final Score	Gross Typical	Net Typical	Abnormal Points	Greatest Spread	Inside Spread	Main Beam R	Main Beam L	Number of Points R	Number of Points L	First Circumference R	First Circumference L	Year	County	Hunter/Owner	Rank
203 0/8	208 6/8	205 4/8	2 4/8	31 7/8	26 0/8	27 5/8	27 4/8	5	7	6 6/8	6 6/8	1994	Harney	Doug White	1
181 2/8	186 1/8	181 2/8	0 0/8	24 4/8	25 2/8	24 6/8	24 6/8	5	5	5 0/8	5 2/8		Harney	Andy Dunbar	2
177 1/8	187 1/3	179 4/8	2 3/8	26 2/8	23 2/8	26 3/8	28 2/8	5	6	4 7/8	4 7/8	1989	Lake	William Kohlhoff	3
176 1/8	179 7/3	176 1/8	0 0/8	26 2/8	22 5/8	24 0/8	23 6/8	5	5	4 7/8	4 6/8	1993	Harney	Tom Metcalf	4
173 4/8	192 2/3	184 7/8	11 3/8	32 7/8	21 7/8	24 7/8	26 0/8	9	7	5 0/8	4 7/8	1978	Lake	Bill Meilick	5
171 3/8	174 6/3	172 5/8	1 2/8	26 6/8	23 5/8	25 2/8	25 0/8	5	6	4 6/8	4 5/8	1990	Jefferson	John Snyder	6
161 0/8	170 1/3	161 0/8	0 0/8	28 4/8	22 0/8	23 5/8	22 4/8	4	5	4 0/8	4 3/8	1973	Lake	Loren Brooks	7
157 4/8	163 6/3	157 4/8	0 0/8	21 7/8	18 4/8	24 2/8	21 3/8	4	4	4 1/8	4 2/8	1995	Malheur	Mark Richards	8
155 0/8	162 5/3	156 4/8	1 4/8	26 4/8	22 4/8	24 2/8	23 0/8	5	5	4 2/8	4 5/8	1986	Lake	William E. Kohlhoff	9
151 5/8	161 0/3	151 5/8	0 0/8	27 0/8	21 3/8	22 7/8	22 1/8	5	5	4 2/8	4 3/8	1995	Lake	William E. Kohlhoff	10
150 3/8	154 7/3	150 3/8	0 0/8	27 4/8	19 7/8	21 6/8	22 5/8	5	5	4 4/8	4 2/8	1975	Lake	Loren Brooks	11
146 0/8	148 5/8	146 0/8	0 0/8	21 0/8	16 6/8	20 6/8	20 6/8	4	4	4 3/8	4 2/8	1987	Lake	Benjamin Brooks/Loren Brooks	12

Typical Mule Deer—Archery (Velvet)
Minimum Score: 145

Final Score	Gross Typical	Net Typical	Abnormal Points	Greatest Spread	Inside Spread	Main Beam R	Main Beam L	Number of Points R	Number of Points L	First Circumference R	First Circumference L	Year	County	Hunter/Owner	Rank
180 6/8	190 6/8	180 6/8	0 0/8	31 0/8	24 4/8	26 2/8	25 3/8	5	5	4 4/8	4 6/8	1994	Harney	Patrick Hagon	1
163 2/8	176 0/8	163 2/8	0 0/8	26 0/8	22 6/8	24 3/8	24 6/8	4	5	5 1/8	5 2/8	1994	Harney	Patrick Wheeler	2
162 0/8	164 7/8	162 0/8	0 0/8	29 0/8	26 5/8	26 4/8	25 4/8	5	5	4 5/8	4 5/8	1995	Morrow	Shane Hoffman	3
156 1/8	173 0/8	166 5/8	10 4/8	25 0/8	21 1/8	23 7/8	23 4/8	8	6	4 6/8	4 5/8	1993	Harney	Patrick E. Wheeler	4

Typical Mule Deer—Shed Antlers
Minimum Score: 70 0/8

Right/Left	Final Score	Subtotal	Abnormal Points	Main Beam	First Point	Second Point	Third Point	Fourth Point	First Circumference	Year	County	Owner's Name	Rank
Left	94 0/8	94 0/8	0 0/8	27 4/8	3 0/8	17 2/8	12 5/8	14 2/8	5 1/8		Grant	Wennie Powell	1
Left	89 3/8	89 3/8	0 0/8	26 4/8	1 7/8	13 6/8	15 1/8	13 1/8	5 7/8			Joey Wood	2
Left	88 7/8	88 7/8	0 0/8	27 2/8	1 3/8	18 5/8	10 4/8	11 7/8	5 4/8			Jim Parmelee	3
Right	88 4/8	88 4/8	0 0/8	27 6/8	1 5/8	17 4/8	10 2/8	11 2/8	5 3/8			Jim Parmelee	4
Right	87 2/8	87 2/8	0 0/8	24 2/8	1 2/8	18 1/8	13 3/8	8 4/8	6 6/8	1995	Crook	Matt Tomseth	5
Left	85 7/8	85 7/8	0 0/8	24 5/8	3 0/8	16 7/8	10 5/8	13 0/8	4 6/8			Jerry Frampton	6
Left	85 0/8	88 4/8	3 4/8	26 4/8	2 5/8	16 0/8	11 5/8	13 2/8	5 0/8			Billy Hueckman	7
Right	84 6/8	84 6/8	0 0/8	24 4/8	1 0/8	18 0/8	12 2/8	13 4/8	4 0/8		Grant	Larry Powell	8
Left	83 5/8	83 5/8	0 0/8	24 0/8	2 3/8	18 3/8	12 0/8	10 2/8	5 1/8	1992	Grant	Cindy Starbuck	9
Right	83 2/8	86 6/8	3 4/8	26 4/8	3 0/8	15 4/8	11 4/8	12 2/8	5 0/8		Grant	Billy Hueckman	10
Left	83 1/8	85 0/8	1 7/8	24 7/8	2 0/8	16 1/8	12 5/8	13 1/8	4 4/8		Grant	David Powell	11
Right	83 0/8	85 0/8	2 0/8	27 7/8	2 0/8	15 6/8	11 1/8	11 0/8	4 2/8		Grant	Joey Wood	12
Right	82 5/8	82 5/8	0 0/8	24 0/8	2 2/8	15 2/8	13 2/8	11 7/8	4 2/8		Grant	Joey Wood	13
Right	81 7/8	81 7/8	0 0/8	24 2/8	1 4/8	16 3/8	12 1/8	12 7/8	4 1/8			Joey Wood	14
Left	81 6/8	89 3/8	7 5/8	24 3/8	3 0/8	17 6/8	13 0/8	12 7/8	5 1/8	1976	Umatilla	Jay Roth	15
Left	81 5/8	83 0/8	1 3/8	23 6/8	1 6/8	16 6/8	11 7/8	11 3/8	4 7/8			Scott Wolff	16
Left	80 6/8	80 6/8	0 0/8	24 0/8	2 0/8	17 4/8	13 0/8	3 3/8	6 3/8	1995	Crook	Matt Tomseth	17
Right	80 3/8	80 3/8	0 0/8	22 2/8	3 0/8	16 0/8	10 6/8	11 5/8	4 7/8		Harney	Joe Baker	18
Right	80 2/8	84 1/8	3 7/8	23 7/8	1 7/8	18 4/8	12 1/8	10 2/8	4 7/8			Scott Wolff	19
Right	80 2/8	80 2/8	0 0/8	21 1/8	1 7/8	16 5/8	9 3/8	10 4/8	5 5/8	1994	Wallowa	Jason Sawin	19
Right	79 5/8	83 1/8	3 4/8	25 1/8	2 1/8	15 2/8	12 0/8	12 1/8	4 5/8		Lake	Tom Neal	21
Left	79 4/8	79 4/8	0 0/8	26 4/8	2 2/8	15 4/8	9 6/8	6 5/8	5 6/8	1996	Grant	Ray Moles	22
Left	79 1/8	80 2/8	1 1/8	25 4/8	1 2/8	14 0/8	10 7/8	10 7/8	5 0/8	1995	Grant	Shannon Egeland	23
Left	79 0/8	79 0/8	0 0/8	23 2/8	1 4/8	16 7/8	10 3/8	11 0/8	4 4/8		Union	Dale Kruse	24
Left	79 0/8	83 1/8	4 1/8	24 6/8	1 4/8	16 4/8	11 4/8	12 1/8	4 5/8		Lake	Tom Neal	25
Left	78 5/8	78 5/8	0 0/8	24 2/8	0 0/8	17 7/8	11 2/8	9 4/8	4 5/8	1993	Grant	Andrew M. Radinovich	26
Right	78 1/8	78 1/8	0 0/8	26 0/8	1 1/8	14 2/8	7 5/8	12 0/8	4 7/8	1995	Grant	Shannon Egeland	27
Left	77 0/8	77 0/8	0 0/8	26 3/8	16 0/8	9 4/8	8 0/8	0 0/8	4 5/8	1990	Grant	Thad Labhart	28
Left	75 6/8	76 6/8	0 0/8	20 7/8	2 4/8	14 4/8	10 5/8	7 2/8	5 3/8	1994	Wallowa	Jason Sawin	29
Right	75 6/8	78 2/8	1 4/8	21 5/8	3 6/8	13 2/8	10 0/8	12 0/8	5 3/8			Steve Holte	29
Right	74 6/8	74 6/8	0 0/8	22 5/8	3 2/8	13 4/8	9 4/8	10 4/8	4 4/8	1996	Jefferson	Terry Valentine	31
Right	74 1/8	78 2/8	4 1/8	23 0/8	2 0/8	15 5/8	9 2/8	11 3/8	5 0/8	1996	Union	Bob Crader	32
Right	73 7/8	73 7/8	0 0/8	22 6/8	1 5/8	13 1/8	10 0/8	9 7/8	4 4/8	1989	Lake	Loren Brooks	33
Right	73 3/8	73 3/8	0 0/8	23 0/8	2 4/8	16 7/8	8 6/8	6 0/8	4 7/8		Klamath	Mike Gerrett	34
Right	73 0/8	75 3/8	2 3/8	20 4/8	2 4/8	15 6/8	9 6/8	10 0/8	4 5/8		Union	Dale Kruse	35
Right	72 5/8	72 5/8	0 0/8	20 3/8	1 7/8	15 7/8	10 0/8	9 5/8	4 3/8		Klamath	Mike Gerrett	36
Left	72 5/8	76 7/8	4 2/8	21 5/8	3 6/8	11 3/8	10 1/8	11 2/8	5 4/8			Mike Benton	36
Right	72 3/8	75 5/8	3 2/8	25 5/8	2 6/8	13 6/8	9 4/8	4 1/8	5 6/8	1996	Grant	Ray Moles	38
Left	7 7/8	71 7/8	0 0/8	22 6/8	1 5/8	12 2/8	10 5/8	8 2/8	5 0/8		Grant	Mike Garrett	39
Right	7 2/8	71 2/8	0 0/8	22 2/8	3 0/8	14 3/8	6 7/8	9 5/8	4 2/8		Klamath	Mike Gerrett	40
Right	70 7/8	72 1/8	1 2/8	22 7/8	1 2/8	14 4/8	9 4/8	7 6/8	4 4/8		Jefferson	Larry W. Vandeburgh	41

Official Scoring System for Oregon Big Game Trophies

NON-TYPICAL
MULE AND BLACKTAIL DEER

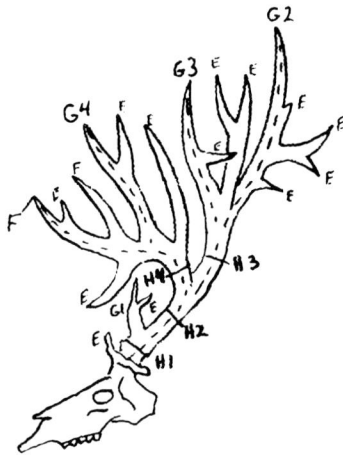

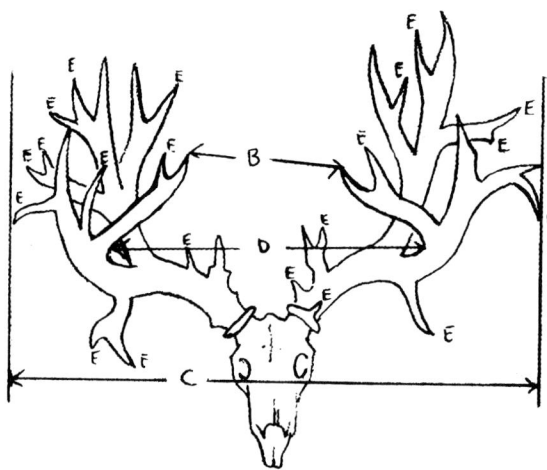

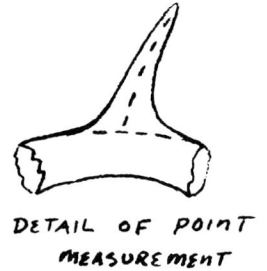

DETAIL OF POINT MEASUREMENT

Abnormal Points	
Right Antler	Left Antler
11 7/8	11 7/8
11 7/8	7 1/8
2 3/8	7 2/8
3 2/8	6 6/8
2 0/8	7 7/8
4 0/8	5 0/8
4 4/8	4 5/8
1 3/8	8 6/8
1 1/8	4 2/8
2 0/8	3 5/8
Subtotals 44 3/8	67 1/8
Total to E	111 4/8

Species	Rifle	Archery	Muzzle	Shed	Archery-Velvet
Mule Deer	200	160	175	85	160
Columbia Blacktail	145	110	115	60	110
Cascade Blacktail	145	110	115	60	110
Northwest Blacktail	145	110	115	60	110

					COLUMN 1	COLUMN 2	COLUMN 3	COLUMN 4
					Spread Credit	Right Antler	Left Antler	Difference
A	Number of Points on Right Antler	17	Number of Points on Left Antler	25				
B	Tip to Tip Spread	27 0/8	C Greatest Spread	34 2/8				
D	Inside Spread of Main Beam	26 5/8	(Credit may be equal to but not exceed longer antler)	26 5/8				
E	Total of Length of Abnormal Points			111 4/8				
F	Length of Main Beam					28 1/8	25 4/8	2 5/8
G-1	Length of First Point, if present					3 7/8	4 2/8	0 3/8
G-2	Length of Second Point					15 4/8	16 2/8	0 6/8
G-3	Length of Third Point, if present					12 6/8	12 5/8	0 1/8
G-4	Length of Fourth Point, if present					11 4/8	10 6/8	0 6/8
H-1	Circumference at smallest place between Burr and First point					6 7/8	6 7/8	0 0/8
H-2	Circumference at smallest place between First and Second points					5 3/8	5 4/8	0 1/8
H-3	Circumference at smallest place between Main Beam and Third point					6 3/8	5 4/8	0 7/8
H-4	Circumference at smallest place between Second and Fourth points					5 6/8	5 4/8	0 2/8
	TOTALS				111 4/8	26 0/8	96 1/8	92 6/8	5 7/8

County where killed:	Umatilla	Date Killed:	1925			
Hunter's Name:	Albert	Peterson		**ADD**	Column 1	26 0/8
Owner's Name:	David	Ayars			Column 2	96 1/8
					Column 3	92 6/8
					Subtotal	214 7/8
					Subtract Column 4	5 7/8
					Result	209 0/8
					Add Line E Total	111 4/8
					FINAL SCORE	**320 4/8**

The Story of the Trophy Buck of Ukiah, Oregon

by Dorene Ayars

Albert Peterson was born in the fall of 1900 and raised near the breaks of the middle fork of the John Day, within a few miles of the present Bud Walton ranch on Highway 395 south. During his short lifetime of thirty years, his experiences were many. He was a respected cattle rancher, a government trapper and at one time contracted the mail-stage route between Pilot Rock and Ritter, a rough route of muddy, rocky dirt roads, taking off out of Pilot Rock through West Birch Creek, over the Yellow Jacket, down through Albee and Ukiah, on over Bridge Creek Flats, down to the NF John Day River, along the river to Dale and on to Ritter. He also owned and operated a mercantile store on Main Street in Ukiah, and he loved rodeos, promoting and di-recting his own in Ukiah from 1920 to 1930, held every Fourth of July on his property at the south edge of town, where horses are now penned.

On a brisk fall morning in 1926, Peterson and his brother-in-law, Bill Huddleston, saddled their horses, shoved 30-30s into gun scabbards tied to their saddles and rode west to hunt a rumored big buck. At this time, the route took them from the foot of the steepest grade, approximately three miles from Ukiah on the Albee Road, on west across Owens Creek and Highway 395, to a trail or forest service road where the western route road to Heppner now exists. From there they rode to an area still known as Sugarbowl where Peterson bagged the big mule deer buck.

In 1991, Peterson's grandson, David Ayars, was observing the trophy heads displayed at the sports show in Pendleton, Oregon. While there, he questioned Roger Sellner, in charge of the

display, about his grandfather's buck. Sellner asked to see the horns and then advised Ayars to contact a professional to score the horns. Glenn Martin of Walla Walla, Washington, was found to be licensed. He scored the horns, and notified Boone and Crockett, who in turn requested the horns be shipped to them so they could be scored again by a panel of five judges. In 1992, Boone and Crockett listed it in their new book as a non-typical mule deer trophy buck, scoring 321 1/8 points. From 1926 to 1996 it held the record as number one in Oregon and fourth largest in the world.

(Final score: 321 1/8 B.C.)

C. F. Cheney,
270 6/8 B.C.,
Grant County, 1962

State Record Non-Typical Mule Deer

by Mike Smith

For the most part, a truly magnificent record-class trophy buck lives only in the imaginations of trophy buck hunters, who often spend a lifetime of hunting, lucky to catch a glimpse of, let alone bag, such an animal. However, for one relatively shy, polite seventeen-year-old high school student, Brad Smith of Prineville, Oregon, such a dream became a reality in November of 1992.

Brad was no stranger to hunting deer. He grew up in a hunting family. His dad, John E. Smith, along with his cousin, Mike Smith, had indoctrinated Brad into deer hunting at the tender age of twelve. This would be the first year that Brad and his cousin Mike would be hunting without the company of Brad's father, as he had passed away in June of that year. Brad speaks warmly of his father, saying that his dad was truly a great deer hunter with several trophies to his credit.

Brad and Mike were headed for Oregon's special late-season archery hunt in an area with which they were both familiar. Mike is an experienced archer, having many good animals to his credit. However, seventeen-year-old Brad had taken only one buck thus far in his young career. Brad and Mike had archery-hunted hard since the opener of the 1992 late-season archery hunt, but to no avail. The end of the season was drawing near, so they decided to give it one more try in mid-November.

While driving through hunting country, Mike suddenly spotted a nice-size buck running with several does. They parked the vehicle, rigged their bows and immediately started their stalk. The buck's rack had not been visible because of dense brush, but Mike knew it was a good, wide-racked buck—at least a good legal buck, Mike had remarked to Brad.

Approximately forty minutes later, Brad finally came upon the buck in the company of four or five does. The buck's antlers were shrouded in a background of dense brush. It looked big, Brad recalled, but its size was still indistinguishable. The buck's body size, which was only about one hundred and fifty pounds, fooled Brad into thinking that he was nothing special.

Brad and Mike had separated during their stalk, and as Brad moved into position for a close shot, he suddenly saw Mike's arrow fly toward the buck. Mike, who wasn't certain that Brad had

actually shot at the deer, had also seen the buck and had let an arrow fly at about fifty yards. The arrow hit the ground short of the buck. Brad did not know why Mike had taken such a long shot, but Mike, who was off at another angle, had seen the huge size of the animal's antlers and had apparently gotten a little eager. Brad said he was surprised that the buck never even flinched when Mike's arrow struck the ground with a thud a short distance from him.

With the buck's attention focused on Mike, Brad managed to sneak within thirty-five yards of where the deer was standing with the does. He could see that it was a wide, big-antlered buck, but brush was obscuring most of the animal's antlers. With careful aim, Brad drew his bow. One doe bolted, and all five deer started running broadside of Brad. Brad said that he placed the aim of his arrow on the running buck's shoulder and released it. He saw the arrow penetrate the buck's left side about mid-section, close to the left back leg. However, the buck kept running as if it hadn't been hit.

Brad whistled for Mike and told him he thought that he had hit the buck. "We both sat down," Brad said, "discussed strategy, then waited another thirty minutes for the buck to bed down."

Brad's shot had been taken at approximately 9:30 a.m. It was now 10:00 and raining hard as Brad and Mike studied the area where Brad had hit the buck. They found a small spot of blood. After discussing the arrow's point of impact, the two archers decided to wait another two hours before they resumed tracking. They hoped that the deer had been hit in a critical area and would lie down. Brad became more excited as Mike explained how big he thought the buck was. "Those two hours seemed like two days, but we knew we had to wait," Brad said.

A little after noon, the two bowhunters continued their tracking. The buck's hoofprints were still very distinguishable in the wet earth, and soon Mike spotted the animal as it lay only fifty yards away. They still could not clearly see the rack because of the thick background brush, and the buck was keeping his head low.

Finally, Brad got within thirty-five yards and took his second and only decent shot. It was a front-on shot, uphill. Brad said that he drew his bow, put his forty-yard pin on the deer's neck and released the arrow. It was a good shot, and the arrow entered just above the brisket area and exited the left shoulder. The buck jumped up and ran off again, the last one-third of the arrow clearly visible out of the top of his left shoulder.

"Good shot!" Mike told Brad, congratulating him at the same time.

Upon walking up to the buck, which had now fallen to his death fifty yards from where Brad had placed his second arrow, Brad finally realized the enormous size of the animal's antlers. They were bigger than anything he'd ever seen. Upon closer examination, the pair began whooping, hollering and rejoicing as they admired the oversized antlers.

Brad's first arrow had clearly penetrated the deer's side just in front of the last rib. Brad's second arrow had cut the buck's esophagus and was still protruding out of the top of the left shoulder. Brad tagged and then field-dressed the buck, while Mike went back to the truck to get packs to haul it out. It took Mike two hours to return,

during which time Brad said he reflected on the moments of the hunt and thought about how much he missed his father and how he would have given anything for his dad to have witnessed him taking this huge-antlered buck. "Dad would have been proud of me, I think," Brad said.

Despite the tragedy of losing his father, 1992 had been a good hunting year for Brad, and for Mike as well. In September, Mike had taken a fine 6×6 bull elk in Oregon with a bow, and now Brad had taken this trophy buck in November. Brad told me that in the stillness of the forest, alone with his deer and waiting for Mike to return, he dedicated this day's hunt and his big buck to his father, the late John E. Smith.

What remains to be told about Brad's buck is history. Pope and Young has officially scored this animal at 257 7/8. It is the number five non-typical mule deer in the world, according to Glenn Hisey of Pope and Young. The massive buck measured 33 1/2″ wide, 25 1/2″ tall and sported 17 legal points on the right beam and 14 legal points on the left beam.

Al Cardens, a taxidermist, drove to Prineville and offered his services to mount the buck for Brad free of charge. Brad accepted, and soon the buck was finished and in his hands again. Brad said that he will continue bowhunting with Mike, but he admits that his chances of ever topping this buck, even in a lifetime of hunting, are slim indeed.
(Final score: 257 7/8 P.Y.)

Official Scoring System for Oregon Big Game Trophies

NON-TYPICAL
MULE AND BLACKTAIL DEER

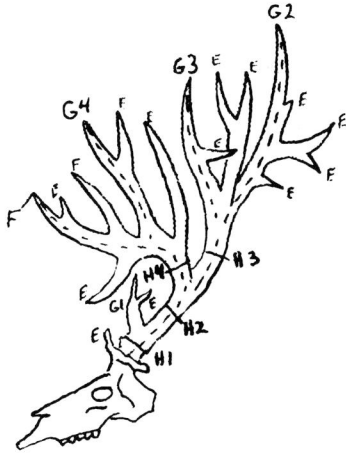

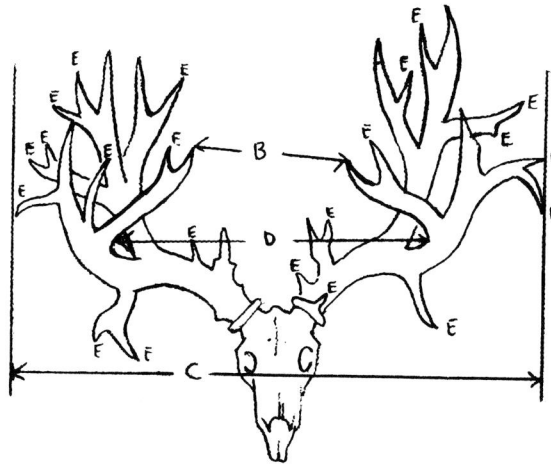

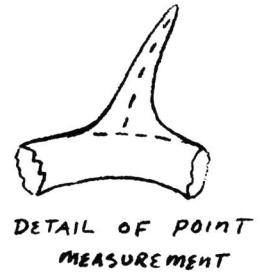

DETAIL OF POINT MEASUREMENT

Abnormal Points	
Right Antler	Left Antler
1 2/8	2 3/8
1 2/8	7 1/8
1 7/8	1 6/8
1 2/8	6 1/8
3 5/8	1 7/8
3 6/8	2 7/8
1 2/8	4 6/8
3 3/8	1 2/8
1 3/8	3 6/8
13 3/8	0 0/8
Subtotals 32 3/8	31 7/8
Total to E	64 2/8

Species	Rifle	Archery	Muzzle	Shed	Archery-Velvet
Mule Deer	200	160	175	85	160
Columbia Blacktail	145	110	115	60	110
Cascade Blacktail	145	110	115	60	110
Northwest Blacktail	145	110	115	60	110

					COLUMN 1	COLUMN 2	COLUMN 3	COLUMN 4
					Spread Credit	Right Antler	Left Antler	Difference
A	Number of Points on Right Antler	18	Number of Points on Left Antler	14				
B	Tip to Tip Spread	13 0/8	C Greatest Spread	32 4/8				
D	Inside Spread of Main Beam	19 1/8	(Credit may be equal to but not exceed longer antler)		19 1/8			
E	Total of Length of Abnormal Points				64 2/8			
F	Length of Main Beam					25 6/8	25 0/8	0 6/8
G-1	Length of First Point, if present					3 7/8	2 5/8	1 2/8
G-2	Length of Second Point					15 6/8	16 1/8	0 3/8
G-3	Length of Third Point, if present					11 4/8	12 6/8	1 2/8
G-4	Length of Fourth Point, if present					13 1/8	12 4/8	0 5/8
H-1	Circumference at smallest place between Burr and First point					5 6/8	5 4/8	0 2/8
H-2	Circumference at smallest place between First and Second points					4 5/8	4 7/8	0 2/8
H-3	Circumference at smallest place between Main Beam and Third point					4 6/8	4 6/8	0 0/8
H-4	Circumference at smallest place between Second and Fourth points					5 0/8	5 3/8	0 3/8
	TOTALS				64 2/8	19 0/8	90 1/8	89 4/8	5 1/8

County where killed: Klamath	Date Killed: 11/18/92	**ADD**	Column 1 19 0/8
Hunter's Name: Brad Smith			Column 2 90 1/8
Owner's Name: Brad Smith /Mike Smith			Column 3 89 4/8
		Subtotal	198 5/8
		Subtract Column 4	5 1/8
		Result	193 4/8
		Add Line E Total	64 2/8
		FINAL SCORE	257 6/8

Official Scoring System for Oregon Big Game Trophies

Records of Oregon
Big Game

RECORD BOOK FOR OREGON

P.O. Box 759
Irrigon, OR 97844

NON-TYPICAL
MULE AND BLACKTAIL DEER

DETAIL OF POINT MEASUREMENT

Abnormal Points	
Right Antler	Left Antler
2 4/8	1 2/8
4 5/8	6 4/8
5 3/8	0 0/8
0 0/8	0 0/8
0 0/8	0 0/8
0 0/8	0 0/8
0 0/8	0 0/8
0 0/8	0 0/8
0 0/8	0 0/8
0 0/8	0 0/8

Species	Rifle	Archery	Muzzle	Shed	Archery-Velvet
Mule Deer	200	160	175	85	160
Columbia Blacktail	145	110	115	60	110
Cascade Blacktail	145	110	115	60	110
Northwest Blacktail	145	110	115	60	110

Subtotals	12 4/8	7 6/8	
Total to E		20 2/8	

					COLUMN 1	COLUMN 2	COLUMN 3	COLUMN 4
					Spread Credit	Right Antler	Left Antler	Difference
A	Number of Points on Right Antler	8	Number of Points on Left Antler	6				
B	Tip to Tip Spread	16 7/8	C Greatest Spread	33 7/8				
D	Inside Spread of Main Beam	20 2/8	(Credit may be equal to but not exceed longer antler)	20 2/8				
E	Total of Length of Abnormal Points			20 2/8				
F	Length of Main Beam					23 3/8	22 4/8	0 7/8
G-1	Length of First Point, if present					2 0/8	0 0/8	2 0/8
G-2	Length of Second Point					15 4/8	16 3/8	0 7/8
G-3	Length of Third Point, if present					11 2/8	11 0/8	0 2/8
G-4	Length of Fourth Point, if present					13 7/8	10 3/8	3 4/8
H-1	Circumference at smallest place between Burr and First point					5 2/8	5 2/8	0 0/8
H-2	Circumference at smallest place between First and Second points					4 7/8	4 6/8	0 1/8
H-3	Circumference at smallest place between Main Beam and Third point					3 4/8	4 1/8	0 5/8
H-4	Circumference at smallest place between Second and Fourth points					4 2/8	4 1/8	0 1/8
	TOTALS				20 2/8	20 0/8	83 7/8	78 4/8	8 3/8

County where killed: Harney	Date Killed: 12/03/95	ADD	Column 1	20 0/8
Hunter's Name: Delwyn Hendrickson			Column 2	83 7/8
Owner's Name: Delwyn Hendrickson			Column 3	78 4/8
			Subtotal	182 3/8
			Subtract Column 4	8 3/8
			Result	174 0/8
			Add Line E Total	20 2/8
			FINAL SCORE	194 2/8

Oregon State Record—
Black Powder (non-typical)
Delwyn Hendrickson,
194 4/8 B.C.,
Malheur County, 1995

Non-Typical Mule Deer—Rifle
Minimum Score: 200 0/8

Final Score	Gross Typical	Net Typical	Abnormal Points	Greatest Spread	Inside Spread	Main Beam R	Main Beam L	Number of Points R	L	First Circumference R	L	Year	County	Hunter/Owner	Rank
321 1/8	215 4/8	209 5/8	111 4/8	34 2/8	26 5/8	28 1/8	25 4/8	17	25	6 7/8	6 7/8	1925	Umatilla	Albert Peterson/David Ayars	1
297 7/8	206 0/8	198 5/8	99 2/8	39 6/8	35 6/8	29 1/8	27 5/8	20	18	5 4/8	5 3/8	1971	Malheur	Bradley Barclay	2
283 7/8	193 5/8	190 7/8	93 0/8	30 3/8	23 3/8	25 4/8	26 2/8	17	17	6 1/8	6 1/8	1965	Harney	Ken Pruitt/Alan Hogan	3
270 5/8	207 0/8	200 0/8	70 5/8	37 0/8	27 6/8	29 3/8	28 4/8	17	16	5 7/8	5 7/8	1962	Grant	C.F. Cheney/Carl Christen	4
268 5/8	162 0/8	155 2/8	113 3/8	38 7/8	27 0/8	28 3/8	22 7/8	14	15	6 0/8	6 3/8	1941	Grant	Lige Davis/Coy Johnston	5
256 4/8	211 0/8	207 6/8	48 6/8	32 5/8	22 0/8	28 3/8	28 4/8	10	9	5 1/8	5 1/8	1988	Baker	Thomas Rosseau	6
252 2/8	198 0/8	196 1/8	56 1/8	35 0/8	25 3/8	25 3/8	25 0/8	13	12	5 0/8	5 0/8			S Centwise Sporting Good	7
250 6/8	173 1/8	168 1/8	82 5/8	34 0/8	20 1/8	23 1/8	22 4/8	17	13	5 4/8	5 4/8	1993	Grant	Stoney E. Gienger	8
248 4/8	195 3/8	186 2/8	62 2/8	34 2/8	20 4/8	29 2/8	27 3/8	15	16	5 2/8	5 3/8	1964	Baker	Duane Hutton/Dwayne Wright	9
246 3/8	203 5/8	198 0/8	48 3/8	33 4/8	24 6/8	24 6/8	24 2/8	11	15	4 6/8	5 0/8	1934	Grant	Clyde Stormer/Mckern's Texaco	10
244 3/8	176 3/8	171 6/8	72 5/8	34 1/8	20 4/8	21 7/8	21 7/8	14	13	4 7/8	5 0/8	1984	Deschutes	M.S. Wattier	11
242 5/8	194 1/8	186 7/8	55 6/8	28 3/8	21 7/8	24 2/8	24 4/8	10	9	4 6/8	4 6/8	1960	Deschutes	Buck D. Matson/Sandy Mergel	12
242 2/8	187 7/8	184 2/8	58 0/8	36 5/8	32 7/8	26 4/8	25 7/8	9	13	6 3/8	6 2/8	1960	Union	Ralph Hardy/Jan Roulet	13
240 2/8	197 4/8	186 3/8	53 7/8	33 5/8	23 1/8	28 4/8	26 4/8	9	8	5 1/8	4 5/8	1995	Crook	Charles H. Kies	14
239 5/8	210 5/8	204 1/8	35 4/8	35 0/8	30 4/8	27 5/8	26 6/8	9	10	6 3/8	6 0/8	1927	Harney	Culver Page/Glen Shelley	15
239 3/8	202 7/8	197 4/8	41 7/8	40 2/8	29 0/8	28 2/8	30 2/8	12	12	6 0/8	6 1/8		Lake	Nolan Greiner	16
238 7/8	178 2/8	167 1/8	71 6/8	25 6/8	16 7/8	22 1/8	23 4/8	22	13	6 1/8	4 3/8	1968	Umatilla	Ray Paynes/Mike Lawkford	17
238 4/8	209 4/8	198 4/8	40 3/8	34 5/8	27 0/8	26 6/8	24 0/8	10	9	5 4/8	6 0/8	1920	Klamath	Harley Hall	17
237 0/8	180 2/8	170 3/8	66 5/8	30 4/8	20 3/8	26 4/8	24 4/8	15	13	6 1/8	6 1/8	1926	Morrow	W.O. Bayless/John Howton	19
236 6/8	213 7/8	207 2/8	29 4/8	39 3/8	34 0/8	30 0/8	29 4/8	9	11	5 5/8	5 7/8	1977	Klamath	George Hessler/Elvis Tillman	20
236 4/8	208 6/8	200 5/8	35 7/8	30 5/8	18 1/8	24 0/8	24 4/8	14	10	5 0/8	5 0/8	1995	Union	Logan Girrard	21
233 7/8	206 3/8	200 6/8	33 1/8	32 0/8	29 3/8	28 2/8	28 4/8	10	8	5 3/8	5 3/8	1991	Lake	Carl Tracy	22
232 6/8	214 0/8	208 2/8	24 4/8	40 0/8	29 0/8	26 2/8	27 4/8	8	9	5 0/8	5 0/8	1952	Harney	The Gun Room	23
232 2/8	215 1/8	209 6/8	22 4/8	27 4/8	25 2/8	29 2/8	29 1/8	7	11	5 5/8	5 4/8	1929	Grant	Dolly Williams/Ed Heid	24
232 0/8	209 0/8	203 5/8	28 3/8	33 6/8	25 1/8	27 5/8	27 5/8	8	8	4 7/8	4 7/8	1995	Sherman	Wendell Clodfelter	25
230 7/8	197 2/8	193 1/8	37 6/8	34 1/8	22 1/8	24 2/8	25 7/8	8	8	5 4/8	5 3/8	1977	Harney	Steve Mayfield	26
229 4/8	213 5/8	209 2/8	28 4/8	35 0/8	27 4/8	26 2/8	27 7/8	7	7	6 0/8	5 4/8	1943	Crook	Harry Sederance	27
229 3/8	205 7/8	202 2/8	27 1/8	32 4/8	26 6/8	25 4/8	26 2/8	11	9	6 2/8	6 2/8			Joseph Hardware	28
228 6/8	188 4/8	185 0/8	43 6/8	31 4/8	26 6/8	24 0/8	23 7/8	13	8	5 0/8	5 1/8	1942	Grant	George Harris/Carl Harris	29
228 5/8	212 4/8	197 6/8	30 7/8	27 0/8	22 6/8	25 2/8	24 6/8	10	11	5 0/8	5 4/8	1935	Grant	Cliff Mulcare/Mike Mulcare	30
228 4/8	189 6/8	184 2/8	44 2/8	32 0/8	23 4/8	25 6/8	24 3/8	12	13	5 6/8	5 6/8	1978	Harney	Mark Curtis	31
226 3/8	206 1/8	197 7/8	28 4/8	42 0/8	24 3/8	27 0/8	26 6/8	9	8	6 0/8	6 0/8	1995	Crook	Larry Powell	32
226 2/8	181 6/8	171 0/8	55 2/8	26 4/8	16 0/8	24 6/8	22 7/8	10	12	8 0/8	8 4/8		Wallowa	Joseph Hardware	33
224 3/8	215 0/8	208 2/8	16 1/8	33 6/8	28 7/8	28 4/8	27 4/8	7	6	6 0/8	5 5/8	1995	Malheur	William T. Monson	34
224 2/8	183 2/8	179 2/8	45 0/8	34 4/8	28 3/8	25 4/8	25 0/8	9	9	5 1/8	5 0/8	1994	Union	Joe Pinkham	35
223 6/8	196 1/8	189 5/8	34 1/8	27 4/8	23 7/8	27 4/8	26 1/8	9	7	6 2/8	6 0/8	1978	Grant	Ken Moore	36
223 5/8	212 1/8	210 3/8	13 2/8	35 4/8	26 3/8	27 6/8	28 3/8	8	6	5 1/8	5 1/8	1962	Jefferson	Harvey Rhoades	37
223 5/8	205 1/8	200 1/8	23 4/8	39 0/8	35 0/8	29 1/8	29 1/8	9	6	5 7/8	5 0/8		Lake	Nolan Greiner	37
222 7/8	193 1/8	185 2/8	37 5/8	31 0/8	23 0/8	27 3/8	26 2/8	10	9	5 4/8	5 2/8	1975	Grant	Karl Lee/Rustin Lee	39
221 3/8	187 5/8	183 6/8	37 5/8	28 3/8	20 6/8	24 3/8	24 3/8	13	8	4 4/8	4 3/8	1975	Baker	Bill Wirth	40

41	Dick Haney	Deschutes	1979	5 4/8	5 2/8	10	13	25 0/8	24 3/8	26 1/8	39 2/8	44 4/8	176 6/8	184 7/8	221 2/8
42	Michael Barden	Jefferson	1993	5 0/8	5 2/8	13	11	26 0/8	24 2/8	24 5/8	37 0/8	58 6/8	162 3/8	171 6/8	221 1/8
43	Cloyd Cox/Jerry Grant	Jefferson	1963	5 1/8	5 2/8	8	10	25 6/8	23 6/8	23 4/8	34 1/8	34 0/8	186 6/8	194 1/8	220 6/8
44	Leon Mawhin	Wallowa	1942	4 6/8	4 6/8	9	7	25 1/8	24 6/8	18 2/8	24 4/8	33 5/8	186 2/8	195 0/8	219 7/8
45	Greg Wagner	Grant	1981	4 5/8	4 5/8	7	9	23 5/8	22 1/8	17 2/8	28 0/8	32 2/8	186 6/8	193 0/8	219 0/8
46	Life Edson/Peggy Winfield	Lake	1962	5 3/8	5 3/8	12	8	22 5/8	23 6/8	23 0/8	33 4/8	33 5/8	185 2/8	190 2/8	218 4/8
47	Fanny Garrett	Deschutes	1936	4 6/8	4 7/8	7	8	23 1/8	22 6/8	23 0/8	32 5/8	33 5/8	184 4/8	188 1/8	218 1/8
48	Bud Dullian			4 4/8	4 4/8	11	10	23 5/8	24 3/8	19 1/8	36 6/8	61 7/8	155 5/8	161 1/8	217 4/8
49	Fran Cherry/Lorraine Cherry	Wheeler	1948	5 0/8	5 0/8	7	6	26 6/8	26 2/8	29 4/8	35 0/8	9 7/8	207 0/8	210 0/8	216 7/8
50	Samuel R. McDaniel	Grant	1993	4 7/8	5 0/8	7	9	28 2/8	27 2/8	22 2/8	28 0/8	31 2/8	185 0/8	194 0/8	216 2/8
51	John Hanna/David Hanna	Morrow	1940	7 3/8	7 4/8	8	9	28 4/8	27 4/8	31 1/8	35 4/8	30 0/8	186 0/8	196 1/8	216 0/8
52	Dave Williams	Baker	1995	4 5/8	4 7/8	8	8	25 5/8	25 0/8	23 7/8	27 4/8	33 5/8	182 1/8	185 7/8	215 6/8
52	Walter D. Gaylord	Umatilla	1970	5 4/8	5 4/8	11	6	25 2/8	25 7/8	27 0/8	33 3/8	27 1/8	188 5/8	195 6/8	215 6/8
54	David Moore	Wasco	1984	4 6/8	4 5/8	12	9	25 2/8	25 1/8	21 5/8	32 2/8	24 6/8	190 7/8	196 5/8	215 5/8
55	Mark Griffith/Jamie Jackson	Gilliam	1993	4 6/8	4 7/8	7	9	23 3/8	23 6/8	23 0/8	31 7/8	36 5/8	178 2/8	183 5/8	214 7/8
56	Gary Engle	Grant	1960	5 4/8	5 3/8	8	6	31 1/8	30 5/8	20 5/8	30 6/8	11 6/8	202 7/8	208 5/8	214 5/8
56	D.G. Dahlgren/Darrell Dahlgren	Grant	1974	6 2/8	6 0/8	8	8	26 6/8	27 6/8	22 7/8	33 2/8	17 0/8	197 5/8	201 0/8	214 5/8
58	Clifton Lemons	Grant	1933	5 3/8	5 1/8	7	7	25 6/8	27 1/8	25 1/8	25 1/8	15 5/8	198 5/8	203 4/8	214 2/8
59	Walter Gaylord	Umatilla	1970	5 4/8	5 4/8	11	6	25 2/8	25 7/8	27 0/8	33 3/8	24 1/8	188 5/8	195 0/8	212 6/8
60	Gary Lovell	Wallowa	1972	5 2/8	5 0/8	8	9	22 5/8	22 5/8	19 0/8	30 4/8	30 1/8	181 6/8	184 5/8	211 7/8
61	Frank McCullough/ The Bowman Museum	Crook		6 2/8	6 0/8	9	10	25 4/8	28 1/8	24 2/8	40 0/8	26 4/8	185 2/8	192 6/8	211 6/8
61	Dan Callaghan	Lake	1975	6 4/8	6 4/8	5	7	26 4/8	25 2/8	26 0/8	31 0/8	6 2/8	205 4/8	211 7/8	211 6/8
63	Dick Faulk/Don Brown	Malheur	1950	5 1/8	5 2/8	6	8	26 3/8	27 0/8	22 0/8	29 3/8	22 1/8	189 4/8	197 1/8	211 5/8
64	Paul Okita	Harney	1984	5 4/8	5 3/8	6	6	25 4/8	26 0/8	26 2/8	28 3/8	21 4/8	190 0/8	198 0/8	211 4/8
65	Charles Wetzel	Lake	1967	4 0/8	4 0/8	10	9	25 4/8	23 7/8	23 7/8	37 0/8	27 5/8	183 5/8	187 2/8	211 2/8
66	Jack Smith	Grant	1973	6 0/8	5 2/8	11	6	25 0/8	25 6/8	25 6/8	25 6/8	37 3/8	173 6/8	177 5/8	211 1/8
67	Katrina Ryder	Jefferson	1994	5 1/8	4 7/8	8	11	25 4/8	23 1/8	25 1/8	31 0/8	25 1/8	184 7/8	189 0/8	210 0/8
68	Molly Wood	Grant		5 0/8	5 2/8	6	9	26 0/8	24 7/8	23 1/8	31 1/8	30 0/8	179 7/8	190 2/8	209 7/8
69	Gordon Mitchell	Grant	1983	4 6/8	4 6/8	11	10	23 0/8	22 3/8	22 3/8	35 4/8	39 7/8	169 5/8	175 0/8	209 4/8
70	Earnest Warrington	Crook	1964	5 0/8	5 0/8	6	9	26 4/8	25 4/8	30 0/8	30 0/8	25 5/8	183 6/8	198 1/8	209 3/8
71	Murry Leslie/Marvin Leslie	Grant	1944	4 6/8	4 6/8	9	8	26 5/8	27 1/8	18 1/8	26 4/8	27 6/8	181 3/8	190 0/8	209 1/8
72	Grant Saunders	Union	1958	5 0/8	5 1/8	8	9	25 5/8	26 3/8	26 4/8	37 6/8	32 3/8	176 1/8	185 2/8	208 4/8
72	Shirley Keagle	Union	1969	5 0/8	5 0/8	10	13	24 5/8	23 2/8	21 1/8	32 5/8	45 3/8	163 1/8	167 4/8	208 4/8
72	Joe D. Brooks	Grant	1982	5 4/8	5 2/8	5	6	27 2/8	27 2/8	26 0/8	31 0/8	7 0/8	201 4/8	207 3/8	208 4/8
75	Jason Smith	Jefferson	1994	4 7/8	4 6/8	11	11	26 0/8	24 5/8	19 4/8	24 6/8	40 4/8	167 6/8	173 3/8	208 2/8
75	Roy Heinz/Gary Arntz	Harney	1930	5 3/8	5 4/8	7	5	26 5/8	24 4/8	22 1/8	31 0/8	9 1/8	199 1/8	207 3/8	208 2/8
77	Floyd W. Ross/Kitty Ross Grauf	Lake	1960	4 6/8	4 7/8	8	7	27 6/8	27 0/8	21 4/8	35 0/8	22 3/8	185 6/8	191 1/8	208 1/8
78	W.V. Masson	Grant	1958	6 1/8	5 6/8	8	9	24 6/8	25 5/8	21 2/8	25 0/8	10 4/8	197 2/8	201 7/8	207 6/8
79	Gordon Mitchell	Grant	1960	5 2/8	4 7/8	9	8	25 6/8	28 0/8	23 4/8	31 0/8	42 5/8	165 0/8	174 0/8	207 5/8
80	Brad Smith	Wallowa	1990	4 6/8	4 7/8	7	9	26 6/8	26 6/8	19 6/8	24 5/8	11 5/8	195 6/8	201 0/8	207 3/8
81	Arthur Dahlgren/Darrell Dahlgren	Deschutes	1949	6 6/8	6 6/8	11	12	26 3/8	27 4/8	25 4/8	33 3/8	35 7/8	171 2/8	179 6/8	207 1/8
82	Pat Moore	Harney	1974	6 2/8	5 5/8	14	9	19 2/8	28 2/8	20 4/8	24 0/8	58 7/8	148 1/8	173 1/8	206 7/8
83	Ron DeRoest	Baker	1965	5 4/8	5 3/8	7	7	23 3/8	26 0/8	36 0/8	36 0/8	19 6/8	187 0/8	198 0/8	206 6/8
84	Steve McKern	Grant	1980	5 2/8	5 2/8	8	10	25 1/8	25 1/8	20 0/8	28 2/8	33 4/8	172 6/8	177 4/8	206 2/8
85	Don Moody	Harney	1963	5 4/8	5 3/8	8	9	27 0/8	26 3/8	22 6/8	31 0/8	19 7/8	186 2/8	190 7/8	206 1/8

Non-Typical Mule Deer—Rifle (continued)

Final Score	Gross Typical	Net Typical	Abnormal Points	Greatest Spread	Inside Spread	Main Beam R	Main Beam L	Number of Points R	Number of Points L	First Circumference R	First Circumference L	Year	County	Hunter/Owner	Rank
205 7/8	199 4/8	192 7/8	13 0/8	30 0/8	18 3/8	22 0/8	24 0/8	8	7	5 6/8	5 4/8	1960		Elmer Frank	86
205 5/8	197 0/8	190 7/8	14 6/8	33 5/8	26 5/8	27 6/8	26 1/8	9	7	5 6/8	5 3/8	1951	Deschutes	Marshal Snearinger/The Tumalo Restaurant	87
205 4/8	193 1/8	187 4/8	18 0/8		20 4/8	24 2/8	25 2/8	7	9	4 2/8	4 2/8	1993	Umatilla	John Wagner	88
204 7/8	177 4/8	170 7/8	34 0/8	28 6/8	22 3/8	24 6/8	24 0/8	11	11	5 5/8	5 2/8	1962	Wallowa	Manford Isley/Joseph Hardware	89
204 6/8	184 4/8	178 1/8	26 5/8	23 5/8	20 1/8	23 2/8	24 5/8	7	7	5 0/8	4 5/8	1980	Wallowa	Wendell Weaver	90
204 4/8	202 0/8	197 7/8	6 5/8	34 0/8	28 5/8	26 0/8	26 3/8	7	6	5 5/8	5 6/8	1969	Malheur	Ron Daniel	91
204 1/8	200 2/8	190 6/8	13 3/8	32 0/8	26 2/8	26 0/8	26 5/8	7	9	4 4/8	4 5/8	1933	Wallowa	Alfred Zollman/Joseph Hardware	92
203 7/8	195 5/8	192 1/8	11 6/8	28 3/8	22 5/8	27 0/8	25 4/8	6	9	4 3/8	4 2/8	1995	Umatilla	Joe L. Gaylord	93
203 4/8	185 0/8	175 0/8	28 4/8	23 5/8	17 4/8	24 6/8	25 4/8	7	13	4 6/8	4 7/8	1994	Jefferson	Lloyd Wagoner	94
203 2/8	189 0/8	184 0/8	19 2/8	31 0/8	22 0/8	24 2/8	25 3/8	7	9	5 0/8	5 0/8	1991	Harney	Greg Quart	95
202 4/8	177 4/8	169 7/8	32 5/8	29 2/8	19 5/8	22 6/8	23 1/8	8	10	4 7/8	5 2/8	1967	Deschutes	Chuck Toftdahl	96
202 4/8	207 0/8	197 3/8	5 1/8	31 0/8	24 1/8	26 6/8	27 0/8	6	5	5 4/8	5 0/8	1959	Wallowa	Gene Roberts	96
202 4/8	166 0/8	161 0/8	41 4/8	24 4/8	18 6/8	24 0/8	24 0/8	9	9	4 4/8	4 6/8	1959	Klamath	June Hamman/Dave Fogelquist	96
202 4/8	195 2/8	190 3/8	12 1/8	33 2/8	24 3/8	27 1/8	25 6/8	7	6	4 6/8	4 6/8	1994	Lake	Fred Dulley	96
202 1/8	199 7/8	191 7/8	10 2/8	36 4/8	28 4/8	26 3/8	27 5/8	8	7	5 5/8	5 6/8		Lake	Nolan Greiner	100
202 0/8	194 2/8	187 0/8	15 0/8	35 4/8	27 2/8	27 3/8	27 6/8	7	6	4 3/8	4 4/8	1976	Baker	Carmen Smallwood	101
201 4/8	183 0/8	178 1/8	23 3/8	33 4/8	21 7/8	26 1/8	27 2/8	8	9	4 6/8	4 5/8	1985	Grant	Ken Moore	102
201 3/8	196 6/8	192 6/8	8 5/8	28 0/8	25 0/8	26 5/8	26 6/8	7	5	5 3/8	5 1/8	1948	Grant	Buster Burnette	103
201 2/8	201 5/8	196 6/8	4 4/8	30 3/8	24 2/8	26 4/8	27 5/8	6	4	5 5/8	5 5/8	1994	Harney	Glen Dobson	104
201 0/8	200 3/8	194 1/8	6 7/8	30 4/8	27 1/8	25 1/8	26 3/8	6	7	4 6/8	4 6/8	1978	Wallowa	Mike Norton	105
201 0/8	173 4/8	163 0/8	38 0/8	35 4/8	24 5/8	24 4/8	23 0/8	8	9	5 0/8	5 0/8	1957	Klamath	Gerald Konopasek	105
200 5/8	193 7/8	186 7/8	13 6/8	31 0/8	22 5/8	26 4/8	26 5/8	5	7	5 4/8	5 5/8	1977	Baker	Kerry Bratcher	107
200 4/8	182 6/8	178 7/8	21 5/8	30 6/8	25 7/8	25 5/8	25 2/8	7	7	4 7/8	4 7/8	1991	Umatilla	Robert C. Hoyt	108
200 4/8	188 1/8	181 6/8	18 6/8	30 0/8	22 2/8	23 4/8	26 1/8	9	8	5 2/8	5 2/8	1991	Grant	Tony Gardner	108
200 3/8	193 0/8	183 2/8	17 1/8	26 3/8	22 2/8	26 1/8	22 6/8	11	6	5 1/8	5 1/8	1995	Umatilla	Justin Skillman	110
200 2/8	194 1/8	184 3/8	15 7/8	32 2/8	23 5/8	27 1/8	26 0/8	7	7	5 0/8	5 1/8	1989	Harney	Scott Ritner	111
200 2/8	188 6/8	171 6/8	28 4/8	31 2/8	25 1/8	23 6/8	25 0/8	10	12	5 3/8	5 2/8	1960	Baker	Dick Crow	111
200 0/8	181 2/8	176 4/8	23 4/8	38 0/8	25 7/8	24 0/8	25 0/8	8	8	4 7/8	5 0/8		Harney	Karen Kelvin/The Gun Room	113
200 0/8	172 5/8	169 0/8	31 0/8	32 0/8	22 5/8	21 6/8	21 0/8	11	9	5 2/8	5 2/8	1992	Lake	Suzan Craven	113
200 0/8	184 2/8	178 5/8	21 3/8	28 2/8	21 1/8	25 0/8	25 4/8	10	10	4 6/8	4 5/8	1961	Morrow	Jim Barnett	113

Non-Typical Mule Deer—Archery
Minimum Score: 160 0/8

Final Score	Gross Typical	Net Typical	Abnormal Points	Greatest Spread	Inside Spread	Main Beam R	Main Beam L	Number of Points R	Number of Points L	First Circumference R	First Circumference L	Year	County	Hunter/Owner	Rank
257 7/8	198 6/8	193 5/8	64 2/8	32 4/8	19 1/8	25 6/8	25 0/8	18	14	5 6/8	5 4/8	1992	Klamath	Brad Smith	1
236 7/8	186 7/8	181 7/8	55 0/8	33 5/8	22 3/8	21 4/8	22 3/8	14	9	5 0/8	5 2/8	1995	Union	Jon D. Silver	2
232 7/8	199 1/8	191 4/8	41 3/8	22 7/8	21 0/8	25 1/8	24 4/8	15	13	6 4/8	5 2/8		Harney	R.L. Brown	3
218 3/8	200 4/8	190 4/8	27 7/8	28 3/8	23 2/8	27 4/8	26 2/8	9	10	5 5/8	6 0/8	1995	Jefferson	Cliff Piper	4
214 2/8	187 7/8	182 4/8	31 6/8	26 4/8	17 2/8	25 4/8	25 5/8	11	12	5 2/8	5 0/8	1982	Umatilla	Dan Follett	5

Final Score	Gross Typical	Net Typical	Abnormal Points	Greatest Spread	Inside Spread	Main Beam R	Main Beam L	Number of Points R	L	First Circumference R	L	Year	County	Hunter/Owner	Rank
213 4/8	183 1/8	175 5/8	37 7/8	24 2/8	18 5/8	21 0/8	22 7/8	12	7	4 5/8	4 6/8	1994	Harney	Glen Shelley	6
191 4/8	169 5/8	164 4/8	27 0/8	24 0/8	20 6/8	23 6/8	23 6/8	7	8	4 4/8	4 3/8	1981	Grant	Joe Mengore	7
175 4/8	163 7/8	157 4/8	18 0/8	29 4/8	18 4/8	23 0/8	21 5/8	9	9	4 2/8	4 2/8	1986	Wheeler	Dave Hyatt	8
168 0/8	150 5/8	141 5/8	26 3/8	21 5/8	17 7/8	21 7/8	21 5/8	6	5	4 0/8	4 1/8	1993	Umatilla	Dan Van Cleave	9
166 5/8	153 5/8	149 0/8	17 5/8	30 4/8	20 2/8	20 3/8	20 1/8	7	7	4 2/8	4 2/8	1980	Linn	Joe Mengore	10

Non-Typical Mule Deer—Black Powder
Minimum Score: 175 0/8

Final Score	Gross Typical	Net Typical	Abnormal Points	Greatest Spread	Inside Spread	Main Beam R	Main Beam L	Number of Points R	L	First Circumference R	L	Year	County	Hunter/Owner	Rank
194 4/8	182 5/8	174 2/8	20 2/8	33 7/8	20 2/8	23 3/8	22 4/8	8	6	5 2/8	5 2/8	1995	Harney	Delwyn Hendrickson	1
192 3/8	185 7/8	177 6/8	14 5/8	31 7/8	29 3/8	26 0/8	26 6/8	8	7	5 4/8	5 5/8		Lake	Ralph N. Jacobson	2
188 4/8	187 7/8	178 5/8	9 7/8	26 2/8	24 1/8	25 2/8	25 6/8	7	8	5 6/8	5 6/8	1995	Harney	Mike DeWitt	3

Non-Typical Mule Deer—Shed Antlers
Minimum Score: 85 0/8

Final Score	Subtotal	Abnormal Points	Main Beam	First Point	Second Point	Third Point	Fourth Point	First Circumference	Right/Left	Year	County	Owner's Name	Rank
125 5/8	79 7/8	45 6/8	27 5/8	2 7/8	11 5/8	10 0/8	4 4/8	5 4/8	Left	1960s	Grant	Ken Moore	1
125 3/8	81 5/8	43 6/8	28 5/8	2 3/8	14 2/8	7 7/8	7 3/8	5 5/8	Right	1960s	Grant	Ken Moore	2
122 0/8	59 1/8	62 7/8	23 5/8	0 0/8	14 0/8	8 4/8	13 0/8	0 0/8	Right		Grant	Joey Wood	3
118 6/8	87 5/8	31 1/8	24 0/8	2 7/8	15 7/8	13 4/8	12 3/8	5 4/8	Left	1940	Wallowa	Ken Moore	4
114 3/8	81 5/8	32 6/8	21 6/8	3 1/8	13 3/8	9 6/8	12 2/8	5 1/8	Right	1995	Crook	John Detrick	5
108 3/8	97 6/8	10 5/8	30 6/8	3 1/8	19 0/8	9 6/8	15 0/8	5 6/8	Right	1996	Crook	Dane Clark	6
105 1/8	78 6/8	26 3/8	24 4/8	2 4/8	11 0/8	11 4/8	11 2/8	5 0/8	Right		Grant	David Powell	7
103 6/8	79 7/8	23 7/8	23 0/8	3 2/8	13 2/8	13 4/8	8 2/8	5 2/8	Right	1940	Wallowa	Ken Moore	8
100 2/8	93 1/8	7 1/8	28 4/8	2 6/8	18 1/8	11 7/8	13 5/8	5 0/8	Left		Grant	Billy Hueckman	9
98 6/8	74 5/8	24 1/8	21 0/8	4 0/8	14 6/8	6 6/8	10 5/8	4 6/8	Left	1992	Wallowa	Dan Bennett	10
97 4/8	87 4/8	10 0/8	27 1/8	3 0/8	16 0/8	11 0/8	11 6/8	5 1/8	Right		Grant	Joey Wood	11
97 0/8	89 3/8	7 5/8	24 3/8	3 0/8	17 6/8	13 0/8	12 7/8	5 1/8	Left	1976	Umatilla	Jay Roth	12
94 3/8	89 2/8	5 1/8	26 0/8	3 1/8	16 2/8	13 2/8	12 0/8	5 1/8	Left	1996	Grant	Larry Powell	13
94 0/8	90 0/8	4 0/8	30 4/8	0 0/8	19 1/8	12 3/8	10 1/8	5 0/8	Right		Grant	Joey Wood	14
93 3/8	71 5/8	21 6/8	22 1/8	2 4/8	13 3/8	7 1/8	9 6/8	4 2/8	Right	1992	Wallowa	Dan Bennett	15
93 1/8	85 6/8	7 3/8	26 4/8	2 4/8	16 3/8	10 3/8	10 6/8	5 1/8	Right		Grant	Joey Wood	16
93 0/8	84 4/8	8 4/8	25 2/8	2 0/8	15 2/8	12 2/8	13 0/8	4 5/8	Left		Grant	Joey Wood	17
92 4/8	85 7/8	6 5/8	26 0/8	2 3/8	16 2/8	10 7/8	11 6/8	5 1/8	Right		Grant	Joey Wood	18
92 1/8	85 7/8	6 2/8	25 0/8	2 2/8	15 4/8	12 2/8	13 0/8	4 6/8	Right			Jerry Frampton	19
92 1/8	81 7/8	10 2/8	22 4/8	2 5/8	14 7/8	12 3/8	12 1/8	4 7/8	Left		Grant	Larry Powell	19
91 0/8	86 5/8	4 3/8	24 6/8	2 0/8	15 4/8	10 7/8	12 7/8	5 2/8	Right		Grant	Joey Wood	21
89 5/8	84 7/8	4 6/8	24 0/8	2 1/8	16 2/8	12 0/8	13 1/8	5 0/8	Right		Grant	Larry Powell	22
87 6/8	79 2/8	8 4/8	23 2/8	3 1/8	13 2/8	11 1/8	11 2/8	5 1/8	Right		Klamath	Mike Gerrett	23
86 6/8	85 0/8	1 6/8	28 0/8	1 5/8	15 5/8	11 0/8	11 0/8	4 5/8	Right		Grant	Joey Wood	24

Boundaries for Blacktail Deer and Mule Deer

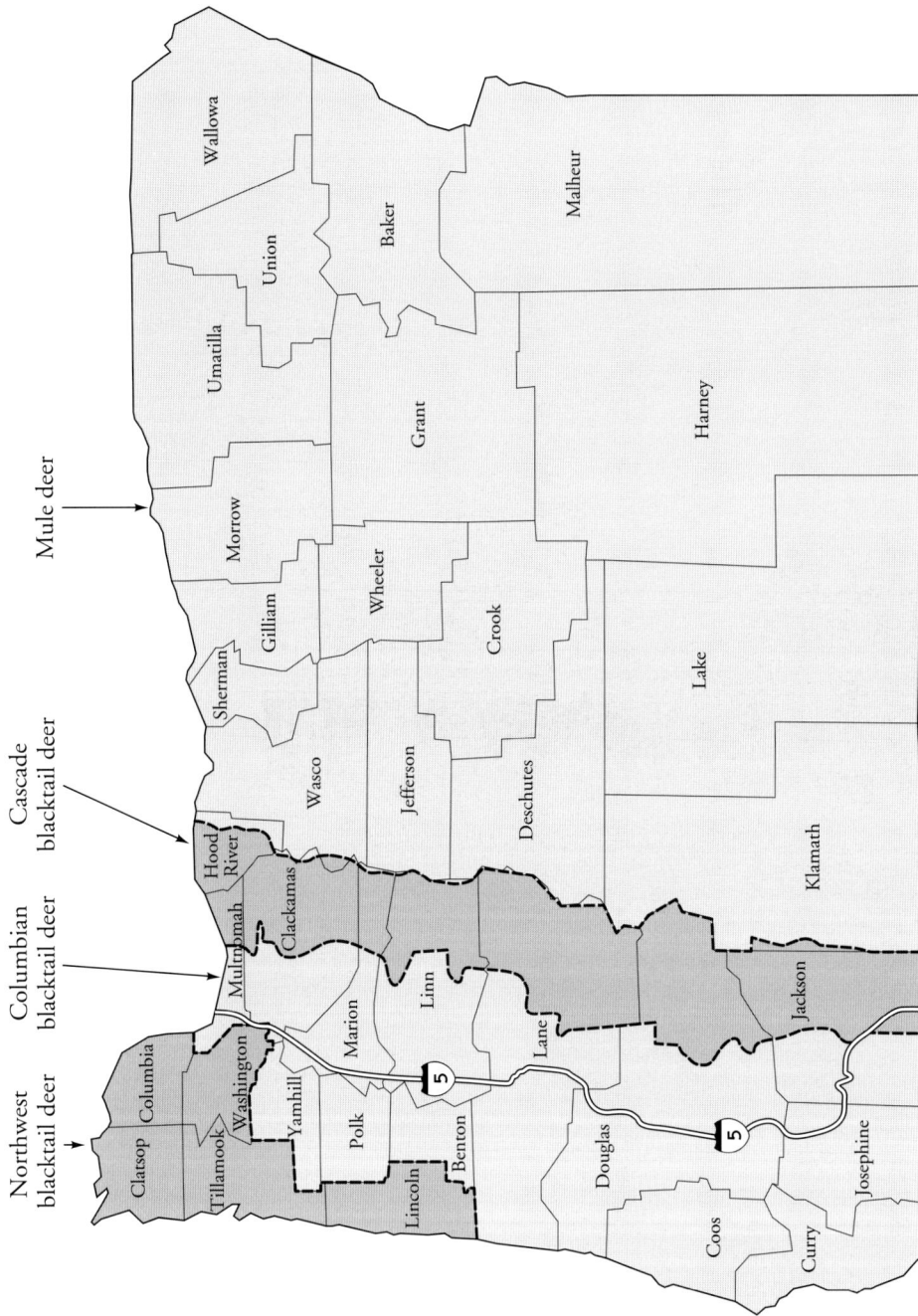

Mule deer →

Cascade blacktail deer →

Columbian blacktail deer →

Northwest blacktail deer →

Three categories have been established for blacktail deer: Northwest, Cascade and Columbian.

Northwest: Deer taken from Columbia, Clatsop, Washington, Tillamook and Lincoln Counties.

Cascade: The eastern boundary begins in Hood River, runs along Highway 35 south until it intersects the Pacific Crest Trail, runs along the Pacific Crest Trail until it leaves the Rogue River National Forest, then south along the Klamath–Jackson County line to the California border. The western boundary is the same as the Columbian blacktail's eastern boundary.

Columbian: The eastern boundary begins at Multnomah Falls on the Columbia River, runs south along the western boundary of the National Forest to Tiller, then south along Highway 227 to Highway 62 at Trail, then south following Highway 62 to Medford, from which the boundary follows the township line between R1W and R2W E.W.M. to the California border.

Mule Deer: Deer taken east of the eastern boundary for Cascade Blacktail.

Whitetail Deer

Boundaries for Whitetail Deer

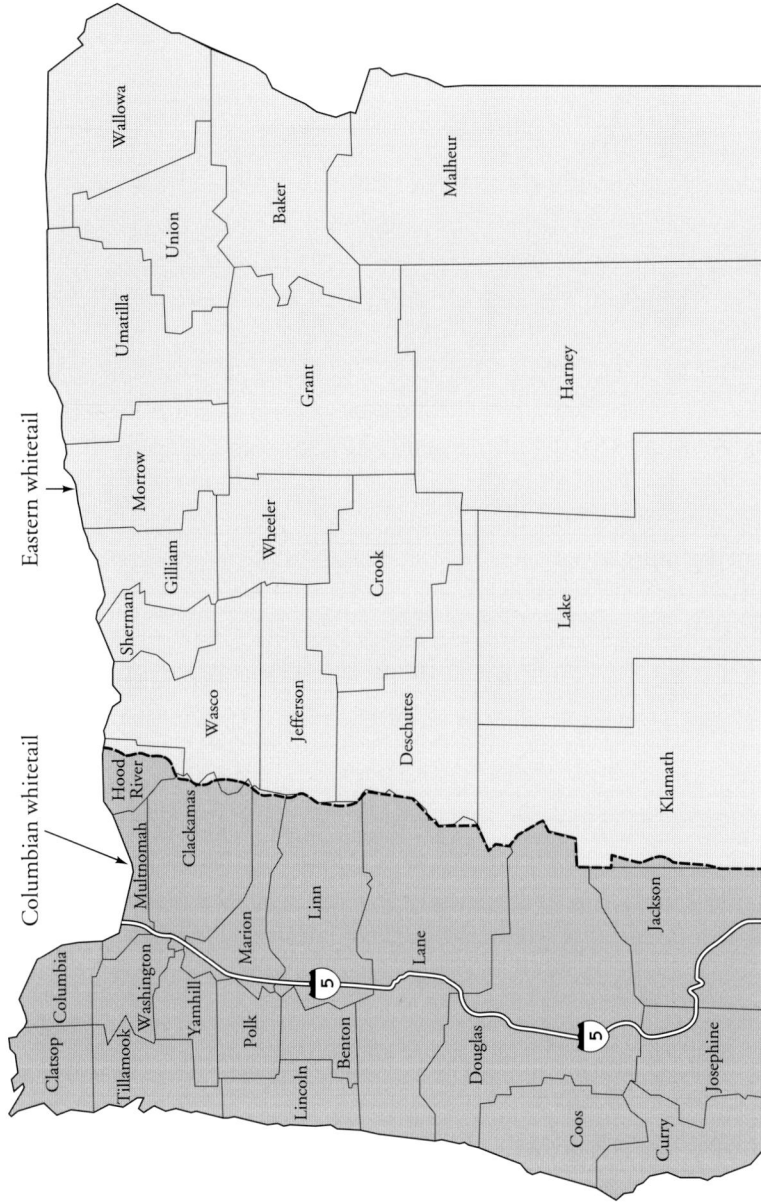

Columbian: the eastern boundary begins in Hood River, runs along Highway 35 south until it intersects the Pacific Crest Trail, south along the Pacific Crest Trail until it leaves the Rogue River National Forest, then south along the Klamath-Jackson County line to the California border.

Eastern: whitetail deer taken east of the above boundary (dashed line).

The Columbian Whitetailed Deer in Oregon

by Steven R. Denney, Wildlife Biologist,
Oregon Department of Fish and Wildlife

The Columbian whitetailed deer (*Odocoileus virginianus leucurus*) is a member of the Cervidae or deer family, which includes, in North America, mule deer, blacktailed deer, elk, moose and caribou. Columbian whitetailed deer is one of thirty subspecies of whitetailed deer in North America and one of two subspecies found in Oregon, the other being Idaho whitetailed deer (*Odocoileus virginianus ochrourus*), which is found in northeast Oregon.

Lewis and Clark observed and killed whitetailed deer in 1805 and 1806 along the Columbia River from the approximate locations of The Dalles, Oregon to Astoria, Oregon. The Columbian whitetailed deer was first described by David Douglas in 1829 as being common along the Cowlitz and Willamette Rivers in Washington and Oregon. The historic range of Columbian whitetailed deer was described as extending as far north as Olympia, Washington, as far east as The Dalles, west along the Columbia River to Astoria and south through the Willamette valley and into the Umpqua River basin near Roseburg. There are some unauthenticated reports of whitetailed deer existing as far south as Grants Pass in the Rogue River basin.

Currently, two subpopulations of Columbian whitetailed deer are found in Oregon. One is found in the lower Columbia River on a series of islands in Clatsop and Columbia counties and on both the Oregon and Washington mainlands adjacent to the Columbia River. The other subpopulation is found in the valley floors of the Umpqua River basin near Roseburg in Douglas County.

The Columbian whitetailed deer was listed as an endangered species in 1967. The species was then included as endangered under the Federal Endangered Species Act in 1978 and was automatically placed on the Oregon Endangered Species List as endangered as required by the Oregon Endangered Species Act, passed in 1987. The Oregon Fish and Wildlife Commission removed the species from the Oregon Endangered Species List in 1995 as a result of increased populations, range expansion and the protection of critical habitat. Efforts continue to have the species removed from the Federal Endangered Species List.

In Oregon, the Columbian whitetailed deer are usually associated with riparian areas. Roseburg area whitetailed deer can be found along creek bottoms and brushy areas of the valley floors using open oak, closed oak, oak-savannah grasslands and riparian areas of the Umpqua River basin. Although also tied to riparian habitats, Columbian whitetailed deer in the Lower Columbia River use a somewhat different habitat. The area is under tidal influence of the ocean and elevations average less than ten feet above sea level. These deer use brushy woodlots associated with tidal lowlands that are characterized by cottonwood, willow, alder, spruce and dogwood. Deer in both populations feed on a variety of items but concentrate on annuals, forbs and browse (shrub) species throughout the year.

The life history of Columbian whitetailed deer is very similar to that of other deer species in Oregon. The rut takes place in November with a peak occurring sometime around the third week of November, depending on weather and other factors. While most of the breeding is over by mid-December, some breeding behavior has been observed as late as January. Most fawns are born from mid-May to mid-June.

Unlike other whitetailed deer subspecies, which may first breed at six months of age, female Columbian whitetailed deer first breed as yearlings (eighteen months) and commonly have a single fawn. Twins are commonly born to does over two years of age, with productivity falling off after the age of eight.

Columbian whitetailed deer can be distinguished in the field from blacktailed deer, which inhabit the same areas. Whitetailed deer have much shorter ears than blacktailed deer, with predominant white eye rings and a white ring behind the nose. The antlers of blacktailed deer grow up and out of the head with dichotomous forking while whitetailed deer antlers grow up and forward with singular points arising from a single main beam. Perhaps the most predominant characteristic is the tail. Blacktailed deer have a relatively narrow tail that is black in color on the dorsal (top) surface, while whitetailed deer have a large, wide, triangular-shaped tail that has a brown dorsal surface fringed with white hair. The blacktailed deer's metatarsal gland, found on the outside of the back leg is long (greater than 275 inches) and tipped with brown or black hairs, while on Columbian whitetailed deer this gland is short (less than 1.65 inches) and tipped with white hairs. Live weights of Columbian whitetailed deer, while similar to blacktailed deer, are smaller than Idaho whitetailed deer with adult does weighing 85–105 pounds and adult bucks weighing 115–150 pounds.

Columbian whitetailed deer were legally hunted in Oregon until they were protected under the Federal Endangered Species Act in 1978.

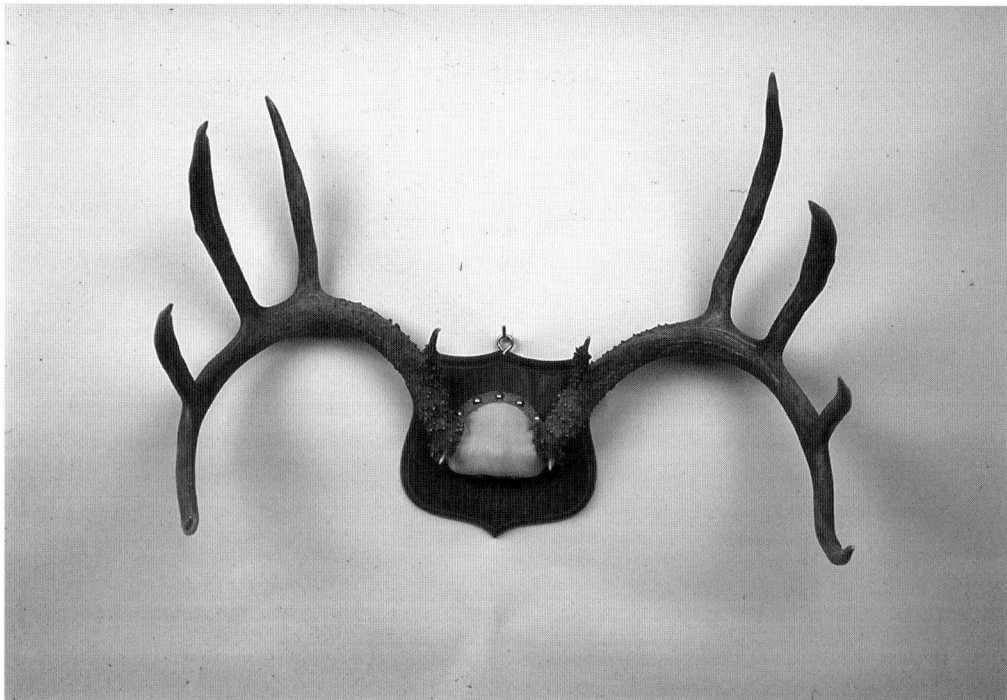

Oregon State Record—Rifle
eastern whitetail (typical), Sterling Shavers, 178 2/8 B.C.,
Wallowa County, 1982

Official Scoring System for Oregon Big Game Trophies

Records of Oregon Big Game

RECORD BOOK FOR OREGON

P.O. Box 759
Irrigon, OR 97844

TYPICAL
WHITETAIL DEER

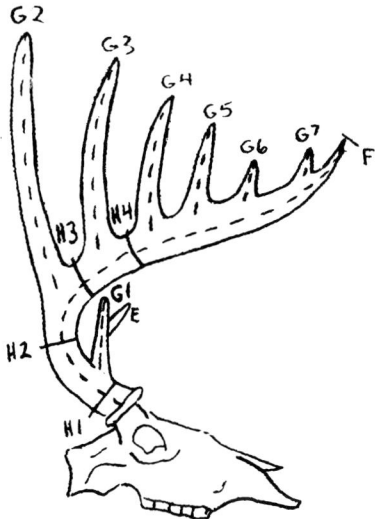

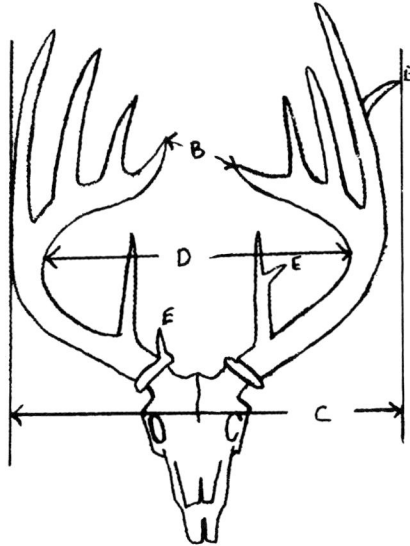

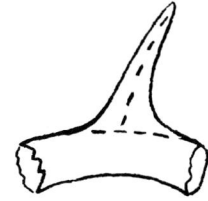

DETAIL OF POINT MEASUREMENT

Abnormal Points			
Right Antler		Left Antler	
1	4/8	1	0/8
0	0/8	0	0/8
0	0/8	0	0/8
0	0/8	0	0/8
0	0/8	0	0/8
0	0/8	0	0/8
0	0/8	0	0/8
0	0/8	0	0/8
0	0/8	0	0/8
0	0/8	0	0/8

Species	Rifle	Archery	Muzzle	Shed	Archery-Velvet
Eastern Whitetail	130	125	125	60	125
Columbia Whitetail	All	All	All	All	All

	Right Antler	Left Antler
Subtotals	1 4/8	1 0/8
Total to E		2 4/8

					COLUMN 1	COLUMN 2	COLUMN 3	COLUMN 4
					Spread Credit	Right Antler	Left Antler	Difference
A	No. of Points on Right Antler	6	No. of Points on Left Antler	6				
B	Tip to Tip Spread	24 0/8	C Greatest Spread	27 0/8				
D	Inside Spread of Main Beam	24 6/8	(Credit may be equal to but not exceed longer antler)		24 6/8			
E	Total of Length of Abnormal Points							2 4/8
F	Length of Main Beam					27 6/8	27 3/8	0 3/8
G-1	Length of First Point					3 5/8	3 3/8	0 2/8
G-2	Length of Second Point					9 3/8	13 2/8	3 7/8
G-3	Length of Third Point					13 0/8	13 0/8	0 0/8
G-4	Length of Fourth Point					10 3/8	8 6/8	1 5/8
G-5	Length of Fifth Point					0 0/8	0 0/8	0 0/8
G-6	Length of Sixth Point, If Present					0 0/8	0 0/8	0 0/8
G-7	Length of Seventh Point, If Present					0 0/8	0 0/8	0 0/8
H-1	Circumference at smallest place between 1st and 2nd points					4 3/8	4 3/8	0 0/8
H-2	Circumference at smallest place between 2nd and 3rd points					4 1/8	4 1/8	0 0/8
H-3	Circumference at smallest place between 3rd and 4th points					4 1/8	4 1/8	0 0/8
H-4	Circumference at smallest place between 4th and 5th points					3 4/8	3 5/8	0 1/8
			TOTALS		24 6/8	80 2/8	82 0/8	8 6/8

County where killed: Wallowa   Date Killed: 1082

Hunter's Name: Sterling Shavers

Owner's Name: Sterling Shavers

ADD	Column 1	24 6/8
	Column 2	80 2/8
	Column 3	82 0/8
	Subtotal	187 0/8
	Subtract Column 4	8 6/8
	FINAL SCORE	178 2/8

Official Scoring System for Oregon Big Game Trophies

Records of Oregon Big Game

RECORD BOOK FOR OREGON

P.O. Box 759
Irrigon, OR 97844

TYPICAL
WHITETAIL DEER

DETAIL OF POINT MEASUREMENT

	Abnormal Points	
	Right Antler	Left Antler
	0 0/8	0 0/8
	0 0/8	0 0/8
	0 0/8	0 0/8
	0 0/8	0 0/8
	0 0/8	0 0/8
	0 0/8	0 0/8
	0 0/8	0 0/8
	0 0/8	0 0/8
	0 0/8	0 0/8
	0 0/8	0 0/8
Subtotals	0 0/8	0 0/8
Total to E		0 0/8

Species	Rifle	Archery	Muzzle	Shed	Archery-Velvet
Eastern Whitetail	130	125	125	60	125
Columbia Whitetail	All	All	All	All	All

						COLUMN 1 Spread Credit	COLUMN 2 Right Antler	COLUMN 3 Left Antler	COLUMN 4 Difference
A	No. of Points on Right Antler	5		No. of Points on Left Antler	5				
B	Tip to Tip Spread	9 3/8	**C**	Greatest Spread	22 7/8				
D	Inside Spread of Main Beam	21 5/8	(Credit may be equal to but not exceed longer antler)			21 5/8			
E	Total of Length of Abnormal Points								0 0/8
F	Length of Main Beam						22 1/8	22 4/8	0 3/8
G-1	Length of First Point						6 1/8	5 0/8	1 1/8
G-2	Length of Second Point						9 3/8	9 3/8	0 0/8
G-3	Length of Third Point						9 1/8	8 4/8	0 5/8
G-4	Length of Fourth Point						3 7/8	3 4/8	0 3/8
G-5	Length of Fifth Point						0 0/8	0 0/8	0 0/8
G-6	Length of Sixth Point, If Present						0 0/8	0 0/8	0 0/8
G-7	Length of Seventh Point, If Present						0 0/8	0 0/8	0 0/8
H-1	Circumference at smallest place between 1st and 2nd points						4 6/8	4 6/8	0 0/8
H-2	Circumference at smallest place between 2nd and 3rd points						4 2/8	4 1/8	0 1/8
H-3	Circumference at smallest place between 3rd and 4th points						3 7/8	4 1/8	0 2/8
H-4	Circumference at smallest place between 4th and 5th points						3 6/8	3 2/8	0 4/8
					TOTALS	21 5/8	67 2/8	65 1/8	3 3/8

County where killed: Umatilla	Date Killed: 09/95		
Hunter's Name: Kenneth C. Lebsock	**ADD**	Column 1	21 5/8
Owner's Name: Kenneth C. Lebsock		Column 2	67 2/8
		Column 3	65 1/8
		Subtotal	154 0/8
	Subtract Column 4		3 3/8
	FINAL SCORE		**150 5/8**

The Adventure I Had in the Harvesting of a Nice Whitetail Buck

by Ken Lebsock

As most hunters know, luck has a lot to do with success. After a lot of scouting trips before the season and watching this buck on many mornings, bow in hand, but not being quite close enough to get a shot, I borrowed a climbing tree stand and tried to set up closer to the deer's travel route. Sure enough, here they came—my buck and a smaller one.

The deer were feeding up the ridge, and as I waited for them to move up to me, I had the feeling that something would go wrong. And it almost did. At one point, my arm was getting tired and I clicked my release. At fifty yards, I had four eyes looking for the location of that minor sound. Luckily enough, they didn't locate me, and they continued to feed up the ridge. At thirty yards, I decided to take a shot. When I was at full draw I noticed that the smaller buck had bedded down right in front of the larger buck. I shot, and the arrow went right over the back of the smaller buck and under the belly of the larger one. The small buck jumped up and locked on to me. I was frozen in the tree. The larger buck then proceeded to bed down eighteen yards below me. There I was, no arrow and bedded below me, the biggest whitetail buck I had ever seen. The smaller buck wasn't sure of what I was, and the big buck must have seen me blink; he got nervous and stood up and walked away. I nocked another arrow as he moved off, and, at twenty-eight yards, leaned out of the tree stand for another broadside shot. This time I didn't miss.

I was very lucky that morning. But it wasn't just luck that put me where I was. It was a lot of preseason scouting and patience on those mornings when I just couldn't get close enough for the shot I wanted.
(Final score: 150 5/8 P.Y.)

Surprise, I'm Back

by James H. Hambleton

It all began near the end of the season of 1991. My wife and I had been hunting for seven days. The season had been fun; as in the past, we had seen a number of nice whitetail buck. This day was snowy and rainy, and we were working along slowly when I spotted a buck, four points on each side, looking straight at me. The distance was long, better than a hundred yards, so I took careful aim at the top of the buck's head and squeezed the trigger. At the crack of my rifle, the buck dropped to the ground. "Nice shot," my wife said. Just then, a huge whitetail buck, much closer to us in the trees, turned and ran to the fallen buck, and hesitated there a moment before turning again and bounding out of sight. All I could do was say, "See you next year."

The thought of that big buck drifted through my mind from time to time during the following year. When my wife and I successfully drew a muzzleloader/whitetail tag for 1992, the thought raced through my mind, "I wonder if we will see that big buck again; I sure hope so." I have heard that whitetails are homebodies, more so than mule deer, though home might consist of ten square miles of timbered country, which is like looking for a needle in the woodpile.

Well, the season finally arrived and we were ready. We had no problems getting to our hunt location, as only a small amount of fresh snow had fallen the night before, making the total about twenty inches. We began our hunt near the location where I had taken my buck the year before, hoping we might get to see the big one that got away. We were moving along slowly, all together, not yet having split up to make our hunt, when I spotted a large buck watching us. I whispered to Steve, our neighbor, who was hunting with us for the weekend, his first time out hunting whitetails, "That's a dandy whitetail buck, take him if you want." So he pulled the hammer back on his rifle and let go. He blew a hole as big as all outdoors right straight through

the sky. That big buck got the message that whitetail season was open, and he ran with his tail speaking for him as it waved off into the dense timber. When I turned to look at Steve, he was standing there looking shocked and dismayed. He said the hammer didn't catch when

he pulled it back. A good black-powder story was all we had to show for that experience. We tracked the buck most of the day to no avail; he was very handy at giving us the slip.

On Tuesday morning, during a big snowstorm, my wife and I returned to our hunting area. We spotted a reasonably fresh track crossing the road. I got out and examined the track: it was a very large deer track. We both thought it might be a mule deer, but since it was in a regular whitetail crossing, I decided to check it out. I did not think that the track could be very old, considering how hard it was snowing. My wife said that she was going to make her regular hunt, and that I should take my time and not hurry on her account. Well, a short time later I jumped a big whitetail buck. It was him: the buck we had seen on the opening weekend! By now I was pretty sure that this buck was the one we had seen the year before, since he was holding pretty close to the same location and his appearance was very similar in all respects.

The timber was dense and getting a good shot was difficult. I chose an opening, took careful aim at his front shoulder, and pulled the trigger. When the smoke cleared I was already moving toward where I had shot: I had just missed a classic buck and I didn't have a good excuse for doing so. That turned what might have been a short hunt into an all-day tracking job in very heavy snow. The buck gave me the slip again when he got into a herd of deer and made tracking a jumbled mess.

On Friday morning it was at least ten degrees below zero in camp, which was at about the fifteen-hundred-foot level, and we were hunting at forty-five hundred feet; a lot colder up there. Steve had returned to hunt with us, so my wife dropped each of us off where we wanted to start. Then she drove down country about five miles to the point where we were to meet. My goal was to cut across country to the location where I had last seen tracks of that big buck, hoping to run across him. Steve was on a more direct route toward the place where the vehicle was to be waiting for us. In near blinding snow, I went down a ridge that I had crossed on Tuesday toward a saddle and the deer crossing. I was within two hundred yards of where I crossed on Tuesday when I found a fresh deer track. I stopped and examined the track and said to myself that it was "him," coming back. I began following the deer in nearly waist-deep snow, flanking to the left of the tracks about ten to fifteen yards. It was about 8:30 in the morning and the going was rough, but the bitter cold was a definite advantage, as the snow was very quiet. Having followed the tracks for about two hundred yards, I came upon the deer's bed. I thought I must have pushed him out of his bed, but upon examining his tracks I noticed that he had never jumped; instead he had gotten out of bed and started feeding. The hunt was back on now and I would have to be extra careful. I moved very cautiously and was only a few steps from his bed when I noticed a movement a short distance to my left. I froze stiff, which wasn't hard to do, as cold as it was. There, reaching up into a tree, was the biggest set of whitetail horns I had ever seen! I could make out the buck's body through the brush; he wasn't more than fifteen yards away. "That's him," I thought to myself, and as I took careful aim at his shoulder, I muttered under my breath, "Surprise, I'm back." My finger touched the trigger on my Hatfield Pennsylvania long rifle. It roared; flame and smoke belched out and for a moment I could not see anything. Then there he stood, about four or five jumps from where I had seen him, broadside and out in the wide open. I had an empty gun in my hand and shock on my face: "Oh, no! Not again." Then it happened: he faltered, and I was relieved! He had just taken a moment before checking out. "What a buck," I thought as I dressed him out and headed for the rendezvous point where Steve and my wife were waiting. Now the work had just begun.

As it turned out, this big buck had exactly the same horn shape and characteristics as the smaller buck I had gotten the year before. We feel certain it was "big daddy," the one we had hoped to see again.

(Final score: 165 5/8 B.C.)

Official Scoring System for Oregon Big Game Trophies

Records of Oregon Big Game

RECORD BOOK FOR OREGON

P.O. Box 759
Irrigon, OR 97844

TYPICAL
WHITETAIL DEER

DETAIL OF POINT MEASUREMENT

Abnormal Points

Right Antler		Left Antler	
0	0/8	0	0/8
0	0/8	0	0/8
0	0/8	0	0/8
0	0/8	0	0/8
0	0/8	0	0/8
0	0/8	0	0/8
0	0/8	0	0/8
0	0/8	0	0/8
0	0/8	0	0/8
0	0/8	0	0/8
Subtotals 0	0/8	0	0/8
Total to E		0	0/8

Species	Rifle	Archery	Muzzle	Shed	Archery-Velvet
Eastern Whitetail	130	125	125	60	125
Columbia Whitetail	All	All	All	All	All

						COLUMN 1 Spread Credit	COLUMN 2 Right Antler	COLUMN 3 Left Antler	COLUMN 4 Difference
A	No. of Points on Right Antler	5	No. of Points on Left Antler	5					
B	Tip to Tip Spread	12 2/8	**C** Greatest Spread	24 5/8					
D	Inside Spread of Main Beam	21 5/8	(Credit may be equal to but not exceed longer antler)		21 5/8				
E	Total of Length of Abnormal Points								0 0/8
F	Length of Main Beam						24 3/8	24 0/8	0 3/8
G-1	Length of First Point						5 3/8	5 5/8	0 2/8
G-2	Length of Second Point						11 3/8	12 3/8	1 0/8
G-3	Length of Third Point						10 4/8	10 4/8	0 0/8
G-4	Length of Fourth Point						6 1/8	4 0/8	2 1/8
G-5	Length of Fifth Point						0 0/8	0 0/8	0 0/8
G-6	Length of Sixth Point, If Present						0 0/8	0 0/8	0 0/8
G-7	Length of Seventh Point, If Present						0 0/8	0 0/8	0 0/8
H 1	Circumference at smallest place between 1st and 2nd points						4 5/8	4 7/8	0 2/8
H-2	Circumference at smallest place between 2nd and 3rd points						4 1/8	4 2/8	0 1/8
H-3	Circumference at smallest place between 3rd and 4th points						4 1/8	4 3/8	0 2/8
H-4	Circumference at smallest place between 4th and 5th points						3 7/8	4 0/8	0 1/8
					TOTALS	21 5/8	74 4/8	74 0/8	4 4/8

County where killed: Wallowa	Date Killed: 12/04/92		
Hunter's Name: James H. Hambleton	**ADD**	Column 1	21 5/8
Owner's Name: James H. Hambleton		Column 2	74 4/8
		Column 3	74 0/8
		Subtotal	170 1/8
		Subtract Column 4	4 4/8
		FINAL SCORE	165 5/8

Typical Eastern Whitetail—Rifle
Minimum Score: 130 0/8

Final Score	Gross Typical	Net Typical	Abnormal Points	Greatest Spread	Inside Spread	Main Beam R	Main Beam L	Number of Points R	L	First Circumference R	L	Year	County	Hunter/Owner	Rank
178 2/8	187 0/8	180 6/8	2 4/8	27 0/8	24 6/8	27 6/8	27 3/8	6	6	4 3/8	4 3/8	1982	Wallowa	Sterling Shavers	1
170 2/8	174 5/8	170 4/8	0 0/8	20 4/8	18 0/8	22 1/8	21 0/8	6	6	4 3/8	4 4/8	1994	Wallowa	Dick Kyriss	2
166 4/8	174 3/8	168 0/8	1 4/8	21 0/8	19 0/8	26 2/8	27 4/8	5	6	3 7/8	4 0/8	1983	Umatilla	Gary Bertelson	3
163 6/8	172 3/8	168 0/8	4 2/8	28 0/8	19 6/8	23 4/8	23 6/8	5	6	4 7/8	4 5/8	1982	Union	Larry Bennett	4
163 1/8	170 5/8	167 0/8	3 7/8	24 1/8	22 2/8	25 0/8	26 2/8	6	5	5 0/8	5 0/8	1987	Umatilla	Jeffrey A. Koorenny	5
149 2/8	154 6/8	151 7/8	0 0/8	19 6/8	18 0/8	20 6/8	20 7/8	6	5	4 3/8	4 3/8	1994	Umatilla	Michael Peterson	6
148 2/8	155 2/8	150 6/8	2 4/8	21 2/8	19 0/8	24 4/8	25 0/8	6	5	3 5/8	3 5/8	1993	Wallowa	Dave Hyatt	7
148 1/8	152 1/8	148 1/8	0 0/8	20 6/8	18 7/8	22 5/8	23 0/8	5	5	4 2/8	4 2/8	1994	Union	Curtis Pedro	8
148 1/8	153 0/8	148 1/8	0 0/8	19 0/8	18 1/8	20 6/8	21 6/8	5	5	4 6/8	4 7/8	1990	Umatilla	Lawrence Wolfgram	8
146 7/8	151 7/8	146 7/8	0 0/8	19 3/8	16 3/8	23 1/8	23 1/8	5	5	4 4/8	4 4/8	1981	Wallowa	Gary Tasakos	10
142 6/8	147 2/8	145 0/8	2 2/8	21 7/8	19 6/8	24 6/8	24 5/8	4	4	4 0/8	4 1/8	1992	Wallowa	Kelly Couch	11
141 4/8	144 5/8	141 4/8	0 0/8	20 4/8	18 4/8	21 5/8	22 2/8	5	5	4 4/8	4 4/8		Wallowa	Dale Dotson	12
141 3/8	154 7/8	151 5/8	10 2/8		17 3/8	23 2/8	22 7/8	6	6	4 4/8	5 0/8	1994	Umatilla	John Wagner	13
141 2/8	146 3/8	141 2/8	0 0/8	25 4/8	23 4/8	24 2/8	24 6/8	4	4	4 6/8	5 0/8	1987	Grant	David M. Morris	14
140 7/8	154 5/8	150 4/8	9 4/8	18 0/8	15 7/8	23 2/8	23 2/8	10	9	5 0/8	4 6/8	1987	Umatilla	Paul Noreen	15
140 7/8	146 6/8	140 7/8	0 0/8	24 0/8	21 1/8	23 7/8	24 1/8	4	4	3 5/8	4 0/8	1969	Wasco	Mike Nicholson, Sr.	15
138 7/8	144 2/8	138 7/8	0 0/8	18 1/8	16 5/8	21 5/8	21 0/8	5	5	4 1/8	4 0/8	1991	Wallowa	Dan Liebe	17
137 6/8	144 4/8	139 6/8	2 0/8	18 4/8	15 6/8	21 7/8	21 3/8	6	5	4 7/8	5 0/8	1983	Wallowa	ODF & W	18
137 3/8	147 6/8	143 7/8	6 4/8	21 0/8	19 1/8	21 7/8	23 1/8	5	7	4 4/8	4 5/8	1993	Union	LarryBennett	19
137 1/8	143 4/8	141 0/8	3 7/8	16 0/8	14 0/8	20 0/8	19 3/8	5	7	5 3/8	5 2/8	1994	Umatilla	Paul Roe	20
136 5/8	147 0/8	141 4/8	4 7/8	20 1/8	18 4/8	21 3/8	20 5/8	6	6	3 7/8	3 7/8	1994	Wallowa	Kyle Couch	21
135 4/8	145 7/8	142 6/8	7 2/8		17 4/8	23 7/8	22 4/8	6	7	5 0/8	5 0/8	1980	Union	Don Townsend	22
135 0/8	142 4/8	138 4/8	3 4/8	18 4/8	16 0/8	21 5/8	21 6/8	5	5	5 0/8	5 0/8	1995	Wallowa	Howard V. Wurdinger, Jr.	23
130 3/8	132 2/8	130 3/8	0 0/8	17 0/8	15 5/8	20 4/8	20 2/8	5	5	3 5/8	3 6/8	1991	Union	Graham Derbyshire	24

Typical Eastern Whitetail—Archery
Minimum Score: 125 0/8

Final Score	Gross Typical	Net Typical	Abnormal Points	Greatest Spread	Inside Spread	Main Beam		Number of Points		First Circumference		Year	County	Hunter/Owner	Rank
						R	L	R	L	R	L				
150 5/8	154 0/8	150 5/8	0 0/8	22 7/8	21 5/8	22 1/8	22 4/8	5	5	4 6/8	4 6/8	1995	Umatilla	Kenneth C. Lebsock	1

Typical Eastern Whitetail—Black Powder
Minimum Score: 125 0/8

Final Score	Gross Typical	Net Typical	Abnormal Points	Greatest Spread	Inside Spread	Main Beam		Number of Points		First Circumference		Year	County	Hunter/Owner	Rank
						R	L	R	L	R	L				
165 5/8	170 1/8	165 5/8	0 0/8	24 5/8	21 5/8	24 3/8	24 0/8	5	5	4 5/8	4 7/8	1992	Wallowa	James H. Hambleton	1
144 4/8	146 1/8	144 4/8	0 0/8	21 7/8	19 2/8	23 2/8	23 0/8	4	4	4 2/8	4 3/8	1991	Wallowa	Wendell Weaver	2
143 2/8	146 4/8	143 2/8	0 0/8	18 2/8	16 0/8	21 0/8	19 6/8	5	5	4 1/8	3 7/8	1995	Umatilla	Dan Evans	3
125 2/8	130 1/8	126 6/8	0 0/8	20 1/8	18 0/8	20 1/8	20 1/8	5	6	3 7/8	3 7/8	1990	Union	Duane Bernard	4

Typical Eastern Whitetail—Shed Antlers
Minimum Score: 60 0/8

Final Score	Subtotal	Abnormal Points	Main Beam	First Point	Second Point	Third Point	Fourth Point	First Circumference	Right/Left	Year	County	Owner's Name	Rank
79 2/8	79 2/8	0 0/8	25 4/8	3 3/8	12 5/8	13 1/8	7 5/8	4 5/8	Right	1995	Umatilla	Mike Bosworth	1
78 5/8	78 5/8	0 0/8	25 3/8	3 5/8	14 2/8	12 5/8	7 0/8	4 6/8	Left	1995	Umatilla	Mike Bosworth	2
72 7/8	72 7/8	0 0/8	23 4/8	4 0/8	12 2/8	10 6/8	6 7/8	4 0/8	Right	1987	Union	Joe Watkins	3

Official Scoring System for Oregon Big Game Trophies

Records of Oregon
Big Game

RECORD BOOK FOR OREGON

P.O. Box 759
Irrigon, OR 97844

NON-TYPICAL
WHITETAIL DEER

DETAIL OF POINT MEASUREMENT

Abnormal Points

Right Antler	Left Antler
0 0/8	9 1/8
0 0/8	0 0/8
0 0/8	0 0/8
0 0/8	0 0/8
0 0/8	0 0/8
0 0/8	0 0/8
0 0/8	0 0/8
0 0/8	0 0/8
0 0/8	0 0/8
0 0/8	0 0/8
Subtotals 0 0/8	9 1/8
Total to E	9 1/8

Species	Rifle	Archery	Muzzle	Shed	Archery - Velvet
Virginia Whitetail	160	140	160	70	140
Columbia Whitetail	All	All	All	All	All

					COLUMN 1 Spread Credit	COLUMN 2 Right Antler	COLUMN 3 Left Antler	COLUMN 4 Difference
A	No. of Points on Right Antler	5	No. of Points on Left Antler	6				
B	Tip to Tip Spread	9 4/8	C Greatest Spread	18 1/8				
D	Inside Spread of Main Beam	15 4/8	(Credit may be equal to but not exceed longer antler)		15 4/8			
E	Total of Length of Abnormal Points			9 1/8				
F	Length of Main Beam					22 6/8	21 6/8	1 0/8
G-1	Length of First Point					4 1/8	3 4/8	0 5/8
G-2	Length of Second Point					8 0/8	8 0/8	0 0/8
G-3	Length of Third Point					8 2/8	9 0/8	0 6/8
G-4	Length of Fourth Point					5 4/8	5 6/8	0 2/8
G-5	Length of Fifth Point					0 0/8	0 0/8	0 0/8
G-6	Length of Sixth Point, If Present					0 0/8	0 0/8	0 0/8
G-7	Length of Seventh Point, If Present					0 0/8	0 0/8	0 0/8
H-1	Circumference at smallest place between 1st and 2nd points					4 3/8	4 2/8	0 1/8
H-2	Circumference at smallest place between 2nd and 3rd points					3 5/8	3 6/8	0 1/8
H-3	Circumference at smallest place between 3rd and 4th points					3 4/8	3 3/8	0 1/8
H-4	Circumference at smallest place between 4th and 5th points					3 4/8	3 3/8	0 1/8
				TOTALS	15 4/8	63 5/8	62 6/8	3 1/8

County where killed: Umatilla Date Killed: 08/95	Column 1	15 4/8
Hunter's Name: Dustin Breshears **ADD**	Column 2	63 5/8
Owner's Name: Dustin Breshears	Column 3	62 6/8
	Subtotal	141 7/8
	Subtract Column 4	3 1/8
	Subtotal	138 6/8
	ADD Line E	9 1/8
	FINAL SCORE	**147 7/8**

Official Scoring System for Oregon Big Game Trophies

Records of Oregon
Big Game

RECORD BOOK FOR OREGON

P.O. Box 759
Irrigon, OR 97844

NON-TYPICAL WHITETAIL DEER

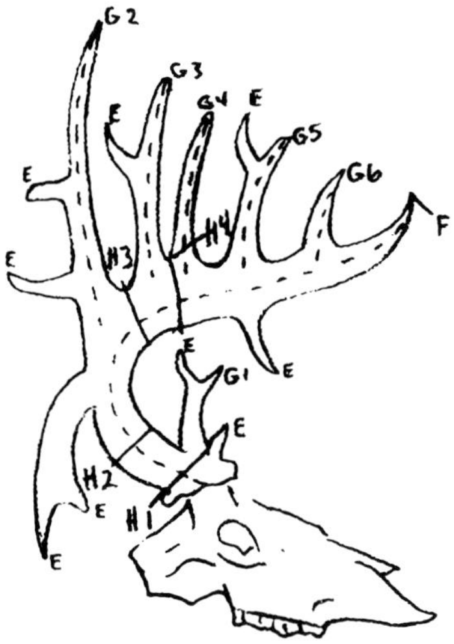

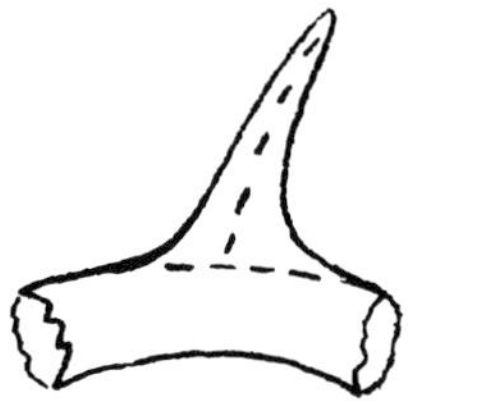

DETAIL OF POINT MEASUREMENT

Abnormal Points

Right Antler	Left Antler
4 5/8	2 1/8
3 4/8	4 3/8
2 6/8	3 1/8
6 3/8	0 0/8
2 4/8	0 0/8
3 0/8	0 0/8
0 0/8	0 0/8
0 0/8	0 0/8
0 0/8	0 0/8
0 0/8	0 0/8
Subtotals 22 6/8	9 5/8
Total to E	32 3/8

Species	Rifle	Archery	Muzzle	Shed	Archery - Velvet
Virginia Whitetail	160	140	160	70	140
Columbia Whitetail	All	All	All	All	All

					COLUMN 1	COLUMN 2	COLUMN 3	COLUMN 4
A	No. of Points on Right Antler	11	No. of Points on Left Antler	9	Spread Credit	Right Antler	Left Antler	Difference
B	Tip to Tip Spread	13 6/8	C Greatest Spread	22 6/8				
D	Inside Spread of Main Beam	20 2/8	(Credit may be equal to but not exceed longer antler)		20 2/8			
E	Total of Length of Abnormal Points			32 3/8				
F	Length of Main Beam					25 7/8	24 1/8	1 6/8
G-1	Length of First Point					7 6/8	7 4/8	0 2/8
G-2	Length of Second Point					8 4/8	8 5/8	0 1/8
G-3	Length of Third Point					10 1/8	9 7/8	0 2/8
G-4	Length of Fourth Point					7 0/8	8 5/8	1 5/8
G-5	Length of Fifth Point					0 0/8	2 7/8	2 7/8
G-6	Length of Sixth Point, If Present					0 0/8	0 0/8	0 0/8
G-7	Length of Seventh Point, If Present					0 0/8	0 0/8	0 0/8
H-1	Circumference at smallest place between 1st and 2nd points					5 5/8	5 3/8	0 2/8
H-2	Circumference at smallest place between 2nd and 3rd points					4 6/8	4 6/8	0 0/8
H-3	Circumference at smallest place between 3rd and 4th points					4 4/8	4 4/8	0 0/8
H-4	Circumference at smallest place between 4th and 5th points					4 0/8	4 0/8	0 0/8
				TOTALS	20 2/8	78 1/8	80 2/8	7 1/8

County where killed: Umatilla	Date Killed: 1982		Column 1	20 2/8
Hunter's Name: Joe Mengore		**ADD**	Column 2	78 1/8
Owner's Name: Joe Mengore			Column 3	80 2/8
			Subtotal	178 5/8
			Subtract Column 4	7 1/8
			Subtotal	171 4/8
			ADD Line E	32 3/8
			FINAL SCORE	203 7/8

Eastern whitetail (non-typical),
Joe Mengore, 203 7/8 P.Y.,
Union County, 1982

Non-Typical Eastern Whitetail—Rifle
Minimum Score: 160 0/8

Final Score	Gross Typical	Net Typical	Abnormal Points	Greatest Spread	Inside Spread	Main Beam R	Main Beam L	Number of Points R	Number of Points L	First Circumference R	First Circumference L	Year	County	Hunter/Owner	Rank
203 7/8	178 5/8	171 4/8	32 3/8	22 6/8	20 3/8	25 7/8	24 1/8	11	9	5 5/8	5 3/8	1982	Union	Joe Mengore	1
198 4/8	192 0/8	180 7/8	17 5/8	20 4/8	18 1/8	26 4/8	26 7/8	10	8	5 0/8	4 7/8	1970	Wallowa	Preston Reynolds/Norm Been	2
178 2/8	158 6/8	153 7/8	24 3/8	24 0/8	20 5/8	21 5/8	20 4/8	7	9	5 5/8	5 4/8	1986	Wallowa	Tom Darnell	3
178 0/8	172 6/8	163 0/8	15 0/8	21 6/8	19 0/8	25 4/8	23 2/8	6	10	4 6/8	6 1/8	1982	Wallowa	ODF & W	4
165 6/8	170 6/8	159 1/8	6 5/8	25 4/8	22 7/8	24 6/8	24 4/8	8	5	5 1/8	5 5/8	1992	Union	Graham Derbyshire	5
157 5/8	147 3/8	144 3/8	13 2/8	18 1/8	18 5/8	22 3/8	22 2/8	9	6	3 6/8	3 7/8	1986	Union	Dan Turley	6

Non-Typical Eastern Whitetail—Archery (Velvet)
Minimum Score: 140 0/8

Final Score	Gross Typical	Net Typical	Abnormal Points	Greatest Spread	Inside Spread	Main Beam R	Main Beam L	Number of Points R	Number of Points L	First Circumference R	First Circumference L	Year	County	Hunter/Owner	Rank
147 7/8	141 7/8	138 6/8	9 1/8	18 1/8	15 4/8	22 6/8	21 6/8	5	6	4 3/8	4 2/8	1995	Umatilla	Dustin Breshears	1

Non-Typical Eastern Whitetail—Shed Antlers
Minimum Score: 70 0/8

Final Score	Subtotal	Abnormal Points	Main Beam	First Point	Second Point	Third Point	Fourth Point	First Circumference	Right/Left	Year	County	Owner's Name	Rank
77 7/8	74 2/8	3 5/8	22 1/8	6 5/8	12 7/8	9 5/8	4 7/8	4 5/8	Left	1992	Wallowa	David M. Morris	1
74 0/8	69 7/8	4 1/8	23 4/8	4 0/8	11 5/8	10 4/8	4 6/8	3 7/8	Left	1987	Union	Joe Watkins	2

Official Scoring System for Oregon Big Game Trophies

Records of Oregon Big Game

RECORD BOOK FOR OREGON

**P.O. Box 759
Irrigon, OR 97844**

TYPICAL
WHITETAIL DEER

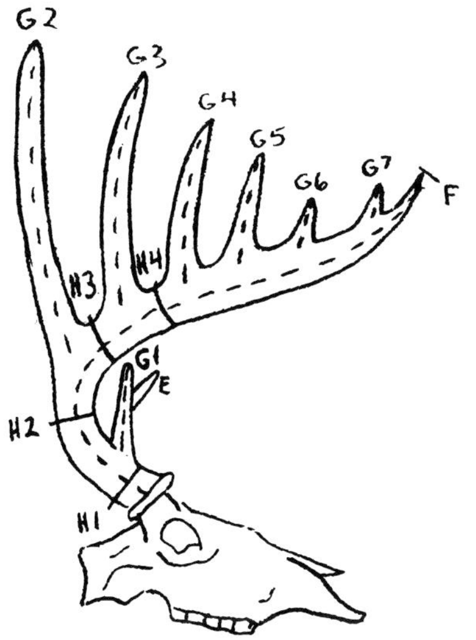

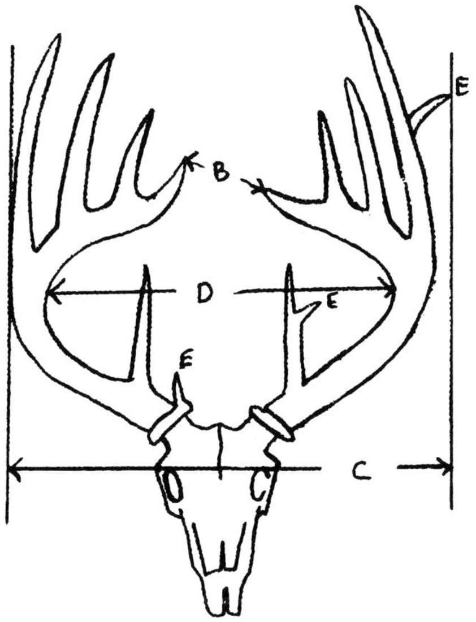

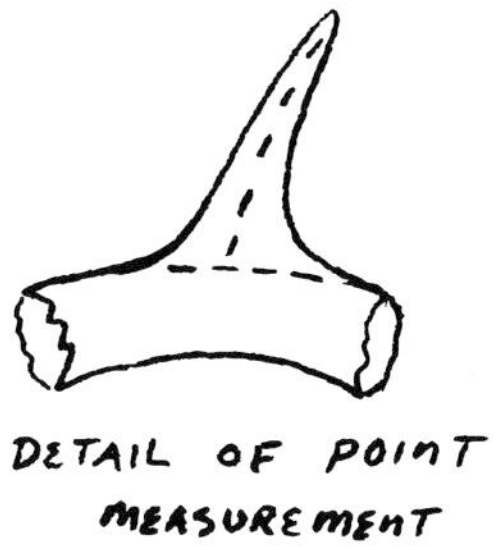

DETAIL OF POINT MEASUREMENT

Abnormal Points	
Right Antler	Left Antler
0 0/8	0 0/8
0 0/8	0 0/8
0 0/8	0 0/8
0 0/8	0 0/8
0 0/8	0 0/8
0 0/8	0 0/8
0 0/8	0 0/8
0 0/8	0 0/8
0 0/8	0 0/8
0 0/8	0 0/8
Subtotals 0 0/8	0 0/8
Total to E	0 0/8

Species	Rifle	Archery	Muzzle	Shed	Archery-Velvet
Eastern Whitetail	130	125	125	60	125
Columbia Whitetail	All	All	All	All	All

					COLUMN 1	COLUMN 2	COLUMN 3	COLUMN 4
A	No. of Points on Right Antler	6	No. of Points on Left Antler	6	Spread Credit	Right Antler	Left Antler	Difference
B	Tip to Tip Spread	12 1/8	**C** Greatest Spread	17 4/8				
D	Inside Spread of Main Beam	15 4/8	(Credit may be equal to but not exceed longer antler)		15 4/8			
E	Total of Length of Abnormal Points							0 0/8
F	Length of Main Beam					21 6/8	20 4/8	1 2/8
G-1	Length of First Point					4 5/8	5 3/8	0 6/8
G-2	Length of Second Point					9 3/8	10 1/8	0 6/8
G-3	Length of Third Point					9 6/8	8 6/8	1 0/8
G-4	Length of Fourth Point					7 3/8	6 1/8	1 2/8
G-5	Length of Fifth Point					2 7/8	2 4/8	0 3/8
G-6	Length of Sixth Point, If Present					0 0/8	0 0/8	0 0/8
G-7	Length of Seventh Point, If Present					0 0/8	0 0/8	0 0/8
H-1	Circumference at smallest place between 1st and 2nd points					4 0/8	4 0/8	0 0/8
H-2	Circumference at smallest place between 2nd and 3rd points					3 6/8	3 7/8	0 1/8
H-3	Circumference at smallest place between 3rd and 4th points					3 6/8	3 7/8	0 1/8
H-4	Circumference at smallest place between 4th and 5th points					3 4/8	3 4/8	0 0/8
				TOTALS	15 4/8	70 6/8	68 5/8	5 5/8

County where killed: Douglas	Date Killed: 1949		
Hunter's Name: Joe DeMarsh	**ADD**	Column 1	15 4/8
Owner's Name: Joe DeMarsh		Column 2	70 6/8
		Column 3	68 5/8
		Subtotal	154 7/8
		Subtract Column 4	5 5/8
		FINAL SCORE	**149 2/8**

Whitetail Buck

by Jon Comstock

From the 1950s through the early 1970s, pheasant hunting around the Roseburg area was great. That was before many of the large farms and ranches were subdivided. Whitetail deer were plentiful and were found in the same fenceline cover and Scotch broom patches as the pheasants. Because the seasons coincided, it was our habit to carry a couple of buckshot and slugloads in case we jumped a whitetail buck. In those days, one seldom saw a whitetail above an elevation of seven hundred to eight hundred feet; they were, and still are, deer of the valley floors. The day I killed the whitetail, I was hunting pheasants on my Uncle Frank's ranch. I saw him go into a Scotch broom patch, and we quickly changed our pheasant loads for slugs and buckshot. We walked through the Scotch broom patch and didn't jump the buck, but the patch was only fifty by one hundred feet and I knew he had to be in it.

After an argument with my partner about my eyesight, I decided to go back through the Scotch broom. After taking a couple of steps, the buck exploded practically under my feet. I snapped off a quick shot just as he went into a scrub oak and ash patch, and I could see that I had hit him a little far back. We decided to let him stiffen up rather than chase him, and we got my Uncle Frank with his 30-30 Winchester to help us. We found the buck after fifteen minutes of tracking. The buck was hit behind the diaphragm in the paunch, liver and the edge of one lung and was still moving. Uncle Frank broke the buck's neck, ending the chase.

Uncle Frank is gone now and without him the buck may have been lost. I'm glad that his name will appear with mine in the *Record Book for Oregon's Big Game Animals.*
(Final score: 142 4/8 B.C.)

Columbian whitetail (non-typical),
174 0/8 B.C.,
Douglas County, 1940

Typical Columbian Whitetail—Rifle
Minimum Score: All

Final Score	Gross Typical	Net Typical	Abnormal Points	Greatest Spread	Inside Spread	Main Beam R	Main Beam L	Number of Points R	Number of Points L	First Circumference R	First Circumference L	Year	County	Hunter/Owner	Rank
149 2/8	154 7/8	149 5/8	0 0/8	17 4/8	15 4/8	21 6/8	20 4/8	6	6	4 0/8	4 0/8	1949	Douglas	Joe DeMarsh	1
142 4/8	149 1/8	145 0/8	2 4/8	20 6/8	17 4/8	23 6/8	23 3/8	6	6	5 1/8	5 1/8	1963	Douglas	Frank Grubbe/Jon Comstock	2
133 6/8	135 6/8	133 6/8	0 0/8	19 0/8	17 0/8	22 6/8	22 2/8	4	4	4 5/8	4 5/8	1962	Clatsop	Robert L. Brown	3
128 4/8	136 0/8	128 4/8	0 0/8	20 4/8	19 0/8	23 3/8	18 2/8	4	4	4 3/8	4 4/8	1995	Douglas	ODF & W	4
118 2/8	122 3/8	118 2/8	0 0/8	17 0/8	15 2/8	20 2/8	20 2/8	4	4	5 3/8	3 6/8	1966	Douglas	W.L. Singleton	5
101 6/8	106 3/8	104 0/8	2 2/8	15 1/8	13 4/8	16 3/8	16 3/8	4	5	3 7/8	3 6/8	1968	Douglas	ODF & W	6
97 1/8	104 6/8	101 7/8	4 6/8	16 4/8	14 7/8	16 6/8	16 5/8	4	6	3 6/8	3 7/8	1985	Douglas	ODF & W	7
95 3/8	106 4/8	101 2/8	5 7/8	17 4/8	14 6/8	17 0/8	17 6/8	6	5	3 4/8	3 4/8	1959	Marion	George Veal/Kerry Veal	8
88 4/8	94 6/8	88 4/8	0 0/8	17 0/8	14 6/8	16 4/8	16 0/8	3	4	3 2/8	3 2/8				9

Non-Typical Columbian Whitetail—Rifle
Minimum Score: All

Final Score	Gross Typical	Net Typical	Abnormal Points	Greatest Spread	Inside Spread	Main Beam R	Main Beam L	Number of Points R	Number of Points L	First Circumference R	First Circumference L	Year	County	Hunter/Owner	Rank
174 0/8	130 4/8	126 5/8	47 3/8	20 5/8	16 7/8	19 3/8	21 1/8	11	8	4 1/8	4 3/8	1940	Douglas	David M. Morris	1
157 7/8	147 0/8	142 4/8	15 3/8	20 4/8	16 4/8	20 6/8	21 6/8	9	8	5 0/8	5 0/8	1957	Douglas	Sharon Polley	2
107 1/8	106 4/8	101 2/8	5 7/8	17 4/8	14 6/8	17 0/8	17 6/8	6	5	3 4/8	3 4/8	1985	Douglas	ODF&W	3
105 1/8	104 0/8	100 3/8	4 6/8	16 4/8	14 7/8	16 6/8	16 5/8	4	6	3 6/8	3 7/8	1968	Douglas	ODF&W	4

Roosevelt Elk

State Record Roosevelt Elk (Rifle)

by Robert Sharp

The season ran from October 25 through November 30, 1949. When it turned out that my falling partner couldn't hunt after all, I had decided to hunt an area I had scouted before, south and west of Saddle Mountain, south of Seaside and Cannon Beach, north of Highway 53, in Clatsop County.

With my .30-06 Enfield rifle, a cleaver, a small knife, a coffee can full of food and Alaskan packboard, I left the Gode Valley camp area before daylight. I had to feel my way across an old railroad trestle: a very dark and story night had preceded, and daylight was long in coming. I was glad of this blustery weather, as it cleans the leaves from the trees—also makes for a quiet approach. Now on the north side of the North Fork of the Nehalem River, with daylight coming on, I thought of my approach into this vast area. Believing I would be the only fool to hunt this area, I felt at ease to hunt on my way: that is, just to get lost and keep the wind in my face as much as possible. I watched carefully for any movement while hunting along very slowly. There were lots of deer, two nice bucks, and above all, there was a coyote packing a large piece of meat—looked like a ham from a deer fawn. He paid me no mind, as I did him.

The weather cleared a bit, but the fog coming in was forming into snow; that happens on the coast, where one has to tolerate numerous and often extreme weather changes in a day. The elk scent was strong, and I was in a low area, so I couldn't see much. (I have argued this with many, but my thought is that if you have never picked up the smell of deer, elk or bear when you're hunting, then you are staying too close to your horse or vehicle.) I crossed a small creek and crested a ridge, and there they were, about twenty or more elk with two spikes. I worked back, trying not to spook them; all went well, and I made tracks getting away from them. The area I was coming into now was one of tall fern and berry vine. I started to go under an area of brush vine maple and hemlock with lots of cedar windfalls, but then something told me, No, go above them . . . gosh knows why. So I proceeded to go above, only to come to a cedar windfall I had to climb like a ladder to get over. On the other side of the log my packboard didn't feel right, so I set down my rifle and took the board off. Set to go again, I checked my scope; I hadn't moved yet, and still didn't, because I had the strangest feeling. I suddenly realized that fifty feet in front of me there stood an enormous bull. I hadn't noticed him before, and now couldn't believe my eyes: such a big, big animal! I wasn't in a position to shoot and all I could see were his rump and horns. I had no place to go, so it was up to the bull to make a move. With my safety off, I stood and waited. Now as I glanced around to see what would happen next, I could not believe it, but there stood another bull, facing me. I supposed he hadn't seen a man before: with his head lowered, his ears perked, he stood like a statue looking straight at me. I placed the cross hairs on his left ear and moved a little to the right, which would put the impact of the bullet on the base of his neck. I didn't really feel the rifle go off when I shot; the bull laid his head back, mouth open and just stood there. I placed the second shot a foot lower and he went down like a ton of bricks. I didn't see the first bull leave, and never knew what happened to him. I can't imagine his big rack; I never really got a good look at any part except for his rump. If his horns matched his hind end, then he was big.

I had his buddy on the ground, though, and I approached this big boy carefully and stuck the barrel into his eye to make sure he was dead. He had slid forward onto his head and I was unable to move him. So I got my cleaver and whacked the head off. It took some time to free the head, but I was careful because this bull was big. I gutted him on his side, and then skinned and butchered him on the hide. I boned the meat as I cut him up, placing the meat on a log next to me.

Official Scoring System for Oregon Big Game Trophies

Records of Oregon
Big Game

RECORD BOOK FOR OREGON

P.O. Box 759
Irrigon, OR 97844

TYPICAL
ROOSEVELT ELK

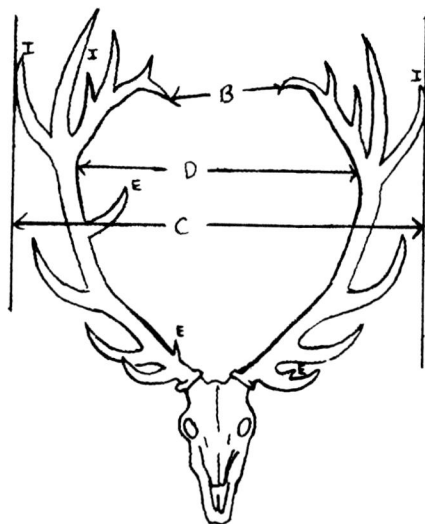

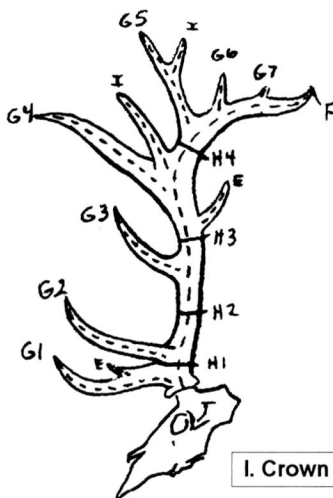

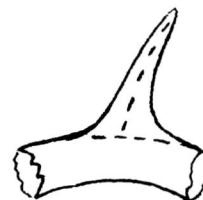

DETAIL OF POINT
MEASUREMENT

Crown Points		
	Right Antler	Left Antler
	10 6/8	11 0/8
	0 0/8	0 0/8
	0 0/8	0 0/8
	0 0/8	0 0/8
	0 0/8	0 0/8
I. Crown Points Total		21 6/8

Abnormal Points		
	Right Antler	Left Antler
	0 0/8	0 0/8
	0 0/8	0 0/8
	0 0/8	0 0/8
	0 0/8	0 0/8
	0 0/8	0 0/8
Subtotals	0 0/8	0 0/8
Total to E		0 0/8

Species	Rifle	Archery	Muzzle	Shed
Roosevelt Elk	260	210	225	100
Cascade Roosevelt Elk	260	210	225	100

					COLUMN 1	COLUMN 2	COLUMN 3	COLUMN 4
					Spread Credit	Right Antler	Left Antler	Difference
A	No. of Points on Right	9	No. of Points on Left Antler	8				
B	Tip to Tip Spread	40 3/8	C Greatest Spread	49 1/8				
D	Inside Spread of Main Beam	41 1/8	(Credit may be equal to but not exceed longer antler)		41 1/8			
E	Total of Length of Abnormal Points							0 0/8
F	Length of Main Beam					48 4/8	49 0/8	0 4/8
G-1	Length of First Point					14 0/8	15 5/8	1 5/8
G-2	Length of Second Point					15 1/8	14 0/8	1 1/8
G-3	Length of Third Point					14 7/8	14 4/8	0 3/8
G-4	Length of Fourth Point					19 5/8	17 4/8	2 1/8
G-5	Length of Fifth Point					13 6/8	12 1/8	
G-6	Length of Sixth Point, If Present					1 7/8	6 6/8	
G-7	Length of Seventh Point, If Present					2 4/8	0 0/8	
H-1	Circumference at smallest place between 1st and 2nd points					8 7/8	9 4/8	0 5/8
H-2	Circumference at smallest place between 2nd and 3rd points					7 4/8	8 0/8	0 4/8
H-3	Circumference at smallest place between 3rd and 4th points					8 2/8	8 0/8	0 2/8
H-4	Circumference at smallest place between 4th and 5th points					9 3/8	10 1/8	0 6/8
				TOTALS	41 1/8	164 2/8	165 1/8	7 7/8

County where killed: Clatsop	Date Killed: 1949			
Hunter's Name:	Bob	Sharp	ADD	Column 1	41 1/8
Owner's Name:	Robert	Sharp		Column 2	164 2/8

Column 1	41 1/8
Column 2	164 2/8
Column 3	165 1/8
Total of I	21 6/8
Subtotal	392 2/8
Subtract Column 4	7 7/8
FINAL SCORE	384 3/8

I had to make a move quickly as time was going fast. I loaded the heart, liver, neck and some small parts in the packboard with the head

upside down on the pack. I didn't get far that way, as the horns got hung up all the time, so I packed them over one shoulder. I went east as fast as possible; I needed to reach the ridge I had been on before, which was a good elk trail. Before I realized where I was, I left the pack and ran up the trail quite a distance, but as luck would have it, I came out on a flat at the end of a railroad grade. Someone had built a fire there earlier in the day and it was still warm. I ran down the hill, gathered my stuff and returned to the fire,

hiding the head. I took the cleaver and can of food and headed out the grade to the east, marking the spans as I came to them. Finally giving in to hunger, I ate; by then it was dark and I was cold, wet and tired. With blood all over me, I knew I was in for a long night, and I had no way of knowing how far it was out.

I had either to feel my way out or hole up, which promised a miserable night. I had no matches so I felt I had let myself down, but there was no use in worrying about that. My main concern was for my family, since they didn't know where I had gone; but I felt good that I had a big bull. I was working my way on the grade, when I heard a vehicle in the distance. It was a good sound and gave me a lot of encouragement.

After quite some time I fell off the railroad grade right onto Highway 53. What a relief. I felt out some big rocks to mark the side of the road. Then I headed west not knowing how far it was to my car; it took forever to get there and no traffic had come by—no one would have loaded me in anyhow. I would have missed my car except for a slight reflection of the sky in the head lamp.

Knowing my family was worried, I got home near midnight. With my friend, Gif Raymond, I returned the next morning with food, a gas lantern, rope, shovel, axe and my rusty old Ford car. We backed up the grade; it took some effort to get the Ford on the grade and I did abuse it a little. With the axe and shovel we cleared the railroad grade to the fire, and then the work began. I hoped a bear, cat or coyote hadn't got into my meat pile. I took another look at the head before I went back down the trail. I knew this was a day to remember, and couldn't believe all the meat on this one animal. We packed all day and into the night. It was a mile uphill to my car from where I had killed the bull, I had put my Ford on the railroad grade some four miles from the highway, and I had covered approximately three miles before I had killed the bull: yes, I was one tired, worn-out dude. (The map showed that I was still a quarter of a mile from Grassy Lake and still in Grassy Lake Creek drainage. I have hunted some of this area for deer, and another time I got a nice five-point elk.)

I took the gas lantern and stopped and cooked myself a piece of meat without salt; it was just filling. My wife said this was the toughest I ever brought home. All my family are successful hunters, now both my sons have killed big bulls and lots of them.

I dedicate all this to my Helen, wife of fifty years, and to my sons Bob and Ben: to my sons for being great outdoorsmen and hunters, and to my wife for her hard work at cutting, wrapping and cleaning up after us.
(Final score: 384 3/8 B.C.)

World Record Roosevelt

by Thomas C. Stacer

In September of 1985, with only two days remaining in Oregon's bowhunting season for elk, Dale Baumgartner was sitting in a tree stand high above a much-used elk trail in an abandoned homestead area that was carved out of the Siuslaw National Forest in the late years of the 1930s. He was intent upon bagging a trophy elk. The trail led from a cedar grove on the edge of the Douglas fir forest into the old farm. An elk herd had been making periodic visits to the area to graze and snip berry bushes.

With his Martin-Lynx Magnum bow, Dale sat patiently waiting for the huge bull elk to enter the old farm area. He felt confident that the big elk, a huge Roosevelt, was master of the herd. The large elk had been seen by Dale and others on the mountain slopes of the coast range, but the animal had not been seen since the bow season started.

The early Oregon season for elk had advantages for a bowhunter: less hunters were present and the bow season was during the start of the elk rut.

Dale purchased his first bow in the spring of 1984 and practiced target shooting during the season of that year. Dale set up a homemade archery range in his backyard with six-inch pie plates as targets and three hay bales. The new archer limited his shooting distance to between ten and thirty yards. During the 1984 bow season, Dale's bowhunting for elk was a bust: he had problems with arrow direction and his first bow broke a limb. He needed advice from veteran bowhunters, but his enthusiasm for the new venture remained high.

During the spring of 1985 Dale was in the Bend, Oregon area. There he met Del and Bobbie Moore of Del's Archery Den. Both owners are avid archers. They became Dale's mentors and, in doing so, determined that the new bowman had problems—mainly with his short draw length. Dale is thirty-four years of age, slightly built and stands a little over five feet three inches in boots. A new bow was needed, so the Martin-Lynx Magnum was chosen to replace Dale's first bow. The Martin bow was set to pull sixty-three pounds.

Elk are among the most popular North American big game animals. The Pope and Young Club, as well as the Boone and Crockett Club, have established records for elk trophies taken by bowhunters. The clubs have recognized

the Roosevelt elk as a separate classification. These elk inhabit the coastal areas of British Columbia, Oregon, Washington and upper California, along with the Alaska coastal areas. Herd sizes vary. It was on the slopes of the Oregon coast range, near Mount Hebo, a 3,174-foot

mountain behind Beaver, Oregon, that Dale had scouted and located the Hebo herd. The elk frequented the upper slopes of the coast range in the summer and moved to lower areas, including the old homestead area, in the fall and winter. Dale was sure the huge Roosevelt that had been seen in the winter and summer was still using the homestead area.

As a native of Hebo, a small town located along the Oregon coast, Dale was familiar with the homestead area and knew the elk claimed the old homestead as a place to make periodic visits during the year. The old place was the size of a football field, but spotted with small fir trees in clumps; grasses were abundant in the area as were bracken fern and some berry bushes. It was ideal elk habitat.

In preparation for the bow season, Dale kept his camouflaged clothing in sealed plastic bags with fir bough tips to avoid any unusual scent. Bull elk urine was obtained and kept for use on boots at hunting time. A tree stand had to be located. A large spruce tree was found immediately adjacent to the old farm just into the forest which fringed the area. The tree was within a short range of a well-used elk trail in the old meadow. The trail stemmed from a cedar grove on the forest edge and continued into the open area and past the tree stand. The fifteen-foot high tree stand would provide the bowhunter with an arrow shot of twenty-five yards.

The 1985 Oregon elk bowhunting season finally arrived. The elk herd had used the homestead area just before the season opened, but abruptly vanished. Dale checked on the homestead area often, but no elk. Thus he found himself at the tail end of the elk season for bowhunters with only a Saturday and Sunday left to bag the fabled elk. But he was confident: the elk rut was on and the Hebo herd had to be near.

He checked the homestead for fresh elk sign Saturday afternoon. There was fresh elk sign. The herd had been at the homestead area early Saturday and should return later in the day.

Dale wore camouflaged clothing with a head net. He crossed the meadow to his tree stand without touching ferns, brush or small fir limbs; his boots left little human scent, since they were painted with bull urine. He climbed the ladder on the spruce tree and seated himself on the tree stand, then placed an arrow to his right for quick use if necessary.

All was quiet. Maybe too quiet. In such a situation, a hunter takes notice of everything; Dale was no exception. He had full view of the homestead and kept a sharp lookout for elk. There was no doubt in his mind that the herd would return.

Dale had been on the stand more than an hour when the sun began sinking into the tips of the tall firs which ringed the homestead. Hunting time was winding down as Dale looked into the last of the sun's rays. Dale waited; things had to happen!

A noise was heard—a small noise only. Near the cedar grove entrance to the old area, Dale sensed something. Then he heard a snapping of underbrush. Small noises, but very distinct. He braced himself, but to no avail; again the whole area was silent. He later recalled:

I heard the brush noise and I knew there was going to be some action. But then, the forest and the old area went silent again. I was getting nervous at the silence. All I could do was wait, look and listen.

A short time afterward, action did come. But it seemed an endless time for the bowhunter sitting on his carpeted stand. Near the cedar grove, above the shoulder-high salmonberries and huckleberry brush, Dale made out the nose of a cow elk. No doubt about it, the herd was returning.

Very slowly the cow elk moved into the open area of the old homestead, her nose still held high. She was a big cow—and a cautious elk. Swinging her head from side to side, the big cow continuously kept sniffing the air. A lead cow! *The vanguard of the Hebo herd*, Dale hoped. The elk moved further into the meadow area, then, apparently satisfied, started to browse on grasses and snip salmonberry leaves. Dale froze on his stand. He recounted:

It was hard to imagine how carefully that cow elk tested the wind. I was shaking! I

knew I had put on bug repellent and figured that was probably a mistake.

Watching from the tree stand, it was only moments later that Dale saw two other cow elk make appearances into the old farm area. The newcomers, following the lead cow, also started grazing and snipping. The three elk moved about, coming near the spruce tree, almost below the tree stand. Dale remained motionless.

With a suddenness, three bull elk burst into the old area: two spikes and a forkhorn. They were immature bulls, but sizable and magnificent. The bulls moved hastily about the homestead area in a skittish manner. None of the bull elk was interested in the cow elk, but each bull kept glancing at the trail entrance to the homestead—as if expecting an immediate challenge.

Both the cows and the bulls were legal game, but Dale still believed there was a bigger elk bull that would appear. He held fire; he knew if he was spotted in his stand, all elk would vanish. All his summer's preparations were at stake. The big elk had to appear with the Hebo herd. Dale was not disappointed.

Suddenly, by no timed signal, the air was shattered by a stupendous elk bugle. The bull elk's piercing cry! The bugle was followed by boisterous, guttural bull grunts: sounds coming from the backside of the spruce tree—only one bugle. Then two more cow elk trotted hurriedly into the old farm area and moved along the elk trail. They joined the other cow elk. Additionally, more of the herd appeared. Six more cow elk came into the homestead on a fast trot. The herd was arriving. Dale, still sitting on the stand, shook with excitement; his patience was being strained.

With a crash of brush and small trees, a big Roosevelt bull made his appearance—a huge animal. He was pushing more cow elk into the old meadow at a fast pace. It was a big animal, with an enormous rack. The antlers on the Roosevelt were of trophy size—maybe even record size. The huge animal instantly saw the three lesser bulls, lowered its head and rushed the smaller elk, which were now running to the far timber cover. Dale related the event:

> The big Roosevelt lit out after the spikes and forked horn on the run. As he rushed the other bulls, the Roosevelt let out enormous grunts. The big animal rushed the lesser bulls the length of the old area—and right into the timber, downslope. Those three bulls didn't hesitate; they left the area.

After ridding the old area of the younger bulls, the huge Roosevelt looked back into the meadow area. Still panting, the huge elk turned and slowly moved in the direction of the cow elk. Dale remembered:

> The big elk came back about seventy-five yards from my tree stand; right in front of him were a bunch of small fir trees. He walked over to the clump of trees and with a big grunt, tackled a twelve-foot fir tree. He really laid into that tree! With that huge rack, he just swung it up and down on the tree—shredding fir limbs and utterly debarking the fir. That tree is dead today. I knew the big elk was mad and had the cows on his mind; the rut was on.

The big Roosevelt took his anger out on the small fir, then moved nearer to the cow elk. A late cow elk had just entered the old farm area and the big elk decided to bring this cow in line with the other cow elk. The huge bull edged closer to the spruce tree, along the elk trail, intent on the cows. Dale knew the elk was nearing the good bow range. He cooled down a bit and quit hyperventilating. By sheer instinct, the Roosevelt stopped, lifted his huge rack and looked directly at Dale in the tree stand. Dale and the bull elk did a staredown. For a time, neither moved. After an eternity, the huge bull lowered its head and resumed along the elk trail to the cows which had continued grazing near the spruce tree. A whole summer's planning was reaching its peak: the fa-

bled Roosevelt was coming within bow range. Dale explains:

> I knew then if the big elk brought the cow back in front of the stand, I would stand up, pull back and release, all in the same motion. And that's exactly what the bull did; he came within twenty-five yards. I stood up and shot! I hit the animal broadside in the chest area. It was a lethal arrow—no doubt. I saw the shot: the arrow struck deep, leaving only some arrow and colored fletch showing.

When hit, the Roosevelt wavered slightly; he knew something had happened. The elk moved around a clump of small trees in the old area, then slowly headed toward the cedar grove entrance to the forested area. The huge bull completely ignored his cows now.

Although hard hit, the elk made it to the cedar grove, then stood at the entrance of the grove for several minutes looking back toward the tree stand area. The huge elk stood stone still, as if waiting for the pursuit of the bowhunter. Dale recounted:

> I knew I had the big bull; he was mine. A giant! I stood on the stand watching the Roosevelt move into the forested area. I slid down the ladder of the spruce to ground level and things went wild. Really wild! Those cow elk spotted me instantly; they just couldn't believe that there had been somebody in that spruce tree.

When Dale touched ground, there was a confused rush of cow elk in the homestead area. Elk cows turned in every direction and beat it into the heavy timber fringing the old farm. The cows were gone in seconds; the herd had vanished.

Quickly the bowhunter crossed the meadow area to the cedar grove entrance. Blood was on leaves, bushes and ground. The huge elk had pushed randomly into the forest undercover and downslope by a creekside. Dale followed. It was, at first, an easy trail, but the late afternoon sunlight into the forest was dimming. Dale reached in his pack for the always present flashlight; it was there, but gave only a faint glimmer of light. Dale sought a roll of plastic tape from his pack—tape to mark trails. The roll was not to be found; it had been packed with other hunting gear. Returning to the homestead area, Dale decided to continue tracking the huge elk on Sunday.

Dale, his brother Richard and buddy Ken Sisco drove the old logging road and went upslope to the old farm area early Sunday morning. Locating the trail of the Roosevelt, they soon retrieved the huge elk, displaying a big seven-by-eight rack and full bodied, heavy stemmed antlers. It was a true trophy elk.

Packing the trophy elk to the pickup on the logging road was a feat in itself—particularly the antlers—because they continually caught brush and small trees along the trail back to the homestead area. The packing job was not completed until noon on Monday.

On Monday afternoon, the rack was on display at Kimmel's Sporting Goods Store at Tillamook, Oregon. Ultimately, David Boys of Artistic Taxidermy of Portland, Oregon, mounted the huge elk head; Boys declared it the most magnificent head done by his shop. The mounted elk head was on exhibition at the Sportsmen's Show at Portland's Expo Center in February. At the show, the huge rack was given preliminary measurement by the founder and patron of the Pope and Young Club, Glenn St. Charles; he keenly predicted that the antlers would score high in the club's classification of Roosevelt elk, possibly in the top five, if not higher. Official measurements of the Roosevelt antlers could be made at the 1987 Pope and Young Club Bowhunters' Convention at Tulsa, Oklahoma, slated for March.

Dale's enthusiasm hit a high peak. He filed application with the Pope and Young Club for an official measurement of the Roosevelt rack. With the mounted head boxed securely, he shipped the trophy to Tulsa by motor freight. Club measurements of the antlers were made in mid-February—just before the convention date. Dale was requested to be present at the convention awards ceremony in late March. Both Dale and his wife, Cheryl, ticketed air flight to Tulsa and attended the three-day bowhunters' convention.

At the awards ceremony, Dale received a plaque for first prize in trophy competition. And, even more important, he received the Pope and Young Club plaque designating him as the holder of the World-Record Roosevelt elk classification for bowhunters. The big elk rack scored 352 1/8, a new record. And the newly-printed publication of the Club revealed Dale at the top of the Club's Roosevelt elk classification. As if to honor the huge Hebo elk, a full-page picture of the mounted head graces the glossy publication of the Club. Measurements of the Hebo elk antlers were published: "R-antler at 43 5/8; L-antler at 45 6/8; with antler spread at 40 0/8." The closest challenge to the Hebo rack is a score of 347 4/8.

Later, as a bonus to the record attained, Dale was informed that the directors of the Pope and Young Club had adopted new Roosevelt elk measurement procedures of the Boone and Crockett Club. Under the newly-adopted procedures the Hebo rack will gain 13 7/8 more points in total score—as the extra crown point on the rack would be considered. A supplemental score would be later issued by the Club, placing the Hebo antlers as a total Roosevelt classification of 366 0/8.

Today, the magnificent Hebo elk head, with its world record rack, hangs for show at Baumgartner's Auto Repair Shop in Hebo, Oregon. The shop is a whistle-clean showroom with numerous antlers and racks of animals taken over several years of hunting by Dale and his brother Richard. But the record Roosevelt rack is the center of attention.

(Final score: 367 3/8 P.Y.)

Official Scoring System for Oregon Big Game Trophies

Records of Oregon
Big Game

RECORD BOOK FOR OREGON

P.O. Box 759
Irrigon, OR 97844

TYPICAL
ROOSEVELT ELK

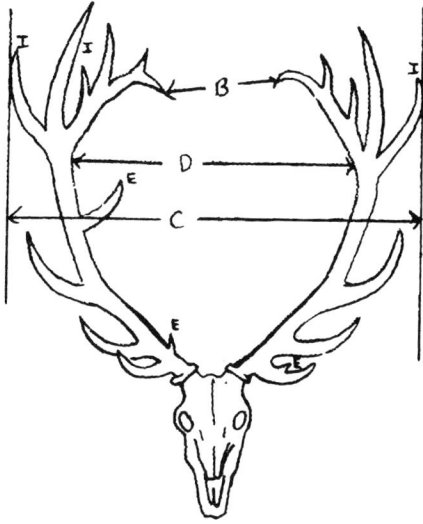

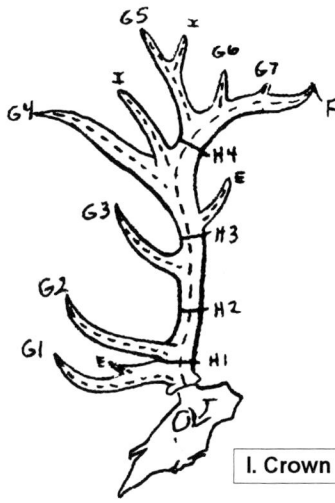

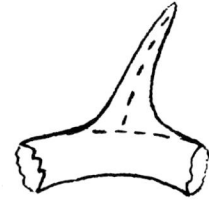

DETAIL OF POINT
MEASUREMENT

Crown Points

Right Antler		Left Antler	
0	0/8	13	7/8
0	0/8	0	0/8
0	0/8	0	0/8
0	0/8	0	0/8
0	0/8	0	0/8
I. Crown Points Total		13	7/8

Abnormal Points

Right Antler		Left Antler	
1	6/8	1	5/8
0	0/8	0	0/8
0	0/8	0	0/8
0	0/8	0	0/8
0	0/8	0	0/8
Subtotals	1	6/8	1	5/8
Total to E			3	3/8

Species	Rifle	Archery	Muzzle	Shed
Roosevelt Elk	260	210	225	100
Cascade Roosevelt Elk	260	210	225	100

					COLUMN 1	COLUMN 2	COLUMN 3	COLUMN 4
					Spread Credit	Right Antler	Left Antler	Difference
A	No. of Points on Right	7	No. of Points on Left Antler	8				
B	Tip to Tip Spread	39 2/8	**C** Greatest Spread	46 6/8				
D	Inside Spread of Main Beam	40 0/8	(Credit may be equal to but not exceed longer antler)		40 0/8			
E	Total of Length of Abnormal Points							3 3/8
F	Length of Main Beam					43 5/8	45 6/8	2 1/8
G-1	Length of First Point					16 2/8	16 4/8	0 2/8
G-2	Length of Second Point					18 0/8	17 3/8	0 5/8
G-3	Length of Third Point					19 2/8	20 2/8	1 0/8
G-4	Length of Fourth Point					17 6/8	15 4/8	2 2/8
G-5	Length of Fifth Point					13 7/8	15 2/8	
G-6	Length of Sixth Point, If Present					0 0/8	0 0/8	
G-7	Length of Seventh Point, If Present					0 0/8	0 0/8	
H-1	Circumference at smallest place between 1st and 2nd points					9 7/8	9 7/8	0 0/8
H-2	Circumference at smallest place between 2nd and 3rd points					7 4/8	8 0/8	0 4/8
H-3	Circumference at smallest place between 3rd and 4th points					7 0/8	7 3/8	0 3/8
H-4	Circumference at smallest place between 4th and 5th points					7 4/8	8 3/8	0 7/8
			TOTALS		40 0/8	160 5/8	164 2/8	11 3/8

County where killed: Tillamook	Date Killed: 1985			
Hunter's Name: Dale Baumgartner		**ADD**	Column 1	40 0/8
Owner's Name: Dale Baumgartner			Column 2	160 5/8
			Column 3	164 2/8
			Total of I	13 7/8
			Subtotal	378 6/8
			Subtract Column 4	11 3/8
			FINAL SCORE	**367 3/8**

Records of Oregon Big Game	**RECORD BOOK FOR OREGON**	P.O. Box 759 Irrigon, OR 97844

TYPICAL and NON-TYPICAL
ROOSEVELT ELK SHED ANTLERS

Crown Points	
Right Antler	Left Antler
3 2/8	8 3/8
8 6/8	6 7/8
2 4/8	14 6/8
0 0/8	0 0/8
0 0/8	0 0/8
14 4/8	30 0/8

Abnormal Points	
Right Antler	Left Antler
1 7/8	0 0/8
0 0/8	0 0/8
0 0/8	0 0/8
0 0/8	0 0/8
0 0/8	0 0/8

Species	Typical	Non-Typical
Roosevelt	100	110
Cascade Roosevelt	100	110

		Right Antler	Left Antler
E	Total of Length of Abnormal Points	1 7/8	0 0/8
F	Length of Main Beam	51 7/8	50 4/8
G-1	Length of First Point, if present	17 7/8	19 4/8
G-2	Length of Second Point	19 1/8	17 6/8
G-3	Length of Third Point, if present	19 6/8	16 5/8
G-4	Length of Fourth Point, if present	19 6/8	20 3/8
G-5	Length of Fifth Point	17 1/8	18 6/8
G-6	Length of Sixth Point, if present	0 0/8	0 0/8
G-7	Length of Seventh Point, if present	0 0/8	0 0/8
H-1	Circumference at smallest place between burr and 1st point	9 4/8	9 1/8
H-2	Circumference at smallest place between 1st and 2nd point	8 0/8	8 0/8
H-3	Circumference at smallest place between main beam and 3rd pt	8 4/8	8 3/8
H-4	Circumference at smallest place between 2nd and 4th points	8 6/8	9 0/8
	TOTALS	180 2/8	178 0/8
	CROWN PTS	14 4/8	30 0/8
	SUBTOTAL	194 6/8	208 0/8
	ABNORMAL POINTS*	1 7/8	0 0/8
	FINAL SCORE	192 7/8	208 0/8

County: Clackamas   Year Found: 1990

Owner's Name: Harold & Belva   Burroughs

Abnormal Points are subtracted if Typical and added if Non-Typical

Typical Roosevelt Elk—Rifle
Minimum Score: 260 0/8

Final Score	Gross Typical	Net Typical	Crown Points	Abnormal Points	Greatest Spread	Inside Spread	Main Beam R	Main Beam L	Number of Points R	Number of Points L	First Circumference R	First Circumference L	Year	County	Hunter/Owner	Rank
384 3/8	392 2/8	384 3/8	21 6/8	0 0/8	49 1/8	41 1/8	48 4/8	49 0/8	9	8	8 7/8	9 4/8	1949	Clatsop	Bob Sharp/Robert Sharp	1
378 5/8	385 4/8	378 5/8	11 2/8	0 0/8	41 3/8	37 0/8	53 2/8	51 3/8	7	9	8 7/8	8 5/8	1947	Clatsop	Fred M. Williamson/ Rusty Lindberg	2
366 5/8	376 1/8	366 5/8	40 7/8	0 0/8	47 2/8	36 1/8	44 3/8	46 4/3	7	8	9 6/8	9 5/8	1962	Columbia	Floyd M. Lindberg	3
363 7/8	369 1/8	363 7/8	15 7/8	0 0/8	42 0/8	37 4/8	46 1/8	45 6/8	7	7	9 4/8	9 1/8	1955	Lincoln	James H. Flescher	4
363 1/8	375 3/8	369 1/8	14 6/8	6 0/8	49 3/8	40 5/8	49 5/8	48 2/8	7	9	9 6/8	9 5/8	1907	Douglas	Bill Mattoon/ Douglas County Museum	5
363 1/8	365 6/8	363 1/8	16 1/8	0 0/8	46 4/8	43 4/8	46 6/8	46 5/8	7	8	9 0/8	9 0/8	1938	Clatsop	Oliver W. Dunsmoor/ Nora Dunsmoor	5
358 3/8	370 0/8	358 3/8	10 4/8	0 0/8	49 6/8	42 2/8	52 2/8	52 5/8	6	7	9 7/8	10 2/8	1938	Clatsop	Donald Schoenborn/ Eric Schoenborn	7
357 6/8	371 2/8	365 1/8	5 3/8	7 3/8	46 4/8	41 3/8	46 2/8	50 0/8	9	7	11 0/8	10 5/8	1958	Coos	Pete Scoville	8
351 7/8	360 6/8	351 7/8	27 2/8	0 0/8	50 4/8	46 6/8	46 4/8	49 2/8	8	7	9 4/8	9 4/8	1995	Clatsop	Steve Fick	9
350 3/8	363 2/8	351 4/8	9 2/8	1 1/8	46 2/8	35 7/8	47 6/8	47 4/8	8	8	11 1/8	11 7/8	1948	Coos	E.V. Schmidt	10
341 4/8	346 6/8	341 4/8	19 2/8	0 0/8	46 0/8	41 0/8	46 1/8	46 1/8	7	7	8 3/8	8 3/8	1928	Lane	Ed Stevens/Warner Pinkey	11
335 2/8	340 7/8	335 2/8	0 0/8	0 0/8	41 4/8	36 4/8	49 2/8	48 3/8	6	6	7 7/8	7 3/8	1992	Curry	Robert Lyons	12
334 6/8	336 5/8	334 6/8	3 7/8	0 0/8	42 4/8	42 2/8	46 4/8	46 2/8	8	8	8 3/8	8 2/8	1965	Clatsop	Perry Lee Haynes/Ronald Haynes	13
327 3/8	351 5/8	338 4/8	30 6/8	9 1/8	52 0/8	39 7/8	46 5/8	49 0/8	7	8	8 5/8	10 6/8			D.A.R. Cabin	14
323 2/8	343 5/8	339 1/8	5 6/8	15 7/8	45 7/8	40 0/8	52 0/8	51 3/8	7	8	10 1/8	9 4/8	1938	Clatsop	David Tweedie/Scott A. Seppa	15
322 3/8	351 5/8	338 5/8	17 3/8	16 2/8	47 1/8	38 1/8	47 6/8	44 5/8	8	7	8 7/8	9 2/8	1952	Columbia	Bill Curtis/Duane Bernard	16
318 1/8	325 1/8	318 1/8	0 0/8	0 0/8	43 2/8	40 5/8	47 1/8	47 0/8	8	6	8 1/8	8 0/8	1993	Douglas	David Williams	17
316 6/8	322 1/8	316 6/8	0 0/8	0 0/8	42 7/8	39 0/8	51 3/8	49 0/8	6	6	8 6/8	9 7/8	1969	Columbia	Harry Olsen/Fay Olsen	18
316 4/8	337 1/8	328 7/8	0 0/8	12 3/8	46 6/8	43 2/8	47 6/8	49 2/8	6	8	11 2/8	10 4/8	1884	Coos	Grandma Miller/Diane Singleton	19
315 4/8	325 2/8	315 4/8	0 0/8	0 0/8	46 0/8	42 0/8	48 2/8	47 7/8	6	6	9 4/8	9 0/8	1965	Columbia	Bill Curtis/Duane Bernard	20
314 5/8	324 4/8	314 5/8	6 1/8	0 0/8	37 2/8	31 3/8	45 3/8	46 3/8	7	7	9 6/8	10 7/8	1951	Clatsop	Mel Parker/Don Pillar	21
312 1/8	320 7/8	313 7/8	8 4/8	1 6/8	46 3/8	40 4/8	42 6/8	41 5/8	7	8	8 6/8	9 5/8	1995	Douglas	Leland Good	22
311 1/8	317 1/8	311 1/8	17 1/8	0 0/8	39 5/8	32 7/8	43 2/8	44 5/8	7	7	8 5/8	8 4/8				23
310 7/8	314 1/8	310 7/8	13 6/8	0 0/8	48 6/8	48 2/8	40 4/8	42 2/8	7	7	8 0/8	8 2/8	1957	Clatsop	Virgil E. Brown	24
305 7/8	310 4/8	305 7/8	0 0/8	0 0/8	41 5/8	37 3/8	44 4/8	44 7/8	6	6	10 2/8	10 5/8		Clatsop	Carol Seabold	25
302 4/8	322 3/8	302 4/8	7 5/8	0 0/8	44 1/8	43 2/8	51 7/8	52 3/8	6	7	9 7/8	9 6/8	1995		Terry Edmonson	26
301 3/8	309 1/8	301 3/8	6 2/8	0 0/8	40 1/8	37 2/8	47 7/8	46 4/8	7	7	8 0/8	7 6/8	1995		Andy Cole	27
294 5/8	299 0/8	294 5/8	0 0/8	0 0/8	46 2/8	43 1/8	46 5/8	46 1/8	6	6	9 0/8	8 3/8	1944	Clatsop	Nolen R. Schoenborn	28
294 1/8	302 3/8	294 1/8	2 6/8	0 0/8	45 2/8	45 2/8	46 1/8	43 2/8	6	7	8 2/8	7 1/8	1976	Washington	John Beavers, Jr.	29
291 7/8	301 7/8	291 7/8	10 5/8	0 0/8	42 2/8	38 6/8	38 3/8	39 4/8	6	7	8 0/8	9 4/8	1994	Douglas	Michael Bridges	30
280 6/8	284 6/8	280 6/8	7 5/8	0 0/8	38 6/8	32 6/8	42 4/8	43 4/8	7	7	8 2/8	8 2/8	1959	Clatsop	Gordon L. Olsen/Duff Olsen	31
277 2/8	286 2/8	279 3/8	5 1/8	2 1/8	39 3/8	36 2/8	39 3/8	39 1/8	7	7	9 5/8	10 0/8	1994	Douglas	Ryan Bennett/Kim Myers	32
275 2/8	282 5/8	275 2/8	0 0/8	0 0/8	39 3/8	35 1/8	42 6/8	43 1/8	6	6	7 1/8	7 2/8	1964	Clatsop	Rusty Lindberg	33
271 4/8	280 1/8	271 4/8	0 0/8	0 0/8	41 0/8	39 0/8	39 0/8	40 3/8	6	6	8 3/8	9 5/8	1987	Coos	C.J. Monroe	34
271 1/8	283 4/8	271 1/8	4 7/8	0 0/8	46 4/8	43 0/8	38 0/8	39 4/8	6	5	7 5/8	8 6/8	1978	Clatsop	Tuck Lepschat	35

Final Score	Gross Typical	Net Typical	Crown Points	Abnormal Points	Greatest Spread	Inside Spread	Main Beam R	Main Beam L	Points R	Points L	Circumf R	Circumf L	Year	County	Hunter/Owner	Rank
270 1/8	273 5/8	270 1/8	0 0/8	0 0/8	37 2/8	32 7/8	42 5/8	43 2/8	6	6	6 6/8	6 7/8	1994	Yamhill	Keith Kershaw	36
268 3/8	275 7/8	268 3/8	0 0/8	0 0/8	39 4/8	37 2/8	40 0/8	37 2/8	6	6	7 7/8	6 6/8	1992	Jackson	Scott Thompson	37
267 7/8	276 3/8	267 7/8	0 0/8	0 0/8	37 7/8	33 5/8	46 2/8	45 5/8	5	5	8 1/8	8 0/8	1965	Clatsop	Joe Roshau	38
267 6/8	273 1/8	267 6/8	1 4/8	0 0/8	34 2/8	32 5/8	41 2/8	42 0/8	6	7	6 2/8	6 4/8	1993	Lincoln	Malin Ensign	39
266 7/8	281 1/8	266 7/8	2 3/8	0 0/8	35 3/8	31 2/8	42 7/8	45 2/8	6	7	9 3/8	9 0/8	1994	Douglas	Harold Good	41
265 0/8	274 0/8	268 3/8	3 2/8	3 3/8	40 3/8	34 5/8	42 0/8	43 5/8	6	7	8 6/8	8 4/8	1992	Tillamook	Nick Hurliman/ Parry M. Hurliman	41
264 3/8	274 2/8	264 3/8	0 0/8	0 0/8	39 3/8	37 5/8	39 0/8	38 0/8	6	6	8 0/8	7 5/8	1992	Coos	Terry L. Stuhlmiller	42
262 7/8	274 4/8	265 5/8	0 0/8	2 6/8		36 1/8	42 3/8	39 0/8	7	6	8 7/8	8 6/8	1963	Clatsop	Buzz Allen	43
260 3/8	265 5/8	260 3/8	7 2/8	0 0/8	38 4/8	37 2/8	35 1/8	34 6/8	5	7	9 0/8	9 4/8	1954	Douglas	Floyd W. Ross/Kitty Ross Grauf	44
*368 4/8	376 6/8	368 4/8	20 0/8	0 0/8	48 7/8	38 6/8	53 4/8	52 7/8	8	6	9 2/8	8 2/8		Douglas	Portland Rebar	

*To be ranked in the top ten, entries must also qualify for Boone and Crockett.

Typical Roosevelt Elk—Archery
Minimum Score: 210 0/8

Final Score	Gross Typical	Net Typical	Crown Points	Abnormal Points	Greatest Spread	Inside Spread	Main Beam R	Main Beam L	Points R	Points L	Circumf R	Circumf L	Year	County	Hunter/Owner	Rank
367 3/8	378 6/8	370 6/8	13 7/8	3 3/8	46 6/8	40 0/8	43 5/8	45 6/8	7	8	9 7/8	9 7/8	1985	Tillamook	Dale Baumgartner	1
362 2/8	369 3/8	362 2/8	8 4/8	0 0/8	46 1/8	43 4/8	51 0/8	48 5/8	7	7	7 7/8	7 4/8	1994	Clatsop	Randy Allen	2
360 1/8	366 5/8	360 1/8	2 6/8	0 0/8	42 6/8	38 5/8	51 5/8	52 4/8	7	7	8 7/8	9 3/8	1985	Columbia	Ken Adamson	3
307 3/8	313 2/8	307 3/8	0 0/8	0 0/8	41 4/8	35 6/8	46 5/8	47 5/8	6	6	7 5/8	7 3/8	1990	Jackson	Armone Foulon	4
296 0/8	302 7/8	296 0/8	0 0/8	0 0/8	37 5/8	35 1/8	45 1/8	47 2/8	6	6	9 0/8	8 4/8	1991	Lincoln	Gary Trommlits	5
295 6/8	304 5/8	295 6/8	5 2/8	0 0/8	45 2/8	41 1/8	43 2/8	43 3/8	6	7	8 1/8	7 5/8	1992	Clatsop	Brian Stanley	6
294 7/8	300 5/8	294 7/8	0 0/8	0 0/8	44 4/8	38 6/8	48 3/8	48 5/8	6	6	7 7/8	8 3/8	1992	Benton	Corey Putney	7
293 6/8	312 1/8	302 0/8	16 2/8	8 2/8	40 3/8	34 3/8	42 7/8	46 4/8	9	7	10 1/8	9 7/8	1993	Yamhill	Dean A. McMullen	8
283 3/8	289 7/8	283 3/8	0 0/8	0 0/8	34 3/8	30 5/8	46 0/8	47 1/8	6	6	9 5/8	9 2/8	1991	Polk	Terry Smith	9
271 4/8	276 6/8	271 4/8	0 0/8	0 0/8	40 4/8	37 2/8	41 3/8	42 0/8	6	6	8 1/8	7 7/8	1995	Douglas	Kenneth A. French	10
256 5/8	271 5/8	256 5/8	0 0/8	0 0/8	0 0/8	32 6/8	40 0/8	40 0/8	6	6	9 1/8	8 2/8	1995	Douglas	John Dickenson	11
255 5/8	260 6/8	255 5/8	5 5/8	0 0/8	40 2/8	38 2/8	36 7/8	36 7/8	7	6	7 1/8	7 1/8	1994	Tillamook	Parry M. Hurliman	12
255 0/8	276 0/8	257 4/8	5 4/8	2 4/8	0 0/8	29 0/8	37 0/8	39 0/8	7	6	8 6/8	8 3/8	1992	Coos	Mark Johnston	13
248 6/8	255 6/8	250 0/8	0 0/8	1 2/8	0 0/8	34 3/8	37 4/8	38 2/8	6	6	8 1/8	7 6/8	1995	Clatsop	Tim Brown	14
245 1/8	250 5/8	246 4/8	0 0/8	1 3/8	37 3/8	34 7/8	38 3/8	37 5/8	7	5	8 1/8	8 0/8	1989	Columbia	Leroy E. Lewis	15
235 0/8	240 1/8	235 0/8	5 2/8	0 0/8	39 5/8	38 0/8	36 2/8	34 1/8	6	6	7 7/8	7 7/8	1995	Tillamook	Parry M. Hurliman	16
228 0/8	233 3/8	229 5/8	0 0/8	1 5/8	34 3/8	32 1/8	36 2/8	36 0/8	6	6	7 5/8	7 7/8	1988	Curry	Kenneth A. French	17
226 4/8	232 1/8	226 4/8	0 0/8	0 0/8	36 0/8	34 2/8	36 0/8	34 4/8	5	6	6 0/8	6 0/8	1987	Coos	William E. Kohlhoff	18
226 3/8	231 1/8	226 3/8	0 0/8	0 0/8	34 0/8	31 5/8	41 4/8	38 7/8	5	5	5 7/8	5 7/8	1993	Coos	Donald L. Phillips, Jr.	19
223 0/8	228 7/8	223 0/8	0 0/8	0 0/8	35 5/8	32 4/8	35 5/8	35 0/8	5	5	6 7/8	7 0/8	1993	Tillamook	Parry M. Hurliman	20
222 4/8	230 3/8	222 4/8	0 0/8	0 0/8	36 1/8	34 0/8	33 6/8	34 5/8	5	5	7 0/8	7 0/8	1990	Tillamook	Ben R. Cook	21
216 5/8	226 7/8	216 5/8	0 0/8	0 0/8	35 0/8	34 1/8	31 5/8	37 5/8	5	6	7 6/8	8 2/8	1995	Clatsop	Jim F. Hendrickson	22

Typical Roosevelt Elk—Shed Antlers
Minimum Score: 100 0/8

Final Score	Subtotal	Crown Points	Abnormal Points	Main Beam	First Point	Second Point	Third Point	Fourth Point	Fifth Point	Sixth Point	First Circumference	Right/Left	Year	County	Owner's Name	Rank
208 0/8	208 0/8	30 0/8	0 0/8	50 4/8	19 4/8	17 6/8	16 5/8	20 3/8	18 6/8	0 0/8	9 1/8	Left	1990	Clackamas	Harold & Belva Burroughs	1
192 7/8	194 6/8	14 4/8	1 7/8	51 7/8	17 7/8	19 1/8	19 6/8	19 6/8	17 1/8	0 0/8	9 4/8	Right	1990	Clackamas	Harold & Belva Burroughs	2
166 4/8	166 4/8	0 0/8	0 0/8	56 7/8	18 7/8	18 2/8	14 3/8	19 7/8	12 4/8	0 0/8	7 0/8	Right	1982	Clatsop	Craig Erickson	3
159 2/8	159 2/8	0 0/8	0 0/8	53 1/8	16 4/8	15 5/8	14 1/8	18 4/8	14 2/8	0 0/8	7 7/8	Left	1982	Clatsop	Craig Erickson	4
157 6/8	157 6/8	9 0/8	0 0/8	48 7/8	12 4/8	14 0/8	12 4/8	18 5/8	14 4/8	0 0/8	8 0/8	Left		Clatsop	Joey Wood	5
140 5/8	140 5/8	0 0/8	0 0/8	44 4/8	15 3/8	14 4/8	10 2/8	13 7/8	12 0/8	3 2/8	7 5/8	Left	1996	Polk	Terry W. Smith	6
133 2/8	133 2/8	0 0/8	0 0/8	46 0/8	15 2/8	11 7/8	8 5/8	12 5/8	11 6/8	1 5/8	6 7/8	Right	1995	Polk	Terry W. Smith	7
130 2/8	136 5/8	0 0/8	6 3/8	50 2/8	11 4/8	12 3/8	12 3/8	18 2/8	3 0/8	0 0/8	8 4/8	Right		Clatsop	Joey Wood	8

Non-Typical Roosevelt Elk—Rifle
Minimum Score: 285 0/8

Final Score	Gross Typical	Net Typical	Crown Points	Abnormal Points	Greatest Spread	Inside Spread	Main Beam R	Main Beam L	Number of Points R	Number of Points L	First Circumference R	First Circumference L	Year	County	Hunter/Owner	Rank
372 4/8	371 2/8	365 1/8	5 3/8	7 3/8	46 4/8	41 3/8	46 2/8	50 0/8	9	7	11 0/8	10 5/8	1958	Coos	Pete Scoville/ Timberline Taxidermy	1
355 0/8	343 5/8	339 1/8	5 6/8	15 7/8	45 7/8	40 0/8	52 0/8	51 3/8	7	8	10 1/8	9 4/8	1938	Clatsop	David Tweedle/Scott A. Seppa	2
354 7/8	351 5/8	338 5/8	17 3/8	16 2/8	47 1/8	38 1/8	47 6/8	44 5/8	8	7	8 7/8	9 2/8	1952	Columbia	Bill Curtis/Duane Bernard	3
347 5/8	351 5/8	338 4/8	30 6/8	9 1/8	52 0/8	39 7/8	46 5/8	49 0/8	7	8	8 5/8	10 6/8			Daughter of American Rev/ Champoeg State Park	4
341 2/8	337 1/8	328 7/8	0 0/8	12 3/8	46 6/8	43 2/8	47 6/8	49 2/8	6	8	11 2/8	10 4/8	1890s	Coos	Grandma Miller/Diane Singleton	5

Non-Typical Roosevelt Elk—Archery
Minimum Score: 235 0/8

Final Score	Gross Typical	Net Typical	Crown Points	Abnormal Points	Greatest Spread	Inside Spread	Main Beam R	Main Beam L	Number of Points R	Number of Points L	First Circumference R	First Circumference L	Year	County	Hunter/Owner	Rank
310 2/8	312 1/8	302 0/8	16 2/8	8 2/8	40 3/8	34 3/8	42 7/8	46 4/8	9	7	10 1/8	9 7/8	1993	Yamhill	Dean A. McMullen	1

Official Scoring System for Oregon Big Game Trophies

Records of Oregon
Big Game

RECORD BOOK FOR OREGON

P.O. Box 759
Irrigon, OR 97844

NON-TYPICAL
ROOSEVELT ELK

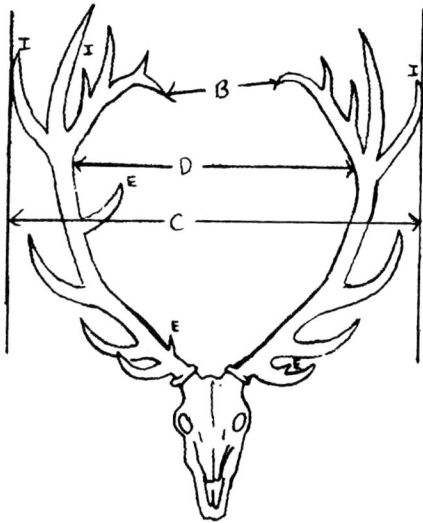

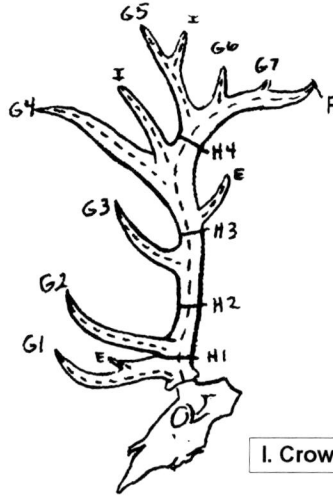

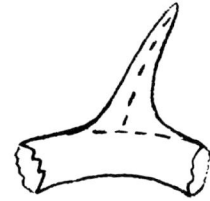

DETAIL OF POINT MEASUREMENT

Crown Points	
Right Antler	Left Antler
5 3/8	0 0/8
0 0/8	0 0/8
0 0/8	0 0/8
0 0/8	0 0/8
0 0/8	0 0/8
I. Crown Points Total	5 3/8

Abnormal Points	
Right Antler	Left Antler
3 3/8	4 0/8
0 0/8	0 0/8
0 0/8	0 0/8
0 0/8	0 0/8
0 0/8	0 0/8

	Right Antler	Left Antler
Subtotals	3 3/8	4 0/8
Total to E		7 3/8

Species	Rifle	Archery	Muzzle
Roosevelt Elk	260	210	225
Cascade Roosevelt Elk	260	210	225

						COLUMN 1	COLUMN 2	COLUMN 3	COLUMN 4
						Spread Credit	Right Antler	Left Antler	Difference
A	No. of Points on Right	9	No. of Points on Left Antler	7					
B	Tip to Tip Spread	38 6/8	**C** Greatest Spread	46 4/8					
D	Inside Spread of Main Beam	41 3/8	(Credit may be equal to but not exceed longer antler)	41 3/8					
E	Total of Length of Abnormal Points								7 3/8
F	Length of Main Beam						46 2/8	50 0/8	3 6/8
G-1	Length of First Point						18 3/8	18 2/8	0 1/8
G-2	Length of Second Point						18 2/8	17 4/8	0 6/8
G-3	Length of Third Point						19 3/8	19 5/8	0 2/8
G-4	Length of Fourth Point						14 0/8	14 1/8	0 1/8
G-5	Length of Fifth Point						11 0/8	10 5/8	
G-6	Length of Sixth Point, If Present						5 4/8	0 0/8	
G-7	Length of Seventh Point, If Present						0 0/8	0 0/8	
H-1	Circumference at smallest place between 1st and 2nd points						11 0/8	10 5/8	0 3/8
H-2	Circumference at smallest place between 2nd and 3rd points						7 2/8	7 1/8	0 1/8
H-3	Circumference at smallest place between 3rd and 4th points						6 4/8	6 3/8	0 1/8
H-4	Circumference at smallest place between 4th and 5th points						6 5/8	6 1/8	0 4/8
				TOTALS		41 3/8	164 1/8	160 3/8	6 1/8

County where killed: Coos	Year Killed: 1958		
Hunter's Name: Pete Scoville	**ADD**	Column 1	41 3/8
Owner's Name: Timberline Taxidermy		Column 2	164 1/8
		Column 3	160 3/8
		Total of I	5 3/8
		Subtotal	371 2/8
		Subtract Column 4	6 1/8
		Result	365 1/8
		Add Line E Total	7 3/8
		Final Score	372 4/8

The Standley Horns

by Linda Diane (Cummings) Singleton

This is the story of the Standley Horns (as it has been passed down).

The elk was killed in Sandy Creek, Oregon, by Grandma Miller in 1896–1898. The oldest Standley daughter of each generation was to get the horns. I am the seventh-generation Standley daughter to have the horns.

During the depression, the horns were in Portland, Oregon, and $100 was offered by the Elks Club of Portland for them.

My grandfather says the elk is a coastal elk. The Roosevelt elk was not introduced to this range until the 1930s.

(Final score: 341 2/8 B.C.)

Roosevelt Elk,
John McIllhenny, Gary Larson,
Allan Johnson, John May, 338 4/8 B.C.,
Clackamas County, 1993

Official Scoring System for Oregon Big Game Trophies

Records of Oregon Big Game	RECORD BOOK FOR OREGON	P.O. Box 759 Irrigon, OR 97844

TYPICAL
ROOSEVELT ELK

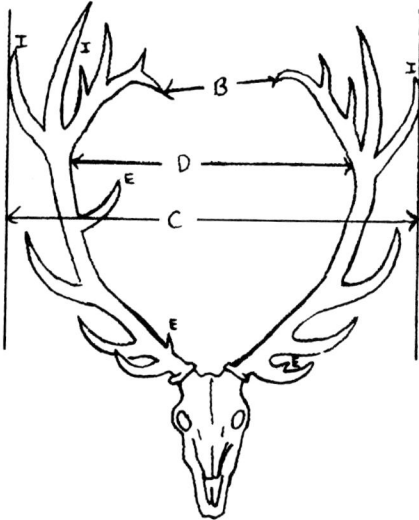

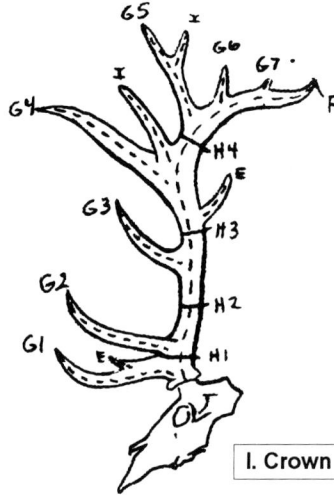

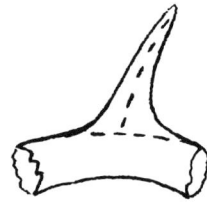

DETAIL OF POINT MEASUREMENT

Crown Points		
	Right Antler	Left Antler
	0 0/8	10 0/8
	0 0/8	0 0/8
	0 0/8	0 0/8
	0 0/8	0 0/8
	0 0/8	0 0/8
I. Crown Points Total		10 0/8

Abnormal Points		
	Right Antler	Left Antler
	0 0/8	0 0/8
	0 0/8	0 0/8
	0 0/8	0 0/8
	0 0/8	0 0/8
	0 0/8	0 0/8
Subtotals	0 0/8	0 0/8
Total to E		0 0/8

Species	Rifle	Archery	Muzzle	Shed
Roosevelt Elk	260	210	225	100
Cascade Roosevelt Elk	260	210	225	100

					COLUMN 1 Spread Credit	COLUMN 2 Right Antler	COLUMN 3 Left Antler	COLUMN 4 Difference
A	No. of Points on Right	6	No. of Points on Left Antler	7				
B	Tip to Tip Spread	35 0/8	C Greatest Spread	46 0/8				
D	Inside Spread of Main Beam	42 3/8	(Credit may be equal to but not exceed longer antler)		42 3/8			
E	Total of Length of Abnormal Points							0 0/8
F	Length of Main Beam					53 6/8	54 6/8	1 0/8
G-1	Length of First Point					17 2/8	17 5/8	0 3/8
G-2	Length of Second Point					18 6/8	19 1/8	0 3/8
G-3	Length of Third Point					13 7/8	15 4/8	1 5/8
G-4	Length of Fourth Point					15 2/8	17 2/8	2 0/8
G-5	Length of Fifth Point					12 4/8	12 1/8	
G-6	Length of Sixth Point, If Present					0 0/8	0 0/8	
G-7	Length of Seventh Point, If Present					0 0/8	0 0/8	
H-1	Circumference at smallest place between 1st and 2nd points					10 5/8	10 0/8	0 5/8
H-2	Circumference at smallest place between 2nd and 3rd points					6 7/8	7 1/8	0 2/8
H-3	Circumference at smallest place between 3rd and 4th points					6 4/8	6 5/8	0 1/8
H-4	Circumference at smallest place between 4th and 5th points					7 1/8	7 4/8	0 3/8
				TOTALS	42 3/8	162 4/8	167 5/8	6 6/8

County where killed: Douglas	Date Killed: 1966		
Hunter's Name: Ron Quimby		Column 1	42 3/8
Owner's Name: Ron Quimby	ADD	Column 2	162 4/8
		Column 3	167 5/8
		Total of I	10 0/8
		Subtotal	382 4/8
	Subtract Column 4		6 6/8
	FINAL SCORE		375 6/8

Typical Cascade Roosevelt Elk—Rifle
Minimum Score: 260 0/8

Final Score	Gross Typical	Net Typical	Crown Points	Abnormal Points	Greatest Spread	Inside Spread	Main Beam R	Main Beam L	Number of Points R	Number of Points L	First Circumference R	First Circumference L	Year	County	Hunter/Owner	Rank
375 6/8	382 4/8	375 6/8	10 0/8	0 0/8	46 0/8	42 3/8	53 6/8	54 6/8	6	7	10 5/8	10 0/8	1966	Douglas	Ron Quimby	1
338 3/8	348 7/8	338 3/8	0 0/8	0 0/8	47 4/8	41 6/8	50 3/8	51 7/8	6	6	7 7/8	9 0/8	1993	Clackamas	John McIllhenny	2
336 4/8	343 2/8	336 4/8	8 0/8	0 0/8	50 0/8	45 6/8	50 5/8	51 7/8	7	7	8 2/8	8 3/8	1969	Douglas	Ernest Thomas	3
323 1/8	345 4/8	340 1/8	0 0/8	17 0/8	41 6/8	34 5/8	50 4/8	49 2/8	7	6	10 1/8	9 7/8	1938	Clatsop	Eldon G. Anderson/ Mike Anderson	4
311 4/8	322 2/8	315 2/8	9 3/8	3 6/8	37 0/8	32 5/8	47 3/8	47 4/8	8	8	8 5/8	8 0/8	1990	Lane	Gerald Riley	5
310 2/8	336 1/8	321 1/8	14 5/8	10 7/8	47 6/8	37 7/8	45 4/8	51 6/8	7	9	9 4/8	9 2/8	1995	Lane	John Williams	6
303 2/8	321 4/8	303 2/8	4 2/8	0 0/8	48 2/8	45 0/8	51 1/8	53 0/8	6	8	8 4/8	9 4/8	1995	Linn	Ernie Kropf	7
289 5/8	295 0/8	289 5/8	0 0/8	0 0/8	39 0/8	35 6/8	46 4/8	47 2/8	6	6	7 4/8	8 0/8	1993	Marion	Roland Brown	8
273 4/8	283 4/8	273 4/8	0 0/8	0 0/8	35 0/8	29 4/8	49 5/8	47 1/8	5	6	9 0/8	9 4/8	1994	Jackson	Sonny Loomis	9

Typical Cascade Roosevelt Elk—Archery
Minimum Score: 210 0/8

Final Score	Gross Typical	Net Typical	Crown Points	Abnormal Points	Greatest Spread	Inside Spread	Main Beam R	Main Beam L	Number of Points R	Number of Points L	First Circumference R	First Circumference L	Year	County	Hunter/Owner	Rank
319 2/8	323 1/8	319 2/8	0 0/8	0 0/8	47 5/8	44 2/8	46 2/8	45 6/8	6	6	8 1/8	7 7/8	1987	Clackamas	Gerald L. Egbert	1
316 0/8	323 2/8	316 0/8	0 0/8	0 0/8	43 4/8	38 0/8	52 2/8	51 0/8	6	6	8 5/8	8 6/8	1989	Clackamas	Randy Allen	2
299 4/8	307 6/8	301 4/8	12 1/8	2 0/8	40 0/8	31 1/8	44 4/8	42 6/8	8	7	7 4/8	7 5/8	1990	Douglas	Kenneth A. French	3
292 2/8	303 5/8	292 2/8	0 0/8	0 0/8	36 4/8	32 4/8	43 6/8	45 4/8	6	6	8 0/8	8 2/8	1993	Clackamas	Randy Allen	4
288 4/8	296 7/3	290 2/8	5 1/8	1 6/8	40 0/8	36 6/8	45 3/8	45 2/8	8	7	7 3/8	7 6/8	1992	Deschutes	Keenan Howard	5
283 2/8	291 5/3	283 2/8	3 0/8	0 0/8	42 5/8	40 3/8	42 3/8	43 6/8	6	7	8 1/8	8 3/8	1995	Deschutes	Nick Parker	6
280 6/8	290 6/8	280 6/8	0 0/8	0 0/8	36 3/8	30 4/8	49 3/8	44 3/8	6	6	8 1/8	7 6/8		Linn	Mike Brady/Shirley Andrews	7
276 4/8	282 1/8	276 4/8	0 0/8	0 0/8	38 0/8	35 4/8	44 1/8	43 6/8	6	6	7 5/8	7 1/8	1980	Linn	Mike Brady/Shirley Andrews	8
264 1/8	279 1/8	270 5/8	7 4/8	6 4/8	42 4/8	37 5/8	36 6/8	37 1/8	7	7	8 0/8	8 3/8	1992	Clackamas	Randy Allen	9
261 5/8	278 7/8	261 5/8	17 1/8	0 0/8	37 0/8	34 0/8	46 0/8	47 4/8	6	6	7 0/8	6 4/8	1995	Douglas	Lyle Curtis, Jr.	10
261 4/8	265 2/8	261 4/8	0 0/8	0 0/8	38 0/8	36 4/8	40 4/8	40 2/8	6	6	6 3/8	7 0/8	1995		Randy Allen	11
258 1/8	262 5/8	258 1/8	0 0/8	0 0/8	39 6/8	31 1/8	42 2/8	41 4/8	5	5	8 0/8	8 1/8	1995	Clackamas	Jacob Hanning	12
257 7/8	276 6/8	257 7/8	0 0/8	0 0/8	39 7/8	31 6/8	45 0/8	48 3/8	5	6	7 3/8	6 2/8		Linn	Mike Brady/Shirley Andrews	13
253 0/8	265 7/8	253 0/8	0 0/8	0 0/8	39 1/8	38 1/8	41 6/8	42 1/8	6	6	6 0/8	6 3/8		Linn	Mike Brady/Shirley Andrews	14
251 7/8	256 2/8	251 7/8	0 0/8	0 0/8	34 0/8	32 3/8	40 5/8	41 6/8	6	6	6 4/8	6 4/8	1991	Clackamas	Randy Allen	15
248 6/8	257 2/8	248 6/8	0 0/8	0 0/8	45 6/8	43 2/8	38 5/8	42 2/8	6	5	7 5/8	7 4/8	1991	Deschutes	Keenan Howard	16
246 7/8	253 0/8	246 7/8	0 0/8	0 0/8	40 3/8	37 5/8	39 4/8	41 4/8	5	6	6 5/8	7 4/8		Linn	Mike Brady/Shirley Andrews	17
244 7/8	259 5/8	244 7/8	0 0/8	0 0/8	35 7/8	33 5/8	43 6/8	36 6/8	6	6	5 6/8	5 6/8	1990	Clackamas	Gerald L. Egbert	18

Typical Cascade Roosevelt Elk—Black Powder
Minimum Score: 225 0/8

Final Score	Gross Typical	Net Typical	Crown Points	Abnormal Points	Greatest Spread	Inside Spread	Main Beam R	Main Beam L	Number of Points R	Number of Points L	First Circumference R	First Circumference L	Year	County	Hunter/Owner	Rank
239 0/8	241 3/8	239 0/8	0 0/8	0 0/8	35 3/8	33 0/8	39 5/8	40 1/8	6	6	7 3/8	7 3/8	1994	Lane	Robert Gwozdz	1

Typical Cascade Roosevelt Elk—Shed Antlers
Minimum Score: 100 0/8

Final Score	Subtotal	Crown Points	Abnormal Points	Main Beam	First Point	Second Point	Third Point	Fourth Point	Fifth Point	Sixth Point	First Circumference	Right/Left	Year	County	Owner's Name	Rank
150 6/8	150 6/8	0 0/8	0 0/8	48 1/8	14 1/8	17 6/8	11 3/8	15 2/8	11 2/8	7 7/8	7 4/8	Left	1989	Lane	Jim Valerio	1
149 6/8	149 6/8	0 0/8	0 0/8	47 3/8	15 6/8	17 4/8	10 7/8	13 7/8	10 6/8	7 6/8	8 0/8	Right	1989	Lane	Jim Valerio	2
141 1/8	141 1/8	0 0/8	0 0/8	50 0/8	12 2/8	12 6/8	11 0/8	17 0/8	10 4/8	0 0/8	7 6/8	Right			Randy Peyton	3

Rocky Mountain Elk

Top 25 Rocky Mountain Elk
Sorted by Combined Main Beam Length

Rank	Hunter/Owner	County	Year	First Circumference R	First Circumference L	Number of Points R	Number of Points L	Inside Spread	Greatest Spread	Abnormal Points	Net Typical	Gross Typical	Final Score	Main Beam R	Main Beam L
1	Elvin Davis	Crook	1963	7 5/8	8 1/8	7	7	46 4/8	54 0/8	0 0/8	371 2/8	394 3/8	371 2/8	65 2/8	63 1/8
2	Hugh Evans/Joseph Jessel, Jr.	Crook	1942	10 1/8	9 6/8	7	7	38 2/8	49 7/8	0 0/8	418 0/8	427 4/8	418 0/8	63 2/8	64 2/8
3	Pat L. Wheeler	Harney	1967	8 6/8	8 6/8	7	8	47 1/8	57 5/8	3 6/8	384 1/8	397 5/8	380 3/8	62 7/8	63 2/8
4	James Sproul	Grant	1972	9 3/8	9 0/8	7	6	43 7/8	49 2/8	0 0/8	401 1/8	421 0/8	401 1/8	60 4/8	64 5/8
5	Frank Bristow	Crook	1974	7 7/8	9 1/8	7	7	45 0/8	52 6/8	6 5/8	381 4/8	385 7/8	374 7/8	59 5/8	59 5/8
6	Mac McKinley	Grant		8 0/8	7 4/8	6	6	41 4/8	46 0/8	0 0/8	325 2/8	337 4/8	325 2/8	58 2/8	59 2/8
7	Jeffrey E. Hale	Crook	1988	9 5/8	9 5/8	6	6	41 5/8	51 5/8	0 0/8	373 1/8	381 4/8	373 1/8	57 5/8	57 6/8
8	Will Bartlett	Wheeler	1986	9 1/8	8 6/8	6	6	42 6/8	48 0/8	0 0/8	375 0/8	380 0/8	375 0/8	58 1/8	58 1/8
9	Mark Barber	Harney	1991	7 3/8	7 7/8	6	6	43 3/8	48 5/8	0 0/8	343 5/8	352 0/8	343 5/8	55 3/8	58 5/8
10	Lyla Johnston	Grant	1948	7 5/8	8 3/8	6	6	37 3/8	41 0/8	0 0/8	332 1/8	340 0/8	332 1/8	56 6/8	57 1/8
11	Lawton McDaniels	Wallowa	1935	9 3/8	10 2/8	7	8	46 5/8	58 6/8	24 1/8	380 3/8	390 2/8	356 2/8	57 2/8	56 4/8
12	Randy Ryerse	Crook	1984	9 1/8	9 1/8	7	7	49 0/8	52 2/8	0 0/8	400 0/8	414 0/8	400 0/8	57 0/8	57 0/8
12	Lawrence Wolfgram	Grant	1980	8 4/8	8 4/8	6	6	44 5/8	48 2/8	0 0/8	368 7/8	372 1/8	368 7/8	56 6/8	56 6/8
14	Brett Puckett	Wheeler	1991	7 1/8	7 3/8	6	6	38 1/8	42 0/8	0 0/8	331 5/8	348 7/8	331 5/8	54 6/8	58 0/8
15	Arnold Tropf	Grant	1966	10 0/8	9 5/8	7	6	37 2/8	50 3/8	1 5/8	389 4/8	399 7/8	387 7/8	55 3/8	57 0/8
16	Jerry Wagner/Greg Wagner	Grant	1973	8 3/8	8 3/8	6	5	47 5/8	53 3/8	0 0/8	348 5/8	357 7/8	348 5/8	55 5/8	56 2/8
17	Jim Myers	Wheeler	1974	9 4/8	8 4/8	7	6	39 4/8	46 0/8	6 3/8	306 7/8	360 6/8	300 4/8	56 4/8	55 2/8
18	Ray Gauge	Wheeler	1957	8 2/8	8 1/8	7	6	45 0/8	56 4/8	0 0/8	376 4/8	395 3/8	376 4/8	56 0/8	56 0/8
19	Taft/La Grande Elks Lodge	Wallowa	1930	10 4/8	9 5/8	8	7	46 6/8	54 2/8	9 6/8	401 2/8	418 2/8	391 4/8	55 7/8	55 7/8
19	David Clayton	Harney	1992	10 1/8	8 0/8	7	8	39 0/8	56 1/8	28 7/8	344 0/8	367 0/8	315 1/8	55 7/8	55 4/8
21	Lee Thompson/The Halfway Museum	Baker	1942	9 3/8	8 4/8	6	7	46 1/8	50 3/8	0 0/8	378 1/8	389 7/8	378 1/8	55 4/8	57 0/8
22	Bill Tensen	Hood River	1980	8 6/8	8 6/8	7	7	49 2/8	55 4/8	0 0/8	390 2/8	400 3/8	390 2/8	55 0/8	55 4/8
22	Chet Hettinga	Wheeler	1988	8 2/8	8 0/8	7	7	45 0/8	47 4/8	0 0/8	352 4/8	359 2/8	352 4/8	55 3/8	55 1/8
24	Donny Worley	Grant	1982	6 4/8	6 6/8	6	6	47 7/8	50 6/8	0 0/8	314 5/8	324 3/8	314 5/8	56 4/8	53 6/8
25	Earl Haney/Dale Dotson	Wallowa	1930	7 7/8	8 4/8	6	7	55 6/8	57 0/8	0 0/8	364 2/8	382 7/8	364 2/8	55 2/8	54 4/8
25	Wayne Marks	Wallowa	1947	8 1/8	7 6/8	7	7	47 3/8	60 1/8	22 6/8	369 3/8	379 1/8	346 5/8	55 0/8	54 6/8

Top 25 Rocky Mountain Elk
Sorted by Greatest Spread

Greatest Spread	Final Score	Gross Typical	Net Typical	Abnormal Points	Inside Spread	Main Beam R	Main Beam L	Number of Points R	Number of Points L	First Circumference R	First Circumference L	Year	County	Hunter/Owner	Rank
64 0/8	341 2/8	371 4/8	355 6/8	14 4/8	58 6/8	52 4/8	50 5/8	6	8	8 1/8	8 1/8	1960	Grant	C.R. Kendall	1
60 1/8	346 5/8	379 1/8	369 3/8	22 6/8	47 3/8	55 0/8	54 6/8	7	7	8 1/8	7 6/8	1947	Wallowa	Wayne Marks	2
58 6/8	356 2/8	390 2/8	380 3/8	24 1/8	46 5/8	57 2/8	56 4/8	7	8	9 3/8	10 2/8	1935	Wallowa	Lawton McDaniels	3
57 5/8	380 3/8	397 5/8	384 1/8	3 6/8	47 1/8	62 7/8	63 2/8	7	8	8 6/8	8 6/8	1967	Harney	Pat L. Wheeler	4
57 0/8	364 2/8	382 7/8	364 2/8	0 0/8	55 6/8	55 2/8	54 4/8	6	7	7 7/8	8 4/8	1930	Wallowa	Earl Haney/Dale Dotson	5
57 0/8	316 0/8	351 6/8	336 4/8	20 4/8	41 4/8	48 4/8	48 0/8	8	7	8 2/8	8 6/8	1935	Union	Wesley H. Townsend/ Wanda De Moss	5
56 4/8	376 4/8	395 3/8	376 4/8	0 0/8	45 0/8	55 5/8	56 0/8	7	6	8 2/8	8 1/8	1957	Wheeler	Ray Gauge	7
56 1/8	315 1/8	367 0/8	344 0/8	28 7/8	39 0/8	55 4/8	55 7/8	7	8	10 1/8	8 0/8	1992	Harney	David Clayton	8
55 4/8	390 2/8	400 3/8	390 2/8	0 0/8	49 2/8	55 0/8	55 4/8	7	7	8 6/8	8 6/8	1980	Hood River	Bill Tensen	9
55 0/8	335 3/8	343 0/8	335 3/8	0 0/8	53 0/8	49 3/8	49 2/8	6	6	7 2/8	6 6/8	1994	Crook	Jason Calarco	10
54 3/8	369 4/8	378 0/8	369 4/8	0 0/8	49 4/8	55 2/8	54 3/8	6	6	8 4/8	8 1/8	1930	Union	Michael Kilby	11
54 2/8	391 4/8	418 2/8	401 2/8	9 6/8	46 6/8	55 4/8	55 7/8	8	7	10 4/8	9 5/8	1930	Wallowa	Taft/La Grande Elks Lodge	12
54 0/8	371 2/8	394 3/8	371 2/8	0 0/8	46 4/8	65 2/8	63 1/8	7	7	7 5/8	8 1/8	1963	Crook	Elvin Davis	13
53 6/8	327 6/8	341 1/8	334 4/8	6 6/8	48 2/8	51 0/8	51 3/8	7	7	8 3/8	8 2/8	1950	Union	Tom Craig	14
53 4/8	350 2/8	360 7/8	350 2/8	0 0/8	52 0/8	47 6/8	47 6/8	6	5	7 2/8	7 2/8	1944		Stratton Store	15
53 3/8	348 5/8	357 7/8	348 5/8	0 0/8	47 5/8	55 5/8	56 2/8	6	7	8 3/8	8 3/8	1973	Grant	Jerry Wagner/Greg Wagner	16
53 0/8	372 4/8	387 6/8	372 4/8	0 0/8	49 2/8	55 1/8	53 5/8	6	7	9 1/8	9 5/8	1962	Grant	Bud Loht	17
53 0/8	329 7/8	340 5/8	329 7/8	0 0/8	46 7/8	53 4/8	54 1/8	6	6	7 4/8	7 4/8		Wallowa	Dean Sprague/The Sports Corral	18
53 0/8	364 6/8	377 3/8	364 6/8	0 0/8	39 2/8	50 3/8	46 2/8	6	6	9 2/8	9 2/8	1976	Grant	Bill Sanowski, III	19
52 6/8	374 7/8	339 7/8	381 4/8	6 5/8	45 0/8	59 5/8	59 5/8	7	7	7 7/8	9 1/8	1974	Crook	Frank Bristow	20
52 4/8	354 3/8	361 7/8	354 3/8	0 0/8	46 5/8	54 5/8	53 6/8	7	6	8 2/8	8 3/8	1935	Crook	Earl H. Baker, Sr./ Charles Baker	21
52 4/8	349 7/8	361 5/8	349 7/8	0 0/8	47 7/8	49 1/8	51 4/8	7	7	7 3/8	7 7/8	1981	Grant	Malcolm Cameron	21
52 4/8	347 0/8	358 1/8	347 0/8	0 0/8	47 6/8	49 3/8	50 2/8	6	6	8 2/8	8 2/8	1981	Grant	Rod Abreu	21
52 3/8	352 2/8	358 2/8	352 2/8	0 0/8	42 4/8	52 0/8	53 2/8	6	6	7 5/8	7 4/8	1941	Harney	Walter Hart/Joe Baker	24
52 2/8	400 0/8	414 0/8	400 0/8	0 0/8	49 0/8	56 2/8	57 0/8	7	7	9 1/8	9 1/8	1984	Crook	Randy Ryerse	25

Top 25 Rocky Mountain Elk
Sorted without Inside Spread Credit

Adjusted Final	Final Score	Gross Typical	Abnormal Points	Greatest Spread	Inside Spread	Main Beam R	Main Beam L	Number of Points R	Number of Points L	First Circumference R	First Circumference L	Year	County	Hunter/Owner	Rank
379 6/8	418 0/8	427 4/8	0 0/8	49 7/8	38 2/8	63 2/8	64 2/8	7	7	10 1/8	9 6/8	1942	Crook	Hugh Evans/Joseph Jessel, Jr.	1
357 2/8	401 1/8	421 0/8	0 0/8	49 2/8	43 7/8	60 4/8	64 5/8	7	6	9 3/8	9 0/8	1972	Grant	James Sproul	2
351 0/8	400 0/8	414 0/8	0 0/8	52 2/8	49 0/8	56 2/8	57 0/8	7	7	9 1/8	9 1/8	1984	Crook	Randy Ryerse	3
350 5/8	387 7/8	399 7/8	1 5/8	50 3/8	37 2/8	55 3/8	57 0/8	7	6	10 0/8	9 5/8	1966	Grant	Arnold Tropf	4
346 0/8	392 3/8	397 0/8	0 0/8	51 2/8	46 3/8	53 4/8	54 4/8	6	6	8 3/8	8 6/8	1982	Umatilla	Robert Brown	5
344 6/8	391 4/8	418 2/8	9 6/8	54 2/8	46 6/8	55 4/8	55 7/8	8	7	10 4/8	9 5/8	1930	Wallowa	Taft/La Grande Elks Lodge	6
341 0/8	390 2/8	400 3/8	0 0/8	55 4/8	49 2/8	55 0/8	55 4/8	7	7	8 6/8	8 6/8	1980	Hood River	Bill Tensen	7
337 2/8	379 4/8	392 7/8	0 0/8	49 4/8	42 2/8	53 4/8	50 1/8	7	7	10 3/8	9 4/8	1941	Union	Frank Rauschkolb, Sr.	8
333 2/8	380 3/8	397 5/8	3 6/8	57 5/8	47 1/8	62 7/8	63 2/8	7	8	8 6/8	8 6/8	1967	Harney	Pat L. Wheeler	9
332 2/8	375 0/8	380 0/8	0 0/8	48 0/8	42 6/8	57 1/8	58 1/8	6	6	9 1/8	8 6/8	1986	Wheeler	Will Bartlett	10
332 0/8	378 1/8	389 7/8	0 0/8	50 3/8	46 1/8	55 4/8	55 4/8	6	7	9 3/8	8 4/8	1942	Baker	Lee Thompson/The Halfway Museum	11
331 4/8	376 4/8	395 3/8	0 0/8	56 4/8	45 0/8	55 5/8	56 0/8	7	6	8 2/8	8 1/8	1957	Wheeler	Ray Gauge	12
331 4/8	373 1/8	381 4/8	0 0/8	51 5/8	41 5/8	57 5/8	57 6/8	6	6	9 5/8	9 5/8	1988	Crook	Jeffrey E. Hale	12
330 6/8	372 4/8	376 5/8	0 0/8		41 6/8	54 5/8	55 0/8	6	6	8 0/8	8 1/8	1981	Grant	Dell Howard	14
330 4/8	376 0/8	379 1/8	0 0/8	48 5/8	45 4/8	48 2/8	48 2/8	6	6	8 6/8	8 7/8	1979	Crook	Carl Ipack	15
329 7/8	374 7/8	339 7/8	6 5/8	52 6/8	45 0/8	59 5/8	59 5/8	7	7	7 7/8	9 1/8	1974	Crook	Frank Bristow	16
325 4/8	364 6/8	377 3/8	0 0/8	53 0/8	39 2/8	50 3/8	46 2/8	6	6	9 2/8	9 2/8	1976	Grant	Bill Sanowski, III	17
325 2/8	364 4/8	372 1/8	0 0/8	44 4/8	39 2/8	53 2/8	51 2/8	6	6	8 2/8	8 5/8	1980	Grant	Cliff Marsh	18
324 6/8	371 2/8	394 3/8	0 0/8	54 0/8	46 4/8	65 2/8	63 1/8	6	7	7 5/8	8 1/8	1963	Crook	Elvin Davis	19
324 2/8	368 7/8	372 1/8	0 0/8	48 2/8	44 5/8	56 4/8	56 6/8	6	6	8 4/8	8 4/8	1980	Grant	Lawrence Wolfgram	20
324 0/8	371 0/8	384 1/8	0 0/8	50 1/8	47 0/8	52 4/8	52 4/8	7	7	8 0/8	7 4/8	1958	Grant	Gale Becker/Harold Burroughs	21
323 4/8	368 0/8	379 1/8	0 0/8	47 6/8	44 4/8	52 7/8	52 3/8	6	6	8 6/8	8 3/8	1988	Grant	Greg E. Willmore	22
323 2/8	372 7/8	378 1/8	0 0/8	52 0/8	49 5/8	50 1/8	50 6/8	6	6	9 4/8	9 0/8	1989	Grant	Bob M. Abbott	23
323 2/8	372 4/8	387 6/8	0 0/8	53 0/8	49 2/8	55 1/8	53 5/8	6	7	9 1/8	9 5/8	1962	Grant	Bud Loht	23
320 0/8	369 4/8	378 0/8	0 0/8	54 3/8	49 4/8	55 2/8	54 3/8	6	6	8 4/8	8 1/8	1930	Union	Michael Kilby	25

State Record Typical Rocky Mountain Elk (Rifle)

by Joe Jessel

In 1991, Joe Jessel was on vacation visiting with Rich Eckert, a part-time taxidermist. Joe asked if Rich could restore an old set of horns that were hanging in an oak tree at his mother's home. Joe was excited to find out that Rich not only could restore the horns, he also could mount them on a head.

Upon returning home from vacation, Joe asked his mother, JoAnne Jessel, if he could have the horns and explained why. She thought it was a great idea and suggested that he also tell his grandmother, Opal, what he intended to do. The horns had belonged to JoAnne's late father, Hugh Evans, and had ended up with her husband in the early 1970s.

At this point, Joe spent some time with his grandmother, asking her questions about how and when the bull was shot. Opal Evans Sexton told Joe that his grandfather, Hugh Evans, had shot the elk in 1942 near Mitchell. She then gave him some old black-and-white photos of the horns strapped to the front of their 1935 Chevrolet pickup. In one photo, Hugh was sitting in the crotch of the horns.

Soon after, Joe's wife, Paula, and his mother-in-law, Pat, strapped the horns to the top of Pat's car and traveled across the state of Oregon to leave the horns with Rich Eckert. While on the way, the women were pulled over and cited for speeding, although they both felt that the officer really pulled them over to get a closer look at the rack.

After the restoration was complete, Eckert told the couple that the mount was the largest he had ever seen and that they probably had a record elk on their hands. He suggested that they contact someone from Boone and Crockett to score it. After returning the trailer they had rented to bring the head home, the couple mounted it in their family room.

Joe tried in vain for over a year to get an official to come out to their home in Molalla to score the mount. Finally, in February of 1993, he rented a truck and took the mounted rack to the Pacific Northwest Sportsmen's Show in Portland, where it was unofficially scored at 419 3/8. At this point, Joe was told that the mount would be considered the largest shot in the state of Oregon and would probably rank in the top ten in the world, if officially scored.

The mount returned to the couple's home until the house was sold in September of 1993. It then went into a local museum for several months before being moved again to be displayed at a local auto parts store.

In September of 1994, Gary Wise, owner of the auto parts store, was finally able to get Charles (Rusty) Lindberg, an official from Boone and Crockett, to come out to Molalla and score the antlers. This time the score was 418 0/8, but it was official.

At this time, Joe went back to his grandmother for more information about the hunt. Below is the story that Opal and her brother Leonard told Joe about the day this record elk was taken.

On a cool November afternoon in 1942, in the Ochoco National Forest near Mitchell, Oregon, Opal Evans was in camp preparing for the evening meal when she heard something crashing through the brush behind her. Looking up, Opal saw a huge bull elk approaching camp. It so

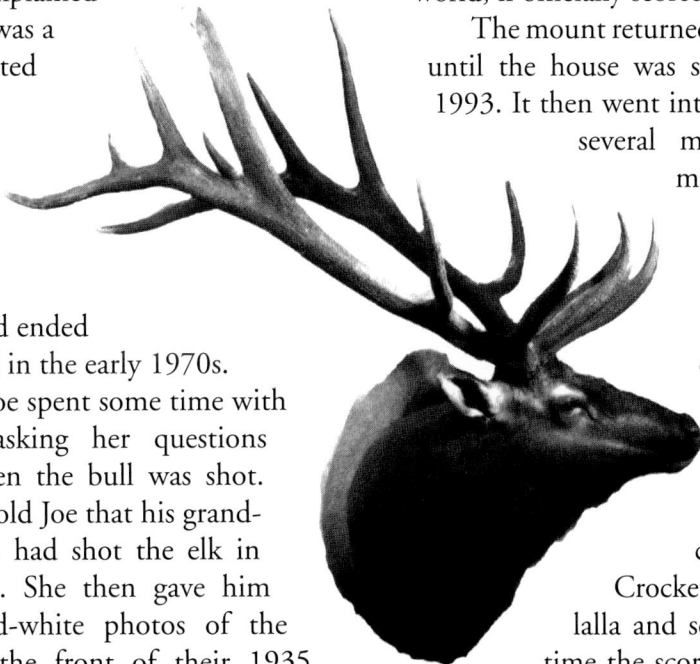

Official Scoring System for Oregon Big Game Trophies

Records of Oregon Big Game	RECORD BOOK FOR OREGON	P.O. Box 759 Irrigon, OR 97844

TYPICAL
ROCKY MT. ELK (WAPITI)

DETAIL OF POINT MEASUREMENT

Abnormal Points	
Right Antler	Left Antler
0 0/8	0 0/8
0 0/8	0 0/8
0 0/8	0 0/8
0 0/8	0 0/8
0 0/8	0 0/8
0 0/8	0 0/8
0 0/8	0 0/8
0 0/8	0 0/8
0 0/8	0 0/8
0 0/8	0 0/8
Subtotals 0 0/8	0 0/8
Total to E	0 0/8

Species	Rifle	Archery	Muzzle	Shed
Rocky Mt. Elk	300	260	255	135

					COLUMN 1	COLUMN 2	COLUMN 3	COLUMN 4
					Spread Credit	Right Antler	Left Antler	Difference
A	No. of Points on Right Antler	7	No. of Points on Left Antler	7				
B	Tip to Tip Spread	25 1/8	C Greatest Spread	49 7/8				
D	Inside Spread of Main Beam	38 2/8	(Credit may be equal to but not exceed longer antler)		38 2/8			
E	Total of Length of Abnormal Points							0 0/8
F	Length of Main Beam					63 2/8	64 2/8	1 0/8
G-1	Length of First Point					18 5/8	18 7/8	0 2/8
G-2	Length of Second Point					20 2/8	19 1/8	1 1/8
G-3	Length of Third Point					19 1/8	18 1/8	1 0/8
G-4	Length of Fourth Point					19 5/8	22 3/8	2 6/8
G-5	Length of Fifth Point					13 5/8	12 6/8	0 7/8
G-6	Length of Sixth Point, If Present					5 7/8	7 2/8	1 3/8
G-7	Length of Seventh Point, If Present					0 0/8	0 0/8	0 0/8
H-1	Circumference at smallest place between 1st and 2nd					10 1/8	9 6/8	0 3/8
H-2	Circumference at smallest place between 2nd and 3rd points					8 1/8	7 6/8	0 3/8
H-3	Circumference at smallest place between 3rd and 4th points					7 4/8	7 4/8	0 0/8
H-4	Circumference at smallest place between 4th and 5th points					7 4/8	7 7/8	0 3/8
				TOTALS	38 2/8	193 5/8	195 5/8	9 4/8

County where killed: Crook	Date Killed: 1942		
Hunter's Name: Hugh Evans		**ADD**	Column 1	38 2/8
Owner's Name: Joseph Jessel, Jr.			Column 2	193 5/8
			Column 3	195 5/8
			Subtotal	427 4/8
		Subtract Column 4	9 4/8
		FINAL SCORE	418 0/8

frightened her that she jumped into the pickup and locked the doors.

Later in the day, when Hugh Evans and Opal's brother, Leonard Ferguson, returned to camp, Opal told the men about the elk. She said it was a large bull with a gray beard and a huge set of antlers. The next morning the men went out on their hunt, and at about 10:00 a.m. Hugh shot a bull with his 300 Savage rifle. When they returned to camp with the elk, Opal told the men it was the same bull she had seen the day before.

Hugh and Opal did not realize the trophy they had, and the antlers were tossed from barn to barn for the next thirty-five years. Opal re-married after Hugh died, and in the early 1970s her second husband suggested that they give the horns to a local tavern. Even though she had no idea what she had, Opal wanted the horns to stay in the family, so she called her son-in-law, Joe Jessel, Sr. and asked him if he would take the horns. He did so and, after bringing them home, the horns were once again resigned to the barn. In 1977, when Joe (Sr.) and JoAnne built their new home, the antlers were nailed to an oak tree in the back yard, where they were used as a flower pot hanger.

After being scored officially, the antlers were re-mounted and are currently on display with Trophy Show Productions. Joe has enjoyed taking time away from his entrepreneurial pursuits to spend time with Roger Selner of Trophy Show Productions, talking about how his grandfather shot this record elk more than fifty years ago. (Final score: 418 0/8 B.C.)

State Record Typical Rocky Mountain Elk (Archery)

by Jeff Hale

I arrived at one of my favorite hunting places in the Ochoco mountains on September 9, 1988. I walked for about a mile before daylight. At first light I bugled and immediately got a response from about four hundred yards away. I pursued the bull for about an hour and a half. I finally got within eighty yards of him and set up. We had a hard-fought bugling contest for several minutes. Then, as quickly as it started, all was quiet.

I listened for any sound out of the ordinary but heard nothing. Suddenly, I caught a movement out of the corner of my eye. The bull had circled and come over the crest of a ridge behind me. He was now about fifteen yards away. He tried to wind me. When he turned to leave, I drew back my bow and shot him behind the front shoulder. I tracked him for about a mile and found the trophy bull I had been looking for all my life. I had no idea I had the state record bull until he was officially scored. (Final score: 373 1/8 P.Y.)

Official Scoring System for Oregon Big Game Trophies

TYPICAL
ROCKY MT. ELK (WAPITI)

DETAIL OF POINT MEASUREMENT

Abnormal Points	
Right Antler	Left Antler
0 0/8	0 0/8
0 0/8	0 0/8
0 0/8	0 0/8
0 0/8	0 0/8
0 0/8	0 0/8
0 0/8	0 0/8
0 0/8	0 0/8
0 0/8	0 0/8
0 0/8	0 0/8
0 0/8	0 0/8

	Right Antler	Left Antler
Subtotals	0 0/8	0 0/8
Total to E		0 0/8

Species	Rifle	Archery	Muzzle	Shed
Rocky Mt. Elk	300	260	255	135

						COLUMN 1 Spread Credit	COLUMN 2 Right Antler	COLUMN 3 Left Antler	COLUMN 4 Difference
A	No. of Points on Right Antler	6	No. of Points on Left Antler	6					
B	Tip to Tip Spread	32 3/8	C Greatest Spread	51 5/8					
D	Inside Spread of Main Beam	41 5/8	(Credit may be equal to but not exceed longer antler)			41 5/8			
E	Total of Length of Abnormal Points								0 0/8
F	Length of Main Beam						57 5/8	57 6/8	0 1/8
G-1	Length of First Point						14 5/8	14 4/8	0 1/8
G-2	Length of Second Point						17 5/8	17 6/8	0 1/8
G-3	Length of Third Point						17 1/8	13 3/8	3 6/8
G-4	Length of Fourth Point						22 2/8	23 3/8	1 1/8
G-5	Length of Fifth Point						10 1/8	11 4/8	1 3/8
G-6	Length of Sixth Point, If Present						0 0/8	0 0/8	0 0/8
G-7	Length of Seventh Point, If Present						0 0/8	0 0/8	0 0/8
H-1	Circumference at smallest place between 1st and 2nd						9 5/8	9 5/8	0 0/8
H-2	Circumference at smallest place between 2nd and 3rd points						7 1/8	7 2/8	0 1/8
H-3	Circumference at smallest place between 3rd and 4th points						7 1/8	8 2/8	1 1/8
H-4	Circumference at smallest place between 4th and 5th points						6 3/8	6 7/8	0 4/8
				TOTALS		41 5/8	169 5/8	170 2/8	8 3/8

County where killed: Crook	Date Killed: 09/09/88		Column 1	41 5/8
Hunter's Name: Jeffrey E. Hale		**ADD**	Column 2	169 5/8
Owner's Name: Jeffrey E. Hale			Column 3	170 2/8
			Subtotal	381 4/8
			Subtract Column 4	8 3/8
			FINAL SCORE	373 1/8

Typical Rocky Mountain Elk—Rifle
Minimum Score: 300 0/8

Final Score	Gross Typical	Net Typical	Abnormal Points	Greatest Spread	Inside Spread	Main Beam R	Main Beam L	No. Points R	No. Points L	First Circ. R	First Circ. L	Year	County	Hunter/Owner	Rank
418 0/8	427 4/8	418 0/8	0 0/8	49 7/8	38 2/8	63 2/8	64 2/8	7	7	10 1/8	9 6/8	1942	Crook	Hugh Evans/Joseph Jessel, Jr.	1
401 1/8	421 0/8	401 1/8	0 0/8	49 2/8	43 7/8	60 4/8	64 5/8	7	6	9 3/8	9 0/8	1972	Grant	James Sproul	2
400 0/8	414 0/8	400 0/8	0 0/8	52 2/8	49 0/8	56 2/8	57 0/8	7	7	9 1/8	9 1/8	1984	Crook	Randy Ryerse	3
392 3/8	397 0/8	392 3/8	0 0/8	51 2/8	46 3/8	53 4/8	54 4/8	6	6	8 3/8	8 6/8	1982	Umatilla	Robert Brown	4
391 4/8	418 2/8	401 2/8	9 6/8	54 2/8	46 6/8	55 4/8	55 7/8	8	7	10 4/8	9 5/8	1930	Wallowa	Tafr/La Grande Elks Lodge	5
390 2/8	400 3/8	390 2/8	0 0/8	55 4/8	49 2/8	55 0/8	55 4/8	7	7	8 6/8	8 6/8	1980	Hood River	Bill Tensen	6
387 7/8	399 7/8	389 4/8	1 5/8	50 3/8	37 2/8	55 3/8	57 0/8	7	6	10 0/8	9 5/8	1966	Grant	Arnold Tropf	7
380 3/8	397 5/8	384 1/8	3 6/8	57 5/8	47 1/8	62 7/8	63 2/8	7	8	8 6/8	8 6/8	1967	Harney	Pat L. Wheeler	8
379 4/8	392 7/8	379 4/8	0 0/8	49 4/8	42 2/8	53 4/8	50 1/8	7	7	10 3/8	9 4/8	1941	Union	Frank Rauschkolb, Sr.	9
378 1/8	389 7/8	378 1/8	0 0/8	50 3/8	46 1/8	55 4/8	55 4/8	6	7	9 3/8	8 4/8	1942	Baker	Lee Thompson/The Halfway Museum	10
376 4/8	395 3/8	376 4/8	0 0/8	56 4/8	45 0/8	55 5/8	56 0/8	7	6	8 2/8	8 1/8	1957	Wheeler	Ray Gauge	11
376 0/8	379 1/8	376 0/8	0 0/8	48 5/8	45 4/8	48 2/8	48 2/8	6	6	8 6/8	8 7/8	1979	Crook	Carl Ipack	12
375 0/8	380 0/8	375 0/8	0 0/8	48 0/8	42 6/8	57 1/8	58 1/8	6	6	9 1/8	8 6/8	1986	Wheeler	Will Bartlett	13
374 7/8	339 7/8	381 4/8	6 5/8	52 6/8	45 0/8	59 5/8	59 5/8	7	7	7 7/8	9 1/8	1974	Crook	Frank Bristow	14
372 7/8	378 1/8	372 7/8	0 0/8	52 0/8	49 5/8	50 1/8	50 6/8	6	6	9 4/8	9 0/8	1989	Grant	Bob M. Abbott	15
372 4/8	376 5/8	372 4/8	0 0/8		41 6/8	54 5/8	55 0/8	6	6	8 0/8	8 1/8	1981	Grant	Dell Howard	16
372 4/8	387 6/8	372 4/8	0 0/8	53 0/8	49 2/8	55 1/8	53 5/8	6	7	9 1/8	9 5/8	1962	Grant	Bud Loht	16
371 2/8	394 3/8	371 2/8	0 0/8	54 0/8	46 4/8	65 2/8	63 1/8	7	7	7 5/8	8 1/8	1963	Crook	Elvin Davis	18
371 0/8	384 1/8	371 0/8	0 0/8	50 1/8	47 0/8	52 4/8	52 4/8	7	7	8 0/8	7 4/8	1958	Grant	Gale Becker/Harold Burroughs	19
369 4/8	378 0/8	369 4/8	0 0/8	54 3/8	49 4/8	55 2/8	54 3/8	6	6	8 4/8	8 1/8	1930	Union	Michael Kilby	20
368 7/8	372 1/8	368 7/8	0 0/8	48 2/8	44 5/8	56 4/8	56 6/8	6	6	8 4/8	8 4/8	1980	Grant	Lawrence Wolfgram	21
364 4/8	372 1/8	364 4/8	0 0/8	44 4/8	39 2/8	53 2/8	51 2/8	6	6	8 2/8	8 5/8	1980	Grant	Cliff Marsh	22
364 2/8	382 7/8	364 2/8	0 0/8	57 0/8	55 6/8	55 2/8	54 4/8	6	7	7 7/8	8 4/8	1930	Wallowa	Earl Haney/Dale Dotson	23
364 1/8	376 5/8	364 1/8	0 0/8	50 0/8	46 5/8	51 2/8	50 2/8	6	6	8 0/8	8 4/8	1930	Wallowa	Tarzan/La Grande Lodge B.P.O.E.	24
362 2/8	379 2/8	362 2/8	0 0/8	45 0/8	42 4/8	53 4/8	52 2/8	7	7	8 2/8	8 0/8	1980	Grant	Pete Hettinga	25
361 5/8	372 1/8	361 5/8	0 0/8	50 0/8	43 7/8	55 0/8	53 6/8	6	6	8 6/8	8 5/8	1982	Grant	Mike Browning	26
360 4/8	385 0/8	360 4/8	0 0/8	48 0/8	42 0/8	46 0/8	54 0/8	6	6	8 0/8	8 1/8	1936	Umatilla	John Blanchet/Jay Britton	27
357 5/8	366 3/8	357 5/8	0 0/8	48 4/8	43 3/8	54 7/8	51 4/8	6	6	9 0/8	9 2/8	1985	Grant	Jody Lance	28
356 2/8	390 2/8	380 3/8	24 1/8	58 6/8	46 5/8	57 2/8	56 4/8	7	8	9 3/8	10 2/8	1935	Wallowa	Lawton McDaniels	29
356 2/8	364 0/8	356 2/8	0 0/8	43 0/8	37 0/8	48 6/8	47 5/8	7	7	8 2/8	8 5/8	1978	Grant	Otis Ricker	29
356 0/8	362 7/8	356 0/8	0 0/8	50 5/8	47 0/8	51 0/8	51 2/8	6	6	7 5/8	7 5/8	1966	Union	John Croghan	31
355 3/8	366 4/8	355 3/8	0 0/8	50 5/8	41 5/8	45 2/8	48 7/8	6	6	7 3/8	7 4/8		Malheur	Joel Moody	32
354 3/8	361 7/8	354 3/8	0 0/8	52 4/8	46 5/8	54 5/8	53 6/8	7	6	8 2/8	8 3/8	1935	Umatilla	Earl H. Baker, Sr./Charles Baker	33
354 2/8	362 2/8	354 2/8	0 0/8	49 0/8	44 0/8	51 5/8	53 3/8	8	6	10 2/8	11 2/8	1940	Umatilla	Glenn Potter/Robert Mawhin	34
352 7/8	367 4/8	359 3/8	6 4/8	48 0/8	43 5/8	54 4/8	53 3/8	8	6	7 5/8	8 1/8	1992	Harney	Roger Reason	35
352 4/8	359 2/8	352 4/8	0 0/8	47 4/8	45 0/8	55 3/8	55 1/8	7	7	8 2/8	8 0/8	1988	Wheeler	Chet Hettinga	36
352 2/8	358 2/8	352 2/8	0 0/8	52 3/8	42 4/8	52 0/8	53 2/8	6	6	7 5/8	7 4/8	1941	Harney	Walter Hart/Joe Baker	37
350 7/8	359 3/8	350 7/8	0 0/8	45 6/8	39 1/8	44 6/8	45 2/8	6	6	7 4/8	7 2/8	1972	Grant	W.V. Masson	38

Typical Rocky Mountain Elk—Rifle (continued)

Final Score	Gross Typical	Net Typical	Abnormal Points	Greatest Spread	Inside Spread	Main Beam R	Main Beam L	Number of Points R	Number of Points L	First Circumference R	First Circumference L	Year	County	Hunter/Owner	Rank
350 3/8	360 5/8	350 3/8	0 0/8	49 4/8	41 5/8	51 0/8	51 2/8	6	6	7 6/8	7 1/8	1958	Baker	Kenneth Musgrove	39
350 2/8	360 7/8	350 2/8	0 0/8	53 4/8	52 0/8	47 6/8	47 6/8	6	6	7 2/8	7 2/8	1944		Stratton Store	40
349 7/8	361 5/8	349 7/8	0 0/8	52 4/8	47 7/8	49 1/8	51 4/8	7	7	7 3/8	7 7/8	1981	Grant	Malcolm Cameron	41
349 6/8	377 5/8	349 6/8	0 0/8	44 0/8	40 0/8	56 0/8	52 4/8	6	7	10 4/8	9 6/8	1946	Wallowa	Merle Hogg	42
349 3/8	360 3/8	349 3/8	0 0/8	52 0/8	46 1/8	53 0/8	52 4/8	6	6	7 0/8	7 4/8	1975	Grant	Roy Hempel, Sr./Mike Hempel	43
349 0/8	369 7/8	349 0/8	0 0/8		45 6/8	54 2/8	50 0/8	8	5	8 3/8	9 4/8	1990	Grant	David G. Powell	44
348 5/8	357 7/8	348 5/8	0 0/8	53 3/8	47 5/8	55 5/8	56 2/8	6	6	8 3/8	8 3/8	1973	Grant	Jerry Wagner/Greg Wagner	45
348 2/8	354 7/8	348 2/8	0 0/8	44 4/8	41 0/8	53 2/8	53 0/8	6	6	8 2/8	8 3/8	1994	Harney	David Bossnot	46
347 4/8	359 2/8	347 4/8	0 0/8	43 5/8	40 2/8	52 3/8	48 0/8	6	6	8 1/8	7 6/8	1964	Harney	George Noble	47
347 2/8	353 6/8	347 2/8	0 0/8	41 7/8	39 2/8	53 3/8	53 4/8	6	6	7 6/8	7 2/8			Joseph Hardware	48
347 0/8	358 1/8	347 0/8	0 0/8	52 4/8	47 6/8	49 3/8	50 2/8	6	6	8 2/8	8 2/8	1981	Grant	Rod Abreu	49
346 5/8	379 1/8	369 3/8	22 6/8	60 1/8	47 3/8	55 0/8	54 6/8	7	7	8 1/8	7 6/8	1947	Wallowa	Wayne Marks	50
345 7/8	355 6/8	345 7/8	0 0/8	44 2/8	38 5/8	48 6/8	48 6/8	6	6	7 4/8	7 6/8	1981	Grant	Gale Wall	51
344 1/8	358 5/8	344 1/8	0 0/8	43 4/8	40 3/8	49 0/8	49 3/8	6	6	8 1/8	8 0/8	1955	Wallowa	Will H. Brown	52
344 0/8	358 5/8	344 0/8	0 0/8	44 4/8	39 6/8	54 1/8	53 3/8	7	6	7 6/8	7 7/8	1978	Grant	Wesley Wilson	53
343 5/8	355 2/8	343 5/8	0 0/8	49 2/8	45 5/8	47 3/8	49 6/8	6	6	7 5/8	7 6/8	1939	Umatilla	Dean Lev Records/Norm Records	54
343 5/8	352 0/8	343 5/8	0 0/8	48 5/8	43 3/8	55 3/8	58 5/8	6	6	7 3/8	7 7/8	1991	Harney	Mark Barber	54
343 5/8	354 5/8	343 5/8	0 0/8	40 5/8	37 3/8	51 5/8	54 4/8	6	6	8 5/8	9 1/8	1950	Umatilla	William Crawford/Jeff Roach	54
341 6/8	350 3/8	343 7/8	2 1/8	46 6/8	40 6/8	49 6/8	50 1/8	6	6	8 6/8	8 5/8	1951	Baker	Ianthus Bennett	57
341 5/8	351 1/8	341 5/8	0 0/8	49 0/8	44 2/8	50 6/8	47 7/8	6	6	6 4/8	6 4/8	1956	Wallowa	Sander Anderson	58
341 4/8	346 1/8	341 4/8	0 0/8	40 2/8	35 2/8	51 0/8	49 7/8	6	7	7 7/8	8 6/8	1965	Umatilla	Leon Olsen/Robert Mawhin	59
341 2/8	371 4/8	355 6/8	14 4/8	64 0/8	58 6/8	52 4/8	50 5/8	6	8	8 1/8	8 1/8	1960	Grant	C.R. Kendall	60
340 2/8	390 4/8	362 4/8	22 2/8	49 4/8	39 4/8	54 1/8	54 0/8	8	7	8 0/8	8 0/8	1939	Wallowa	Alva J. Victor	61
340 0/8	349 6/8	340 0/8	0 0/8	44 4/8	36 6/8	49 2/8	46 4/8	7	7	10 2/8	11 2/8		Grant	Elmer Bennett	62
339 5/8	362 2/8	339 5/8	0 0/8	46 4/8	37 7/8	56 7/8	52 6/8	6	6	8 3/8	8 2/8	1936	Union	Verne Gilalund/Paul Ellis	63
339 3/8	346 7/8	339 3/8	0 0/8	46 3/8	43 1/8	53 0/8	51 7/8	6	6	9 6/8	9 1/8	1985		Don Herman	64
339 2/8	347 3/8	339 2/8	0 0/8	51 0/8	49 5/8	48 2/8	48 6/8	6	6	8 3/8	8 2/8	1988	Crook	Richard Reynolds	65
338 1/8	347 2/8	338 1/8	0 0/8	46 0/8	39 5/8	49 7/8	50 1/8	6	6	8 1/8	7 7/8	1986	Harney	Roy L. Kneriem	66
338 0/8	344 4/8	338 0/8	0 0/8		42 4/8	48 6/8	46 3/8	6	6	7 4/8	7 6/8	1984	Grant	Ray Moles	67
337 4/8	348 3/8	337 4/8	0 0/8	42 2/8	38 4/8	48 7/8	50 1/8	7	6	7 2/8	7 1/8	1980	Harney	Stan Sturza/Mike Sturza	68
336 6/8	354 4/8	336 6/8	0 0/8	46 4/8	43 6/8	51 5/8	50 2/8	6	6	7 3/8	6 6/8	1969	Wallowa	Wayne Norton/Mike Norton	69
336 6/8	349 2/8	336 6/8	0 0/8	41 0/8	37 2/8	49 7/8	49 4/8	7	6	8 2/8	8 0/8	1965	Harney	Jim Connelly	69
336 1/8	341 3/8	336 1/8	0 0/8	44 4/8	42 1/8	52 2/8	50 4/8	6	6	8 3/8	9 1/8	1992	Hood River	Tom Scranton	71
334 6/8	345 0/8	334 6/8	0 0/8	46 2/8	41 0/8	47 1/8	45 1/8	6	6	8 5/8	8 4/8		Wallowa	The Gun Room	72
333 4/8	346 1/8	333 4/8	0 0/8	48 0/8	45 2/8	51 2/8	51 1/8	6	6	8 5/8	8 2/8	1995	Jefferson	Ed & John Pugh	73
333 1/8	346 5/8	333 1/8	0 0/8	52 0/8	45 1/8	47 3/8	47 5/8	8	8	7 4/8	8 1/8	1962	Grant	Eldon Deardorff	74
332 7/8	346 6/8	332 7/8	0 0/8	49 0/8	41 7/8	53 6/8	53 1/8	7	6	7 1/8	8 5/8	1980	Grant	Dennis Ferguson	75
332 5/8	337 3/8	332 5/8	0 0/8	45 2/8	39 5/8	50 3/8	50 6/8	6	6	7 5/8	7 4/8	1968	Wallowa	Marvin Burnette	76
332 4/8	338 3/8	332 4/8	0 0/8	43 4/8	37 2/8	49 5/8	51 5/8	6	6	7 6/8	7 5/8	1935	Crook	John Snyder	77
332 1/8	340 0/8	332 1/8	0 0/8	41 0/8	37 3/8	56 6/8	57 1/8	6	6	7 5/8	8 3/8	1948	Grant	Lyla Johnston	78
332 1/8	339 7/8	333 5/8	1 4/8	45 6/8	42 3/8	49 1/8	48 6/8	6	7	8 1/8	8 1/8	1994	Grant	Gil Okita	78
331 7/8	347 5/8	331 7/8	0 0/8	42 4/8	33 3/8	45 4/8	50 3/8	6	6	7 5/8	7 3/8	1994	Wallowa	Marilyn Riggs/Karlee Riggs	80

81	Allen Currier	Wheeler	1991	8 2/8	8 5/8	7	6	57 2/8	52 2/8	41 4/8	47 2/8	14 2/8	346 0/8	331 6/8	367 0/8
82	Brett Puckett	Umatilla	1995	7 3/8	7 1/8	6	6	58 0/8	54 6/8	38 1/8	42 0/8	0 0/8	331 5/8	331 5/8	348 7/8
83	Ken McCullough	Union	1973	7 0/8	7 0/8	6	6	46 3/8	46 2/8	37 4/8	47 0/8	0 0/8	331 0/8	331 0/8	340 3/8
83	Bob Chandler	Union	1981	7 4/8	8 0/8	6	6	47 7/8	52 0/8	42 6/8	47 7/8	0 0/8	331 0/8	331 0/8	345 4/8
83	Joe De Marsh	Grant	1995	7 7/8	8 2/8	6	6	44 2/8	42 6/8	38 4/8	45 5/8	0 0/8	331 0/8	331 0/8	340 6/8
86	Phillip Nance	Crook	1962	7 2/8	7 4/8	7	6	55 3/8	53 0/8	41 6/8	45 6/8	0 0/8	330 6/8	330 6/8	344 6/8
86	Mike Browning	Malheur	1954	7 3/8	7 1/8	6	6	48 3/8	49 3/8	42 2/8	45 0/8	0 0/8	330 6/8	330 6/8	339 6/8
86	Don De Moss	Union		8 4/8	9 1/8	7	6	54 0/8	54 5/8	40 4/8	45 0/8	0 0/8	330 6/8	330 6/8	344 7/8
89	Dean Sprague/The Sports Corral	Wallowa		7 4/8	7 4/8	6	7	54 1/8	53 4/8	46 7/8	53 0/8	0 0/8	329 7/8	329 7/8	340 5/8
90	Chris Wood	Grant	1984	7 3/8	7 7/8	7	6	46 6/8	45 7/8	46 2/8	50 4/8	0 0/8	329 4/8	329 4/8	340 5/8
91	Arnold Tropf	Grant	1976	7 2/8	7 4/8	6	6	56 4/8	53 0/8	37 5/8	43 0/8	0 0/8	328 5/8	328 5/8	341 2/8
92	Ronnie Hill	Harney	1994	7 5/8	7 2/8	6	6	49 4/8	48 6/8	37 5/8	44 2/8	0 0/8	328 1/8	328 1/8	332 3/8
93	Tom Craig	Union	1950	8 2/8	8 3/8	7	7	51 3/8	51 0/8	48 2/8	53 6/8	6 6/8	334 4/8	327 6/8	341 1/8
94	Walter Hart/Joe Baker	Malheur	1940	7 1/8	7 1/8	6	6	49 1/8	49 0/8	44 0/8	47 0/8	0 0/8	326 4/8	326 4/8	330 0/8
95	Elmer Meltebeke	Wallowa	1990	7 2/8	7 1/8	6	6	45 2/8	46 1/8	40 0/8	43 4/8	6 3/8	332 6/8	326 3/8	340 6/8
96	Patrick Wheeler	Harney	1988	7 4/8	7 0/8	6	6	48 1/8	46 2/8	39 5/8	45 0/8	0 0/8	326 0/8	326 0/8	332 4/8
97	Mac McKinley	Grant		7 4/8	8 0/8	6	6	59 2/8	58 2/8	41 4/8	46 0/8	0 0/8	325 2/8	325 2/8	337 4/8
98	Kevin Loveland	Harney	1994	8 1/8	7 7/8	7	6	51 0/8	49 2/8	36 0/8		2 4/8	327 2/8	324 6/8	332 6/8
99	Jerry McClellan	Grant	1984	6 6/8	6 5/8	6	6	50 5/8	49 7/8	40 1/8	52 1/8	0 0/8	324 5/8	324 5/8	328 4/8
100	Beverley Karstens	Malheur	1994	7 4/8	7 6/8	6	6	51 0/8	51 2/8	41 6/8	45 2/8	0 0/8	324 4/8	324 4/8	333 4/8
101	W.W. York	Wallowa	1993	8 1/8	8 0/8	6	6	47 3/8	49 4/8	40 1/8	48 6/8	0 0/8	324 1/8	324 1/8	332 2/8
102	Bob Chadwick	Baker	1986	7 4/8	7 4/8	6	6	46 2/8	48 2/8	44 2/8	49 2/8	0 0/8	323 6/8	323 6/8	329 6/8
103	The Sports Corral	Wallowa		9 2/8	8 4/8	8	6	46 6/8	46 5/8	47 2/8	49 6/8	0 0/8	323 4/8	323 4/8	355 7/8
104	Benny G. Parmele/Ben Parmele	Harney	1977	8 0/8	8 1/8	6	6	48 1/8	47 5/8	47 0/8		0 0/8	323 0/8	323 0/8	330 7/8
105	Jake Nash	Grant	1986	7 5/8	7 7/8	7	7	48 7/8	50 0/8	41 1/8	44 6/8	0 0/8	322 3/8	322 3/8	330 7/8
106	Dick Blashill	Grant	1983	7 1/8	7 1/8	6	6	49 6/8	51 2/8	44 6/8	48 3/8	0 0/8	321 6/8	321 6/8	331 0/8
107	Jim McPhetridge	Wheeler	1992	7 0/8	6 7/8	6	6	50 7/8	52 3/8	38 0/8	41 4/8	0 0/8	320 2/8	320 2/8	330 0/8
108	Larry Blakeslee	Grant	1987	7 5/8	7 7/8	6	6	46 4/8	45 2/8	36 0/8	40 0/8	0 0/8	319 2/8	319 2/8	325 2/8
109	Jay Don Greenwood	Baker		8 0/8	9 0/8	6	7	50 0/8	51 4/8	37 2/8	47 0/8	0 0/8	319 0/8	319 0/8	330 4/8
110	Cheryl Durgan	Jefferson	1980	7 6/8	7 6/8	6	6	51 4/8	50 5/8	38 3/8	42 4/8	0 0/8	318 7/8	318 7/8	326 4/8
111	Vernon Case	Umatilla	1931	7 4/8	7 2/8	7	6	51 0/8	52 0/8	39 5/8	43 0/8	5 0/8	323 5/8	318 5/8	334 1/8
112	Ken Nagel	Grant	1995	7 6/8	7 6/8	6	6	50 0/8	50 1/8	44 3/8	44 4/8	0 0/8	318 1/8	318 1/8	327 3/8
113	Walter Hart/Joe Baker	Harney	1916	7 1/8	6 6/8	6	6	50 4/8	50 3/8	42 1/8	48 2/8	0 0/8	317 7/8	317 7/8	327 7/8
114	Bob Frazier	Jefferson	1991	8 0/8	7 5/8	6	6	47 4/8	49 5/8	41 1/8	41 4/8	0 0/8	317 5/8	317 5/8	327 2/8
114	Annie Girdner	Grant	1990	7 6/8	8 0/8	6	6	50 3/8	50 0/8	42 3/8	47 0/8	0 0/8	317 5/8	317 5/8	324 4/8
116	Burton Asher/Jack Grimes	Wallowa	1939	6 5/8	6 5/8	6	6	51 5/8	50 5/8	39 6/8	44 2/8	0 0/8	317 4/8	317 4/8	325 0/8
117	Dan Hooker	Grant	1980	7 3/8	7 3/8	6	6	52 2/8	52 1/8	44 2/8	44 7/8	0 0/8	317 2/8	317 2/8	321 3/8
118	Lucy Woodward	Wheeler	1995	7 5/8	8 2/8	7	8	50 1/8	52 1/8	36 2/8	41 4/8	0 0/8	316 6/8	316 6/8	321 5/8
119	Wesley H. Townsend/Wanda De Moss	Union	1935	8 6/8	8 2/8			48 0/8	48 4/8	41 4/8	57 0/8	20 4/8	336 4/8	316 0/8	351 6/8
120	Jesse Crader/Gladys Nobles	Wallowa	1958	7 3/8	7 4/8	6	6	47 4/8	47 1/8	42 1/8	44 3/8	0 0/8	315 5/8	315 5/8	324 6/8
121	Benny G. Parmele/Ben Parmele	Harney	1965	4 7/8	5 1/8	7	8	49 0/8	47 4/8	44 6/8	52 1/8	7 4/8	322 6/8	315 2/8	336 3/8
122	David Clayton	Harney	1992	8 0/8	10 1/8	8	7	55 7/8	55 4/8	39 0/8	56 1/8	28 7/8	344 0/8	315 1/8	367 0/8
123	Ralph Holcomb/Doug Holcomb	Umatilla	1948	7 3/8	8 0/8	6	6	43 4/8	45 5/8	41 0/8	45 2/8	0 0/8	315 0/8	315 0/8	326 3/8
124	Donny Worley	Grant	1982	6 6/8	6 4/8	6	6	53 6/8	56 4/8	47 7/8	50 6/8	0 0/8	314 5/8	314 5/8	324 3/8
125	Joey Wood	Grant		8 2/8	7 7/8	6	6	52 0/8	51 2/8	40 0/8	44 0/8	0 0/8	314 4/8	314 4/8	326 7/8

Typical Rocky Mountain Elk—Rifle (continued)

Final Score	Gross Typical	Net Typical	Abnormal Points	Greatest Spread	Inside Spread	Main Beam R	Main Beam L	Number of Points R	Number of Points L	First Circumference R	First Circumference L	Year	County	Hunter/Owner	Rank
314 1/8	353 5/8	342 2/8	28 1/8	51 0/8	45 2/8	51 6/8	52 0/8	7	8	7 2/8	7 1/8	1994	Harney	Glen Shelley	126
314 1/8	324 0/8	314 1/8	0 0/8	43 4/8	39 1/8	50 4/8	50 3/8	6	6	7 0/8	6 5/8			Mickey Ochs	126
313 3/8	318 1/8	313 3/8	0 0/8	41 4/8	37 7/8	48 2/8	47 2/8	6	6	7 4/8	7 2/8	1994	Deschutes	Clay Walker	128
312 6/8	323 4/8	312 6/8	0 0/8	48 3/8	46 0/8	49 1/8	47 3/8	6	6	7 7/8	7 7/8	1948	Wallowa	Ken Jones	129
312 5/8	319 0/8	312 5/8	0 0/8	43 4/8	40 1/8	48 0/8	48 0/8	6	6	6 6/8	6 6/8	1991	Grant	Larry Powell	130
312 4/8	319 4/8	312 4/8	0 0/8	45 5/8	41 4/8	47 2/8	46 0/8	6	6	9 5/8	9 3/8		Grant	Mac McKinley	131
312 0/8	318 1/8	312 0/8	0 0/8	41 0/8	36 0/8	47 0/8	49 1/8	6	6	7 6/8	7 6/8	1989	Grant	David G. Powell	132
311 7/8	323 4/8	311 7/8	0 0/8	43 0/8	41 3/8	49 0/8	48 5/8	6	6	7 6/8	7 5/8	1973	Grant	Ken Moore	133
311 5/8	316 7/8	311 5/8	0 0/8	42 4/8	38 7/8	49 1/8	50 0/8	6	6	6 5/8	6 4/8	1978	Grant	Craig Hansen	134
311 4/8	320 2/8	311 4/8	0 0/8	48 7/8	43 4/8	48 4/8	47 6/8	6	6	8 2/8	7 6/8	1983	Harney	Robbie Presley	135
310 7/8	338 0/8	331 0/8	20 1/8	43 2/8	33 6/8	50 4/8	48 0/8	9	8	7 4/8	6 1/8	1952	Wallowa	Duane Brown	136
310 4/8	317 7/8	310 4/8	0 0/8	42 0/8	38 2/8	43 2/8	45 1/8	6	6	6 6/8	6 7/8	1995	Wheeler	David Armstrong	137
310 0/8	318 0/8	311 0/8	1 2/8	43 4/8	39 6/8	49 4/8	49 6/8	7	7	7 5/8	8 1/8	1995	Grant	M. Andrew Shown	138
309 2/8	314 1/8	309 2/8	0 0/8	39 1/8	35 4/8	48 3/8	48 4/8	6	5	8 4/8	8 3/8	1941	Wallowa	Al Victor	139
308 6/8	313 4/8	308 6/8	0 0/8	41 4/8	33 4/8	46 3/8	46 3/8	6	6	6 6/8	6 7/8	1994	Malheur	Evelyn Heid	140
308 5/8	319 3/8	310 3/8	1 6/8	45 5/8	41 5/8	50 3/8	51 4/8	7	7	9 0/8	8 2/8	1995	Jefferson	Jay Roth	141
308 4/8	316 5/8	308 4/8	0 0/8	46 0/8	42 2/8	48 4/8	49 6/8	6	6	7 1/8	6 7/8	1957	Grant	Jack DeRosier	142
307 7/8	318 1/8	307 7/8	0 0/8	43 3/8	39 5/8	49 2/8	47 0/8	6	7	6 7/8	7 0/8	1984	Grant	Larry Wolfgram	143
307 7/8	322 3/8	315 1/8	7 2/8	46 0/8	38 5/8	48 2/8	48 4/8	6	7	6 6/8	7 2/8	1995	Harney	Rob Littleton	143
307 3/8	308 4/8	307 3/8	0 0/8	41 5/8	32 1/8	50 1/8	50 4/8	6	6	8 2/8	7 6/8	1992	Harney	Darin Daniel	145
307 1/8	314 5/8	307 1/8	0 0/8	45 2/8	44 5/8	45 0/8	43 4/8	6	6	7 6/8	8 1/8			Albert Letsch/Mike Letsch	146
306 1/8	316 0/8	308 5/8	2 4/8	48 0/8	45 3/8	49 4/8	49 5/8	6	6	7 7/8	7 3/8	1967	Grant	Jack DeRosier	147
306 1/8	324 4/8	306 1/8	0 0/8	43 1/8	36 7/8	50 7/8	51 5/8	7	7	6 6/8	7 2/8	1995	Malheur	Mike Selleck	147
306 0/8	317 7/8	308 1/8	2 1/8	41 5/8	38 5/8	44 3/8	48 5/8	6	6	6 2/8	6 1/8	1961	Wallowa	C. Donald Gibbs	149
306 0/8	314 5/8	306 0/8	0 0/8	38 6/8	35 4/8	47 3/8	47 4/8	6	6	7 0/8	7 3/8	1995	Baker	John Carolson	149
304 0/8	308 6/8	304 0/8	0 0/8		40 0/8	49 5/8	50 2/8	6	6	7 4/8	7 0/8	1994	Grant	Michael P. Gray	151
304 0/8	319 0/8	304 0/8	0 0/8	45 0/8	39 6/8	49 1/8	51 4/8	6	6	7 2/8	7 6/8	1994	Wheeler	Scott Wolff	151
303 5/8	312 3/8	303 5/8	0 0/8	47 4/8	42 3/8	45 5/8	46 4/8	7	7	7 4/8	7 2/8	1994	Union	Terry Hayward	153
303 3/8	320 3/8	303 3/8	0 0/8	44 4/8	37 3/8	47 0/8	49 7/8	6	6	7 6/8	7 7/8	1952	Umatilla	Fred Pearson/Rusty Lindberg	154
303 1/8	314 3/8	303 1/8	0 0/8	46 0/8	38 3/8	48 6/8	45 3/8	6	6	6 4/8	6 2/8	1950	Grant	Allen Anthony	155
303 0/8	320 4/8	303 0/8	0 0/8	45 0/8	40 0/8	50 4/8	48 5/8	6	6	9 3/8	9 3/8	1995	Union	Jim Willis	156
301 6/8	307 0/8	301 6/8	0 0/8	38 4/8	35 4/8	47 0/8	47 4/8	6	6	7 1/8	8 1/8	1992	Wallowa	Dennis Botts	157
300 6/8	318 2/8	306 4/8	5 6/8	46 6/8	39 2/8	46 5/8	44 2/8	6	7	6 6/8	7 2/8	1983	Umatilla	Dave A. Russell	158
300 5/8	311 6/8	305 7/8	5 2/8	45 6/8	41 7/8	45 7/8	46 4/8	7	7	7 1/8	7 5/8	1912	Umatilla	Isaac/Myrtle Winslow	159
300 5/8	308 7/8	300 5/8	0 0/8	48 6/8	44 5/8	45 7/8	46 3/8	6	6	6 1/8	6 7/8	1984	Grant	Jake Nash	159
300 4/8	360 6/8	306 7/8	6 3/8	46 0/8	39 4/8	56 4/8	55 2/8	7	6	9 4/8	8 4/8	1974	Wheeler	Jim Myers	161
300 3/8	311 1/8	300 3/8	0 0/8	43 4/8	38 3/8	48 4/8	50 1/8	6	7	6 6/8	7 1/8	1990	Grant	Bill L. Loving	162
300 0/8	308 6/8	300 0/8	0 0/8	45 0/8	42 2/8	47 0/8	49 4/8	5	5	7 2/8	7 0/8		Grant	Pete Hettinga	163
300 0/8	307 5/8	300 0/8	0 0/8	42 5/8	40 0/8	46 4/8	47 7/8	6	6	6 6/8	6 3/8	1965	Baker	Lovell Bennett	163

Typical Rocky Mountain Elk—Archery
Minimum Score: 260 0/8

Final Score	Gross Typical	Net Typical	Abnormal Points	Greatest Spread	Inside Spread	Main Beam R	Main Beam L	Number of Points R	Number of Points L	First Circumference R	First Circumference L	Year	County	Hunter/Owner	Rank
373 1/8	381 4/8	373 1/8	0 0/8	51 5/8	41 5/8	57 5/8	57 6/8	6	6	9 5/8	9 5/8	1988	Crook	Jeffrey E. Hale	1
368 0/8	379 1/8	368 0/8	0 0/8	47 6/8	44 4/8	52 7/8	52 3/8	6	6	8 6/8	8 3/8	1988	Grant	Greg E. Willmore	2
364 6/8	377 3/8	364 6/8	0 0/8	53 0/8	39 2/8	50 3/8	46 2/8	6	6	9 2/8	9 2/8	1976	Grant	Bill Sanowski, III	3
353 0/8	359 6/8	353 0/8	0 0/8	42 2/8	38 0/8	47 2/8	46 1/8	6	7	8 6/8	8 2/8	1983	Grant	Kenneth Mills	4
342 4/8	356 3/8	342 4/8	0 0/8	45 6/8	45 0/8	50 0/8	48 1/8	6	6	10 5/8	10 0/8	1949	Wallowa	John Kriwox	5
339 1/8	360 2/8	339 1/8	0 0/8	46 0/8	42 1/8	52 2/8	52 2/8	6	8	7 2/8	7 4/8	1988	Grant	Brad Miller	6
335 3/8	343 0/8	335 3/8	0 0/8	55 0/8	53 0/8	49 3/8	49 2/8	6	6	7 2/8	6 6/8	1994	Crook	Jason Calarco	7
335 0/8	342 7/8	335 0/8	0 0/8	43 6/8	38 4/8	48 0/8	48 3/8	7	7	7 0/8	7 0/8	1993	Harney	Joel R. Griffin	8
332 0/8	336 1/8	332 0/8	0 0/8	42 6/8	37 2/8	50 3/8	49 6/8	6	6	8 1/8	8 3/8	1992	Grant	Robert Reed	9
325 6/8	333 6/8	325 6/8	0 0/8	42 0/8	37 4/8	51 2/8	50 2/8	6	6	8 6/8	8 6/8	1992	Deschutes	Royce Nelson	10
324 1/8	334 5/8	326 1/8	2 0/8	40 3/8	35 7/8	46 4/8	44 7/8	6	7	8 3/8	8 3/8	1994	Harney	Jeff Nichols	11
323 4/8	339 3/8	323 4/8	0 0/8	42 6/8	39 0/8	49 2/8	47 6/8	6	7	9 4/8	9 2/8	1987	Crook	Todd Catterson	12
321 6/8	329 4/8	323 0/8	1 2/8	43 2/8	40 2/8	49 1/8	47 7/8	6	7	7 4/8	7 3/8	1995	Grant	Randy Walz	13
321 3/8	331 4/8	321 3/8	0 0/8	42 3/8	37 1/8	49 1/8	49 3/8	6	6	8 0/8	8 0/8	1994	Grant	Tim Hedeman	14
320 7/8	328 4/8	320 7/8	0 0/8	50 5/8	45 5/8	49 2/8	52 0/8	6	6	7 2/8	7 0/8	1991	Jefferson	Steve Yeoman	15
313 3/8	323 3/8	318 1/8	4 6/8	39 4/8	37 5/8	47 2/8	47 2/8	6	7	7 0/8	7 2/8	1990	Harney	Robert M. Chaste	16
308 7/8	315 2/8	308 7/8	0 0/8	43 0/8	38 3/8	50 0/8	49 7/8	7	6	7 4/8	7 0/8	1987	Grant	Ron De Roest	17
304 0/8	310 3/8	304 0/8	0 0/8	34 4/8	32 4/8	43 5/8	42 5/8	6	6	7 3/8	7 4/8	1993	Harney	Patrick E. Wheeler	18
301 6/8	310 0/8	301 6/8	0 0/8	41 4/8	38 0/8	51 6/8	54 0/8	6	6	7 6/8	8 0/8	1995	Harney	Patrick Wheeler	19
301 0/8	315 5/8	301 0/8	0 0/8	45 4/8	32 4/8	45 7/8	46 4/8	6	6	6 7/8	7 2/8	1992	Crook	Roger Norris	20
291 3/8	299 6/8	291 3/8	0 0/8	38 6/8	36 3/8	45 4/8	46 2/8	7	6	7 6/8	6 7/8	1994	Grant	Terry Harling	21
286 4/8	290 2/8	286 4/8	0 0/8	36 5/8	31 0/8	46 2/8	46 2/8	6	6	7 2/8	7 2/8		Grant	Kelly Thrasher	22
286 2/8	292 7/8	286 2/8	0 0/8	40 0/8	34 0/8	36 4/8	36 4/8	6	6	8 0/8	8 4/8	1991	Grant	David M. Morris	23
284 0/8	289 2/8	284 0/8	0 0/8	38 3/8	36 0/8	51 3/8	51 0/8	6	6	6 3/8	6 2/8	1995	Baker	Gerald E. Johnson	24
283 6/8	304 3/8	283 6/8	0 0/8	39 1/8	35 4/8	48 2/8	48 6/8	6	6	8 7/8	8 6/8	1994	Deschutes	Royce Nelson	25
283 3/8	292 0/8	283 3/8	0 0/8	40 1/8	36 1/8	45 1/8	46 2/8	6	6	6 4/8	6 7/8	1994	Baker	Carl Duke	26
282 7/8	290 3/8	282 7/8	0 0/8	41 6/8	38 7/8	41 7/8	41 4/8	6	6	6 4/8	6 6/8	1986	Wallowa	Steven R. Zollman	27
277 6/8	298 3/8	277 6/8	0 0/8	40 0/8	32 6/8	50 4/8	46 0/8	6	6	7 6/8	7 7/8	1989	Grant	Ray Moles	28
277 0/8	289 4/8	277 0/8	0 0/8	46 0/8	39 2/8	47 7/8	48 4/8	5	6	6 6/8	6 6/8	1993	Baker	Kevin Zemmer	29
276 7/8	282 2/8	276 7/8	0 0/8	37 6/8	33 5/8	46 1/8	45 4/8	6	6	7 3/8	7 1/8	1984	Grant	Gary Nyden	30
275 7/8	280 6/8	275 7/8	0 0/8	36 4/8	33 1/8	43 7/8	43 6/8	6	6	6 6/8	6 4/8	1990	Wallowa	Dale Dotson	31
273 4/8	282 6/8	273 4/8	0 0/8	39 7/8	37 0/8	48 7/8	50 7/8	6	6	5 6/8	6 0/8	1994	Grant	Dan Klicker	32
272 5/8	280 0/8	272 5/8	0 0/8	40 1/8	35 7/8	44 0/8	45 1/8	6	6	6 2/8	6 6/8	1987	Baker	Lloyd V. Christensen	33
271 0/8	298 3/8	271 0/8	0 0/8		40 0/8	53 0/8	53 0/8	5	5	6 7/8	8 0/8		Grant	Tim Hedeman	34
269 2/8	275 0/8	269 2/8	0 0/8	37 0/8	34 4/8	40 3/8	42 1/8	6	6	6 6/8	7 1/8	1993	Union	Richard Goben	35
260 4/8	273 1/8	260 4/8	0 0/8	44 6/8	43 1/8	38 2/8	41 0/8	5	6	7 3/8	8 3/8	1995	Wallowa	Fred Walasavage	36

Typical Rocky Mountain Elk—Shed Antlers
Minimum Score: 135 0/8

Final Score	Subtotal	Crown Points	Abnormal Points	Main Beam	First Point	Second Point	Third Point	Fourth Point	Fifth Point	Sixth Point	First Circumference	Right/Left	Year	County	Owner's Name	Rank
184 6/8	184 6/8	0 0/8	55 0/8	24 4/8	23 0/8	20 3/8	19 5/8	12 1/8	0 0/8	0 0/8	9 3/8	Left	1925	Wallowa	Jerry Hudson (Taft)	1
181 0/8	181 0/8	0 0/8	49 2/8	18 0/8	19 6/8	17 4/8	22 4/8	17 5/8	5 6/8	0 0/8	8 0/8	Left	1984	Grant	Larry Powell	2
177 6/8	177 6/8	0 0/8	55 3/8	19 5/8	17 1/8	18 3/8	22 6/8	9 7/8	2 1/8	0 0/8	9 3/8	Right	1987	Grant	Joey Wood	3
177 5/8	177 5/8	0 0/8	59 1/8	15 0/8	14 0/8	10 3/8	22 4/8	17 0/8	9 7/8	0 0/8	8 1/8	Right	1995	Grant	Brad Browning	4
174 5/8	174 5/8	0 0/8	54 2/8	19 0/8	16 6/8	18 0/8	22 0/8	9 4/8	2 2/8	0 0/8	9 4/8	Right		Harney	Joey Wood	5
174 0/8	174 0/8	0 0/8	54 5/8	16 0/8	19 1/8	22 6/8	19 7/8	12 7/8	0 0/8	0 0/8	9 2/8	Right		Harney	Rod Abreu	6
173 5/8	182 0/8	8 3/8	54 4/8	22 7/8	24 5/8	20 1/8	19 5/8	9 3/8	0 0/8	0 0/8	9 4/8	Right	1925	Wallowa	Jerry Hudson (Taft)	7
173 4/8	173 4/8	0 0/8	55 3/8	17 7/8	15 0/8	18 3/8	23 7/8	11 7/8	0 0/8	0 0/8	9 2/8	Right	1979	Grant	Ken Moore	8
173 0/8	174 6/8	1 6/8	54 0/8	21 4/8	24 5/8	18 3/8	17 0/8	8 6/8	0 0/8	0 0/8	9 3/8	Right	1927	Wallowa	Wallowa Lake Lodge (Taft)	9
172 2/8	172 2/8	0 0/8	55 2/8	18 6/8	17 6/8	12 5/8	20 2/8	17 4/8	0 0/8	0 0/8	9 0/8	Left	1980	Grant	Mike Browning	10
171 5/8	188 2/8	16 5/8	53 6/8	23 6/8	24 4/8	19 4/8	18 4/8	14 0/8	3 6/8	0 0/8	9 1/8	Left	1927	Wallowa	Wallowa Lake Lodge (Taft)	11
170 0/8	170 0/8	0 0/8	56 0/8	16 0/8	15 6/8	15 6/8	18 1/8	14 3/8	4 0/8	0 0/8	8 4/8	Left	1994	Grant	Thad Labhart	12
168 4/8	168 4/8	0 0/8	54 2/8	16 3/8	18 2/8	19 7/8	17 0/8	12 2/8	0 0/8	0 0/8	9 1/8	Right		Grant	Walt Gentis	13
168 3/8	168 3/8	0 0/8	53 2/8	17 0/8	18 7/8	17 2/8	19 2/8	13 0/8	0 0/8	0 0/8	9 0/8	Left		Grant	Walt Gentis	14
168 1/8	168 1/8	0 0/8	52 6/8	18 4/8	14 7/8	16 1/8	22 5/8	12 1/8	0 0/8	0 0/8	9 6/8	Left		Harney	Rod Abreu	15
166 6/8	166 6/8	0 0/8	53 3/8	15 5/8	14 7/8	17 1/8	20 3/8	15 0/8	0 0/8	0 0/8	9 2/8	Right		Grant	Joey Wood	16
166 3/8	166 3/8	0 0/8	53 4/8	16 4/8	17 0/8	13 5/8	21 2/8	15 4/8	0 0/8	0 0/8	8 4/8	Right	1930	Umatilla	Richard Kopp	17
166 2/8	166 2/8	0 0/8	52 7/8	16 0/8	16 0/8	13 2/8	19 6/8	16 2/8	6 4/8	0 0/8	7 5/8	Left		Harney	Patrick Wheeler	18
165 6/8	165 6/8	0 0/8	51 0/8	19 4/8	20 6/8	18 7/8	17 1/8	10 4/8	0 0/8	0 0/8	7 1/8	Right	1940	Harney	Joe Baker	19
164 7/8	164 7/8	0 0/8	55 0/8	15 5/8	16 7/8	11 6/8	19 2/8	17 1/8	0 0/8	0 0/8	8 6/8	Left	1930	Umatilla	Richard Kopp	20
164 3/8	164 3/8	0 0/8	52 5/8	18 4/8	21 4/8	14 4/8	19 6/8	10 2/8	0 0/8	0 0/8	8 3/8	Left		Grant	Joey Wood	21
161 1/8	161 1/8	0 0/8	56 4/8	16 6/8	17 4/8	14 5/8	19 1/8	9 6/8	0 0/8	0 0/8	7 6/8	Right	1950	Grant	Ken Moore	22
160 4/8	160 4/8	0 0/8	56 3/8	17 5/8	15 4/8	9 4/8	20 0/8	11 3/8	0 0/8	0 0/8	8 6/8	Left	1985		Haskel Junior Neal	23
159 1/8	159 1/8	0 0/8	57 6/8	13 1/8	12 4/8	9 0/8	18 4/8	15 6/8	4 7/8	0 0/8	7 6/8	Right	1995	Grant	Brad Browning	24
158 4/8	158 4/8	0 0/8	55 1/8	19 2/8	15 1/8	7 1/8	18 7/8	11 2/8	0 0/8	0 0/8	8 7/8	Right	1985		Haskel Junior Neal	25
157 3/8	157 3/8	0 0/8	54 5/8	19 0/8	14 4/8	14 5/8	18 5/8	8 7/8	0 0/8	0 0/8	7 5/8	Left	1950	Grant	Ken Moore	26
156 7/8	156 7/8	0 0/8	48 5/8	17 4/8	18 2/8	16 1/8	17 4/8	12 0/8	0 0/8	0 0/8	7 6/8	Left		Grant	Pauline Powell	27
156 6/8	156 6/8	0 0/8	54 6/8	15 0/8	14 2/8	10 4/8	21 6/8	14 0/8	0 0/8	0 0/8	6 7/8	Right	1996	Crook	Mike A. Borden	28
156 2/8	156 2/8	0 0/8	50 2/8	15 6/8	17 1/8	13 3/8	17 5/8	10 1/8	0 0/8	0 0/8	9 4/8	Right		Harney	Kim Rowlins	29
154 4/8	154 4/8	0 0/8	55 3/8	15 4/8	12 4/8	10 5/8	19 6/8	14 1/8	0 0/8	0 0/8	7 6/8	Right		Crook	Bob Wanker	30
153 2/8	153 2/8	0 0/8	48 0/8	16 4/8	17 0/8	15 4/8	17 6/8	13 2/8	0 0/8	0 0/8	7 5/8	Right		Harney	Glen Shelley	31
150 6/8	150 6/8	0 0/8	48 6/8	13 6/8	16 2/8	12 0/8	19 7/8	9 3/8	0 0/8	0 0/8	8 7/8	Left	1995	Crook	Mike Bristow	32
150 1/8	150 1/8	0 0/8	50 2/8	13 4/8	13 0/8	12 5/8	15 0/8	4 0/8	7 5/8	5 3/8	7 0/8	Left		Grant	Scott Powell	33
148 1/8	148 1/8	0 0/8	50 1/8	14 6/8	17 0/8	15 0/8	15 3/8	10 1/8	0 0/8	0 0/8	7 1/8	Right	1996	Crook	Mike W. Borden	34
146 6/8	151 5/8	4 7/8	48 5/8	15 1/8	16 5/8	12 6/8	17 3/8	13 4/8	0 0/8	0 0/8	7 7/8	Left	1995		Chris F. Adams	35
144 0/8	144 0/8	0 0/8	50 0/8	14 1/8	18 1/8	9 4/8	16 0/8	10 5/8	0 0/8	0 0/8	7 4/8	Right	1989	Grant	Todd Hueckman	36
144 0/8	144 0/8	0 0/8	47 3/8	13 4/8	14 6/8	11 6/8	19 0/8	8 4/8	0 0/8	0 0/8	9 1/8	Right		Crook	Mike Bristow	36
143 6/8	143 6/8	0 0/8	48 0/8	15 0/8	14 1/8	15 6/8	17 4/8	5 2/8	0 0/8	0 0/8	7 6/8	Right	1995	Wasco	Ron Bozarth	38
143 5/8	143 5/8	0 0/8	50 3/8	16 1/8	16 7/8	11 0/8	16 4/8	7 5/8	0 0/8	0 0/8	7 3/8	Right		Crook	Scott La Franchi	39
143 0/8	143 0/8	0 0/8	46 1/8	14 1/8	14 2/8	17 6/8	17 0/8	2 2/8	3 3/8	0 0/8	8 0/8	Left	1995	Wasco	Ron Bozarth	40

41	Gene Rolen	Grant	1989	Left	8 2/8	0 0/8	0 0/8	12 1/8	18 0/8	12 0/8	14 6/8	13 6/8	48 4/8	4 6/8	147 0/8	142 2/8
42	Mike Piazza	Lake	1989	Right	6 7/8	0 0/8	0 0/8	11 0/8	17 0/8	12 2/8	13 0/8	11 6/8	51 3/8	0 0/8	141 6/8	141 6/8
43	Todd Hueckman	Grant	1989	Left	7 3/8	0 0/8	0 0/8	10 3/8	16 0/8	9 6/8	14 5/8	15 1/8	50 5/8	1 4/8	142 2/8	140 6/8
44	Sandi Howell	Crook	1989	Right	6 6/8	0 0/8	0 0/8	10 4/8	16 6/8	8 2/8	15 2/8	13 2/8	51 4/8	0 0/8	139 7/8	139 7/8
45	Gene Rolen	Grant	1989	Right	7 7/8	0 0/8	0 0/8	12 1/8	16 5/8	12 6/8	12 4/8	15 3/8	48 6/8	7 0/8	146 2/8	139 2/8
46	Mike Piazza	Lake	1989	Left	6 7/8	0 0/8	0 0/8	9 7/8	16 2/8	10 6/8	12 0/8	12 2/8	51 4/8	0 0/8	137 6/8	137 6/8
47	Mike Garrett	Grant		Right	7 5/8	0 0/8	0 0/8	7 7/8	16 2/8	10 0/8	12 7/8	10 1/8	55 0/8	0 0/8	137 0/8	137 0/8
48	L. Wolfgram	Grant	1992	Right	6 6/8	0 0/8	0 0/8	11 1/8	15 2/8	11 6/8	13 0/8	14 4/8	46 2/8	0 0/8	136 5/8	136 5/8
49	Mike Agidius	Umatilla	1995	Right	8 0/8	0 0/8	0 0/8	9 3/8	17 0/8	16 4/8	15 4/8	14 0/8	43 2/8	6 0/8	142 0/8	136 0/8
50	Larry Bennett	Wallowa	1996	Right	8 0/8	0 0/8	0 0/8	9 0/8	14 7/8	13 1/8	16 1/8	14 0/8	42 1/8	0 0/8	135 0/8	135 0/8

Official Scoring System for Oregon Big Game Trophies

NON-TYPICAL
ROCKY MT. ELK (WAPITI)

DETAIL OF POINT MEASUREMENT

Abnormal Points

Right Antler		Left Antler	
2	4/8	0	0/8
7	2/8	0	0/8
0	0/8	0	0/8
0	0/8	0	0/8
0	0/8	0	0/8
0	0/8	0	0/8
0	0/8	0	0/8
0	0/8	0	0/8
0	0/8	0	0/8
0	0/8	0	0/8
Subtotals 9	6/8	0	0/8
Total to E		9	6/8

Species	Rifle	Archery	Muzzle	Shed
Rocky Mt. Elk	300	260	255	135

					COLUMN 1 Spread Credit	COLUMN 2 Right Antler	COLUMN 3 Left Antler	COLUMN 4 Difference
A	No. of Points on Right Antler	8	No. of Points on Left Antler	7				
B	Tip to Tip Spread	39 3/8	C Greatest Spread	54 2/8				
D	Inside Spread of Main Beam	46 6/8	(Credit may be equal to but not exceed longer antler)		46 6/8			
E	Total of Length of Abnormal Points			9 6/8				
F	Length of Main Beam					55 4/8	55 7/8	0 3/8
G-1	Length of First Point					24 0/8	25 2/8	1 2/8
G-2	Length of Second Point					25 4/8	22 7/8	2 5/8
G-3	Length of Third Point					18 5/8	20 6/8	2 1/8
G-4	Length of Fourth Point					18 2/8	21 3/8	3 1/8
G-5	Length of Fifth Point					7 0/8	11 5/8	4 5/8
G-6	Length of Sixth Point, If Present					0 0/8	1 3/8	1 3/8
G-7	Length of Seventh Point, If Present					0 0/8	0 0/8	0 0/8
H-1	Circumference at smallest place between 1st and 2nd					10 4/8	9 5/8	0 7/8
H-2	Circumference at smallest place between 2nd and 3rd points					7 2/8	7 2/8	0 0/8
H-3	Circumference at smallest place between 3rd and 4th points					7 7/8	7 5/8	0 2/8
H-4	Circumference at smallest place between 4th and 5th points					6 4/8	6 7/8	0 3/8
			TOTALS		46 6/8	181 0/8	190 4/8	17 0/8

County where killed: Wallowa	Date Killed: 09/30			
Hunter's Name: Tarzan		**ADD**	Column 1	46 6/8
Owner's Name: La Grande Elks Lodge			Column 2	181 0/8
			Column 3	190 4/8
			Subtotal	418 2/8
			Subtract Column 4	17 0/8
			Subtotal	401 2/8
			ADD Line E Total	9 6/8
			FINAL SCORE	411 0/8

Official Scoring System for Oregon Big Game Trophies

Records of Oregon
Big Game

RECORD BOOK FOR OREGON

P.O. Box 759
Irrigon, OR 97844

NON-TYPICAL
ROCKY MT. ELK (WAPITI)

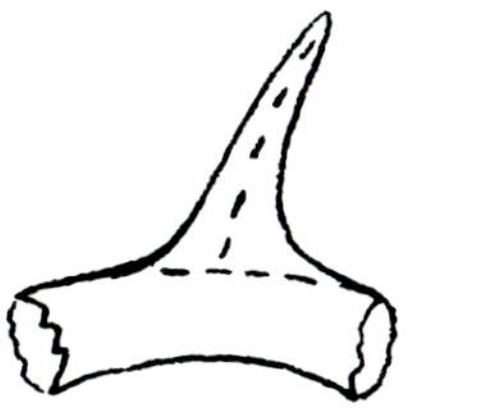

DETAIL OF POINT MEASUREMENT

Abnormal Points			
Right Antler		Left Antler	
13	0/8	13	2/8
3	4/8	0	0/8
3	4/8	0	0/8
3	6/8	0	0/8
0	0/8	0	0/8
0	0/8	0	0/8
0	0/8	0	0/8
0	0/8	0	0/8
0	0/8	0	0/8
0	0/8	0	0/8
Subtotals		23 6/8	13 2/8
Total to E			37 0/8

RECEIPT

OREGON BIG GAME, INC.
5283 HWY 35
PARKDALE, OR 97041
(541) 352-HUNT

RECEIVED FROM: JAMES BETHEL
ADDRESS: 6091 WALISH Ct. S.E.
Salem, Oregon 97301
FOR: One big Game Animals
DATE: 3-2— 19 99
DOLLARS $ 45
001089

		COLUMN 1	COLUMN 2	COLUMN 3	COLUMN 4
		Spread Credit	Right Antler	Left Antler	Difference
A	No. of Points on Right Antler	8			
B	Tip to Tip Spread	3/8			
D	Inside Spread of Main Beam	41 6/8			
E	Total of Lengths of Abnormal Points	37 0/8			
F	Length of Main Beam		55 1/8	53 0/8	2 1/8
G-1	Length of 1st Point		15 6/8	16 0/8	0 2/8
G-2	Length of 2nd Point		16 5/8	17 1/8	0 4/8
G-3	Length of 3rd Point		13 6/8	21 0/8	7 2/8
G-4	Length of 4th Point		21 0/8	12 4/8	8 4/8
G-5	Length of 5th Point		16 4/8	14 0/8	2 4/8
G-6	Length of 6th Point		1 6/8	14 3/8	12 5/8
G-7	Length of 7th Point		2 2/8	0 0/8	2 2/8
H-1	Circumference		9 0/8	10 0/8	1 0/8
H-2	Circumference		7 6/8	7 7/8	0 1/8
H-3	Circumference		8 2/8	7 6/8	0 4/8
H-4	Circumference		8 6/8	10 1/8	1 3/8
	TOTALS	41 6/8	176 4/8	183 6/8	39 0/8

County where killed: Wallowa	Date Killed: 09/14/82			
Hunter's Name:	Bill	Hamilton	**ADD**	Column 1	41 6/8
Owner's Name:	Bill	Hamilton		Column 2	176 4/8

ADD	Column 1	41 6/8
	Column 2	176 4/8
	Column 3	183 6/8
	Subtotal	402 0/8
	Subtract Column 4	39 0/8
	Subtotal	363 0/8
	ADD Line E Total	37 0/8
	FINAL SCORE	**400 0/8**

Rocky Mountain Elk—
Archery (non-typical),
Bill Hamilton, 400 0/8 P.Y.,
Wallowa County, 1982

Rocky Mountain Elk—
Black Powder,
Don Sargent, 265 0/8 B.C.,
Jefferson County, 1994

Official Scoring System for Oregon Big Game Trophies

Records of Oregon
Big Game

RECORD BOOK FOR OREGON

P.O. Box 759
Irrigon, OR 97844

TYPICAL and NON-TYPICAL
ROCKY MT. ELK SHED ANTLERS

Abnormal Points			
Right Antler		Left Antler	
8	3/8	0	0/8
0	0/8	0	0/8
0	0/8	0	0/8
0	0/8	0	0/8
0	0/8	0	0/8
0	0/8	0	0/8
0	0/8	0	0/8
0	0/8	0	0/8
0	0/8	0	0/8
0	0/8	0	0/8

Species   **Typical**   **Non-Typical**

Rocky Mt. Elk   135   150

		Right Antler		Left Antler	
E	Total of Length of Abnormal Points	8	3/8	0	0/8
F	Length of Main Beam	54	4/8	55	0/8
G-1	Length of First Point, if present	22	7/8	24	4/8
G-2	Length of Second Point	24	5/8	23	0/8
G-3	Length of Third Point, if present	20	1/8	20	3/8
G-4	Length of Fourth Point, if present	19	5/8	19	5/8
G-5	Length of Fifth Point	9	3/8	12	1/8
G-6	Length of Sixth Point, if present	0	0/8	0	0/8
G-7	Length of Seventh Point, if present	0	0/8	0	0/8
H-1	Circumference at smallest place between burr and 1st point	9	4/8	9	3/8
H-2	Circumference at smallest place between 1st and 2nd point	7	0/8	7	2/8
H-3	Circumference at smallest place between main beam and 3rd pt	7	3/8	7	2/8
H-4	Circumference at smallest place between 2nd and 4th points	7	0/8	6	2/8
	TOTALS	182	0/8	184	6/8

County: Wallowa   Year Found: 1925

Owner's Name: Jerry Hudson

ABNORMAL POINTS*	8	3/8	0	0/8
FINAL SCORE	190	3/8	184	6/8

Abnormal Points are subtracted if Typical and added if Non-Typical

Official Scoring System for Oregon Big Game Trophies

Records of Oregon
Big Game

RECORD BOOK FOR OREGON

P.O. Box 759
Irrigon, OR 97844

TYPICAL and NON-TYPICAL
ROCKY MT. ELK SHED ANTLERS

Species	Typical	Non-Typical
Rocky Mt. Elk	135	150

Abnormal Points		
Right Antler	**Left Antler**	
1	6/8	15	0/8
0	0/8	1	5/8
0	0/8	0	0/8
0	0/8	0	0/8
0	0/8	0	0/8
0	0/8	0	0/8
0	0/8	0	0/8
0	0/8	0	0/8
0	0/8	0	0/8
0	0/8	0	0/8

		Right Antler		Left Antler	
E	Total of Length of Abnormal Points	1	6/8	16	5/8
F	Length of Main Beam	54	0/8	53	6/8
G-1	Length of First Point, if present	21	4/8	23	6/8
G-2	Length of Second Point	24	5/8	24	4/8
G-3	Length of Third Point, if present	18	3/8	19	4/8
G-4	Length of Fourth Point, if present	17	0/8	18	4/8
G-5	Length of Fifth Point	8	6/8	14	0/8
G-6	Length of Sixth Point, if present	0	0/8	3	6/8
G-7	Length of Seventh Point, if present	0	0/8	0	0/8
H-1	Circumference at smallest place between burr and 1st point	9	3/8	9	1/8
H-2	Circumference at smallest place between 1st and 2nd point	7	0/8	7	0/8
H-3	Circumference at smallest place between main beam and 3rd pt	7	2/8	7	5/8
H-4	Circumference at smallest place between 2nd and 4th points	6	7/8	6	6/8
	TOTALS	174	6/8	188	2/8

County: Wallowa	Year Found: 1927				
Owner's Name:	Wallowa Lake Lodge	**ABNORMAL POINTS***	1	6/8	16	5/8
		FINAL SCORE	176	4/8	204	7/8

*Abnormal Points are subtracted if Typical and added if Non-Typical

Non-Typical Rocky Mountain Elk—Rifle
Minimum Score: 325 0/8

Final Score	Gross Typical	Net Typical	Abnormal Points	Greatest Spread	Inside Spread	Main Beam R	Main Beam L	Number of Points R	Number of Points L	First Circumference R	First Circumference L	Year	County	Hunter/Owner	Rank
411 0/8	418 2/8	401 2/8	9 6/8	54 2/8	46 6/8	55 4/8	55 7/8	8	7	10 4/8	9 5/8	1930	Wallowa	Taft/La Grande Elks Lodge	1
404 4/8	390 2/8	380 3/8	24 1/8	58 6/8	46 5/8	57 2/8	56 4/8	7	8	9 3/8	10 2/8	1935	Wallowa	Lawton McDaniels	2
392 1/8	374 3/8	369 3/8	22 6/8	60 4/8	47 3/8	55 0/8	54 6/8	7	7	8 1/8	7 6/8	1947	Wallowa	Wayne Marks	3
388 1/8	393 7/8	381 4/8	6 5/8	52 6/8	45 0/8	59 5/8	59 5/8	7	7	7 7/8	9 1/8	1974	Crook	Frank Bristow	4
384 6/8	390 1/8	362 4/8	22 2/8	49 4/8	39 4/8	54 1/8	54 0/8	8	7	8 0/8	8 0/8	1939	Wallowa	John C. Victor	5
372 7/8	367 0/8	344 0/8	28 7/8	56 1/8	39 0/8	55 4/8	55 7/8	7	8	10 1/8	8 0/8	1992	Harney	David Clayton	6
370 3/8	353 5/8	342 2/8	28 1/8	51 0/8	45 2/8	51 6/8	52 0/8	7	8	7 2/8	7 1/8	1994	Harney	Glen Shelly	7
370 2/8	371 4/8	355 6/8	14 4/8	64 0/8	58 6/8	52 4/8	50 5/8	6	8	8 1/8	8 1/8	1960	Grant	C.R. Kendall/Prineville Elks Lodge	8
365 7/8	367 4/8	359 3/8	6 4/8	48 0/8	43 5/8	54 4/8	53 3/8	8	6	7 5/8	8 1/8	1992	Harney	Roger Reason	9
360 2/8	367 0/8	346 0/8	14 2/8	47 2/8	41 4/8	52 2/8	57 2/8	6	7	8 5/8	8 2/8			Allen Currier	10
357 0/8	351 6/8	336 4/8	20 4/8	57 0/8	41 4/8	48 4/8	48 0/8	8	7	8 2/8	8 6/8	1935	Union	Wesley H. Townsend/Wanda De Moss	11
351 1/8	338 0/8	331 0/8	20 1/8	43 2/8	33 6/8	50 4/8	48 0/8	9	8	7 4/8	8 1/8	1952	Wallowa	Duane Brown	12
348 1/8	338 6/8	315 4/8	32 5/8	41 6/8	35 6/8	49 0/8	48 0/8	6	8	8 2/8	9 6/8	1966	Grant	Larry Powell	13
341 6/8	325 6/8	313 4/8	28 2/8	43 6/8	41 6/8	43 6/8	45 0/8	8	7	8 4/8	9 4/8	1992	Wallowa	Bob Harris	14
333 4/8	327 2/8	316 5/8	16 7/8	51 6/8	47 1/8	46 3/8	45 3/8	6	9	7 6/8	8 1/8	1981	Crook	Jessie Fuller	15
329 4/8	352 6/8	317 6/8	11 6/8	56 4/8	46 4/8	48 0/8	54 1/8	6	6	7 0/8	7 0/8	1945		Stratton Store	16

Non-Typical Rocky Mountain Elk—Archery
Minimum Score: 300 0/8

Final Score	Gross Typical	Net Typical	Abnormal Points	Greatest Spread	Inside Spread	Main Beam R	Main Beam L	Number of Points R	Number of Points L	First Circumference R	First Circumference L	Year	County	Hunter/Owner	Rank
400 0/8	402 0/8	363 0/8	37 0/8	51 3/8	41 6/8	55 1/8	53 0/8	12	8	9 0/8	10 0/8	1982	Wallowa	Bill Hamilton	1

Non-Typical Rocky Mountain Elk—Black Powder
Minimum Score: 265 0/8

Final Score	Gross Typical	Net Typical	Abnormal Points	Greatest Spread	Inside Spread	Main Beam		Number of Points		First Circumference		Year	County	Hunter/Owner	Rank
						R	L	R	L	R	L				
265 0/8	277 1/8	259 0/8	6 0/8	38 5/8	33 0/8	42 7/8	46 0/8	6	7	8 7/8	7 5/8	1994	Jefferson	Don Sargent	1

Non-Typical Rocky Mountain Elk—Shed Antlers
Minimum Score: 150 0/8

Final Score	Subtotal	Crown Points	Abnormal Points	Main Beam	First Point	Second Point	Third Point	Fourth Point	Fifth Point	Sixth Point	First Circumference	Right/Left	Year	County	Owner's Name	Rank
204 7/8	188 2/8	16 5/8	53 6/8	23 6/8	24 4/8	19 4/8	18 4/8	14 0/8	3 6/8	0 0/8	9 1/8	Left	1927	Wallowa	Wallowa Lake Lodge (Taft)	1
190 3/8	182 0/8	8 3/8	54 4/8	22 7/8	24 5/8	20 1/8	19 5/8	9 3/8	0 0/8	0 0/8	9 4/8	Right	1925	Wallowa	Jerry Hudson (Taft)	2
184 6/8	184 6/8	0 0/8	55 0/8	24 4/8	23 0/8	20 3/8	19 5/8	12 1/8	0 0/8	0 0/8	9 3/8	Left	1925	Wallowa	Jerry Hudson (Taft)	3
180 1/8	159 4/8	20 5/8	46 4/8	15 4/8	11 6/8	12 5/8	22 0/8	17 4/8	0 0/8	0 0/8	7 4/8	Left	1940	Union	Harry Thomas	4
179 2/8	168 7/8	10 3/8	52 2/8	14 6/8	15 6/8	12 3/8	19 5/8	17 2/8	9 1/8	0 0/8	8 0/8	Right		Harney	Glenn Shelly	5
176 4/8	174 6/8	1 6/8	54 0/8	21 4/8	24 5/8	18 3/8	17 0/8	8 6/8	0 0/8	0 0/8	9 3/8	Right	1927	Wallowa	Wallowa Lake Lodge (Taft)	6
166 2/8	158 4/8	7 6/8	56 4/8	15 6/8	15 3/8	12 0/8	16 4/8	11 6/8	0 0/8	0 0/8	10 6/8	Right	1993	Crook	Scott La Franchi	7
161 5/8	157 2/8	4 3/8	47 5/8	14 0/8	12 6/8	12 4/8	20 5/8	17 5/8	0 0/8	0 0/8	7 3/8	Right	1940	Union	Harry Thomas	8
158 1/8	145 7/8	12 2/8	50 0/8	13 0/8	12 4/8	12 7/8	13 5/8	15 6/8	0 0/8	0 0/8	7 4/8	Left	1995	Jackson	Chris Wood	9
155 1/8	144 3/8	10 6/8	44 4/8	14 6/8	14 4/8	15 1/8	17 1/8	11 7/8	0 0/8	0 0/8	7 2/8	Left	1995	Umatilla	Mike Agidius	10

Boundaries for Roosevelt and Rocky Mountain Elk

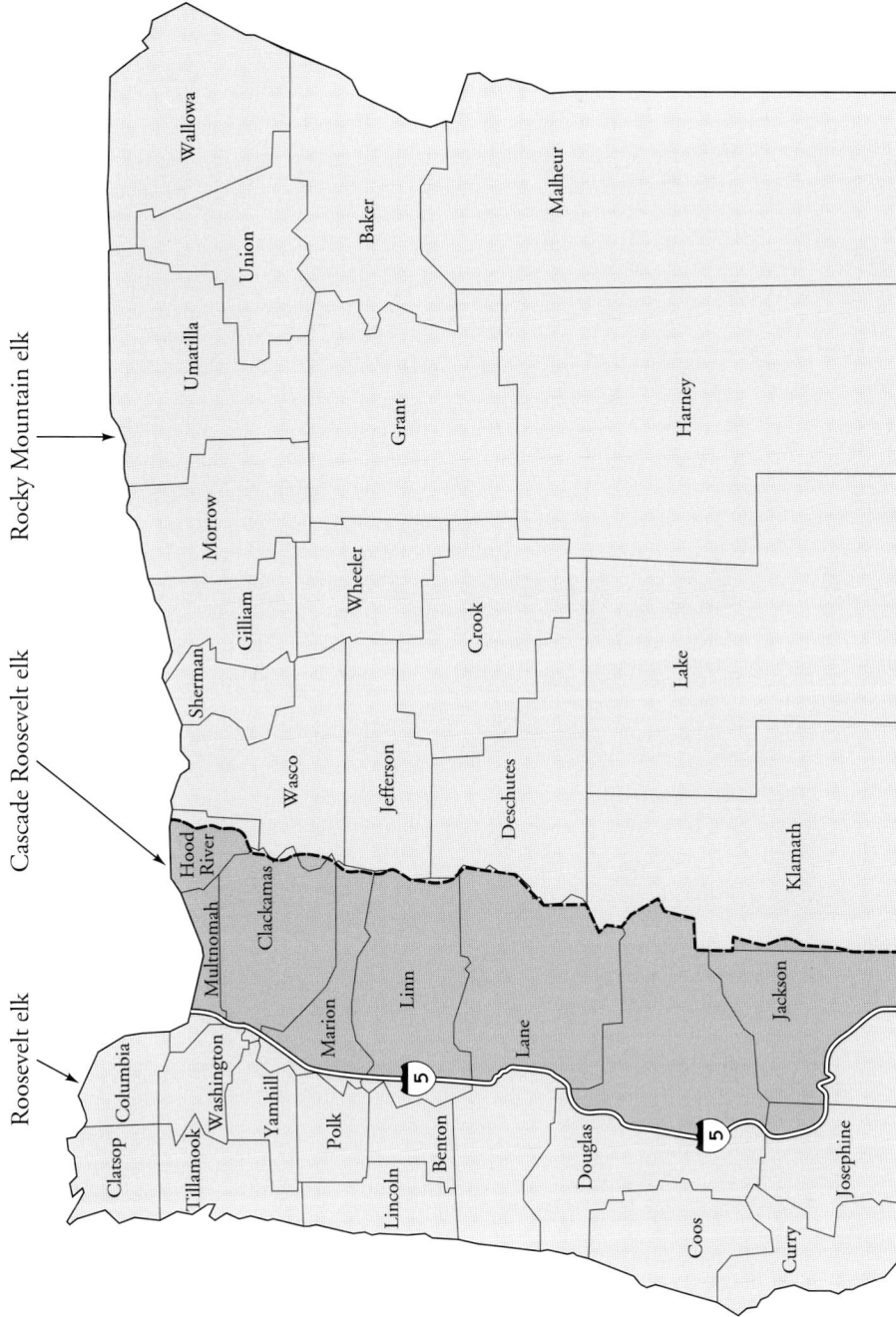

Roosevelt elk: elk taken west of Interstate 5 from the Washington border to the California border.

Cascade Roosevelt elk: elk taken east of Interstate 5 to the boundary beginning at Hood River, along Highway 35 south to the intersection of the Pacific Crest Trail, south along the Pacific Crest Trail until it leaves the Rogue River National Forest, then along the Klamath–Jackson County line to the California border.

Rocky Mountain elk: elk taken east of the above boundary (dashed line).

Mule deer illustration by Josh Zabransky

Whitetail illustration by Josh Zabransky

Coming in late '97...

UPDATE

❧ 1 9 9 7 ❧

Oregon's Big Game

YEARLY

- AN ANNUAL SUPPLEMENT TO THE *RECORD BOOK*
- RECORDING PERIOD: JULY 1996–JUNE 1997
- PHOTOGRAPHS AND ACCOUNTS OF OREGON'S LARGEST BIG GAME ANIMALS
- HISTORICAL HUNTING PHOTOGRAPHS
- CATEGORIES FOR EACH BIG GAME SPECIES:
  - RIFLE • ARCHERY • BLACK POWDER • SHED ANTLERS

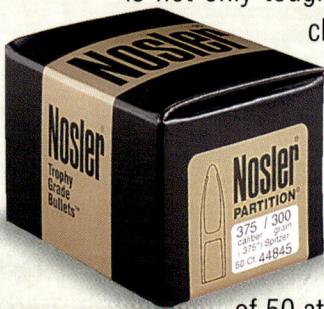

NORTHWEST LEATHER DESIGN

unique , creative designs of superior quality and craftsmanship

Northwest Leather Design works entirely in leather and suede, creating western and Native American pieces that include full hide throws, pillows, garments and wall shields. Each intricate design is unique in shape and color and many incorporate brands, silver or other unusual focal points.

Trish Davidson Box 229, Beavercreek, OR 97004 (503) 632-7650

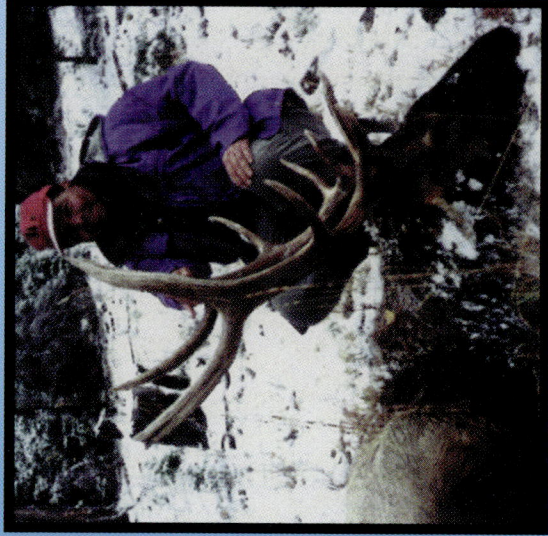

Outdoor
Adventures from
the High Desert to
The Summit

Big Game Hunting, Fishing and Camping

- Private leases in the Ochoco, Grizzly, Fossil, Silvies and Maury Units
- Catering to avid rifle hunters and dedicated archery hunters
- State licensed, bonded and a member in good standing of the Oregon Guides & Packers Association

Come join us on one of our large private ranches. Over 225,000 acres of some of the best Central Oregon has to offer!

Centerfire Outfitters
— PRINEVILLE, OREGON —

P.O. Box 663
Prineville, Oregon 97754

Call

Clay Woodward or Stan Rogers:
541-447-3841 Eve. 541-447-6055

Eric Ovens: 541-447-5611

LEUPOLD & STEVENS

L90

NINETY YEARS

1907 · 1997

LEUPOLD